BEATLES '66

BEATLES '66

THE REVOLUTIONARY YEAR

STEVE TURNER

An Imprint of HarperCollinsPublishers

HarperCollins books may be purchased for educational, business, or sales promotional use. For information please e-mail the Special Markets Department at SPsales@harpercollins.com.

FIRST EDITION

Library of Congress Cataloging-in-Publication Data has been applied for.

ISBN 978-0-06-247548-0

16 17 18 19 20   RS/RRD   10 9 8 7 6 5 4 3 2 1

To my class of 1966—Robert Benjamin, John Chandler, Don Eales, Sue Engall, Stephen Goodwin, Bob James, Peter Kay, Keith Newitt, Dave Nightingale, Wanda Pasciewicz, Linda Rainbow, Malcolm Rock, Danny Smedley, Neil Spencer, Geoff Thompson, and Andrew Windsor

To Abby Gibson and the new generation of Beatlemaniacs

CONTENTS

ACKNOWLEDGMENTS

Thanks to Hunter Davies for permission to quote from his 1966 interview with Paul McCartney as reprinted in his book *The Beatles Lyrics*. Thanks to the BBC Written Archive Centre (Caversham Park) for permission to quote from Donald Milner's interview with George Harrison that was broadcast on *The Lively Arts* on December 11, 1966. Thanks to Mike Barrow for permission to quote from correspondence written by his father, Tony Barrow.

PROLOGUE

We were all on this ship in the sixties, our generation–a ship going to discover the new world. And the Beatles were in the crow's nest of that ship.
–JOHN, 1974

Nineteen sixty-six was without question the pivotal year in the life of the Beatles as performers and recording artists. Before that they were the four loveable guys from Liverpool who wore identical suits on stage, played to packed houses of screaming (largely female) teenagers, played themselves in movie capers, and wrote jaunty songs chiefly about love. After 1966, they were serious studio-based musicians who no longer toured, wore individually selected clothes from Chelsea boutiques, wrote songs that explored their psyches and the nature of society, and were frequently considered a threat to the established order by governments around the world.

During that twelve-month period they went through changes that would have crushed men with less resilience and vision. The marriage of John and Cynthia and the live-in relationship of Paul and Jane Asher were disintegrating. John began consuming LSD so recklessly that it affected his self-worth and sense of identity. "I got a message on acid that you should destroy your ego," he told *Rolling Stone* in 1970. "And I did." As a group they had their lives threatened in Japan, America, and the Philippines. Church leaders, senators, governments, radical political groups, and the Ku Klux Klan denounced them. They saw their critical acclaim rise and shares in their publishing company fall. Records were sold and records were burned.

It was the year that Ringo met Charlie Chaplin, Paul met philosopher Bertrand Russell, George met sitar maestro Ravi Shankar, and John met Yoko Ono. It was also the year that the group recorded *Revolver*, the album that many critics consider their greatest artistic achievement, and started recording *Sgt. Pepper's Lonely Hearts Club Band*, the other LP that vies for top place in reviews not only of the Beatles' personal legacy but also of the history of rock albums.

So how was it that this quartet of slightly undereducated musicians from a working-class city in the north of England came to create such a mold-breaking record in 1966 and prepare themselves to do something similar in 1967? How did the Beatles go from chart-oriented pop to progressive rock in such a short time, from adulation in high schools to respect on college campuses, and what were the creative and social forces that combined to turn them from artistes into artists?

In books covering the whole career of the Beatles, this period necessarily has to be compressed into thirty or forty pages. Some of the best authors have had to chronicle the Beatles' final tour of America in a few paragraphs and gloss over the weeks when they were neither recording nor playing.

But the only way to fully understand this transitional period is to slow it down, in order to examine the details. The times when the group was out of the public eye are as revealing as those when they were at work, because this was when they enjoyed the newfound freedom to explore their personal passions and develop individual points of view. It was away from the cameras and the security guards that they absorbed the art and thought later implemented in their own creations.

David Crosby, a member of the Byrds and friend of the Beatles, has made the point that the most creative musicians, the ones who ultimately alter their genre, tend to be synthesizers. "By taking widely disparate streams that haven't been formally in contact with each other, you become a synthesist and create new forms," he said. "The Beatles took folk music chord changes and a rock backbeat and synthesized a new form."

But these fusions are rarely done consciously. The musical artist, as Crosby also observed, listens to various forms of music and allows the influences to permeate the creative consciousness in a natural way. The Byrds listened to Ravi Shankar and John Coltrane, and this led to them writing songs like "Eight Miles High." In 1966, the Beatles listened to artists as varied as Smokey Robinson, Karlheinz Stockhausen, Albert Ayler, Bob Dylan, Bernard Herrmann, and the Beach Boys and came up with *Revolver*.

For at least six years—virtually since the end of their teenage years—they had been working nonstop. When they weren't on stage, they were in the recording studio. When they weren't recording, they were writing. When they weren't doing any of these things, they were promoting themselves on TV and radio. John used to say that he was only a Beatle once he exited the front door of wherever he was living, but between 1959 and 1965 he was out of the house more than he was in it.

This was all good for business, but it didn't encourage personal growth. There was little time to reflect, explore, or develop meaningful friendships beyond their small circles of family, school friends, and business associates. Their identity was bound up in that of four people who wore the same clothes, had the same haircuts, and spoke in the same accents. There was little incentive for John, Paul, George, or Ringo to pursue independence of thought, image, or creativity. "We were an entity," Paul admitted in 2011. "Mick Jagger used to call us the Four-Headed Monster."

It was only when they cut back on tour dates, and then stopped touring altogether, that they began to contemplate how different they might be in their individual interests, values, and aims. As they did this, each group member began delving into new areas of thought and culture and enriching the work of the Beatles with their findings. In turn, slowing things in this book down allows me to look in more depth at apparently incidental people, places, and art that helped to mold the Beatles' attitudes and, ultimately, their work during this period.

The Beatles were already the market leaders in pop. They not only sold more records than anyone else but also set recording standards and heralded artistic changes. Everyone looked to them to see in which direction pop would be heading. But in 1966 that influence began to spread to creative people working in forms other than music. Photographers, designers, and painters became inspired by their example. After hearing "Taxman," the American poet and Trappist monk Thomas Merton confided in his diary: "They are good. Good beat, independence, wit, insight, voice originality." "Eleanor Rigby," with its image of a face kept "in a jar by the door" stopped illustrator Alan Aldridge in his tracks, because he saw parallels between it and his own exploration of surrealism. "The music and the lyrics of the Beatles," he said, "are a tremendous springboard into the imagination."

As they became more influential, they also became more influenced. They knew that the more they gave out, the more they needed to take in, and therefore they actively sought material that might challenge and stir them. At the same time they were sought out by those who wanted to piggyback on their fame, prestige, and power. There was no shortage of entrepreneurs keen to turn the Beatles on to new fashions, music, art, books, experiences, philosophies, and even new technology.

This had obvious downsides—they were deluged with useless information and risked being conned by fraudulent inventors, spiritual leaders, and even dieticians—but it ultimately proved beneficial, since it enabled them to remain that vital one step ahead by availing them of a wide range of contemporary ideas, tastes, and products well before the general public got to hear of them.

What surprised me most when examining this period of the Beatles' lives was how unpremeditated the developments were. They wanted to progress, but there was no grand career plan. Their basic approach to *Revolver* was no different than it had been to *With the Beatles* or *Rubber Soul*. They wrote each of the songs close to the time of recording, had no overarching theme in mind, and stopped when they'd recorded enough for fourteen tracks and two sides of a single. A title wasn't decided on until the sessions were completed, within weeks of the LP's release. An old friend was commissioned on the spur of the moment to design the cover, and he wasn't given a detailed briefing or a title. George put their work ethic in a nutshell when he said: "We're not trying to do anything. That's the big joke. . . . Everyone gets our records and says 'Wonder how they thought of that?' or 'Wonder what they're planning next?' or whatever they do say. But we don't plan anything. We don't do anything. All we do is just keep on being ourselves. It just comes out. It's the Beatles."

When they discussed the emergent songs with each other before they were recorded, the Beatles often had little more than a tune, partial lyrics, and the suggestion of a feeling they wanted to communicate, but most of the magic took place in the studio. It was a combined effort of the players and writers along with producer George Martin, with his wealth of knowledge about the business of recording, his impeccable connections with classically trained session musicians, and his ability to score music, and younger technicians such as engineer Geoff Emerick who were always eager to find solutions to meet the seemingly impossible demands of John and Paul.

When George said that they did no more than be themselves—"It just comes out"—he was telling the truth, from his perspective, but not taking into account the fact that in order to "be themselves" they first had to find out who they were. This involved self-reflection and a willingness to uncover and pursue their inclinations. It also required informal research into music and other art forms to see what they really liked. They each exposed themselves to new cultural experiences, some of which they'd previously dismissed, and were surprised how their tastes changed in the process.

But inner changes and fresh influences don't always combine to create new art. Not everyone has the capacity to forge new forms in this way. Good work doesn't just "come out" if you pour in the right ingredients. The artist has to resist the temptation to play it safe or appeal to the lowest common denominator. It only seems to "come out" if the creator has courage and vision and doesn't mind swimming against the tide for a while. Paul admitted as much in 1966 when he said, "Pinching ideas from other people is like abstract art. Anybody can throw paint on canvas just like anybody can pinch bits from songs, but not everybody gets the same result."

Before the Beatles in 1966, there was no precedent for a successful pop group retiring from live performances to focus on making records. There was also no precedent for pop music that drew not only from rock 'n' roll but also from traditions as diverse as Hindustani and European classical, experimental electronic, and southern soul. In their approach to their work they were now closer to contemporary jazz musicians than to fellow pop stars.

From our contemporary perspective, this sort of progression and artistic ambition seems natural in pop, but at the time it was a high-risk enterprise. The group repeatedly spoke about the possibility that, as a result of their artistic experimentation, they could lose an audience that basically wanted the Beatles to say, in different ways, "I love you" and to produce guitar-and-drum music capable of exciting passions. Girls who went nuts over "I Want to Hold Your Hand" wouldn't necessarily know how to respond to "Paperback Writer," "Eleanor Rigby" or "Strawberry Fields Forever." How could you shake or shimmy to songs about loneliness, death, and the alteration of consciousness through the use of psychedelic drugs? At the time these songs were referred to as "dark," an awkward fit in the world of show business, whose function was seen to be the promotion of good feelings.

The Beatles were imagining a type of popular music that didn't yet exist and that without their influence would possibly not have come into being. Without it, there would have been no Pink Floyd, REM, Radiohead, Talking Heads, or possibly even Cream or Led Zeppelin as we know them. There would be no *Tommy* by the Who, *What's Going On* by Marvin Gaye, *Tales from Topographic Oceans* by Yes, *The Rise and Fall of Ziggy Stardust and the Spiders from Mars* by David Bowie, *Horses* by Patti Smith, or *The Slim Shady LP* by Eminem.

Wherever possible I've used comments the Beatles made in 1966 rather than their later reflections. From past experience I have found that it's safer to trust what John, Paul, George, and Ringo said at the time or immediately after than what they said in retrospect. Memories are often unreliable. Paul, for example, continues to say that he grew his Sgt. Pepper mustache to conceal a lip injury, but he damaged his lip in December 1965 and grew the mustache in November 1966 as a disguise when vacationing in France. He's on record as saying that his guitar solo on "Taxman" was inspired by Jimi Hendrix, yet he'd neither seen nor heard Hendrix when that track was recorded. He also says that he didn't take LSD until 1966, but I show that his first trip took place in December 1965, which throws a new light on his state of mind when composing and recording *Revolver*.

In discussing the Beatles and their work I've tried to bear in mind what we knew back then and how we described things at the time rather than imposing later readings. So, for example, I deliberately refer to *Revolver* as an LP, as it would have been spoken of in 1966, rather than as an album. For the same reason I will talk about EMI Recording Studios rather than Abbey Road, because it was only after the album *Abbey Road* that the studios became known by the street on which they were located rather than by the record company that owned the property.

I will refer to the Beatles as a "group" rather than as a "band," because that's how they described themselves in the mid-sixties. The term "band" only started being used toward the end of the decade when musicianship took priority over image and showmanship (a change that the Beatles, of course, ushered in). Similarly, it was only toward the end of 1966 that some forms of pop started being spoken of as "rock." Until then, the Beatles were seen as pop musicians. Rock was sometimes used as a shorthand term for rock 'n' roll, but there was, as yet, no concept of something called rock culture, let alone a rock revolution.

When the Beatles began recording in 1962, they were thought of as a pop group playing "beat music." As far as I can determine, this was a musical description coined by British TV producer Jack Good in 1959 to describe music that had evolved out of rock 'n' roll but which incorporated a broader range of styles, from R & B to ballads, and used lead guitar, rhythm guitar, bass, and drums. In his 1961 book *The Big Beat Scene*, Royston Ellis spoke of "rock groups," but meant groups

The Big Beat Scene by Royston Ellis, 1961.

that still played 1950s-style rock 'n' roll, and he predicted that the future would belong to "the big beat," a sound that embraced elements of rock 'n' roll, jazz, R & B, mainstream pop, and that acoustic blend of American jug band, folk, and blues known in Britain as skiffle.

When writing about the Beatles in Britain I refer to their UK LPs and singles and the relevant charts published in papers like *New Musical Express* and *Melody Maker*. When writing about them in America I take into account their releases on the Capitol label and the all-important *Billboard* chart, although, when referring to *Revolver*, it will be to the fourteen-track release that first came out in the UK, not the eleven-track version put out in America. This is not only because it's what I first heard and have lived with ever since but also because this is the LP as the Beatles conceived it with the running order that they decided on.

I CAN REMEMBER 1966. IT WAS THE YEAR I LEFT SCHOOL AND started work. I remember the excitement of buying *Revolver* and hearing it played in boutiques along the King's Road, Chelsea, during my weekly visits to London. On October 13 I met Keith Richards

A business card for Granny Takes a Trip, 1966.

at the Chelsea Antiques Market and got him to autograph a Stones picture in one of the music papers I happened to have with me. The only thing I could think to ask him was how his recently completed tour of Britain had been. "The kids were great," he said, causing me to realize that to him teenage record buyers like me were just "kids."

I picked up my first copy of the radical "underground" newspaper *International Times* at the hip new King's Road boutique Granny Takes a Trip that year and visited the alternative bookshop Indica, where John and Paul shopped for literature. At the time I found it hard to put my finger on exactly what it was that united the satin shirts at Granny's and the underground literature at Indica, but I knew for sure that with *Revolver* the Beatles had their finger on that particular pulse and that from it I was getting a sneak preview of the future. In 1994 Paul McCartney said, "I feel like the sixties is about to happen. It feels like a period in the future to me, rather than a period in the past." I know what he meant, and hopefully, by the end of this book, you'll know, too.

DECEMBER 1965

We don't progress because we play the same
things every time we play somewhere. We used
to improve at a much faster rate before we
ever made records. You've got to reproduce,
as near as you can, the records, so you don't
really get a chance to improvise or improve
your style.
–GEORGE, 1965

A black Austin Princess limousine with tinted windows pulled out of
William Mews in Belgravia on the morning of Thursday, December 2,
and turned right into Knightsbridge, driving past Harrods toward
Hyde Park Corner. In the front was thirty-seven-year-old chauffeur
Alf Bicknell, bespectacled and wearing a formal gray suit and tie. On
the other side of the glass partition behind him were five young men
sitting in two rows: Ringo Starr, George Harrison, John Lennon, Paul
McCartney, and their personal assistant / road manager, Neil "Nell"
Aspinall, who they'd known since their early days in Liverpool when
they were a local beat group and he was training to be an accountant.

Traveling up Park Lane they could see on their right the twenty-
eight-story tower of the Hilton Hotel (the third tallest building in

the capital), which had opened two years before, the first in Britain
built by an American hotel chain and a convenient symbol of the
new, modern London. Close by was 45 Park Lane, where Playboy was
soon to open a new club.

At Marble Arch, the car turned into Edgware Road and slid toward Maida Vale and St John's Wood, where they were just yards away
from the EMI Recording Studios on Abbey Road, the building where
every Beatles song from "Love Me Do" in 1962 to the just-released
double-A-sided single "We Can Work It Out" / "Day Tripper" had
been recorded.

They were heading out to the start of the M1 motorway, the first
dual three-lane highway linking the south of England with the north.
There were still only 360 miles of motorway in the country, and city
bypasses accounted for much of this. To travel long distances by road
in Britain still meant driving on category-A roads that often had only
two lanes, were unlit at night, had no hard shoulders to pull onto in
the case of emergencies, and frequently twisted and turned. The only
refreshment stops were at cheap cafés, designed for long-haul lorry
drivers and where there was dark brown tea, a selection of stale sand-
wiches, a jukebox, and possibly a pinball machine.

Ahead of them was a 350-mile journey to the north of England,
where they would stop overnight before driving into Scotland for the
first of their nine-date 1965 tour of Britain. Probably already there
by now was Mal Evans, their other road manager, who'd set out the
night before in the van with seven electric guitars and the amplifiers,
leaving behind only the acoustic guitars the Beatles used for rehearsals and songwriting.

Almost two weeks before, on November 20 and 21, they'd had
a full-scale practice at the Donmar Rehearsal Theatre on Earl-
ham Street, Covent Garden, a space used by ballet companies,
opera houses, and theatres to develop new productions. The four
of them had stood facing each other, dwarfed by the vast empty
space, with only their instruments, some speakers, chairs, and a

The Beatles rehearsing for their final UK tour at the Donmar Rehearsal Theatre in London, November 20, 1965.

table for refreshments and ashtrays. The lights were dimmed. To the side of the electric piano was a copy of the new LP *B. B. King Live at the Regal,* which had been recorded almost exactly a year ago in Chicago.

They finalized eleven songs that would make up their thirty-five-minute set. Boldly, they had chosen to leave out their traditional barnstormers such as "Please Please Me," "She Loves You," "I Want to Hold Your Hand," "I Saw Her Standing There," and "Twist and Shout" to concentrate on songs released over the past twelve months. They planned to start with "I Feel Fine" and follow with its B-side, "She's a Woman," George's "If I Needed Someone" (just covered by the Hollies), Ringo's vocal number "Act Naturally," and John's more introspective "Nowhere Man." The show would continue with "Baby's in Black," "Help!," "We Can Work It Out" (with John on keyboards), "Yesterday" (with Paul on keyboards), the new single "Day Tripper," and end triumphantly with Paul's Little Richard pastiche

"I'm Down," successfully used as a closer during their tour of America in August.

This was the first year they'd played so few dates in their home country. In 1962 they'd played 188; in 1963, 117; and in 1964, 50. In the early days, when their fame was limited to the Merseyside area, it wasn't unusual for them to play three gigs in a day—a lunchtime appearance at the Cavern Club followed by two evening shows elsewhere in Liverpool. This decrease was because of their choice to limit touring in general and also the need to satisfy demand in other territories. The bigger they became, the less significant the home market was in terms of concert revenue.

Thursday was the day that Britain's music papers reached the newsstands. These papers played a vital role in building excitement about the new beat music: exaggerating rivalries between various groups, introducing new acts, and keeping music fans well informed about musical developments. They all featured the latest news, charts of the bestselling singles and LPs, interviews with pop stars, record reviews, ads, and gossip.

There was the long-established *Melody Maker* with its bias toward jazz and serious musicianship, as befitted its origin in 1926; *New Musical Express* (*NME*), which focused more on pop, as befitted its origin in 1949; *Record Mirror*, which pioneered appreciation of American R & B; *Music Echo,* which was what the Liverpool fan paper *Merseybeat* had turned into; and the more chart-oriented *Disc.* The combined sales of these papers was well over half a million copies, and most young people in Britain got their pop education from them, along with girls' comics such as *Boyfriend* and *Valentine,* unisex teenage magazines like *Rave* and *Fabulous,* the European radio station Radio Luxemburg, and the new "pirate ships" Radio Caroline and Radio London. The pirate ships outwitted Britain's ban on commercial radio and the subsequent monopoly of the airwaves by the BBC by broadcasting from just outside British territorial waters and introducing twenty-four-hour pop and American-style DJ patter after decades of fairly prim officially sanctioned presentation.

On this day, as the Beatles headed north on the motorway, the early verdicts on both the LP *Rubber Soul* and the single "We Can Work It Out" / "Day Tripper" were out, Friday being the official release date for both records. The music press had been integral to the group's rise, and the group had developed close relationships with its younger reporters, who often traveled with them. But some of the older writers, who'd grown up on music by Frank Sinatra and Count Basie rather than Elvis and Buddy Holly, didn't fully comprehend what was going on. *NME*'s Derek Johnson, who was thirty-seven, described "Day Tripper" as having a "steadily rocking shake beat" and decided that it was "not one of the boys' strongest melodically." "We Can Work It Out," on the other hand, with its "mid-tempo shuffle rhythm" was, he thought, "more startling in conception."

Allen Evans, who'd been writing for *NME* since 1957, was equally restrained in his review of *Rubber Soul,* concluding merely that it was "a good album with plenty of tracks you'll want to hear again and again." His song-by-song descriptions left much to be desired. "Norwegian Wood" was a "folksy bit of fun by John," and the music of George's sitar was misidentified as "Arabic-sounding guitar chords." "Nowhere Man" reminded him of the Everly Brothers, and "The Word" of gospel music. "What Goes On" was "jogging" and "tuneful," "I'm Looking Through You" was "a quiet, rocking song," and "Wait" was a "jerky" song. His entire description of John's breakthrough composition "In My Life" was "A slow song, with a beat and spinet-sounding solo in the middle. Song tells of reminiscences of life."

Record Mirror concluded, "One marvels and wonders at the constant stream of melodic ingenuity stemming from the boys, both as performers and composers. Keeping up their pace of creativeness is quite fantastic. Not, perhaps, their best LP in terms of variety, though instrumentally it's a gas!" *Melody Maker* declared after one hearing that *Rubber Soul* was "not their best." Its reviewer thought tracks like "You Won't See Me" and "Nowhere Man" were monotonous. "With-

out a shade of doubt, the Beatles sound has matured but unfortunately it also seems to have become a little subdued."

The Beatles were frustrated that pop music journalism had not
caught up with what they were doing. The reviewers had neither the
critical vocabulary nor the broad musical perspective to evaluate
the advances that they were making in the studio. If songs weren't
pounding, head-shaking rock numbers or toe-tapping melodies, the
writers concluded that the band was slipping or becoming complacent. A month before, speaking to Keith Altham, one of *NME*'s new
generation of writers, John had reluctantly conceded, "There are only
about a hundred people in the world who really understand what
our music is all about."

By late 1965 the British press was anticipating, not without a
smidgen of relish, that the Beatles might be nearing their end as the
Kings of Pop and so were scrutinizing the group's output and image,

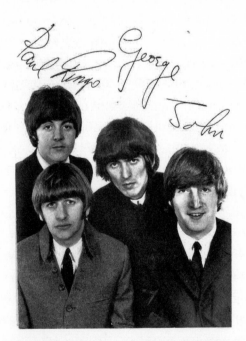

A machine-autographed publicity photo for
the Beatles, late 1965.

as well as the behavior of fans, for the first signs of decline. Two to three years was the predicted lifespan of pop stars dependent on a largely teenage market. After this they either diversified into film actors and "all-round entertainers" or risked turning up in "Where Are They Now?" columns.

British pop history was littered with people who had shone for a few singles and then either retired, hit rock bottom, or tried to woo the parents: the Vipers, the King Brothers, the Mudlarks, Terry Dene and the Dene-Agers, Emile Ford and the Checkmates, Tommy Bruce and the Bruisers. Because of this, the Beatles were frequently asked what they would do once the "bubble has burst," and none of them doubted that this was the inevitable end. John and Paul imagined their future selves as songsmiths smoking briar pipes and wearing tweed jackets with leather arm patches, and they were already writing material for other artists with this end in view. Pop stardom was transient, but songwriting was a worthy profession that involved people of all ages. For George and Ringo, putting their earnings in a business was regarded as the most sensible move.

Initially, there was no planned winter tour of Britain, because the Beatles were due to make a movie in Spain for Pickfair Films Limited, a company set up by their manager Brian Epstein and George "Bud" Ornstein, the former European head of production for United Artists films. According to press releases, this was outside of the Beatles' three-film deal with United Artists. Ornstein was a nephew of the actress Mary Pickford, who helped found United Artists in 1919 with Charlie Chaplin, D. W. Griffith, and Douglas Fairbanks, and Pickfair had been the name of the Pickford-Fairbanks studios.

Epstein, who'd spent a year studying at the Royal Academy of Dramatic Arts in London, was a great lover of theatre and film and particularly enjoyed it when his pop management brought him close to the world of actors, directors, and producers. The world of beat music and screaming teens was not his natural milieu. He was happier with classical music, ballet, and Broadway.

In February 1965, Pickfair had announced that it had commissioned Richard Condon, the American author of the 1959 bestseller *The Manchurian Candidate,* to produce a screenplay of his 1961 Western novel *A Talent for Loving.* The month before, John had invited the Geneva-based Condon out to St. Moritz, where John and his wife, Cynthia, were vacationing with producer George Martin and his then mistress, Judy Lockhart-Smith. According to Condon, John wanted him to recount the whole story so that he could be sure of getting a plum role (and wouldn't have to read the book). Then the group had doubts about Condon's script, and Epstein announced that they were delaying a planned autumn shoot due to the unpredictability of the Spanish weather, not a plausible excuse. This allowed for a short tour to be scheduled, the first in Britain for a year.

Compared to tours nowadays that involve months of rehearsals, containers full of equipment, light shows, complex staging, security teams, and hundreds of technicians, caterers, assistants, drivers, and media managers, the Beatles' 1965 tour of Britain looks positively primitive. The entire road team consisted of Mal Evans, Neil Aspinall, Brian Epstein, publicist Tony Barrow, and chauffeur Alf Bicknell. Promoter Arthur Howes came to some of the shows with his secretary, Susan Fuller.

They arrived at Berwick-upon-Tweed in Northumberland, three miles south of the Scottish border, under the cover of darkness and checked in for a night's sleep at the King's Arms Hotel, an eighteenth-century coaching inn close to the river at the center of the town. The staff and local police had been advised of the visit but were sworn to secrecy. As a result the rest of the town knew nothing about it until a week later when the *Berwick Advertiser* ran a story headlined "Beatles Came in Night and Slipped Away" with an accompanying photo of John, George, Ringo, and driver Alf Bicknell descending the hotel's main staircase.

The next day the Beatles slept late, had breakfast in bed, and then left at lunchtime dressed in thick, dark coats over jackets and turtlenecks (except for Paul, who wore a shirt and tie) and carrying small

John, followed by Ringo, George, and driver Alf Bicknell, leaving the King's Arms Hotel, Berwick-upon-Tweed, December 3, 1965.

overnight bags. During the 130-mile trip from Berwick to Glasgow in driving rain, one of George's guitars, a £300 Gretsch Country Gentleman, fell from its position strapped to the trunk and into the path of traffic behind them. It was hit by a truck and wrecked. Years later George attributed the event to karma, though he didn't take it so philosophically at the time: "Some people would say I shouldn't worry because I could buy as many replacement guitars as I wanted, but you know how it is. I kind of got attached to it." The only consolation was that it wasn't the guitar he played on stage.

Once in Glasgow they checked into the Central Hotel on Gordon Street, and at 5:10 (seventy minutes late) were ready at the Odeon for their first press conference of the tour. John was wearing his trademark Greek fisherman's cap, Ringo had on the brown suede jacket he'd worn for the cover shoot of *Rubber Soul*, George wore a baggy gray turtleneck pullover, and Paul sported a black collared button-down shirt with a floral "mod" tie bought a week earlier during a three-hour private shopping spree at the Harrods department store in Knightsbridge.

Q: How do you feel at the start of another UK tour?

JOHN: It's funny. It's always the same at the start of a tour. We are nervous. But, once we get on stage, it all goes.

Q: Why did you drive up to Glasgow instead of flying?

JOHN: We don't like flying. If we can go by road, we do. We've done so much flying without really having any accidents, so that the more we do, the more we worry. I suppose we think that, sooner or later, something might happen.

Q: What about having the Moody Blues on tour with you?

GEORGE: We've always been good friends with them. We seem to get on well. I don't think we specifically asked for them, but I know we all agreed when their name was mentioned. They go down well with the kids. Their style is different to ours, but we follow the same trends.

As with all the dates on this short tour, there were two evening shows in Glasgow, and the Beatles were supported by four groups—the Moody Blues (including Denny Laine, who would go on to be a member of Wings), the Paramounts (whose keyboard player, Gary Brooker, would form Procol Harum), the Marionettes (featuring Trinidad-born vocalist Mac Kissoon), the Koobas from Liverpool, and two solo acts from Liverpool—Beryl Marsden and Steve Aldo—who were backed by the Paramounts. An MC from Sheffield, Jerry Stevens, introduced each act and told jokes as the stage was set up between performances.

There wasn't the normal fraternizing associated with tours. The Beatles always had a separate dressing room, the groups stayed in different hotels according to what they could afford, and everyone made it to the venues with their own transport. After each show the Beatles were bundled off so quickly to an awaiting car that the Koobas never had the chance to talk to them until they went to a club after the last of the London concerts.

Exclusive access to the tour was given to twenty-five-year-old *New Musical Express* reporter Alan Smith, who'd been interviewing the Beatles since early 1963. The same age as John, and brought up on the other side of the Mersey in affluent Birkenhead, he was more attuned to the group's music and social origins than most journalists. He stayed with the tour for a few days in the north and then rejoined it when it reached London. He socialized with them in their dressing room at Glasgow's Odeon, listening to them discussing work and watching John carefully disarrange his hair before showtime ("It takes me hours to look this scruffy"). He concluded that they were a lot more serious than they had been on previous tours. They were calmer and more mature. There was less joking, drinking, and partying.

This may have been due to the fact that they'd replaced drinking with pot smoking. When they arrived at a theatre they would seek out an empty, unused room in the backstage area and disappear with Steve Aldo to have a smoke before the show. This was extremely risky at the time. A pop star caught with pot would have been as scandalous as one found with heroin today, and since pot smoking was so out of keeping with their clean and cheerful image, the Beatles' reputation would have been irreparably damaged.

The calmness may also have been a result of accepting their lot in show business life. They had wanted to ascend to the "toppermost of the poppermost" (as John would jokingly describe it in the days when they traveled in the back of a van along with their equipment), make lots of money, and become bigger than Elvis, and now that they had achieved these things, they found themselves prisoners of their own adolescent dreams. They had achieved their early ambitions, and yet their freedom of movement was now restricted because of their fame, their musical development was impeded by not being able to hear themselves play, and the sheer joy that they had experienced on stage when unknown was fast evaporating.

Fifteen years later, in one of his last interviews, John said, "The idea of being a rock 'n' roll musician sort of suited my talents and mentality, and the freedom was great. But then I found out I wasn't free. I'd got boxed in. It wasn't just because of my contract, but the contract was the physical manifestation of being in prison. And with that I might as well have gone to a nine-to-five job as to carry on the way I was carrying on. Rock 'n' roll was not fun anymore."

There were conflicting reports about the intensity of Beatlemania as 1965 drew to a close. Newspapers had a vested interest in keeping the phenomenon alive (it spiced up news and sold copies), but they also wanted to be the first on the scene when it began to experience its death throes. The unspoken rule was that those who benefitted from huge acclaim, financial reward, and natural talent should eventually suffer for their success.

On December 4, the *Daily Mirror* reported that 131 teenage girls had to be treated by ambulance staff during the two Glasgow shows and that six fans were taken to the hospital—a third of the casualties had fainted, and two-thirds had succumbed to "hysteria." It said that there had been "a continuous chorus of screaming," at times so loud that the music was drowned out. Alan Smith, however, heard the same screams and judged that they were less intense than at past shows. "Crazy Beatlemania is over, certainly," he would conclude in his December 10 report. "Beatles fans are now a little bit more sophisticated than Rolling Stones followers, for instance, and there were certainly no riots at the Glasgow opening night. But there were two jam-packed houses, some fainting fits, and thunderous waves of screams that set the city's Odeon theatre trembling."

If the fans were screaming at lower volumes and fainting in smaller numbers, it may have been because of the Beatles' change of material. "People who expect things to always be the same are stupid," Paul told Smith. "You can't live in the past. I suppose things would be that little bit wilder if we did big raving, rocking numbers all the time, just like we did at the beginning. But how long could we last if we did that? We'd be called old fashioned in no time. And doing the same thing all the time would just drive us round the bend."

The next day began with a 150-mile drive to Newcastle, where they checked into the Royal Turk's Head Hotel on Grey Street. At the venue, City Hall, they were given a darkened TV room next to their dressing room to relax in. When they weren't on stage, they watched the Saturday night ITV schedule, including the American TV series *Lost In Space,* an episode of *The Avengers* starring Patrick Macnee as John Steed and Diana Rigg as Emma Peel in which the duo tracked down a criminal businessman who was bumping off financiers through use of new-fangled paging devices that triggered heart attacks ("Dial a Deadly Number"), and an edition of the light entertainment show *Thank Your Lucky Stars,* presented by Jim Dale, in which the Beatles were featured in a film clip playing "We Can Work It Out" and "Day Tripper." Other guests included Tom Jones, the Shadows, the Kinks, Dennis Lotis, and Mark Wynter.

The clips had been filmed at Twickenham Film Studios on November 23 and were intended to satisfy the demand of TV stations without the group having to sacrifice time by traveling to them all. It was a time- and cost-effective way of promoting their music while retaining control of presentation. All the clips were shot in the studio, and other than changing their clothes and the sets no effort at visual storytelling was made. Renting the set cost £750, and the BBC paid £1,750 for the rights to be the first to screen them. It was the birth of the promotional pop video, something the group would develop further in 1966. "We had great ideas for it," John told Alan Smith. "We thought it was going to be an outdoor thing, and with more of a visual appeal. I'm not really happy the way it's turned out, but it hasn't put me off this kind of idea for the future. I've no objection to filming TV appearances. For a start, it means we can film them all in one day instead of traipsing round the country to do different programmes."

The Newcastle dates were notable not for rioting or collapsing fans but for the showers of jelly beans and "gonks" (small egg-shaped novelty toys with frizzy hair) hurled onto the stage. Between shows the Beatles were served dinner and were interviewed by local news-paper journalist Philip Norman, who would much later become a staff writer with the *Sunday Times* and a celebrated biographer of the Beatles, John Lennon, and Paul McCartney. When the second show ended, they again retreated to the TV room to watch the play *The Paraffin Season* by Donald Churchill as part of the *Armchair Theatre* se-ries, which had recently been moved from its coveted spot on Sunday night. Hotels in those days rarely provided in-room TVs, and one of the stars of *The Paraffin Season,* the Liverpudlian actor Norman Ross-ington, had acted with the Beatles the previous year in *A Hard Day's Night* (where he played the group's manager, Norm).

According to Alan Smith it was a quiet night, and the boys all returned to the hotel after the show. According to another source, some of them at least stayed up late, partying with the Moody Blues and playing LPs by the Isley Brothers and B. B. King.

The next day they rose late from bed and didn't leave for Liv-erpool until 1:00 p.m. No other British city had seen more of the Beatles. Since the group's earliest incarnation in 1957 they'd made over five hundred local appearances. Their uncles, aunts, school friends, parents, and cousins all still lived there, as did many of the fans who'd faithfully stuck by them in the days when they played cover versions and dreamed of international stardom. "Liverpool is home," said John. "As they all know us, we'll be expected to do well, and we'll get nervous."

The two shows they played at the Empire Theatre would be their last ever in Liverpool. The Empire had played a role at key times in their career. It was here that both Paul and George had seen the Ca-nadian vocal quarter the Crew-Cuts in concert in September 1955, and where Paul had lined up at the stage door to collect their auto-graphs. It was here that John had (unsuccessfully) auditioned with the Quarry Men for talent scout Carroll Levis in 1957 and John, Paul, and George had auditioned as Johnny and the Moondogs for Levis in 1959. In October 1962 it had been the scene of their first major theatre show, on a bill headlined by Little Richard. In December 1963 they'd played here before fan club members in a special afternoon event, part of which was screened on BBC TV as *It's the Beatles.*

It was sadly appropriate that on the day of their final Liverpool engagement they were approached by fans campaigning to prevent the closure of the Cavern, the cellar club close to the docks where they'd played almost three hundred of their early gigs. The city council was demanding that it modernize its sanitation and drainage, but the owner couldn't afford the expense. The Beatles were not about to bail out a failing business. As yet there was no Beatles tourist industry in the city, and no one was thinking of plaques, preservation orders, or the involvement of the National Trust. It was Paul who suggested that it could be turned into a local attraction, while John announced, "We don't feel we owe the Cavern anything physical." Two months later it closed down, and despite a brief reprieve it was filled in and covered by a parking lot in 1973.

As with the Glasgow concerts, the level of fan enthusiasm was hard to calculate. Careful policing prevented the street riots of previous years, and the count of fainters (a mere seventeen out of a total audience of five thousand) made it appear less hysterical in press reports, but the screaming and dancing in the aisles persisted. The noise was loud enough for Paul to ask anxiously whether his voice was being picked up by the microphones and for Ringo to comment later, "You heard them. You saw them. That's the answer to the knockers who say we're on the way out." Yet Alan Smith could still write in *New Musical Express*: "Even in 'the Pool,' however, I noticed a quietening down of audience reaction compared with previous concerts. I'm not knocking in any way—I just think the group's fans are getting a bit more sensible lately. There was tons of thunderous applause to compensate for the lowered screaming decibel rate!"

Friends and family were on hand to greet the group backstage, including the Labour MP for Liverpool Exchange, Bessie Braddock; the young comedian Jimmy Tarbuck, who had been at school with John; Ringo's mother, Elsie, and stepfather, Harry Graves; and George's parents, Harold and Louise, and his model girlfriend, Pattie Boyd, whom he'd met in 1964 on the set of *A Hard Day's Night*. There had initially been plans for more shows that Monday, but the Beatles preferred time off to spend with relatives and friends.

The Beatles were proud Liverpudlians. Unlike previous generations of entertainers from the north of Britain they didn't try to modify their regional accents or disguise their working-class roots. They loved the community feeling that had been fostered by hard times, the natural unpretentiousness, the droll sense of humor, and the cosmopolitanism that came from generations of immigration.

So much of what made the Beatles unique—their wit, their word-play, their grass-roots left-wing sympathies—was an inheritance of having been born and raised in Liverpool. Yet Liverpool was also a place that young people with ambition like them strained to escape from. The people were warm and overwhelmingly working class, yet the architecture in the city center was austere and grandly imperial. There were exciting connections with the major ports of the world because of the ships that sailed from the Mersey, yet culturally it lagged behind the south. In the 1950s and early 1960s all of Britain's regional cities were two to three years behind the capital when it came to trends in fashion and lifestyle. It was to London that the Beatles looked for all the latest changes in pop music and to London that they moved in the first year of their fame. Said George: "I get a funny feeling when I go back to Liverpool. I feel sad because the people there are living in a circle. They're missing out on so much. I'd like them to know about everything—everything that I've learnt by getting out of the rut."

As soon as they came into money Paul, George, and Ringo improved the lives of their parents by moving them out of their government-subsidized housing to large properties in more prestigious areas. Ironically, it was John, the "working class hero," who had grown up in the most middle-class home, who moved his Aunt

Mimi to one of the most expensive areas of Britain's South Coast—
Sandbanks, in Dorset. When he bought her six-bedroom house on
Panorama Road in 1965, it cost eight times the average British home
of the day.

Tuesday's concerts in Ardwick, Manchester, were affected by bad
road conditions. A heavy fog brought traffic on the Liverpool–East
Lancashire Road to a standstill, and the Beatles didn't arrive at the
ABC Cinema until twelve minutes after they were due on stage. An
extra interval had to be inserted to compensate, the support acts extended their spots, and MC Jerry Stevens was left frantically thinking
of things to say to prevent fans from rioting.

From Manchester they moved on to the steel city of Sheffield,
where they played the Gaumont Cinema on Wednesday, December 8,
and then drove to Birmingham on December 9 to play at the Odeon.
In Sheffield twenty fans fainted, and Paul was hit in the eye by a pear
drop that left him blinking throughout the show. Fred Norris, the
thirty-eight-year-old theatre critic for the *Birmingham Evening Mail*,
summarized the Beatles' thirty-minute set as "one long ear-aching,
head-reeling blast" and said that the behavior of the fans ranked as
some of the worst he'd ever witnessed. "If this is modern 'live' music,"
he concluded, "one understands why The Beatles themselves spent
most of their time backstage, watching television."

When "We Can Work It Out" / "Day Tripper" reached only No. 3
on *Melody Maker*'s new chart (beaten out by the Seekers' "The Carnival Is Over" and "My Generation" by the Who), the *Daily Mirror*
headline was "Beatles' New Disc Misses No 1 Spot" over a story that
began, "A two year Beatles' record went west yesterday. For the first
time since December 7, 1963 a newly-issued single disc by the Mer-
seysiders failed to fly automatically to No 1 in the *Melody Maker* pops
chart."

The *Daily Express* featured a subdued photo of John and Paul
dressed in black next to the headline "From the Revealing Album
of David Bailey . . . to Mark What Might Be a New Phase in the Era

The double-A-sided single "We Can Work It Out" / "Day Tripper" made the British charts in December 1965.

of the Beatles." After making the same point as the *Daily Mirror* that the new single had "failed to reach the top spot" (despite making No. 1 on a rival chart by *New Musical Express*), show business correspondent Judith Simons posed the question "Does this mark a change in Beatlemania?" George Harrison didn't think it did. He felt it was the result of marketing the single as a double A side, the first time any artist had done so. In the end "We Can Work It Out," composed predominantly by Paul, was deemed the more popular song.

Contained in these stories was other news that would reveal the deeper nature of what was happening. UK advance orders for the new LP, *Rubber Soul,* stood at five hundred thousand, almost the same as the number of singles that had been sold. It was, Simons noted, "believed to be the biggest ever advance demand" for a British LP. In other words, the big story wasn't that the Beatles had failed to take the top spot of the singles charts immediately after their new release but that fans were now buying LPs in equal volumes. An LP by the

Beatles was changing from something bought as a nonessential supplement to the singles—often as a special birthday treat or Christmas
gift—to the very focus of their music-making career.

The pinnacle of the tour was the two London dates—the first at
the Odeon Cinema in Hammersmith and the second at the Astoria
Cinema in Finsbury Park. The expectation had been that these would
be the toughest shows, because Londoners had more opportunity to
see great entertainment and therefore prided themselves on their
cool restraint. Audiences in the provinces were expected to go wild,
but London fans usually made performers work hard for applause.

This time the opposite proved to be true. The audiences in both
venues erupted. After the second show at Finsbury Park Alan Smith
reported,

This was the wildest, rip-it-up Beatles performance I have
watched in over two years. Girls have been running amok
on the stage chased by hefty attendants. Some were hysterical and I have just seen one girl carried out of the theatre
screaming and kicking and with tears streaming down her
contorted face.

Finsbury Park Astoria holds 3,000 people and I swear
that almost every one of them has been standing on a seat.
Now, after the show, some of the seats in the front stalls lie
battered out of existence. They tell me the hysteria and the
fan scenes were even worse at Hammersmith last night. I did
not think I would say this again but, without question, BEA-
TLEMANIA IS BACK! Don't get me wrong. In saying that, I
have not been swayed simply by the screams. In the NME last
week I told of the tremendous reception given to the Beatles
in Glasgow, Newcastle, Liverpool and Manchester. But these
London concerts were different. I have not seen hysteria like
this at a Beatles show since the word Beatlemania erupted
into headlines!

Backstage at Hammersmith the Beatles socialized with Gary Leeds and John Maus of the Walker Brothers, themselves now the object of screaming fans after the success of the single "Make It Easy on Yourself" and their debut LP, *Take It Easy with the Walker Brothers*. The Americans discussed the technical aspects of guitar playing with the Beatles, then watched the concert from the wings. After the show they accompanied the Beatles to the newly opened Scotch of St James, a club that had become the headquarters of London's cool and fashionable elite.

Their final British tour date was at the Capitol Theatre in Cardiff on Sunday, December 12, the day after Finsbury Park. Toward the end of the second set there was a worrying incident when a man managed to get on stage while John was introducing "Day Tripper" and made a lunge for Paul and George before being grabbed by security guards. He was swiftly ejected, but it was a salient reminder of how vulnerable the Beatles were to attack.

John was also involved in mild religious controversy. Oxfam had recently used his illustration accompanying his poem "The Fat Budgie" from *A Spaniard in the Works*, his second book of poems and drawings, for one of its 1965 Christmas cards. This didn't go down well with some supporters of the Oxford Committee for Famine Relief (to give the charity its full title). They felt it was in poor taste to use a pop star's cartoon of a budgie to celebrate the birth of Jesus Christ. One such opponent, Rev. Frederick Nickalls of Barnehurst, Kent, was quoted as saying, "The John Lennon card has nothing to do with Christmas. It is a pity that Oxfam should choose such a card. Those old world pictures of stage coaches, snow and candles are more Christian than The Fat Budgie."

After the second show in Cardiff the Beatles got into the Austin Princess, and Alf Bicknell drove them out of the city, from where they were escorted by police cars and onto the road back to London. They were delivered to the Scotch, where they celebrated the end of the tour.

Paul returned to the Scotch the next night, December 13, for what would turn out to be a memorable occasion for him. John,

The Fat Budgie

An Oxfam Christmas card featuring John's drawing
"The Fat Budgie" from *A Spaniard in the Works*,
December 1965.

Ringo, and George had taken LSD by this time and were enthusiastic about the way in which they felt the drug made them more creative, open-minded, and loving. They argued that it unleashed human potential by revealing how artificial many of the restrictions are that we place on our understanding. Their campaigning made Paul feel like an outsider. It was as though the three of them possessed some special knowledge and were leaving Paul behind. The closer that John got to George, the more of a threat it was to the Lennon-McCartney partnership.

Many others in Paul's London coterie were converts to LSD, but Paul was cautious by nature. He'd heard the rumors of depression, schizophrenia, and madness that could be triggered by LSD and was reluctant to experiment foolishly with something as finely tuned and fragile as the brain. He was sensible, responsible, and loath to do anything that could damage his career or his mental health. He always remembered his father's advice of "moderation in all things, son." At the same time, he was adventurous and keen not to dismiss out of hand any tool that offered to expand his consciousness and liberate his imagination.

Paul had become friendly with the Honourable Tara Browne, the son of Oonagh Guinness and Dominick Geoffrey Edward Browne (Fourth Baron Oranmoore and Browne, member of the House of Lords since 1927), who at twenty had already been schooled at Eton, privately tutored in Paris, and married and was the father of two sons. The young Irishman had become the archetypal swinging Londoner from the aristocratic set. He didn't need to work, owned a house in Belgravia, and was due a million-pound inheritance when he turned twenty-five, so he spent his time partying, driving fast cars, taking drugs, and dressing like a pop star. It was an indication of class barriers buckling, if not altogether crumbling, that Browne's set of friends was defined more by wealth, looks, and available leisure time than blood, education, or family connections. Lords and ladies now mingled with the sons and daughters of cotton salesmen, factory workers, bus drivers, and coal miners, probably because the ascendant working class wanted what they had (wealth, property, manners, style) and they wanted what the ascendant working class had (drive, creative talent, fame, acclaim, and street smarts).

In the early hours of December 14, Viv Prince, the twenty-one-year-old recently deported drummer of the Pretty Things, an R & B band from London that made the Stones look well-groomed, restrained, and conventional, arrived at the Scotch with the Who's bass player, John Entwistle. The two of them had just driven 120 miles down from Norwich, where the Who had played the Federation Club on Oak Street with Prince deputizing for Keith Moon, who was out of action for two weeks with whooping cough. At the Scotch they met Paul, John, and Tara Browne's wife, Nicky. She invited Prince back to the couple's mews cottage in Belgravia along with Paul, John, dancer Patrick Kerr, and a few attractive girls. John declined the offer,

The Pretty Things: Dick Taylor, Brian Pendleton, Viv Prince, Phil May, and John Stax. Prince left the group in November 1965.

because he'd promised to get back to Cynthia at their home in Weybridge.

When the revelers got to Eaton Row, Tara Browne was at home and suggested that they take LSD. Paul was still apprehensive. He was more in the mood for a joint and some drinks but the relief of the tour being over and the relaxing of responsibility that came with a few weeks of not having to write, record, perform, or be interviewed persuaded him that now was as good a time as ever to take the plunge. Prince had heard about LSD from his friend Brian Jones of the Rolling Stones but had never taken it and had no clear idea what the effects would be. The liquid drug was pure and was dropped onto sugar lumps that Nicky served with the tea, saying, "One lump or two?"

The trippers stayed up all night. Paul saw paisley shapes and experienced "weird things" that made him feel slightly disturbed. He looked at his shirtsleeves, and the dirt on the cuffs was so intensified that it made him feel angry. He became sensitive to every kind of stimulus—light, sound, color, even the touch of fabric. There suddenly seemed to be so much more to be gleaned from the simple things of life—depths of experience that he had so far ignored or glossed over.

Prince reacted in a very different way. Rather than becoming quiet and reflective he started drinking heavily while Paul sat leafing through a book of art. One particular image that caught Paul's eye transfixed him for over an hour as he processed all the detail.

Paul has since wrongly dated this experience to late 1966, leading critics to believe that everything he wrote for *Revolver* was done before he, to adopt the language of Timothy Leary, had turned on and tuned in. Some writers have even speculated that Paul's artistry on the LP was the result of him resisting John and George's pressure to trip by showing them that he could outperform them without chemical assistance. But Prince's revelation in interviews with me that this took place immediately after the Beatles' last tour date of 1965 alters our understanding. After all, Paul has agreed with John's statement that no one is the same after taking LSD and had called his experiences "amazing" and "deeply emotional." In 1967 he told the *Daily Mirror* that his initial trip was "quite an incredible experience" that lasted for six hours; he said, "[It] opened my eyes to the fact that there is a God" and "made me a better person."

The first of Paul's songs recorded by the Beatles after December 1965, and therefore almost certainly the first song he composed after tripping, was "Got to Get You Into My Life." Believing he first took LSD in late 1966, he has said in interviews (and in his book *Many Years from Now*) that the song was about pot, but the language of taking "a ride," seeing "another kind of mind," and not knowing what he "would find there" is more consistent with the language of a psychedelic trip than a marijuana high. In the song he's talking about getting this new perspective, this new consciousness, into his life. "Far from harming me," he told the *Daily Mirror,* "it helped me to see a lot more truth. I am more mature. I am less cynical. I have started to be honest with myself." It turns out that John was right after all when he told *Playboy*, "It ["Got to Get You Into My Life"] actually describes his experience taking acid. I think that's what he's talking about. I couldn't swear to it, but I think it was a result of that."

The psychedelic experience had a reputation for challenging people's basic assumptions, often leading them to believe that their lives up to that point had been based on false information or a shared fiction. Users began to question what was "real," "normal," or "proper" as the old standards and guideposts began to crumble. When it came to music, this manifested itself in a new attitude of openness. The dividers that separated pop from classical, Western from Eastern, and low art from high art no longer appeared relevant. Neither did the rules about the length of songs or the volume of recordings. Everything was more fluid than we had been led to believe.

But despite the changes that were taking place in the outlook of the Beatles, they were still wedded to many old show business practices. For example, they had become a part of the British Christmas experience. The season of goodwill was also the season of good business. *With the Beatles* had been released in late November 1963 and *Beatles for Sale* in December 1964. It made sound commercial sense. In both those years they'd also had the top spot on the singles chart, with "She Loves You" in 1963 and "I Feel Fine" in 1964. This year was no different in that respect. "Day Tripper" / "We Can Work It Out" topped the Christmas hit parade, while *Rubber Soul* was the bestselling album. However, the normal effusive jollity was at odds with their newly emerging seriousness as artists.

In 1965, they continued the tradition of making a Christmas flexi-disc recording exclusively for members of the Official Beatles Fan Club in the UK, but they were less cuddly and congratulatory. They sent up the idea of giving a message by spending the entire six minutes and twenty seconds of recording time messing about, adopting silly voices, and trying to make each other giggle. They sang a raucous version of "Auld Lang Syne," changed the words of "Yesterday" to "Christmas Day," and almost plowed through the Four Tops' summer hit "It's the Same Old Song" until George shouted out "Copyright! You can't sing that."

For the past two years the Beatles had headlined special Christmas shows in London that lasted almost three weeks and involved other acts managed by Brian Epstein's company, NEMS Enterprises. For these festive spectaculars they would dress up in costumes and take part in sketches as well as sing as a group. In August 1965 it had been announced that Epstein's artists would again be putting on a Christmas special, with Cilla Black, Gerry and the Pacemakers, and Billy J. Kramer and the Dakotas, but noticeably no Beatles. Asked in a Canadian press conference whether they'd be appearing, John had said, "Ask Mr. Christmas Epstein."

Simply put, they were butting against the boundaries of "light" entertainment. It would have been incongruous for them to dress up in capes, shawls, top hats, and cloth caps to sing recent songs such as "The Word," "In My Life," or "Norwegian Wood." They didn't want to be like previous British pop stars Cliff Richard and Tommy Steele, who'd broadened their audience by doing musicals, revues, and vaudeville-style shows that appealed to adults. This strategy may have fulfilled some of Epstein's dreams of a life in the theatre, but it fulfilled none of theirs.

Besides, they hadn't had a proper Christmas break since 1959. Every year since then they'd had engagements between Christmas Eve and New Year's Day. In 1962 they'd spent fourteen days in Hamburg with only December 25 off. This year John and Ringo wanted to remain at home in Weybridge with their children (Ringo's son, Zak Starkey, had been born on September 13), and Paul and George wanted to travel north to visit their parents.

On December 23, while they were driving together through London, George proposed to Pattie. He'd had to get Epstein's permission beforehand, because this was still an era when the marriage of a male pop star could cost them fans and even end a career. Under existing moral codes, a married man was no longer available, and eligibility was crucial to pop stardom. As Epstein had said in his biography *A Cellarful of Noise,* published in 1964, "It is unwise for pop singers to marry, and so they stay single. But if they [Paul, George, and Ringo] were determined to wed, there is nothing I would wish to do to stop them."

Paul's long-term

THEATRE ROYAL, BRISTOL
Licensee: *Douglas Morris*
Monday, 27th December 1965 to Saturday, 29th January 1966.
The Bristol Old Vic Trust Ltd.
in association with The Arts Council of Gt. Britain
presents
THE BRISTOL OLD VIC COMPANY
in
THE HAPPIEST DAYS OF YOUR LIFE
by JOHN DIGHTON
Characters in order of appearance:

Dick Tassell .... MATTHEW ROBERTON
  Assistant Master at Hilary Hall
Rainbow .... TERRENCE HARDIMAN
  School Porter and Groundsman
Rupert Billings .... PETER FRENCH
  Senior Assistant Master at Hilary Hall
Godfrey Pond .... FRANK MIDDLEMASS
  Headmaster at Hilary Hall
Miss Evelyn Whitchurch .... HAZEL HUGHES
  Principal of St. Swithins School for Girls
Miss Gossage .... THELMA BARLOW
  Senior Assistant Mistress at St. Swithins
Hopcroft Mi. .... STANLEY BATES
  Pupil at Hilary Hall
Barbara Cahoun .... JANE ASHER
  Pupil at St. Swithins
Joyce Harper .... JANE LAPOTAIRE
  Assistant Mistress at St. Swithins
The Reverend Edward Peck .... TOM MINNIKIN
Mrs. Peck. .... JOSEPHINE SHORE
  his wife
Edgar Sowter .... PATRICK STEWART
Mrs. Sowter. .... MARGARET LAMB
  his wife

Directed by DENIS CAREY
Setting designed by GRAHAM BARLOW
Lighting by Kenneth Vowles

The action of the play takes place in the Masters' Common Room at Hilary Hall School for Boys, in Hampshire.
ACT I. The first day of the Summer Term. Afternoon.
ACT II. Saturday afternoon. Three weeks later.
ACT III. Two hours later.

There will be Two Intervals of Twelve Minutes

A theater program for the Bristol Old Vic production of John Dighton's play *The Happiest Days of Your Life,* which featured Jane Asher.

girlfriend, Jane Asher, had arrived in Bristol to play the schoolgirl Barbara Cahoun in John Dighton's play *The Happiest Days of Your Life* at the Theatre Royal, opening on December 27. Paul spent a couple of days at Rembrandt, the house on the Wirral close to Liverpool that he'd bought his father in 1964, only to find that his brother, Mike, had invited Tara Browne as a houseguest. (Although they were married for less than three years, the Brownes were on the verge of separation, and Tara was living an independent life).

On the night of Boxing Day Paul invited Browne to travel five miles to visit his cousin Bette, who lived in Higher Bebington. He had bought two new Raleigh mopeds from Camerons' Cycles in nearby Neston to make the trip more adventurous than a normal drive. Riding along the narrow Brimstage Road, slightly high on pot, Paul was pointing out local landmarks and staring up at the bright crescent moon when his front wheel hit a stone and he was thrown off. His face hit the ground, causing an upper front left tooth to chip and forcing it through his lip. His left eyebrow was also gashed. Despite the damage and the flow of blood he continued the journey, and when they arrived Bette called up the family practitioner, Dr. "Pip" Jones, to attend to the wound.

According to Paul in the *Anthology* book, the doctor proceeded to try to give him stitches despite having no local anesthetic and a shaky hand. He lost the thread on the first attempt and so had to go back and resew the cut. Paul didn't get the tooth capped until June 1966 despite Brian Epstein urging him to do so, and the gap was visible in May when the video for "Paperback Writer" was shot (despite an attempt to temporarily fill it with a piece of chewing gum).

Paul's left eye was swollen and the eyebrow above was matted with blood. The gash on the lip looked to be at least an inch long and quite deep. News leaked out, and on December 31 the *Daily Mirror* ran a news story with the headline "No Fight, Says Injured Beatle." It read: "Beatle Paul McCartney denied last night that his gashed eyebrow and cut lip were the result of a fight. He said he had fallen off his moped during his Christmas stay with his father near Liverpool." Later a photo of his damaged face (taken by brother Mike and stolen from Paul's home by a dishonest chauffeur) surfaced in an Italian magazine as evidence of "wild Beatle drug parties in swinging London." (Incidentally, this disproves a story frequently told by Paul that his Sgt. Pepper–era mustache was occasioned by the need to conceal the damage from this moped accident. Over ten months separated the two events.)

Meanwhile, John's Christmas was slightly marred by the reemergence of his father, Alf (now "Freddie") Lennon. Singer Tom Jones's dad had discovered him washing dishes at a restaurant in Shepperton, Surrey, and one of Jones's management team, Tony Cartwright, had made contact with him with a view to cutting a novelty record. They managed to get a recording contract with Piccadilly (distributed by Pye), and a publishing deal with Leeds Music, and Cartwright set about composing a "song" based on Freddie's reminiscences. The result, produced in Twickenham by John Schroeder (cowriter of Helen Shapiro's hit "Walking Back to Happiness" and leader of the easy-listening instrumental group Sounds Orchestral), was a cloying spoken-word track titled "That's My Life" replete with crashing waves, sobbing violins, and choral voices, over which Freddie recited platitudes about his up-and-down life. It began to get a lot of airplay because of the Lennon name.

Flushed with newfound fame, Freddie decided to pay his long-abandoned son an unannounced visit at his Weybridge home. It did not have a happy ending. "It was only the second time in my life I'd seen him," John later revealed. "I showed him the door. I wasn't having him in the house."

Irritated by what he saw as his father's exploitation of the family name, John asked Epstein to use his power to get the record suppressed. Epstein wanted Pye to withdraw it and stop the publicity campaign. Cartwright and Freddie were discreetly compensated for their potential losses (probably with funds supplied by John) to the tune of eight thousand pounds, and Pye was rewarded for its compliance in dropping the record by being given permission to use the Lennon-McCartney song "Michelle" with a group called the Overlanders that it had been recording without success since 1963. (Their version would top the UK charts in January and be the group's only hit.)

It's easy to forget that in 1965 rock 'n' roll–inspired pop did not yet dominate the British charts. Of the ten bestselling singles for this year, only the Beatles' "Help!" and "I'm Alive" by the Hollies

would have qualified. The rest were comprised of folk ("I'll Never
Find Another You" by the Seekers), ballads ("Tears" by the Liverpool
comedian Ken Dodd and "Crying in the Chapel" by Elvis Presley),
instrumentals ("A Walk in the Black Forest" by classically trained
German pianist Horst Jankowski and "Zorba's Dance" by Italian
bouzouki player Marcello Minerbi), pop (Cliff Richard's "The Minute You're Gone"), and the country sound of Roger Miller's "King of
the Road."

Half of the Top 10 albums were taken up with the soundtracks
of three musicals (*Mary Poppins, The Sound of Music,* and *My Fair Lady*)
and easy listening LPs by Andy Williams (*Almost There*) and Irish entertainer Val Doonican (*The Lucky 13 Shades of Val Doonican*). The other
half had two recordings each by Bob Dylan (*Freewheelin'* and *Bringing
It All Back Home*) and the Beatles (*Beatles for Sale* and *Help!*) and one by
the Stones (*Rolling Stones No. 2*).

Epstein threw an end-of-year party for his artists at his Belgravia
home. After most of the guests had left, Epstein gathered the Beatles,
his assistant Peter Brown, and Steve Aldo in a room at the top of
the house he called the smoking room. There were gold discs on the
walls, a small jukebox on top of a desk, modernistic cube seats, and,
between the windows, a ship's wheel. Brian said he had Christmas
gifts from Capitol Records for the boys. He presented a small balsa-
wood box filled with straw. When the Beatles broke it open they
found several eggs, all numbered, and instructions to open them in
order. Inside each egg was a clue to the identity of the real gift, and
in the final one a photograph of a new-fangled piece of technology.
It was called a video recorder. None of them had even heard of such
an invention at the time. Early in the new year a VTR machine was
delivered to each of the Beatles' homes.

Three months later Paul talked about his recorder. "It's the
greatest little present ever," he would say. "You just plug it into your
set and you record the program straight off, just like onto a tape. You
can record BBC while you're watching ITV and show the film on your

telly at one o'clock in the morning if you want to. They said we'd be the first people in England to have them."

The Beatles' position at the top of the record industry gave them privileged access to such advances. They traveled more widely than most of their contemporaries, listened to a greater variety of music, and were kept abreast of all the latest cultural trends. If a new club opened, they were on the invitation list. If a new style of cuisine was introduced, they'd be among the first to taste it. They were magnets for some of the most creative people in the popular arts, many of whom became part of their inner circle and benefitted from their patronage.

Paul's Christmas gift to his fellow Beatles was an acetate disc of a radio-style show that he'd taped at home featuring music tracks by artists he thought they should take note of, linked by Paul speaking in the style of a New York DJ. "It was something crazy, something left-field just for the Beatles . . . that they could play late in the evening," he later explained. "It was called *Unforgettable* and started with Nat King Cole's 'Unforgettable.' It was like a magazine programme full of weird interviews, experimental music, tape loops and some tracks that I knew the others hadn't heard."

He was clearly hinting at the direction the Beatles might go when they reconvened in the studio, offering the sort of rich palette from which they might choose. Besides "Unforgettable" and the experimental sounds there was "Down Home Girl" by the Rolling Stones, "Don't Be Cruel" by Elvis, Martha and the Vandellas singing "Heat Wave," the Beach Boys with "I Get Around," and the Peter and Gordon LP track "Someone Ain't Right."

Reflecting on the record selection a few months later George said, "It was a peculiar overall sound. John, Ringo and I played it and realized Paul was on to something new. Paul has done a lot in making us realize that there are a lot of electronic sounds to investigate. If we're in the studio we don't mentally think that this is the Beatles making a new hit LP or single. It's just us, four blokes with some ideas, good and bad, to thrash out."

USING JOHN'S LATER ANALOGY OF THE BEATLES BEING PART of a ship that a whole generation had climbed aboard, it's easy to see how he saw them as being in the crow's nest. They were high up and therefore visible to everyone, and, because of their vantage point, they were the first to spot storms and the first to spy landfall. This was the position they found themselves in at the start of 1966. The things they would see from the crow's nest over the next twelve months would reverberate through the decades to come.

JANUARY 1966

I think we are being influenced at the moment
by what we know we could do, and what we
know we will eventually be able to do.
-PAUL, 1966

Brian Epstein didn't exactly raise expectations when asked for his predictions for 1966. In his typically measured tones he said, "I see 1966 as being very similar to last year for the Beatles, with progress being made musically as ever. On the other hand, I must state that no film plans have been finalised for the New Year."

The early reports from America on the sales of *Rubber Soul* were encouraging. *Billboard* announced that in the first nine days of its release it had already sold 1.2 million copies—breaking all previous records.

The LP may have perplexed the old guard of entertainment correspondents, but it was a beacon for fledgling rock critics (as they would soon be called) as well as for a new generation of musicians who knew exactly what the Beatles were trying to do.

Chief among these musicians was Brian Wilson, leader of California's Beach Boys. His group's career had shared a similar trajectory to the Beatles': the musicians started out with a clean-cut look and appealed to screaming teenagers, but then had made their music more complex and the lyrics more introspective and adult. Wilson had been born in Hawthorne, California, two days after Paul was born in Liverpool, and both had become bass players and songwriters with a keen ear for melody and harmony. Both were eager to extend the parameters of pop.

When Wilson heard *Rubber Soul* for the first time, he was at his home on Laurel Way in Beverly Hills smoking marijuana with Terry Melcher (producer of the Byrds and son of actor and singer Doris Day). The musical experience affected him so profoundly he claimed not to have slept for the next two nights. He marveled at the expansion of the group's subject matter and Paul's more intricate bass playing, and also at the fact that the record sounded like a cohesive whole rather than a collection of potential singles with not-so-good songs added as padding. According to Wilson, it was the next day that he sat down at the piano with his new lyricist, Tony Asher, and began work on "God Only Knows," the first song for the Beach Boys' LP that would be titled *Pet Sounds*.

"Hearing *Rubber Soul* was really a challenge to me," he said. "I told Marilyn [his wife] that I was going to make the greatest rock album ever. That's how blown out I was over the Beatles. I had the feeling in my gut that I could do it. *Rubber Soul* got to my soul, and I wanted to do something as good as that. I just made up my mind to do something that expressed what was in my heart and soul. I didn't care about sales. I just cared about the artistic merit of it."

Thus began the pop equivalent of an arms race where, inspired by the advances of those they considered to be their most worthy opposition, singers and groups tried to maintain or advance their positions by developing challenging new sounds. The hard core of this movement included the Beatles, the Beach Boys, the Stones, the Byrds, the Who, the Animals, the Yardbirds, the Kinks, Bob Dylan, the Impressions, Smokey Robinson, and the Motown writing, arranging, and producing team Holland-Dozier-Holland. There was no resentment between the participants, but they all kept a close watch on each other and tried to come up with new material that would top everyone else's achievements.

The fertility of Paul's mind at the time was well captured in a remarkable interview he had given in November to the British writer and literary critic Francis Wyndham for a short-lived upmarket weekly magazine called *London Life*. Wyndham was by then forty-one, compared to Paul's twenty-three, and had only a glancing interest in rock and pop. He was the son of a soldier and diplomat, had been educated at Eton, and contributed to publications such as *Queen* and the *Times Literary Supplement*. Perhaps the fact that Wyndham wasn't a journalist from a music or teen magazine gave Paul the confidence to talk about his work in a broader social and cul-

tural context. He was now eager to establish the fact that Lennon-McCartney was a serious writing partnership drawing from a rich variety of influences, both literary and musical, and that rock 'n' roll was a vital part of the dramatic cultural changes taking place.

Wyndham had first met with both John and Paul but described the meeting by saying, "They gave an impenetrable performance—a double act with John facetiously

This Gerald Scarfe cartoon of the Beatles accompanied an in-depth interview with Paul published in *London Life*.

punning on clichés and Paul obligingly feeding him. The jokes were good but no better than Beatle jokes on the cinema or television screens." The resulting quotes were unusable, so he rebooked Paul on his own, and they spoke for two hours at Brian Epstein's office in London's West End. "He was ready to talk about his music," Wyndham wrote, "and did so with the minimum of suspicion or self-consciousness." The result was an almost four-thousand-word open quote that stands as a unique record of Paul's intellectual and artistic aspirations at this crucial juncture in the history of the Beatles.

What stood out was Paul's aspiration to develop as both a writer and performer in order to avoid simply repeating a successful hit-making formula. The breadth of his influences had increased exponentially over the past two years. Although he mentioned pop contemporaries, he also referred to Handel, the painter Francis Bacon, the playwrights John Osborne and Eugene O'Neill, the actors Tom Courtenay and Albert Finney, and the poets Robert Graves and Dylan Thomas. Being present when the Beatles' producer George Martin transformed ragged acoustic sketches of new numbers into polished master tapes, often with altered time signatures and unusual instruments (unusual for a pop group, that is), and hearing the interpretations of their songs by other artists had enlarged his imagination. He spoke excitedly of plans to write songs that had fewer musical notes in their melodies but used each one more potently. "Melodic songs are in fact quite easy to write," he explained. "To write a good song with just one note [sic] in it—like 'Long Tall Sally'—is really very hard. . . . We get near it in 'The Word.'"

In an interesting aside he mentioned having recently seen a TV program in which the journalist and broadcaster Malcolm Muggeridge interviewed the renowned poet, classicist, and former World War I soldier Robert Graves. Paul identified with Graves's comment that he wrote poetry because he had to. The program was screened on the then-new BBC2 channel on November 16, 1965, and was part of a series called *Intimations* that explored influences in the lives of artists, writers, and thinkers. The fact that Paul even watched BBC2 was itself an indication of his changing cultural tastes and his appetite to learn from art forms other than popular music.

The comment that caught his attention came at the conclusion of the half-hour program. Muggeridge asked if the motivation behind Graves' prose differed from that behind his poetry. He answered, "I write prose as a man breeds dogs in order to feed his cat. I write poems because I damn well must."

Britain was changing, and Paul was proud that the Beatles were a significant part of that change. Although heavily involved in the cultural maelstrom, he knew that they could lose their position if they ever became complacent. "It's an interesting time just now because something's got to happen," he said. "There's got to be some kind of change. It probably won't be drastic but I think the good thing about us is that we keep contradicting ourselves. I saw someone on TV asked what he wanted out of life and he said 'a cozy rut.' To be in a cozy rut is about the sickest thing ever, I think. You can enjoy it, but what's the point of living in a cozy rut? We could stay in one now forever, repeating our early hits, and if we did come up with something exciting we'd have to scrap it."

Creative restlessness propelled the Beatles forward. Once they'd achieved an artistic breakthrough, they instinctively felt the need to move on. Despite the then-current wisdom of show business, they were not satisfied with duplicating previously successful techniques or giving the public exactly what it wanted. As Paul said, "Everything we've done we get sick of. We've got some comedy songs on our new LP. There's one called 'Norwegian Wood.' . . . It's something new for us. It's just that we're a bit sick so we thought we'd write something funny. You can't be singing 15-year old songs at 20 because you don't think 15-year old thoughts at 20—a fact that escapes some people."

The two contemporary pop influences Paul cited were Bob Dylan and the Who (latest UK singles, respectively, "Positively 4th Street" and "My Generation"). "They are the two great influences on

1965. They definitely started us thinking again—Dylan about lyrics, and The Who about backings, bigger feedback, that sort of thing. We had that feedback idea in 'I Feel Fine' but The Who went further and made all kinds of weird new sounds."

Rubber Soul had been the group's idea of value for money. It had a memorable cover that accurately indicated the mood of the music, a snappy punning title, and a collection of songs that most artists would have kept in store for future singles. There was no dip in standards on the basis that fans would buy the record anyway, even if the quality was uneven: "We want to do what *we* would have liked when we were record buyers ourselves. A 14-track LP and a separate single is unheard of in the States. There you'd have just 12 tracks, and the single would just be two numbers from the LP."

An ever-present guide to their choices when it came to making LPs was how they had felt as teenagers when they bought the latest rock 'n' roll records. John and Paul never forgot the excitement they felt from seeing such apparently peripheral things as the color of the label at the center of the disc, the songwriting credits beneath each song. The packaging—even the feel and smell of the cover—was an important part of the total experience of record buying.

The piece closed with Paul's reflections on his future. "Writing songs and performing are equally rewarding—that is, when it goes well. But the songwriting thing looks like being the only thing you could do at 60. I wouldn't mind being a white-haired old man writing songs, but I'd hate to be a white-haired old Beatle at the Empress [*sic*] Stadium playing for people."

Paul and John wrote very different songs. Paul was more melodic yet less revealing. He developed stories and characters and loved the sound of language, but his songs told you little about his personal experiences or desires. "Mine are a bit soppier than John's," he admitted to Wyndham. "That's because I am a bit soppier than John." John couldn't help but explore his longings and fears. "In My Life" wasn't a work of fiction; it was a heartfelt assessment of the passing years and the inevitability of death and decay. When writing the original lyrics he took the then-unusual step of mentioning the names of specific Liverpool sites but later removed them because he thought they made the song sound too much like the familiar school essay "What I Did on My Vacation."

An important artistic transition had taken place during the previous year. After John published *A Spaniard in the Works*, he had been interviewed for BBC TV by reporter Kenneth Allsop. On camera Allsop asked him, "When you write a song for the group, is your approach completely different [from the way you write your books] or do you look on Beatle lyrics as really another form of nonsense rhyming?" According to Allsop's biographer Mark Andresen, the interviewer pushed the question further with John at the bar of the BBC studio after the show. "He suggested that . . . he could afford a broader and more ambiguous range in his song lyrics than those on teenage love currently in vogue." The influence of Allsop's comments and the example of Bob Dylan produced such recent songs as "Nowhere Man," "The Word," and "Norwegian Wood," where John broadened his subject base to address issues of marital infidelity, universal love, and existential angst. His lyrics were now about his personal beliefs and his lived experience rather than rehashes of previous pop songs.

Despite Paul's reticence to write autobiographically and his natural bent toward traditional song formats, he was gregarious, open-minded, and always ready to seek out work by others that would challenge him. Conscious of not having completed the educational path expected of him (if music hadn't intervened he would almost certainly have gone to college and into teaching), he was now gobbling up information at a furious rate and anxious to delve into the nooks and crannies of contemporary culture. The experimental and bizarre, far from repelling him, aroused his curiosity. He respected artistic outlaws because of their determination to resist the comfort of the cozy and the safety of the tried and tested.

John was confined to a less adventurous life in the twenty-two-room countryside mansion he had bought the previous year in Weybridge, the home territory for successful City of London stockbrokers. Whereas Paul absorbed influences through contact—conversations, parties, visits to galleries, and events—John, being a loner, was happy to catch up through listening to records and reading books. In the interview for *London Life* Paul confessed that whereas he was a bedtime and vacation reader, John read all the time. The two of them had recently visited the Times Bookshop on Wigmore Street, where in an hour John had spent £150 on books. This was in the day when one pound could buy six paperbacks.

Cynthia Lennon remembered him most typically lying in bed with a notepad and then getting up, going to his piano and sketching out a few chords for a new song. When I interviewed her in 1987 she told me, "He'd go from one thing to another, from his notepad to the piano, and then he'd listen to music, gawp at television and read newspapers. He was basically dropping out from what was happening, thinking about things and resting. Everything he was doing outside the home was pretty high-powered."

In a 1964 interview John had declared his ambition was to buy a detached house "standing in its own grounds" so that he wouldn't be disturbed while working. "That way I can get away from everyone when I feel like it," he said. "No distractions at all. Then I think I could write more."

John had never been much of a social animal, and he found alcohol difficult to handle. His preference for his own company was rooted in a childhood spent with an aunt, uncle, and adult lodgers but no siblings. Paul's dad, like many working-class fathers, welcomed any excuse to have relatives and friends over for sing-alongs, but Aunt Mimi was more reserved. As a consequence, the activities that John took part in as a child were solitary—writing stories and poems, creating comics, reading, drawing, playing records, listening to the radio, daydreaming.

As an adult he was little different. He still lounged around at home, watched endless TV, and in the years before his death was proud to be an Upper West Side househusband. When asked in 1980 whether he checked out the latest music acts in New York clubs, he snappishly responded, "Did Picasso go down to some studio and watch somebody paint? I don't want to see other people paint. I'm just not interested in other people's work—only inasmuch as it affects me. . . . I don't go to clubs to listen. The only person I ever went to see in London during the Swinging Sixties era was Jimi Hendrix and Bob Dylan at the Isle of Wight. I was too busy doing to be watching other people."

Yet observation has its limitations. The solitary life doesn't demand that opinions be sharpened through argument. Listening to records is no substitute for going out to gigs and being moved (or repelled) by the music in an environment where you can witness the responses of others. John was envious of Paul's freedom and gregariousness, because in late-1950s Liverpool he'd been the one socializing with artists, arguing in pubs, and visiting the latest exhibitions. The art of surrealism, abstraction, and provocation had been John's natural habitat as a student at Liverpool College of Art, and consequently he should have been the Beatle most likely to be found in art galleries or smoking pot while listening to jazz in bohemian pads.

At the same time that John bought Kenwood in Weybridge, George bought a bungalow named Kinfauns five and a half miles away in Esher, built on land that was originally part of Clive of India's Palladian mansion Clermont (later Claremont). He was becoming increasingly serious about his musicianship and feared that the Beatles' inability to hear themselves play on stage was having a deleterious effect on their musical progress. In September he had told Mike Hennessey of *Rave* he felt that if they had carried on playing to their original Cavern Club audience, they would have made greater musical advances, because they'd have grown up with their listeners. Now there was a battle between amplified sound and crowd screams that deprived both sides of enrichment. "We have different audiences all the time and we play the same numbers—so we don't get much chance to develop. . . . I suppose I should have improved much more. If we pack it in one day I'll probably learn to play the guitar properly. Or chop it up."

The guitar wasn't the only instrument George was now playing. In April 1965, while filming *Help!* at Twickenham Film Studios, he'd fooled around with a sitar used as a prop in the set of an Indian restaurant and had become intensely curious about it. In August, when touring America, he'd met with David Crosby of the Byrds in Los Angeles, and Crosby had recommended that George listen to recordings by Ravi Shankar (already an influence on the music of the Byrds). On his return to London George bought a cheap sitar at Indiacraft on Oxford Street and learned enough about it to play it on "Norwegian Wood" when recording *Rubber Soul*.

A sitar string broke during one of the "Norwegian Wood" sessions, and George didn't know where to go for a replacement. He called the High Commission of India, based in the Aldwych, who referred him to a small organization called the Asian Music Circle that had good connections with British-based Indian musicians and promoted Asian cultural events in the UK. Ayana Angadi and his wife, Patricia, ran the group from their home on Fitzalan Road in Finchley. Ringo was designated to make contact with the Angadis.

This turned out to be a significant connection for the Beatles, eventually leading to their exploration of Eastern thought and culture. Ayana Angadi, then sixty-two, was an Indian intellectual and writer who'd lived in Britain since 1924. He'd been sent to London by his parents to take exams designed to prepare him for a good job in the Indian Civil Service but had instead become a Trotskyite and a harsh critic of colonialism. In 1943, he married a rebellious English debutante, Patricia Fell-Clarke, who was eleven years his junior.

In 1953 the Angadis founded the Asian Music Circle with the aim of bringing Eastern musicians and dancers to Britain and fos-

tering an appreciation of Indian culture. Over the years
they were responsible for inviting players such as Vilayat
Khan, Ali Akbar Khan, Alla
Rakha, Chatur Lal, and
Ravi Shankar to Britain. In
1961, the renowned teacher
B. K. S. Iyengar gave yoga
classes at their home. Iyengar had met their friend Yehudi Menuhin in 1954 and
had taught the violinist to meditate.

The logo for the Asian Music Circle.

George was the youngest Beatle and, as a composer, wrote in the
shadow of John and Paul. Yet he was a conscientious musician, keen
to emulate favorite players such as Carl Perkins and Chet Atkins, and

George and Pattie Boyd with Ayana and Patricia Angadi, the founders of the Asian Music
Circle, in the garden of the Angadis' house at 116 Fitzalan Road, Finchley, London.

aspired to develop his writing. He sketched out music at home using a reel-to-reel tape recorder but was a slow worker and had problems completing lyrics (and thinking up titles). In August 1965 he'd said, "I don't think it's worth writing songs and getting somebody else to do the lyrics. . . . You don't feel as though you've done it, really. If I get something going then I'll tape it, and I'll leave it for about five weeks and I'll suddenly remember. Then I'll add a bit more to it and so probably it will take me about three months before I've really finished one song. I'm so lazy, you know, it's ridiculous. But I'd like to write more."

Although less formally educated than John and Paul—he'd left school at sixteen to become an apprentice electrician—George was conscious of the opportunities for exploration opened up by being a Beatle and took advantage of them. Being around the Angadis and their friends introduced him to new worlds of art, culture, politics, and music. He and Pattie spent many evenings at the couple's home, and Patricia painted their portrait.

When it came to writing songs, Ringo, by contrast, had problems with both words and music. Since 1964 he'd been playing with an idea called "Don't Pass Me By" but could never advance beyond the chorus. Occasionally he'd think he'd discovered a great melody only to be told by his fellow Beatles that it had already been written by someone else and been a worldwide hit.

Ringo's home in Weybridge had a top-of-the-line sound system fitted in the living room, but unlike John, Paul, and George his priorities were pleasure rather than work. His current obsessions were military memorabilia and Hollywood films. He didn't rehearse on his drums at home (he believed that touring was the only practice he needed) and had turned one room into a bar called the Flying Cow, with paneled walls, mirrors, beer taps, and even a cash register. In 1965 he'd had his own cinema built onto the house.

The Beatles were entering their longest period of inactivity so far. Almost four months would elapse between the final date of their

1965 tour and their first day back in the studio. They filled it with what for most people would be normal activities—holidays, house improvement, movie watching, gardening, entertaining—but which they'd had to sacrifice for fame. They also spent time discovering who they were and pondering the purpose of the Beatles.

In the meantime, Beatle business continued. On January 4, Brian Epstein flew to New York to work out the details of the group's expected summer tour of the United States. Back in London the Beatles met up at CTS Studios in Bayswater to improve the soundtrack of a film that had been shot for TV by Sullivan Productions, Inc., of their groundbreaking August 1965 concert at New York's gigantic Shea Stadium. The audience of 55,600 was the largest ever for a pop music show at the time, and while it was undoubtedly a great achievement in terms of their popularity, it raised serious questions about the group's direction and the very function of a concert. How much bigger could these shows get? What was the point of them when the fans couldn't hear the music and the musicians couldn't hear each other?

In commentary added to the footage from interviews they did with journalist Larry Kane, the Beatles sounded a positive note, but the images showed them battling to make sense of their roles. John was fooling around much of the time—making faces, laughing, striking the electric piano with his elbow—as if testing how sloppily he could perform while still receiving mass adulation. The howls and tears of the fans came not as a response to the songs but from the collective hysteria generated by those ecstatic to be in the presence of the group they loved.

As a consequence the quality of the live soundtrack was poor. There were musical errors and recording glitches, and the primitive mobile equipment had trouble in separating the songs from the screams. Some tracks needed overdubbing, and some needed replacing with rerecordings synchronized to the movements of the Beatles' lips and fingers on the screen. For "Twist and Shout," unreleased audio from the August 30 Hollywood Bowl concert was used.

"Ticket to Ride" and "Help!" had to be totally rerecorded, and "Act Naturally" was replaced with the original LP recording. Watching the color images on the screen at CTS reminded the group of the increasing gap between public expectations of what the Beatles should be and their current interest in pushing the pop envelope.

The resulting fifty-minute documentary was shown on American TV on January 10. The next day, Paul was driving back to London after a weekend spent with his father on the Wirral when he heard the play *Ubu Cocu* being broadcast on the Third Programme, the BBC's twenty-year-old "high-brow" radio channel of arts, culture, science, and intellectual debate, a channel that its founders believed would contribute to "the refinement of society." The play, written by Frenchman Alfred Jarry in the final years of the nineteenth century, had been translated into English in 1945 by the author and literary critic Cyril Connolly, and this version was produced by Martin Esslin, the critic who coined the term "theater of the absurd."

Alfred Jarry was regarded as the original absurdist. He invented a deliberately antiscientific science he named pataphysics; shocked Parisian audiences with his first play, *Ubu Roi*, by having Papa Ubu utter the word "merdre" (almost, but not quite, "merde") in the opening line and made a name for himself by taking nothing seriously (except the business of taking nothing seriously). He drank absinthe and took ether to create states of transcendental perception and died at the age of thirty-four. His plays defied all the conventions of drama and storytelling, being full of nonsensical dialogue, invented language, and inconsequential action.

There are no obvious inspirations from Jarry in subsequent Beatles songs—although John comes close in songs like "I Am the Walrus," "Mean Mr Mustard," "Polythene Pam," and "Cry Baby Cry," and Paul mentioned pataphysics in "Maxwell's Silver Hammer,"—but, as with the free jazz that Paul was now listening to, the most profound effect came from exposure to art that defied existing conventions. Speaking about Jarry a couple of months later Paul said, "He's great—

weird." One of Jarry's translators, Kenneth McLeish, said, "Jarry's work liberated other people's creative imagination. His irreverence towards pre-existing culture, to his audience, his performers and the world at large, and the plays' absolute self-certainty . . . prefigured a whole twentieth-century approach to the arts and their audiences."

By contrast, the same day that Paul came across Jarry's work, Peter and Gordon's new single "Woman" was released in the United States. They'd had three previous hits with unreleased Lennon-McCartney songs (actually McCartney songs), "World Without Love," "Nobody I Know," and "I Don't Want to See You Again," but because the duo was often accused of simply riding the Beatles' coattails, it was decided that Paul would this time disguise his songwriting identity as

"Woman," written by Paul under the nom de plume Bernard Webb, was a hit in both Britain and America for Peter and Gordon.

"Bernard Webb," supposedly a student currently living in Paris who didn't like publicity. The ruse didn't fool many people for very long. The style was too distinctively Paul McCartney.

There was no hint in a song like "Woman" of the new ideas that Paul had discussed in his *London Life* interview. There was no influence of Dylan or the Who and no attempt to break the mold of contemporary songwriting. It was an expertly written number but hailed back to early influences like Buddy Holly rather than forward to the genre-busting musicians and artists he was now in awe of.

On January 12, John and Ringo, along with their respective wives, Cynthia and Maureen, left for a ten-day vacation in the Caribbean. John said at the time: "We asked a girl in our office to find a place that was hot and good for a holiday. She contacted travel agents and they suggested Tobago." Ringo surprised journalists and photographers at London Airport when he arrived wearing a beard, something he'd last sported in 1962 as a member of the Liverpool band the Hurricanes. He'd had to be clean-shaven when he joined the Beatles and adapt his hairstyle to conform to the group image. The beard was an advanced warning of the break from the loveable mop-top image that was about to take place. "I suppose the beard will come off when the Beatles start working again," he reassured the press. "That'll probably be in about a month's time."

They arrived in Trinidad's Piarco International Airport in Port of Spain on a BOAC flight and then chartered a fifty-three-seat Viscount for eight hundred dollars to take them on to the nearby island of Tobago. Here they checked into a private cottage at the Arnos Vale Hotel and over the next few days spent time shopping in the nearby town of Scarborough, sunbathing by their pool, fishing off the coast of Bloody Bay, and lunching with British society photographer Norman Parkinson at his spectacular hilltop home, Galera Point, in Runnymede. In the evenings they played board games like Monopoly.

They only had two engagements as Beatles. The first was to pose for photographs and talk to the local press at Arnos Vale Beach on

January 15. Wearing their swimming suits they paraded down the largely empty strip of sand and then sat on sun loungers while journalists posed rapid-fire questions. (John hated the resulting photographs, because they revealed him to be flabby and overweight. As a result, he would lose fourteen pounds by the time of the summer tour.)

The second appointment, on January 20, was a meeting and island tour with Dr. Eric Williams, the first prime minister of the newly independent Trinidad and Tobago. The fact that two of the best-known entertainers in the Western world had chosen to vacation on Tobago was a great PR coup for the island. In the words of an edito-

John and Ringo's walkabout in Tobago as reported in a local newspaper.

rial in the local *Daily Mirror,* "Here is a tremendous opportunity for the country as a whole to make capital of the charms and the fame of Tobago." When Williams arrived at the Crown Point Hotel to lunch with the two Beatles, he was accompanied by his fourteen-year-old daughter, Erica; the minister of agriculture; the manager of the Trinidad and Tobago Tourist Office; and a posse of journalists, photographers, security guards, and minor officials.

Erica, who was at boarding school in England and a huge fan

of the Beatles, found John and Ringo charming and attentive, even though she was often at a loss for words to say to the stars. Her father spoke to them about the pressures of his job and his plans for improving the quality of life on the islands. Ringo pressed him for information on two local calypso singers that he had recently discovered—Mighty Sparrow and King Fighter. Erica shared with John the problem she was having finding good contact lenses, and he gave her the address of his Harley Street optician, whom she subsequently visited.

The fact that two Beatles chose Tobago as their holiday destination was seen as a huge publicity coup by the tourist board of the Caribbean island.

After a long lunch that featured tropical punch, pigeon pea soup, and crab back, the prime minister took the two couples on a four-hour tour of recent building developments that involved a seventy-mile drive and a two-mile walk. The highlight of the expedition was the still-incomplete North Coast Road from Bloody Bay to Roxborough. When it was all over Williams gave Cynthia and Maureen gold earrings. Ringo diplomatically told a local journalist, "I enjoyed it."

It's likely that it was while John and Ringo were away that Paul drove down to Bristol from London to see Jane perform in her new production for the Bristol Old Vic Company. Their relationship was under strain. Paul wanted her to adopt the more conventional role of a pop star's consort, but she was adamant that she wanted to maintain the career that she'd embarked on as a child actor. He wanted her to stay in London, but she wanted to go wherever her work took her. The tension had in the past erupted into songs like "I'm Looking Through You" and "We Can Work It Out."

By this time Paul already had a song germinating that was different than anything he'd written before. Every previous Beatles song contained personal pronouns such as "I," "me," and "you," and was in the voice of the singer confessing his feelings and often appealing to a girl to respond. Indeed, in the early days they made a point of using "you" and "me" in their titles ("Love Me Do," "From Me to You," "Please Please Me," "She Loves You") because they deduced from fan mail that many listeners experienced the songs as being personally addressed to them when these pronouns were used.

Paul's new song, about a spinster cleaning up rice after a wedding and a lonely priest, had no first- or second-person pronouns. It was written from the point of view of a detached observer, using the techniques of a novelist or a screenwriter. Paul was testing fresh approaches to songs just as John had recently done with "Nowhere Man" and "Norwegian Wood." The two verses written so far were brief vignettes of the two main characters, with no connections between them. All they had in common were the church and implications of loneliness, isolation, and lack of fulfilment.

The songwriting of Ray Davies, who as leader of the Kinks had had a hit with "Well Respected Man" in September 1965 and had just released "Dedicated Follower of Fashion," could have suggested this direction. Both Kinks songs commented on social issues, and involved characters. The well-respected man was an archetypal middle-class male of the period, and the dedicated follower of fashion was a style chaser in the mod tradition. Later in the year, when George was questioned about the new LP, he said that this song of Paul's was unusual and that it would "probably only appeal to Ray Davies types," implying that this is how the group viewed the song.

The Kinks' characters didn't have names. Paul's did. The woman was Miss Daisy Hawkins, yet something wasn't right about the choice, and he was searching for an alternative that sounded less contrived. Later that year he explained the song's evolution to Hunter Davies, a *Sunday Times* journalist and soon-to-be authorized biographer of the Beatles. "I was sitting at the piano when I thought of it," he said.

> Just like Jimmy Durante. The first few bars just came to me. And I got this name in my head—"Daisy Hawkins picks up the rice in the church where a wedding has been." I don't know why. I can hear a whole song in one chord. In fact, I think you can hear a whole song in one note, if you listen hard enough.
>
> I couldn't think of much more, so I put it away for a day. Then the name "Father McCartney" came to me—and "all the lonely people." But I thought people would think it was supposed to be my dad, sitting knitting his socks. Dad's a happy lad. So I went through the telephone book and I got the name McKenzie. I was in Bristol when I decided Daisy Hawkins wasn't a good name. I walked round looking at the shops and I saw the name Rigby. You got that? *Quick pan to Bristol.* I can just see this all as a Hollywood musical.

What Paul had seen in Bristol was not a shop but the office of a wine-and-spirits importer named Rigby & Evens at 22 King Street, just across the road from the Theatre Royal (the base for the Bristol Old Vic) at number 35. Paul had taken a stroll while waiting to meet Jane and had seen the name on a sign hanging over the front door of this corner building. He has since said that the first name of the woman in the finished version of the song came from the actress Eleanor Bron, who had acted with the Beatles the previous year in *Help!* But could Eleanor have evolved out of Evens? Could he have sung to himself "Evens & Rigby" before deciding on Eleanor Rigby?

The now-demolished premises of Bristol wine exporters Rigby & Evens. After seeing the company sign above the door, Paul changed the surname of the main character in the song he was writing from Hawkins to Rigby.

Coincidentally, there was a gravestone for an Eleanor Rigby in the churchyard of St Peter's in Woolton, not many yards from the field where John and Paul first set eyes on each other at the church fete on July 6, 1957, where John's group the Quarry Men had played. Beatles fans only became aware of it in the 1990s, and Paul has since said that although he'd often walked through the churchyard (this was the church where John attended Sunday school for many years), he couldn't recall noticing this gravestone. Still, there's a chance that it registered all those years ago as a pleasant sounding name and that the Rigby & Evens sign was merely a trigger that helped him retrieve it from his subconscious.

The song, even at this early stage, was more mature than anything Paul had attempted so far and his first venture away from the traditional love song. The problem of loneliness, particularly the loneliness

The gravestone of an Eleanor Rigby in the churchyard of St Peter's Church, Woolton, Liverpool.

of the elderly, was being discussed in the House of Commons in 1965. Isolation and alienation were popular topics in drama, poetry, and fiction as well as in new songs by Paul Simon (recorded by Simon and Garfunkel) such as "The Sounds of Silence" and "I Am a Rock." Later in the year homelessness would be highlighted in the powerful TV drama *Cathy Comes Home*, directed by Ken Loach, and the formation of the charity Shelter.

Paul pictured Eleanor Rigby putting on a face "that she keeps in a jar by the door" which may have been taken from T. S. Eliot's line about preparing "a face to meet the faces that you meet" in his 1920 poem "The Love Song of J. Alfred Prufrock" (Eliot, who had died the year before, was a distant relative of Jane Asher's mother, Margaret). It was a striking image to use in a pop song, reflecting a feeling among the young that the older generation was faking it—that they were more concerned about how others perceived them than about being true to themselves. Hypocrisy was seen as the abiding sin of the middle class. It was an attitude explored by the young working-class playwright Joe Orton in plays like *Entertaining Mr Sloane* and *Loot*. The latter, first staged in 1965, had the memorable closing line, delivered by the main female character Fay, "We must keep up appearances."

There was a slightly dismissive tone to Paul's song, in that it assumed that all spinsters and celibate priests were plagued by loneliness and regret. This was the natural view of someone young, talented, and popular and particularly someone taking full advantage of the sexual adventures available in the new "permissive society." Speaking about Eleanor Rigby in 1967 Paul said, "She didn't make it. She never made it with anyone. She didn't even look as if she was going to."

The song, when completed, would also allude to a church that "no one comes near." Father McKenzie preaches sermons but no one hears them and, as a consequence, "no one was saved." It wasn't an attack on Christianity, but it showed that the Beatles believed that the church had become a lifeless and irrelevant institution in England, associated by the young with weddings, funerals, and lonely old people. The contrast with Beatlemania couldn't have been greater. They were aware of which direction people were looking today for community, inspiration, and uplift.

John had made a more theological comment in his song "Girl," although it wasn't seen as such at the time. John revealed to *Rolling Stone* in 1970 that when he'd asked the girl in the song whether she thought that "pain would lead to pleasure," he was addressing the misconception that salvation was a reward for self-denial and suffering. "I was just talking about Christianity in that," he explained. "The thing like you have to be tortured to attain heaven." Paul had told Francis Wyndham, "John's been reading a book about pain and pleasure, about the idea behind Christianity that to have pleasure you have to have pain. The book says that's all rubbish. It often happens that pain leads to pleasure but you don't *have* to have it. All that's a drag. So we've written a song about it with, I suppose, a little bit of protest."

The group had made no secret of the atheism and agnosticism of its members, but since their experiences with LSD and reading of books about Buddhism and Hinduism they were less dismissive of religion in general. They would even talk about God and the significance of the spiritual, but this was no return to the creeds of Catholicism or Anglicanism. They were neo-pantheists who believed that everything was a part of God and God was a part of everything.

The Beatle most interested in religion was George, because of his new passion for Indian thought and culture. His experience after taking LSD for the first time had profoundly shaken his secular view of the world, and he was looking for teachings that made sense of his new outlook.

AFTER LESS THAN A MONTH'S ENGAGEMENT, GEORGE AND Pattie were married on January 21. John, Cynthia, Ringo, and Maureen were still in Tobago, which meant that Paul was the only Beatle present at the morning ceremony at the Register Office in Epsom, Surrey. The location was Brian Epstein's choice, because he thought a low-key venue and an early start would avoid too much attention. Pattie's mother was only told of the date on January 12, and George's parents five days later.

Pattie had always wanted a white wedding in a church, but George had told writer Mike Hennessey just a few months before, "I don't want a white wedding. If it weren't for all that business with vicars and snivelling people I might have been married ten times by now." In accordance with his wishes Pattie wore the latest hip clothing rather than a

Patricia Angadi's painting of George and Pattie.

wedding dress—creamy stockings, red shoes with pointed toes, and a short silk dress made by Mary Quant.

There was no music at the ceremony and only a handful of invited guests—Paul, best man Brian Epstein (just returned from a Virgin Islands break added to his New York business visit), Neil Aspinall, Tony Barrow, model Venetia Cuninghame, ad man Terry Howard, George's parents and three brothers, Pattie's brothers and sisters, and her mother, Diana, and her mother's cousin Penny Evans. Her mother's brother, John Drysdale, a former Foreign Office diplomat who had worked in the Gold Coast (now Ghana) and was now a permanent resident in Somalia, gave Pattie away in the absence of her divorced father, Jock Boyd. Pattie's wide gold ring had been bought at Garrard & Co, the royal jeweler's on Regent Street.

John and Ringo had married girls who were working-class and from the Liverpool area. Cynthia Powell had been an art student and Maureen Cox a hairdresser. Pattie, a model, was instead from a prosperous middle-class background. The men on her mother's side had served in the army in India, and her great-grandfather, born near Lucknow, had been rewarded for his service with indigo and sugar plantations. Pattie's mother was born in India, and Pattie spent a lot of her early life in Kenya. In an earlier era, Pattie would have become a debutante and then settled down to marriage and a family with a landowner, stockbroker, or minor aristocrat. In these changing times she had married a guitarist and former electrician raised in government-subsidized housing in Speke, Liverpool.

Pattie's mother, Diana Gaymer-Jones, was full of praise for her new son-in-law, telling *Motion Picture Magazine*: "It was so exciting the day she told me that she would like to bring George home to dinner. The children and I loved him immediately. He's such a fine boy and such a gentleman."

Despite the hushed nature of the wedding planning, it was unrealistic to expect no press attention, so Tony Barrow arranged a brief photo session and press conference where Pattie was asked how many children she would like ("Three would be ideal") and George was asked when he'd like to start having them ("I don't want children yet but I'd like some a little later on"). After the ceremony it was back to the Harrison bungalow, Kinfauns, in a chauffeur-driven Rolls-Royce Princess, for a low-key reception where incense was burned.

In the diary where she had previously written "Getting married" and surrounded it with hearts, Pattie recorded the day's events:

8:00	Got up.
8:30	Press man came.
9:20	Left for registry office.
10:40	We were married. (Yippee)
11:10	Arrived home. From then on party.

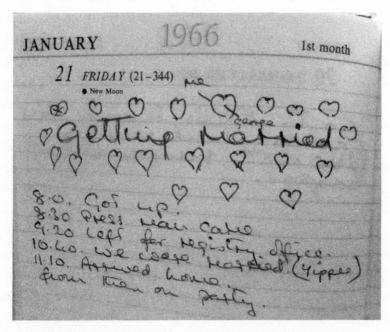

The entry in Pattie Boyd's diary from the day she married George.

This left Paul as the only single Beatle at a time when such things mattered in pop, even though as far as Beatles fans were concerned his almost three-year relationship with Jane Asher was a marriage in all but name. What none of them knew at the time was that she wasn't the exclusive focus of his amorous intentions; not even Jane knew that.

At the launch party for the Indica Books and Gallery, held on January 28, Paul was seen with Maggie McGivern, a twenty-year-old nanny hired by Marianne Faithfull and her husband, John Dunbar, for their baby son, Nicholas. The former model and Marquee Club disc jockey was wearing a crop top and had her dark hair in pigtails. By April their affectionate friendship would develop into a full-blown affair. "She was a very earthy, working class girl," observed Dunbar. "Unlike Jane."

McGivern had a boyfriend at the time, so the fact that both she and Paul were cheating on their partners meant that their meetings either had to be clandestine or were engineered "accidental" encounters at public functions. This loose arrangement suited them both. "I was doing my thing, and Paul was seeing me when he could," she told me. "I didn't question where he was going or what he was doing. It was one of those things. When we were together, we were together. The fact that it was secret suited me down to the ground."

The composition of attendees for the Indica launch was indicative of the changes taking place in London society, where it wasn't only the barriers between classes that were coming down but the barriers between high art and popular culture. There was theatre producer Michael White, educated at the Sorbonne, and Animals singer Eric Burdon, a graduate of Newcastle College of Art; pop music photographer Gered Mankowitz, whose studio was nearby in Mason's Yard; tailor John Pearse, who was about to open the trendsetting boutique Granny Takes a Trip in Chelsea; mod-turned-hippie Mark Feld, soon to become Marc Bolan of the acoustic duo Tyrannosaurus

Rex; Beat writer William Burroughs; old Etonian art collector Robert Fraser; and aristocrat fashion designer Jane Ormsby-Gore, whose father, Lord Harlech, had been the British ambassador to America when the Beatles first played in Washington, DC. Things were organized so haphazardly that at the last minute before opening, as drinks were being set out on trays, Marianne Faithfull found herself on her hands and knees scrubbing the toilets.

The media loved what was happening. What was better for colorful copy than this mélange of bright young models, pop singers, actors, artists, writers, and entrepreneurs right in the heart of London's old establishment, close to the gentlemen's clubs, gunsmiths, wine stores, bespoke shirt makers, and antique shops? The *International Herald Tribune* and *Life* magazine both popped down to interview Barry Miles. The *Observer Magazine,* one of the earliest newspaper color supplements, launched in September 1964, ran a spread. Even

Maggie McGivern, Paul, and Barry Miles at a party launching the Indica Books and Gallery, Mason's Yard, London.

teenage pop magazines became interested because of the Beatles connection.

"Miles was there, and a few other people like John Dunbar and Marianne who knew about our relationship," says McGivern. "But we managed to disappear out of that party. I can't remember where we went but we disappeared. In those days everyone was quite loyal. More to Paul rather than to me because I was an unknown entity. It wasn't like today where news of such a liaison would be everywhere within three minutes."

Two days later Jane returned to London, and Paul's boulevardier ways had to be reined in. The next night the two of them went to Wyndham's Theatre in Charing Cross Road with Pattie and George to see Roger Milner's hot new screwball comedy *How's the World Treating You?* starring Peter Bayliss, James Bolam, and Patricia Routledge. The play had already enjoyed successful runs at the Hampstead Theatre Club (where the *Times* had called it "one of the funniest, best directed, best acted and most sharply timed comedies ever seen in Hampstead") and the New Arts Theatre Club on Great Newport Street.

With John and Ringo back from Tobago, Epstein finally at home in London, and George delaying his honeymoon because of unfounded expectations that the songs for the next LP would have been written by now, there was time to reconvene and plan the new year. Would there be a new film, and, if so, would it be yet another caper where they played themselves as Beatles or something more serious that made demands of them as actors? Should the planned tour of Germany, Japan, and America be extended to other territories? How much time should they set aside for the recording of a new LP?

Behind all these questions was the bigger question of what the career of a maturing Beatles would look like. Was it going to be a continual cycle of writing, recording, promoting, touring, and filming until their luck ran out, or was there another way of doing things?

FEBRUARY

I'd rather have a couple of hundred people who really dug the music than two million who didn't know what was going on.
–JOHN, 1966

It was all very well wanting to develop artistically in order to avoid standing still, but the Beatles' large audience was on average ten years younger than the group members and not as sophisticated in its tastes. It was content with "I Want to Hold Your Hand" and such hits and wasn't demanding that the Beatles become more adult, experiment with new sounds, or explore the darker side of human experience. By changing tack, the group risked alienating the very people who'd put them where they were.

However, by this point they were all agreed that they needed to extend their capabilities whatever the cost. They couldn't live with themselves if they tried to secure their position simply by repeating the same hit recipe. "If they ever said 'You're too way out and you've got to go back to then' [the way they were playing in 1962]—we'd give up," said Paul. John concurred: "We just do the music. If more people like it then all is well and good. If less people like it, that's just the way it's going to go."

But where John appeared not to be alarmed by the prospect of a smaller but more sympathetic audience, Paul wanted to educate existing fans by gradually introducing more challenging work rather than confusing them with esoteric material before they were ready to assimilate it. "If we did a whole album of way-out things we'd be doing what the people who do electronic music do, which is to go too far out, too suddenly, and no-one stays with them. Everyone gets left behind because they're miles ahead, digging all this electronic stuff. What we try to do is—*Rubber Soul* was a bit more towards that, the next album will be a bit more, and the one after that should be a bit more. If people stay with us, it's great."

Specifically asked if the Beatles were trying "to lead the kids, little by little," into deeper music, John replied, "There's no plan. It just went that way. The next one will just happen. There are no plans to it. We only think—let's make one better than the last LP. How did the last LP go? Oh, yeah. Let's go. We have no specific plans. We just always go forwards. That's all."

Paul explained to one journalist in 1966 that the crowd-pleasing music they'd played in the early days of the Beatles' career had been necessary for them to get noticed in a busy marketplace. Now that they had the attention they'd craved, they could relax and experiment. "In 1960 there was a whole different attitude and a different thing from our side because back then we were unknown and had to go mad to get known. That was what we did, but we gradually changed. It's just a development."

George looked back on songs such as "P.S. I Love You" as being "basic pop." "We got typecast as the 'Yeah, yeah, yeah' mob, and I'm so glad we've grown out of that into thinking players. It would have been easy—with all the rubbish written in the papers about how great we were—to settle back with the money and not bother. Well, it would have been a cosy rut but there are so many things to do. Everybody realizes that if they're a musician they've got to keep moving."

Maureen Cleave was a journalist close to the Beatles during those changes. She first met them in January 1963 when she was twenty-eight years old and authoring a pop column called "Disc Date" for London's *Evening Standard* newspaper. She was well-spoken, educated, and darkly attractive. Born in Mussoorie, India, where her father was a major in the Seventh Rajput Regiment of the British Indian Army, she had studied history in the 1950s at St Anne's College, Oxford, and then started work in Fleet Street, where she soon gained a reputation for picking up on changing social mores. She was naturally inquisitive, observant, and straightforward in her opinions.

Ironically, she wasn't really a pop fan. She'd been given the column only because the incumbent was thought to be getting too old and she seemed relatively young. She began writing about British stars like Cliff Richard, Billy Fury, and Adam Faith, and then a university friend, future *Daily Telegraph* radio critic Gillian Reynolds, alerted her to this new group who was causing a bit of a stir in her hometown of Liverpool. "They look beat-up and depraved in the nicest possible way," she informed Cleave.

Journalist Maureen Cleave with the Beatles in 1964.

Cleave went to talk to them, and the resulting seven-hundred-word piece, published on February 2, 1963, under the headline "Why the Beatles Create All That Frenzy," was the first major newspaper story outside of Liverpool to explain what she called "the darlings of Merseyside" to the wider world. "They are a vocal-instrumental group, three guitars and drums," she wrote, "and they don't sound a bit like the Shadows, or anybody else for that matter."

At this time the Beatles had one partial hit in Britain with "Love Me Do," and the follow-up, "Please Please Me," was selling well, but Cleave took them seriously, and her report was full of perceptive observations. They looked scruffy, she noticed, but "scruffy on purpose." Their hairstyles were French-influenced. They bursted with self-confidence and professional polish, mostly because they'd been working at their craft since 1958.

Her thumbnail sketches of each Beatle were often unflattering but unerringly accurate. John had "an upper lip which is brutal in a devastating way." George was "handsome, whimsical and untidy." Paul had "a round baby face." Ringo was "ugly but cute." She didn't need to spend long with them to distill their essence.

She realized that they were more intelligent than the average pop group and mentioned this to John. "It helps being intelligent, I suppose," John responded. "Though, mind you, I've met people in this business who aren't as thick as they look. On second thoughts, I'd rather be thick and rich than bright and otherwise. We all want to be rich so we can retire. We don't want to go straight or get to be all-round entertainers."

This was a very different type of interview from the ones being run in pop weeklies and teen magazines at the time. In 1963, British newspapers rarely gave space to the thoughts of pop stars, but Cleave respected them as intelligent young men with valued opinions and genuine artistic aspirations, and they responded by being candid in their conversations with her. She later deduced that her success with them came because she was an outsider. She was a grown-up unpacking the Beatles phenomenon for fellow grown-ups.

The Beatles liked the way Cleave dealt with them, and she became one of their most trusted newspaper allies. At the end of 1963, just before they played the Royal Command Performance at the Palladium in front of the Queen Mother and Princess Margaret, she did a series under the title *The Year of the Beatles* that ran over three consecutive days. When they headed to America in February 1964, she was with them on the plane. She became particularly friendly with John and Cynthia and would occasionally stay overnight at their home. She famously challenged John over his lyrics (in 1965 when he was composing the movie title track "Help!"), encouraging him to ditch clichés and empty phrases and to use more multisyllabic words.

In January 1966, three years after Cleave's first encounter with the group, she pursued the idea of an unprecedented series of in-depth interviews that would result in a double-page feature on each Beatle and one on Brian Epstein, the pieces to be run as a series over a five-week period. From the perspective of today's media landscape this is unusual, because by the time the stories were run, the Beatles' last album would have been out for over three months and the follow-up hadn't even been started. As the biggest pop group in the world, they only needed to cooperate with publicity that was pegged to a new product.

But that wasn't how Maureen Cleave thought. She felt that they'd each gone through such huge changes recently that the world deserved to know who they were becoming. She would, if possible, meet them on their home territory and look carefully for signs of how the four boys were becoming men. The theme of her interviews, used throughout the series, was "how a Beatle lives."

The series provided sharply focused portraits of each member of the group on the cusp of their new incarnation as "philosopher-poets of the new religion," as LSD guru Timothy Leary would call them. Significantly, it presented them as four individuals who were each developing different interests rather than as the four-headed monster that Mick Jagger joked about. Cleave approached them with the dissecting eye of a historian and the objectivity of a good reporter. She was not at all swayed by their fame or overwhelmed by their charm. She noticed all the details—their mannerisms, the books on their shelves, their tastes in home décor—and used them as clues to a fuller understanding of who they were away from their caricatures as Cynical, Mystical, Cute, and Funny.

The order in which Cleave did the interviews is uncertain. The only thing we can know for sure is that Paul was the last to be spoken to, by which time the pieces on the three other Beatles had already appeared in print. John, Ringo, George, and Brian Epstein were interviewed at their homes, while Paul was spoken to over a meal in a restaurant close to the Asher home on Wimpole Street.

Cleave met Ringo on a Monday morning in February, and he took her for a tour of his house and garden. She saw each room of his home—including the bedroom where the marital bed had a wicker headboard—as well as the sloping lawns, the goldfish pond, a tree house, the kennel for the two Airedale dogs he had named Daisy and Donovan, a wartime air raid shelter, and a patch of newly flowering crocuses.

Ringo didn't discuss music, and there was no sight of a drum kit on the premises. He confessed to another reporter that he never rehearsed between tours, as he never learned anything new when playing unaccompanied and without an audience. His tastes were those of an uncultured person who'd suddenly come into money. He'd been able to indulge his childhood passions for cars (two Minis, one Rolls-Royce, one Facel Vega), weaponry (guns, knives, pikes, air rifles, canons), military memorabilia, trophies, uniforms, and the Wild West. The only books on display that weren't merely decorative were science fiction.

Having once called him "ugly," Cleave now found him "the least brilliant Beatle" but thought that he was also "the most sensible and the most mature." She was impressed with the aura of contentment that surrounded him. His wife, Maureen, then nineteen, was by his side most of the time, and both of them doted on their five-month old son, Zak.

Ringo's simple tastes reflected his impoverished background and the years of schooling he missed because of illness. He could read okay, but found it hard to write because of problems with spelling. "I'm not thick," he assured Cleave. "It's just that I'm not educated. People can use words and I won't know what they mean. I say 'me' instead of 'my.' . . . Odd things like that I would like to correct."

He expressed disgruntlement with the state of the world but in a general rather than partisan political way. He mused on the possibility of aliens visiting our planet, suggesting that such an invasion would shake up our priorities. "That would get us all sorted out," he said, "fighting over atom bombs and doing nothing about famine and all that." The background was the arms race between America and Russia (with China beginning nuclear tests in 1964) and the recent food shortage in India's state of Bihar.

Ringo's disposition, even before the hippie era, was of peace and love. As a child he'd thought that in an ideal world tunnels would link our homes with those of our best friends. His dining room pub was made in the same spirit of conviviality, as was his move to Weybridge to be close to John and George. While Cleave ate lunch with the Starr family, Pattie Boyd called on the phone, and John popped over with Julian. "I wish I had a club in my house," Ringo told her. "Of course, that's the great thing about being married—you have a house to sit in and company all the time. And you can still go to clubs, a bonus for being married. I love being a family man."

AROUND THE TIME THAT RINGO WAS BEING INTERVIEWED for a mass market publication, moves were afoot that would transform the nature of pop journalism by encouraging criticism that was as sophisticated, intelligent, and wide-ranging as the music under scrutiny. On February 7, at Swarthmore College in Pennsylvania, seventeen-year-old music fan Paul Williams had taken delivery of five hundred copies of the first mimeographed edition of a magazine he had named *Crawdaddy* after the R & B club in Richmond, England, where the Rolling Stones had played regularly in their early days. This was the first publication dedicated to regarding pop as something other than either a commercial phenomenon that could be measured in revenue and chart positions or a collective teenage spasm that could be measured in decibels.

Williams outlined his vision in the editorial:

> You are looking at the first issue of a magazine of rock and roll criticism. Crawdaddy will feature neither pin-ups nor news-briefs; the specialty of this magazine is intelligent writing about pop music. Billboard, Cash Box, etc. serve very well as trade news magazines; but their idea of a review is: "a hard-driving rhythm number that should spiral rapidly up the charts just, as (previous hit by the same group) slides." And the teen magazines are devoted to rock and roll, but their idea of discussion is a string of superlatives below a foldout photograph. Crawdaddy believes that someone in the United States might be interested in what others have to say about the music they like.

The Beatles would benefit from this development when writers schooled in the new approach to music journalism emerged as respected critics and national newspapers began to discuss music as art rather than news or entertainment. As *Crawdaddy* extended its reach across America, building up a circulation of twenty-five thousand within the first eighteen months, it caught the attention of University of California dropout Jann Wenner, who in October 1967 would launch *Rolling Stone* in its image and likeness.

On February 8, George and Pattie flew off to the British colony of Barbados for sixteen days in the sun. They rented a villa called Benclare on the west coast of the island that was perched on a hillside overlooking the Sandy Lane Hotel and had its own cook and house keeper. Scottish photographer Harry Benson, a friend to the Beatles from their early days, arrived from his new home city of New York with a commission to snap pictures of the newlyweds and, after finding George on the beach, was invited to take a series of romantic shots of the couple in their vacation living room, in the gardens, and by the sea. George wore a large, red mod-style cap and a short-sleeved crochet tee shirt that exemplified the new feminine influence in men's fashion being pioneered by the boutiques of London's Carnaby Street.

"They didn't want people to know where they were going for their honeymoon," says Benson. "But they were photographed at London airport by passengers so everyone knew they were going to Barbados. I came in on the second or third day they were there. It was very quick. I was walking along a beach, I didn't know where they were and I walked straight into them! George thought it was a complete coincidence. 'Gosh! You're here. I can't believe it.'"

Joining them for the second week were two friends from London, advertising copywriter Terry Howard and his twenty-year-old model girlfriend, Venetia Cuninghame. They all knew each other from the London scene—Pattie and Venetia had modeled together—and Venetia and Howard had been backstage when Dylan played at the Royal Albert Hall the year before.

It was while they were at George and Pattie's wedding that they were invited to Barbados. They were already planning to meet Mick Jagger and Keith Richards in New York, and so it made an attractive side visit. They found Benclare a "comfortable" villa but noticed that it lacked luxuries. It didn't even have a pool.

One day they all went to the North Point Surf Resort but instead of using its Olympic-size outdoor pool, they chose to swim in the

ocean. Pattie and George swam out too far and for a tense few minutes were afraid that the swell would pull them into deep waters and
drown them. Another night they attended the launch of a weather
rocket sent up to analyze the behavior of high-altitude winds.

Barbados was awash with rich and often eccentric British expats
who clung to colonial lifestyles, living in weather-beaten mansions
with spacious verandas where servants served them evening cocktails
as the sun went down. One of them, twenty-two-year-old George Albert Harley de Vere-Drummond, had been born at Windsor Castle
and could claim King George VI as his godfather. He'd met Pattie in
the fall of 1965 when the American magazine *Seventeen* arranged for
them both to appear in a fashion shoot. Pattie was to model the latest designs alongside a number of swinging British males who both
dressed well and had money. The caption for this photo was "Pattie
posing with sports enthusiast George Drummond, one of the richest
young men in England."

Drummond had plenty of free time on his hands and good connections with the upper echelons of Barbadian society. Picnics were
organized on the lawn of his crumbling mansion. George enjoyed the
situation because he didn't have to encounter ordinary people who
might recognize him as a Beatle. He cherished anonymity wherever
he could find it.

Drummond took them to hear the Merrymen, who'd started recording the same year as the Beatles and were on their way to becoming the island's best-loved calypso group. One night he arranged a
party to which he invited Formula One driver Innes Ireland, motor-
cyclist Mike Hailwood, and the Barbadian premier, Errol Barrow. At
one point George got into a heated debate with Ireland about war
and peace. Ireland, who'd served as a British army officer during the
Suez crisis, was not in favor of pacifism. George was not in favor of
the military. Drummond sought out Errol Barrow to resolve the con-
flict, only to find him hard at work in the kitchen.

George and Pattie honeymooning on the Caribbean island of Barbados.

During the days Pattie sunbathed and George practiced on his sitar. George even had a better sitar flown to Barbados for him, and when it arrived he gave his old one—probably the one he had bought from Indiacraft—to Drummond as a gift.

On their return to England Maureen Cleave visited George and Pattie at Kinfauns. Cleave was aware that the public then knew very little about George, often referred to as "the quiet one." He was the Beatle best known for not being John, Paul, or Ringo. He wasn't characterized by cynicism, cuteness, or knockabout humor. He was just "good old George." But Cleave sensed steeliness beneath the gauche exterior. She found him strong-willed and uncompromising, with a high regard for truth and rights, and she pointed out that he was more likely than the others to act independently. He was the first Beatle to move out of London and the first to embrace the music of India. He would later introduce the rest of the group to Transcendental Meditation and the International Society for Krishna Consciousness.

He was also the first Beatle to voice disenchantment with his pop star status and with materialism. "I asked to be successful," he told her. "I didn't ask to be famous. I can tell you, I got more famous than I wanted to be. . . . OK—we're famous Beatles. So what? There are other things apart from being famous Beatles. It's not the living end, is it? On the other hand, I feel I've seen twice as much as most people do when they peg out. I'm very pleased that I'm me. After all, I could have been somebody else, couldn't I?"

His passion was for craft rather than celebrity. He spent hours practicing on his guitar, playing through tunes ranging from Bach's Prelude in C Major to songs from the 1964 stage musical *Hello, Dolly!* and had a music room with tape recorders, walls full of guitars, and a jukebox. He revealed that he'd thought of going to India to study the sitar even if it took up six years of his life. "I couldn't believe it," he said of his first exposure to the music of Ravi Shankar. "It was just like everything you have ever thought of as great music all coming out at once."

He believed Pattie was improving his tastes. He now wore an expensive Cartier watch, drove a Ferrari (two Minis were in the garage), and had graduated from standard northern working-class fare such as toast, steak, chicken, beans, eggs, and chips to what he referred to as "the avocado scene." The house had a conservatory with plants, a print by the Australian artist Sidney Nolan on the living room wall, decorative bound volumes of French books on natural history, and furniture that was updated to reflect his current outlook.

The Beatles had always presented a unified front. The view of any one of them was the view of the Beatles. As they grew up, found partners, and developed their own interests, this impression was harder to sustain. They wanted to give their own opinions on the hot issues of the day. They wanted to be free to offend if necessary. In their early days in Hamburg they'd been rude, outspoken, and slightly uncouth. It irked them that Brian Epstein had domesticated them in order to achieve popularity. "We should have stuck out for all that." said George. "We only cut our hair and said all the 'yes-sir, no-sir, three-bags-full-sir' bit to get in."

George went on to discuss war, religion, and authority with Cleave, sensitive topics in America but not as much in Britain, where irreverence and even eccentricity were respected. He spoke to her about the seven-month-old war in Vietnam, which had initiated a protest movement among the young. "I think about it every day and it's wrong. Anything to do with war is wrong. They're all wrapped up in their Nelsons and their Churchills and their Montys—always talking about war heroes. Look at *All Our Yesterdays* [a weekly TV series on Granada Television that showed TV newsreels from exactly twenty-five years ago]—how we killed a few more Huns here and there. Makes me sick. They're the sort who are leaning on their walking sticks and telling us a few years in the army would do us good."

George revealed a deep-seated dislike of authority figures, ranging from teachers and Roman Catholic priests to the current prime minister of Britain, Harold Wilson. Religion was still an influence in British culture, and as children the Beatles had intermittently attended either Sunday school (John and Ringo), visited churches with friends (Paul), or attended mass (George). However, the doctrines of Christianity and the authority of the churches were being challenged by a generation that resented being told what to do, found popular culture more invigorating than sermons, rituals, and hymns, and was more interested in self-discovery than discovering God.

"And to go on to religion," George told Cleave,

I think religion falls flat on its face. All this "love thy neighbour," but none of them are doing it. How can anybody get into the position of being Pope and accept all the glory and the money and the Mercedes-Benz and that? I could never be Pope until I'd sold my rich gates and my posh hat. I couldn't sit there with all that money on me and believe I was religious. Why can't we bring all this out in the open? Why is

there all this stuff about blasphemy? If Christianity's as good
as they say it is, it should stand up to a bit of discussion.

During 1966, the Beatles made it clear that they didn't approve
of America's involvement in Vietnam, but they were less than outspoken critics. Asked about the war by *Melody Maker* in January,
John only commented, "I don't like what's happening there." Seven
months later, when asked what the role of an entertainer should be
with reference to Vietnam, Paul said: "I dunno, you know. If you can
say that war is no good, and a few people believe you, then it might be
good. I don't know. I can't say too much, though. That's the trouble."

At the time few thought show business people were qualified to
comment on complex issues of foreign policy. Active involvement in
politics was seen as okay if you were supporting your government,
but not if you were a critic. The Beatles' reason for opposing Vietnam
appeared to be no more than a preference for peace over war. They
didn't discuss the virtues of communism versus those of capitalism
or the domino theory. Nevertheless, their increasing willingness during 1966 to speak negatively of American policy in Southeast Asia,
however mildly, put them on the side of the draft dodgers, doves,
and peaceniks.

Paul has since claimed that a turning point came when he met
the celebrated British philosopher Bertrand Russell, who was a
founder member of CND (the Campaign for Nuclear Disarmament)
and an outspoken critic of America's policy in Southeast Asia since
April 1963, when in a letter to the *New York Times* he accused the
country of "conducting a war of annihilation."

Now in his nineties, Russell remained a prominent cultural
commenter and was the only living British philosopher that most
British people knew of. When Paul discovered that Russell had a
London house on Hasker Street, only three streets away from the
apartment shared by John Dunbar and Marianne Faithfull, he
made an appointment to meet him when the great man made one

of his infrequent visits south from his home at Penrhyndeudraeth in North Wales.

Russell's thirty-year-old American assistant, Ralph Schoenman, a formidable antiwar campaigner in his own right and an original signatory of the Committee of 100, which promoted civil disobedience in the cause of peace, had known Paul since 1964 and was instrumental in setting up this meeting between the author of "I Want to Hold Your Hand" and "Can't Buy Me Love" and the author of *A History of Western Philosophy* and *Has Man a Future?* He recalls Paul's nervousness on the day: "He was rather self-conscious during the conversation and at one point gestured awkwardly, his arm causing the lamp to the left of his chair to go flying. Russell was gracious, put Paul at his ease and the conversation resumed seamlessly."

It was Russell's involvement in the peace movement rather than his humanistic philosophy that interested Paul. Almost forty years later Paul would claim that it was Russell who made him aware of what was taking place in Vietnam and that later that day, at EMI Studios: "I said to the guys 'Hey, I met Bertrand Russell and he's really against this war.' So I explained to everyone the issue."

Told this way, the account raises awkward questions. The American military had been in Vietnam since 1961 and Russell had been voluble about it since 1963; could the four members of the Beatles really have been ignorant of what was going on? If Paul passed on Russell's analysis to the rest of the group, why weren't they more inspired to protest at an earlier stage? (The only reference Paul made to Russell at the time was when he told Maureen Cleave, in an exchange expressing his feelings about getting old, "If our bodies stayed young our minds would have to stay young, and nobody wants that. But Bertrand Russell seems all right—I wouldn't mind being like him at all.")

Yet it wasn't George's quotes about the pope or the war in Vietnam that would prove to be the most controversial in Cleave's series but an offhand comment from John on the popularity of the

Beatles compared to the popularity of Jesus. It would threaten their record sales in America, endanger their lives, and contribute to the end of their career as stage performers. "I always remember to thank Jesus for the end of my touring days," John would later observe. "If I hadn't said that the Beatles were 'bigger than Jesus' and upset the very Christian Ku Klux Klan, well, Lord, I might still be up there with all the other performing fleas."

Of all the Beatles, Cleave was probably closest to John. She respected his sharp, humorous, and untrained mind, while he respected her intellect, perceptiveness, and learning. She could see that John was more complex and original in this thought than the other Beatles. He was also full of contradictions. He was the hard-working musician and songwriter who was terminally lazy; the champion of the downtrodden who liked to be chauffeur-driven in a Rolls-Royce with tinted windows and a TV; the dedicated artist who could say, "I want the money just to be rich." She described him as imperious, unpredictable, indolent, disorganized, childish, vague, charming, easy-going, tough, and quick-witted.

As with John's fellow Beatles, Cleave surveyed his possessions to work out what they said about him. In John's case they showed his immense curiosity and his unsystematic way of learning—volumes on natural history and India side by side with Tolstoy, Huxley, Tennyson, Wilde, and Richmal Crompton's series of William books for children. They also showed his impulsiveness and low boredom threshold—a suit of armor, an old family Bible picked up at a shop in Chester, a gorilla suit, model racing cars, records of sitar music, a porcelain cat, and a slot machine.

In the sitting room there were eight little green boxes with blinking red lights. John told her that he'd bought them as Christmas presents but hadn't given them away and that they'd carry on blinking for a year. These were marketed at $25 and were a short-lived craze in late 1965 and early 1966 when some boutiques on the King's Road sold them. Their pointlessness was the point, although they had another use for the stoned or tripped-out, to whom flashing lights could be entrancing and even meaningful.

John was naturally introspective, although it was only recently that he had used self-examination as a stimulus to his songwriting. "Nowhere Man" questioned life's purpose; "In My Life" explored loss, decay, and change; and "The Word," which he later referred to as his first "message" song, was a tub-thumping sermon for the liberating power of love full of biblical phrases such as "in the beginning," "the light," "the way," and "the word" (all to be found, as it happens, in the Gospel of John). "This could be a Salvation Army song," Paul had told Francis Wyndham in November. "The word is love. It could be Jesus. It *isn't*, mind you, but it could be."

For John, any exploration into the spiritual involved revisiting the Christianity of his past. Although not raised in a strong Christian environment, he was sent to Sunday school at an early age because his Aunt Mimi thought it would keep him out of trouble; he joined the church choir, was confirmed, and for a brief time went to a Bible study for older boys. The experience gave him a framework that he would constantly return to, even if only to challenge it, as well as words and phrases that would creep into his conversation and lyrics for the rest of his life.

He spoke most extensively about his Christian roots in a 1964 interview for a one-off American Beatles special publication. "I was brought up Church of England by my aunt," he explained.

She used to pack me off to Sunday school. At sixteen I was confirmed—and I must confess the reason was because I'd heard that you couldn't get a job unless you were confirmed. Then, when I was twenty, my aunt finally confessed that she didn't really believe in God at all and I realized why it was she'd always made me go to church but had never gone herself. But she was so right to send me, so right, for it gave me the chance to decide for myself whether to believe in God or not. She didn't try to prejudice me one way or the other. She was completely fair, and very wise I'd say, to have handled the situation the way she did.

One of my friends told me I ought to become a choirboy. "You get paid for it," he said. "It's marvelous." Well, that really impressed me—getting paid for dressing up in a lot of choirboy gear. And singing was something I could do easily, and I always loved it anyway.

Once he left school and music began to take up more of his free time, John stopped attending church, but wealth, adulation, and his drug experiences made him reconsider spirituality.

John in particular saw parallels between pop stars and messianic figures. He had firsthand experience of mass devotion and was aware of the power he had to influence people through his words and actions. Jesus became someone he could relate to as a young leader who was revered by some, misunderstood by others, and hated by a few.

Five years later, during an interview at the Apple office in Savile Row, John showed me an open letter written to him by a recent Christian convert in the center pages of a newspaper published by an American Jesus movement commune. This led to him telling me his views on those who sought to convert him to Christianity. It appeared that he had not yet finished ruminating about the gospel message, the character of Jesus, and the construction of myths and legends.

He explained to me:

I think Jesus was probably a very hip guy. I think a lot of the stuff about magic and miracles is probably a lot of bullshit that was written about years later. I think he was just a very hip guy and you can read his messages. What he really says is, "You are here. Be true to yourselves. Try to love people. Love your neighbor. Help someone if they're down." They are quite radical statements. It's very aligned to communism, what he says.

Now you can imagine, if it wasn't the twentieth century, [with the] kind of mysticism and guru-ism [that] has been said and put out about the Beatles. Imagine what they would put out if we were in a primitive society, if we were "four young men with long hair and strange apparel" who "appeared and drew thousands" and all that! You can imagine how this bullshit came about.

A recent book that had affected John's beliefs was *The Passover Plot: New Interpretation of the Life and Death of Jesus* by the liberal British biblical scholar Hugh Schonfield. Published in October 1965, this book would go on to become a bestseller. It posited the controversial theory that Jesus was a very religious Jew who understood the Messianic prophecies in the Jewish scriptures and determined to fulfill them in every detail. His mistake came when, with the collusion of Joseph of Arimathea, he decided to fake his own death. This went wrong when a Roman soldier, assuming he was dying, speared his side and killed him.

Cleave didn't quote John referring to Schonfield's theory—although he would later admit the connection— but he appears to have been affected by the idea that Jesus

The Passover Plot by British Bible scholar Hugh Schonfield, which influenced the controversial comments about Jesus that John made to Maureen Cleave.

may have been a wise and well-meaning individual who got swept up in the enthusiasms of his era. He also seems to have been swayed by Schonfield's assessment of the disciples as "loyal in their own way, but of limited intelligence, simple Galileans for the most part, who would not be at all at home in the sophisticated atmosphere of Jerusalem."

But what John actually said to Cleave was, "Christianity will go. It will vanish and shrink. I needn't argue about that; I'm right and I will be proved right. We're more popular than Jesus now; I don't know which will go first—rock 'n' roll or Christianity. Jesus was all right but his disciples were thick and ordinary. It's them twisting it that ruins it for me."

It wasn't unusual for Cleave to ask the Beatles about religion. It had come up with both John and Paul in her October 1963 feature when John had said, "Everybody's drumming on about the future, but I'm not letting it interfere with my laughs, if you see what I mean. Perhaps I worried more when I was working it out about God. I used him, like everybody else, for things I wanted." Paul, who had admitted that religion didn't fit in with his life, added, "I might need it as I grow older to comfort me when I'm dying."

The feature didn't say what prompted John's comment about Jesus, but the quote printed immediately before it (and therefore likely to be a relevant link in the conversation) was about India. John had just been playing Cleave a record of sitar music, and one of the books on his shelf that Cleave had noticed was *Forty-One Years in India* by Field Marshal Lord Roberts, a British soldier involved in quelling the Indian Mutiny of 1857 who went on to have a long and successful career. "Don't the Indians appear cool to you?" he'd asked her. "Are you listening? This music is thousands of years old. It makes me laugh, the British going over there and telling them what to do. Quite amazing."

Possibly the conversation had turned to the religion of India and comparisons between the passionately held beliefs of ordinary Indians and the lukewarm beliefs of nominal Christians in England.

Cleave may have added her own reflections on Indian religious culture and British colonialism from her childhood at the hill station of
Mussoorie. All she could remember six months later was that, in her
words, "we discussed how the power of Christianity had declined in
the modern world and his remarks were intended to illustrate this."

He was almost certainly thinking of Britain rather than America or mainland Europe and, because of his childhood experience in
Woolton, specifically of the Church of England. There's no record
of him at this point having attended a church in any other country.

Globally, Christianity hasn't diminished in the way John thought
it would. It's the most populous religion, with almost a third of the
world's population as adherents. But in Britain things have turned
out as he anticipated. In 1964 the Survey of British Social Attitudes
reported that 74 percent of the country "belonged to a religion and
attended services." By 2011 that figure had plunged to 13.1 percent.
In 1964 the number of British people claiming to belong to no religion was only 3 percent. In 2011 it stood at 45 percent and in 2014,
48.5 percent. In June 2015 the former Archbishop of Canterbury
Lord Carey warned that the Church of England was "one generation
away from extinction."

John also must have been thinking of the young rather than all
generations when he made the comment about religion. The evidence, as he saw it, was that there was a greater passion among them
for music and popular culture than there was for church and religious practice. The movie A Hard Day's Night (1964) caused far more
excitement among both critics and audiences than did the biblical
epic The Greatest Story Ever Told (1965) and made around a third more
at the box office. A magazine special about the Beatles would have
sold more copies to the young than a special about Jesus.

John's view was that the essence of Christianity had become corrupted during transmission. He had witnessed myths building up
about himself and the Beatles and had firsthand experience of the
way in which quotes could be wrongly translated and misconstrued.

He also knew that ordinary people could be elevated to positions that they had never desired and could have powers attributed to them that they didn't possess. Sick children were being wheeled into the dressing rooms of the Beatles in the hopes that a pat on the head or a shake of the hand by John, Paul, George, or Ringo would bring about healing.

Through his life John would speak warmly of the values of Jesus but was critical of priests, popes, bishops, evangelists, Jesus freaks, and organized religion. Shortly before his death in 1980 he told David Sheff of *Playboy,* "People got the impression I was anti-Christ or anti-religion. I'm not at all. I'm a most religious fellow. . . . I'm certainly not an atheist."

When he said he didn't know which would go first—rock 'n' roll or Christianity—the equation of a form of music and a centuries-old religion sounded inappropriate. It would have been natural to compare rock 'n' roll with jazz or folk or compare Christianity with Islam or Buddhism. By comparing rock with Christianity John seems to have intuited that rock 'n' roll was becoming more than a form of entertainment and was fulfilling a religious role in many people's lives. There was as yet no "rock culture" by that name, but John may have anticipated the time, not far in the future, when rock festivals would take on aspects of open-air revivals, rock stars would become treated as gurus, and music would be deliberately used (often in conjunction with light shows and drugs) to bring about altered states of consciousness in ceremonies that bore similarities to shamanistic rituals.

Could it have been in connection with this that John made the following cryptic comment about his own calling? "Weybridge," he told Cleave, "won't do at all. I'm just stopping at it, like a bus stop. Bankers and stockbrokers live there; they can add figures and Weybridge is what they live in and they think it's the end, they really do. I think of it every day—me in my Hansel and Gretel house. I'll take my time; I'll get my real house when I know what I want. You see, there's something else I'm going to do, something I must do—only

I don't know what it is. That's why I go round painting and taping and drawing and writing because it may be one of them. All I know is, it isn't for me."

This was the most prescient comment of the whole interview. Like George, John wasn't content with fame and wealth. He valued these things for the security and power they provided but had learned that they didn't satisfy the deepest level of his being. He was still restless and searching for something. He was also looking for a role that would take him beyond that of a "mere" entertainer.

"He was always prepared to be interested in anything," Cleave told me when reflecting on the interview in 2005. "He was clever. He was clever but badly organized. Clever and lazy. The thing about John Lennon was that his mind just darted around."

During February, Paul was continuing his musical explorations as well as adding finishing touches to the £40,000 house he'd bought the previous April on Cavendish Avenue, St. John's Wood, close to EMI Studios, and was having renovated. The three-story Regency town house would become his permanent home in London and, because of its proximity to the studio, became the base for the group to meet. Paul would write and demo songs in the top-floor music room that he'd had purpose-built.

Moving there would give him space and freedom while at the same time allow him to be close to the clubs, cinemas, art galleries, theatres, and performance spaces of central London. He had the house fitted with the latest in ovens and rotisseries, the best sound system for his record players, and a movie screen in the dining room. He had brought in John Dunbar's designer sister, Marina, and her architect husband, John Adams, to redesign the interior of the property. An art school friend of Barry Miles, Pete Simpson, was hired to paint decorative scenes on the cupboard doors in his music room.

From an architect's point of view, Paul's demands were basic. He wanted the house renovated as quickly as possible and within a budget of six thousand pounds. There were no major structural changes.

He favored hominess over modernity, even to the point of asking Adams to design the ground floor in such a way that the kitchen smells would waft into the living room as they had done at the Ashers' house (and presumably did at his Liverpool council home). He bought his furniture from auction rooms on Old Brompton Road—a

Paul's newly purchased house in St John's Wood undergoing renovations in 1966.

metal clock for seven pounds, a mahogany table for ten pounds, a three-piece suite for twenty pounds. "I don't go for this modern stuff," he said. "It always looks as though it needs something doing to it. I like it to be comfortable." In the basement was an apartment for a couple, the Kellys, who cooked and looked after the house.

During the refurbishment, freshly burned-off paint fell on the wooden floorboards and caused a small fire. When neighbors called the fire department, one of the officers referred to the building as "Paul McCartney's home," and the secret of the owner's identity was out. Not even the construction workers had known whose property they were working on. When the *Evening Standard* reported it as news, fans turned up and made off with souvenir fixtures and fittings. This resulted in Adams fitting large wooden gates with an expanded metal sheet across the front. It was not only meant to look good, but the rough surface stopped people from writing messages in lipstick and chalk; there was no aerosol paint graffiti in 1966.

Despite his opposition to modernism in furniture and his preference for comfort over experiment when it came to interior design, Paul's more adventurous side was revealed in his art collecting. Although he was only beginning to become interested in collecting, he had already bought a four-square-foot oil painting by pop artist Peter Blake (soon to become widely known for coproducing the cover of *Sgt. Pepper's Lonely Hearts Club Band*) that was a contemporary take on Sir Edward Landseer's 1851 painting *The Monarch of the Glen*. This purchase was made on the advice of gallery owner Robert Fraser, who was becoming his mentor on contemporary art.

Paul's other major purchase was a metal sculpture titled *Solo* made by the Scottish artist Eduardo Paolozzi that stood in the music room. Paolozzi had also exhibited at Fraser's gallery and was highly celebrated, but there was another important connection for Paul. The sculptor had tutored the former bass guitarist of the Beatles, Stuart Sutcliffe, before Sutcliffe's sudden death in 1962.

Earlier in the month, Paul had seen Stevie Wonder playing at the Scotch of St James. The Beatles had loved Motown music from its inception, covering Barrett Strong's 1960 track "Money (That's What I Want)" (cowritten by Motown founder Berry Gordy), the Marvelettes' 1961 hit "Please Mr. Postman," and, from 1962, "You've Really Got a Hold on Me" by the Miracles. In interviews they specifically mentioned records by Marvin Gaye, Chuck Jackson, Mary Wells, and the Miracles as being among their favorites. In October 1963, Ringo, who was sent every Motown record by the Oriole label, which licensed them in the UK, was photographed holding the recently released album *Recorded Live: The 12 Year Old Genius* by Little Stevie Wonder. When this image was used in the Beatles' official 1964 calendar, it introduced Wonder to new audiences around the world.

The backing on all the Motown tracks was played by a group of session musicians known informally as the Funk Brothers. They were never mentioned on record sleeves, received no writing credits for their often-considerable musical input, and were paid by the hour. Their resident bass player was James Jamerson. "His style was one of the major influences on me when I was learning to play electric bass," Paul would later say, although at the time he didn't know his name.

Surprisingly, in December 1965, a press release was put out by Al Abrams of Motown saying that George Martin had made tentative enquiries to see if Motown's hit-making team of writer-producers Brian Holland, Lamont Dozier, and Eddie Holland (Holland-Dozier-Holland), currently riding high with a run of hits for both the Supremes and the Four Tops, would write the Beatles' next single. If true, it was an unusual move, as the Beatles had never released covers of other people's songs as singles—Holland-Dozier-Holland were their closest competitors as commercially successful songwriters, and they would inevitably have had to record in Detroit. Lamont Dozier told me while I was researching this book that the call came from Brian Epstein rather than Martin and was a general inquiry about collaboration rather than about a single, and that after the songwriting team showed interest, the subject was never raised again.

In 1983 he had been more expansive. "We were supposed to do an album along the lines of *The Beatles Meet Holland-Dozier-Holland*, but Berry Gordy refused to do it. We were going to write each other songs and perform them but we couldn't put it together because we were primarily known as writers and I don't think Berry wanted to disturb that."

Eddie Holland told me the team was so busy working with Motown artists that there wasn't time to pursue the project and that no songs ever got written by them with the Beatles in mind. It was just an idea that disappeared as quickly as it came, and probably only became a press release because Al Abrams could see the value in publicizing the admiration expressed by the Liverpool group for the Detroit songwriters.

"We would have done something if we could," said Holland. "If we could have merged the talent that we had as Holland-Dozier-Holland with the tremendous talent the Beatles had, we would have come up with some very different, interesting things. It would have been exciting. It would have been very dynamic. My brother Brian, being the head of Holland-Dozier-Holland, was so magnificent. He could hear things that the average producer couldn't hear. Lamont Dozier had a feeling for rhythm. It would have been a lot of fun and very exciting, but unfortunately it didn't happen."

Now fifteen, Stevie Wonder was on a British tour to promote his new single "Uptight (Everything's Alright)," backed by a popular London club band, the Sidewinders. Impeccable in a well-cut mohair suit and wearing his trademark shades, Wonder played a short set that included "High Heel Sneakers," Dylan's "Blowing in the Wind," "Fingertips," and, of course, "Uptight," which had that day entered the UK Top 40 chart. He was a mesmerizing performer who sang with a broad grin and a harmonica in his hand while waving his arms in time to the music and shaking his head. He was blind since shortly after his birth, and it seemed that his lack of sight was compensated for by a heightened sense of rhythm.

At the end of the month Paul attended a lecture at the Italian Institute in London given by the forty-year-old avant-garde composer Luciano Berio, who had worked with Pierre Boulez, John Cage, and Karlheinz Stockhausen and had recently taught Steve Reich as a graduate student at Mills College in California. The talk was based around a presentation of his latest work, *Laborintus II,* a collage of voices, musical instruments, and cut-up tapes commissioned by a French TV station to celebrate the seven hundredth anniversary of the birth of Dante. Berio described the composition as "a laboratory reduced to the dimensions of performance, where we test theories and practices which can be used as experimental models of real life." It was at the opposite end of the musical spectrum from Stevie Wonder's foot-stomping "Uptight."

Paul must have found the tunelessness irritating, but the deconstruction of sound and the questions the piece raised about the very nature of music connected with his shaken-up post-LSD view of the world. Although pop music was widely considered to be rebellious and daring, many unwritten rules governed it, from the length of a typical song to the verse/chorus structure and the types of instruments that could be used. Exposure to the work of composers like Berio prompted Paul to consider how the rules of pop could be effectively challenged while still holding on to a mainstream audience.

One recording of Berio's work that Paul had already heard, through Barry Miles, was "Thema (Omaggio a Joyce)," which cut and spliced a tape recording of Armenian mezzo-soprano Cathy Berberian reading from James Joyce's *Ulysses* to create what has been described as an "electro-acoustic composition." No instruments were used in the piece. The musicality was all derived from the naked voice and Berio's choice of tape edits, speeds, distortions, echoes, repeats, and reverberations.

After the lecture Paul and Miles spoke with Berio, but the conversation was cut short by the crush of photographers and the attention of the Italian embassy staff. The press had been tipped off about

Paul and Barry Miles (*at table right*) listening to a presentation by the avant-garde Italian composer Luciano Berio (*seated second from left*) at the Italian Cultural Institute in London, February 23, 1966.

the presence of a Beatle. Photos subsequently appeared in publications ranging from the *Daily Mail* ("What a Beatle Does in the Evenings") to the *Musical Times* ("Beatle Meets Modern Italian Composer Luciano Berio"). On February 24, the *Times* briefly commented on the event, although it didn't mention Paul's attendance. "Everything that Luciano Berio does is interesting even when it isn't entirely convincing," it reported. "Last night at the Italian Institute he talked for almost an hour about his new work, *Homage to Dante* [*sic*]—mostly about what it was not, and what is the only possible way of creating a work of art, and suchlike topics."

Paul's frenetic self-education program was the subject of a revealing interview with radio disc jockey Alan Freeman that took place at Freeman's apartment at Wellesley Court in Maida Vale. Paul arrived smartly dressed in gray trousers, a dark jacket, white shirt, and polka dot tie. The first thing he did on entering the apartment was to sit down at Freeman's piano for ninety minutes, working on a new song idea (which Freeman didn't identify). "That's all I've got so far," he said. "I must work on it a bit more."

When he finally left the piano stool for the sofa, he told Freeman that the biggest change in the Beatles of late was the broadening of their artistic experiences. "We've all got interested in things that just never used to occur to us. I've got thousands, millions, of new ideas myself. What I really want to do now is to see whether I could write all the music for a film. Not just to write tunes, but the music of the film itself. I want to read a lot more than I do. It annoys me that so many million books came out last year and I only read twenty of them. It's a drag."

He reiterated the point he'd made three months ago to Francis Wyndham that he wanted the Beatles to move forward rather than tread water. "We've only made records which *we* think are good, and that's the only standard we've gone by. Eventually we may get a bit too way-out. I hope not, but I don't know. . . . There are still too many groups who are trying just to keep up. That's no good. That's what makes the whole pop thing dull in the end. You ought to be able to move on a bit further with every record, like the Who."

Significantly, his only references to pop music were brief mentions of the Who and the Stones. He was keener to talk of reading plays (mentioning Alfred Jarry), investigating reports of the Kennedy assassination, learning to read music, making home movies, and listening to classical music.

"I made myself listen to classical records, though nobody in our house ever liked them. When one came on [the radio] they'd just turn it off. But I thought, 'I'd better sort this out for myself and see whether I like it or not.' And in fact I don't like a lot of it. It's too fruity and sentimental. But from that you get on to what modern composers are doing and it's suddenly great. Then I play them to John and he says, 'What a drag! All these millions of records coming out all the time and we've not been getting on to them.' Then we rush out and buy loads of modern compositions. The only thing is to *listen* to everything and then make up your mind about it."

The modern composer he spoke about by name was Karlheinz

The British DJ Alan Freeman interviewing Paul for *Rave* magazine.

Stockhausen, a thirty-seven-year-old German recommended to him by Barry Miles and John Dunbar. "His ideas are fantastic," Paul enthused. "It's the farthest-out music yet. He uses electronic stuff that nobody else has got round to. And his records are listed under the classical section in the catalogues. So if you've got it in your head that you don't dig classical music, look what you're shutting out. You can't go putting music into little categories like 'Serious' and 'Merseybeat' and so on. The great thing is that it's *music,* whatever label they try to stick on it."

His plans for the Beatles in 1966 were to push forward, absorb fresh influences, and break new artistic ground: "We can't just stop where we are or there's nothing left to do. We can go on trying to make popular records and it can get dead dull if we're not trying to expand at all and move on into other things. Unless you're careful, you can be successful and unsuccessful at the same time."

MARCH

I'd say that the really big change is in our
tastes, in finding out about things we didn't
know before.
–PAUL, 1966

On March 3, during a visit to New York, Brian Epstein announced the Beatles' tour plans for the year. He spoke of them playing in America, Britain, Germany, and Japan (although Britain would eventually be dropped and the Philippines added). The long talked-about third film was not going to be shot any time soon.

It appears that Epstein was coaxing the group out of its hibernation and easing their fears about touring by taking them to places that had some additional appeal. The Far East seemed exotic, and Japan was the biggest record-buying market in the region. Germany too was a big market, but it had also played a crucial role in the development of the group when they played night after night in Hamburg clubs between 1960 and 1962. It was here that they developed their distinctive haircuts and posed for their first artistic photo portraits with Astrid Kirchherr. Returning to Germany offered an opportunity to bathe in nostalgia and reconnect with old friends.

The day after Epstein's announcement, the first of Maureen

Cleave's profiles appeared in the *Evening Standard*—a double-page spread on John headlined "How Does a Beatle Live? John Lennon Lives Like This."

Ironically, in light of the furor that was to follow, the only quote to be pulled out and enlarged in the paper was "They keep telling me I'm all right for money but then I think I may have spent it all by the time I'm 40 so I keep going" and the three crossheads were "Small Hours," "Mock Tudor," and "Bus Stop." The strapline running along the top of the page was "On a hill in Surrey . . . A young man, famous, loaded, and waiting for something." No attention was drawn to John's soon-to-be-infamous comment about Jesus, either in the layout or in Cleave's text.

It's commonly reported that the irreligious British didn't even notice the quote, but that is not so. On March 7, the historian John Grigg, writing in his column for the *Guardian*, quoted John's view about the "thick and ordinary" disciples and commented, "The same fate has befallen other great men. Beatle maniacs are a distinct obstacle to higher appreciation of the Beatles. In the disciples' day, people who were 'thick and ordinary' could win fame (and martyrdom) by throwing up their careers and associating with a man of genius. Nowadays they can win fame (without martyrdom) through a combination of bad taste and good publicity."

Two days later the *Evening Standard* published a letter from "a loyal reader" who found John's assertion "impudent" but was nevertheless more outraged that the Beatle had spoken of ejecting his estranged father from his Weybridge home. "No gentleman," wrote the correspondent, "would discuss his private family affairs for publication in a national newspaper." John's words must have become reasonably well known, because cartoonist Gerald Scarfe (later to marry Jane Asher) made them the subject of a cartoon for the satirical magazine *Private Eye*. In the drawing John was dressed in heavenly robes and playing a cross-shaped guitar with a halo made out of a vinyl LP.

The interview was on the newsstands in time to be picked up by some of the two hundred guests being flown out from London to Dublin on two private jets to celebrate Tara Browne's twenty-first birthday in grand style. The party, held at his mother's eighteenth-century hunting lodge, Luggala, on a five-thousand-acre estate in the beautiful Wicklow Mountains, would become legendary for its extravagance (the American folk-rock group the Lovin' Spoonful was flown in to provide entertainment), its density of "beautiful people" (Mick Jagger and Brian Jones; models Anita Pallenberg and Suki Potier; John Paul Getty and his wife, Talitha; art dealer Robert Fraser), and the copious amounts of hallucinogenic drugs available.

Mike McCartney was there but Paul wasn't, presumably because he was making the final preparations to move into Cavendish Avenue. Two days later Paul and Jane crossed the English Channel and drove to the small Swiss ski resort of Klosters, near Davos, for a two-week vacation. The Beatles had spent three days in Obertauern, Austria, the previous year filming skiing sequences for *Help!,* and this introduction to the sport had given Paul the appetite to learn to ski properly.

The couple rented La Casa Rosemarie, a chalet on the road to Davos overlooking the town and the Alps beyond and built by local restaurant owner Tino Meisser for his daughter. In the bathroom of the chalet Paul began writing his song "For No One," at first with the title "Why Did It Die?" He already had a portion of "Got to Get You Into My Life" written, based on his December LSD experience, and had "Eleanor Rigby" in good enough shape to play it on a piano in a private room at Gasthaus Casanna (a hotel also run by Meisser) for three or four guests, so this meant that half of his eventual contributions to the next LP were already at least started.

"For No One" showed Paul experimenting again with perspective, using the second-person narrative mode in order to create distance between him and the actions and emotions described. It's almost as if it is written in the voice of a stage or film director explaining motivations to a pair of actors. "I'm reading plays like mad," he'd told Alan Freeman. "I don't know if I'll ever write one but there are so many things I'd like to have a try at."

The song describes a man's rejection by a woman who no longer needs him. In "I'm Looking Through You" it had been Paul who'd set himself up as self-sufficient, but now the woman is in control. He had looked through her, but now, assuming the song is autobiographical (Paul later said it must have been written after "another argument" with Jane), she looks through him.

In "We Can Work It Out" Paul assumed that all would be well if both parties could only see things in the same way—his way. He's no longer so arrogant. He can see that he's changed a lot since they first met, and he's no longer the same person she fell in love with. In "For No One" he predicts a time when "all the things she said" will come back to haunt him, surely a reference to one of Paul's earliest songs about Jane, "Things We Said Today," which he wrote while sailing around the Virgin Islands with Jane, Ringo, and Maureen. In a similar way his provisional title, "Why Did It Die?," echoes the earlier hope in "And I Love Her" that "a love like ours could never die."

Every day in Klosters Paul and Jane started at 9:00 a.m. with their twenty-two-year-old ski instructor, John Christoffel, and were taught until 4:00 p.m. Their visit wasn't announced, and so no journalists or photographers trailed them. Even Christoffel wasn't told the identity of his new students and didn't discover it until he casually asked Paul what he did for a living. At the time Paul was driving his Aston Martin to the ski lift, and he just put on a record and said, "This is what I do." The record was "Michelle."

Christoffel wasn't aware of any problems between Paul and Jane. As far as he could detect, they were a happy couple, both keen to learn as much as they could in the short time available. On some evenings the three of them remained together after the lessons to eat or drink. On one night Christoffel took them to a town hall dance in

Saas where bands played traditional Swiss folk music on accordions, clarinets, and upright basses.

Despite its ups and downs, Paul's relationship with Jane was a vital component in the broadening of his outlook. He was quickly absorbed into the Asher family after beginning to date her in April 1963 (when she was more famous than him in Britain) and was soon given his own room on the top floor of their home at 57 Wimpole Street in an area of the West End famed for its private medical practices. This became his London base for three years.

The Ashers were a sophisticated and educated family with liberal views and a passion for the arts. Jane and her sister, Clare, were actresses; their brother, Peter, was a pupil at the prestigious Westminster School and sang in a musical duo with his friend Gordon Waller (Peter and Gordon) that Paul would give Lennon-McCartney songs to for them to record and later write specifically for them; mother Margaret was an oboe professor at the Guildhall School of Music and Drama (where a young George Martin had been one of her pupils); and father Richard, although now prematurely retired, had been an endocrinologist and hematologist with a special interest in the physical effects of mental illness.

This environment was intellectually invigorating for Paul, whose home not long before had been a Liverpool council house with his cotton worker father and apprentice hairdresser brother. At the Ashers' home, books, pictures, and musical instruments surrounded him, as did conversations covering classical concerts, the latest West End plays, breakthroughs in medicine, and international news as reported by the broadsheet newspapers. Margaret Asher gave him some lessons in playing the recorder, and he started doing the *Times* crossword.

Richard Asher was also committed to improving the style and language of medical writing and wrote articles urging practitioners to be clearer in their communication. He had a reputation for challenging received opinion in medicine—one of his most influential papers criticized the practice of telling sick people that they were better off in bed—and this may have accentuated Paul's questioning of songwriting conventions. Asher's penchant for the ringing phrase as opposed to the off-the-peg sentence can only have helped Paul in his approach to lyrics. In an article published in the *British Medical Journal* in 1958 Asher urged contributors to such magazines to liven up their prose: "I believe if a man has something to say which interests him, and he knows how to say it, then he need never be dull. Unfortunately some people have a desire for publication but nothing more. They have nothing to say, and they do not know how to say it."

But most significant was the coterie of young bohemians who were either friends of Peter Asher or friends of his friends. Through them Paul was introduced to the small but burgeoning "underground" scene of art galleries, poetry readings, happenings, lectures, and protests that had been brought into being by young creative people reacting against what they saw as the dull, conformist culture of postwar Britain.

The connection had started with Peter Asher's friend and musical partner Gordon Waller, who had dated Jenny Dunbar, from nearby Bentinck Street. Through Jenny they got to know her brother, John Dunbar, who had studied science and art at Cambridge and married singer Marianne Faithfull in May 1965. He wrote a weekly art column for the *Scotsman* and had a knack of being the first to pick up on emerging trends. He would become an important mentor to both Paul and John.

A frequent guest at Wimpole Street, Dunbar knew a lot about contemporary art, music from other cultures, American and European literature, and psychedelic drugs. A friend of his was Barry Miles, an art college graduate (Gloucestershire College of Art) and expert on Beat generation writing who knew the poets Allen Ginsberg and Gregory Corso and the novelist William Burroughs. At the time he was introduced into the Wimpole Street circle he was managing Better Books on Charing Cross Road, a shop inspired by Lawrence Ferlinghetti's bohemian City Lights Bookstore in San Francisco.

The art critic and artist John Dunbar, the husband of singer Marianne Faithful, was a part owner of the Indica gallery and bookstore.

This meant that Paul was now engaging with classical music and free jazz, medical journals and Beat literature, West End theatre and southern soul, the *Village Voice* and the *Times*. He found this clash of cultures enlivening and loved life in the heart of London, where all the important events seem to happen within a twenty-minute drive.

"We had books around and by osmosis he absorbed a lot of these things," says Dunbar. "He learned about films as well. My father had a film school and Truffaut came over and those guys and I had watched a lot of movies by that time. I had an 8mm camera and John and Paul had 16mm cameras and I showed them both how to use them. They'd send things through twice so they'd get double exposures. They learned by trying things out."

Paul impressed his new friends with his appetite for learning. It seemed to them that he felt he had a lot of catching up to do and was trying to reconcile the standards of classical art, literature, and music with those of popular culture. Once he asked Jenny Dunbar why anyone would bother to study Chaucer. Although he'd enjoyed "The Miller's Tale" at school because of its earthy humor, he couldn't see the possible relevance of medieval poetry to life in the sixties.

With Jane increasingly away from London and the Beatles not yet back at work, Paul had time to pursue these new cultural interests. He spent time with Miles, who left Better Books in late 1965 to found the Indica Books and Gallery with John Dunbar and Peter Asher as business partners. Like Better Books, Indica catered to the experimental and countercultural. Its stock of books explored New Left politics, New Age religions, drugs, sex, alternative lifestyles, and rock music, and it also carried small press poetry magazines and underground newspapers from America and Europe. The *Village Voice* in New York declared Indica "the spiritual center of the new movement."

At the time few London bookstores specialized in such topics, and the target market was still relatively small. Paul would often glance through copies of imported books that Miles kept in the basement at Wimpole Street and as a result borrowed volumes of poetry and books on subjects such as drugs and the antiwar movement. He would smoke pot at Miles's home on Hanson Street, at John Dunbar and Marianne Faithfull's flat in Lennox Gardens, or at Michael Hollingshead's World Psychedelic Centre on Pont Street.

In these safe places he would listen to music as varied as John Cage's *Indeterminacy*, *Spirits Awake* by Albert Ayler, and new jazz by Pharoah Saunders, Ron Blake, Sun Ra, Eric Dolphy, and Ornette Coleman. Ayler was quoted in *Jazz Monthly* as saying, "Our music is pure art. It's like I'm moving, like I'm creating truth. I'm not trying to entertain people. I'm playing the truth for those that can listen." Impromptu jam sessions would often ensue when musicians were present. Influential blues player John Mayall would sometimes hold court and show off his ability to set any text to music. Mayall also invited Paul over to his flat in Bayswater, where he played him the records of American blues artists like Freddie King, Albert King, and J. B. Lenoir.

Paul had acquired an early Phillips cassette tape player and had it installed in his car (British cars at the time only had radios, if they had any sound system at all). He made compilation tapes of R & B records and played them as he drove around London or down to Weybridge to see John. Each week he and the other Beatles were sent all the new entries in the *Billboard* singles charts, many of them never to be released in the UK or only to come out two to three months later, by an American subscription service, for which they each paid thirty pounds a month. Doing this guaranteed that they were always in touch with changing tastes in the US record market. In March they would have been sent "Lightnin' Strikes" by Lou Christie, "Elusive Butterfly" by Bob Lind, "Working My Way Back to You" by the Four Seasons, "I Fought The Law" by the Bobby Fuller Four, "Don't Mess With Bill" by the Marvelettes, "Crying Time" by Ray Charles, and "Batman Theme" by the Marketts.

Paul was also reading the avant-garde literary magazines *Evergreen Review* and *Big Table*, underground newspapers such as New York's *East Village Other* and San Francisco's *Berkeley Barb,* and poetry by Finnish poet Anselm Hollo, American writer and singer Ed Sanders, and Allen Ginsberg. Miles lent him a copy of *The Fugs First Album* (by Ed Sanders's group), which contained the tracks "Slum Goddess," "I Couldn't Get High," and "I Feel like Homemade Shit." The Fugs, who emerged from the New York poetry scene rather than the folk or rock scene, hijacked pop to say things previously only said in Beat poetry or "sick" comedy. They swore, were explicit about sex, and sang about drugs. Paul called it "a new development in discord" and "new and very funny."

Press officer Tony Barrow thought the Beatles' eagerness to learn during this period came from the fact that they'd gone straight from the classroom to the Cavern thus leapfrogging the university experi-

The Fugs (*standing:* Steve Weber, Peter Stampfel; *seated:* Ken Weaver, Tuli Kupferberg, Ed Sanders).

ence. He was amazed at their almost adolescent capacity for surprise when it came to religion, literature, and art. Being almost constantly on the road had made them streetwise and professional but had deprived them of the cultural education that for many of their contemporaries was a matter of course.

Before Indica opened, Barry Miles and assorted volunteers redecorated the space in Mason's Yard for the book shop and gallery. Paul was among them, totally enthusiastic about the project and not at all ashamed to pick up a paintbrush. He even designed and had printed a thousand sheets of wrapping paper that he then presented to the shop for its use. When the American teen magazine *16* published the news, fans wrote to request sample sheets of the paper.

The poet Pete Brown, later to become a significant lyricist for Eric Clapton's power trio Cream, was another friend of Dunbar's drafted to decorate. Along with Michael Horovitz, he'd been an important part of Britain's oral poetry revival starting in the late 1950s and had appeared at a Royal Albert Hall reading in June 1965 with (among others) Allen Ginsberg, Lawrence Ferlinghetti, and Gregory Corso. "I think Paul wanted some identification with progressive policies and the movement," says Brown. "He didn't want to be seen as Mr. Bland. Which was great."

In 1965, the Beatles' music publisher, Dick James, had supplied John and Paul with Brenell Mark 5 reel-to-reel tape recorders. There were practical reasons for this gift. It enabled them to work more confidently on their songwriting at home—none of them being able to write music—and they would be able to take these sketches of songs into the studio at the start of recording sessions.

It also affected the way they wrote. They could approach a song a number of different ways and keep all the results for review. They could take more risks away from the watchful eye of George Martin and hear their material in a more finished form. "If you write a song on tape you have a much better idea in your head of how it sounds and you can take it from there," said George.

Paul had two machines in his small room at the Ashers' and was using them not only to preserve melodies but also to tinker with sounds. William Burroughs had recently arrived in London with his boyfriend, Ian Sommerville, a British-born electronics technician and computer programmer. Sommerville had worked with Burroughs on some of his earliest spoken word experiments, including "Silver Smoke of Dreams," where tapes were physically cut up in sections and then randomly spliced back together. There were plans to establish a studio in a new building that Brian Epstein had acquired where Sommerville would produce a regular audio magazine for Indica. The first edition, scheduled for March 1966, was going to include an electronic music composition by Paul and a poem read by Pete Brown.

When Epstein didn't move his office to the new building, the recording equipment was taken to Ringo's recently vacated London flat at 34 Montagu Square. The audio magazine didn't happen, and so Burroughs took advantage of the unused studio to record his sto-

ries and experiment with more cut-ups, and Paul used it to work on
new songs. Using two machines he could record himself singing with
an acoustic guitar and then play it back while playing along on bass
or electric piano, everything being recorded on the second machine.
The results could be bounced back any number of times while building up layers of sound. Paul's demos soon sounded almost like finished products.

Back at the Ashers', Paul was creating tape loops with a mixture
of music, spoken word, recorded sounds, and reversed tapes. If he dis-
abled the erase head (the device that wipes out previous recordings
by demagnetization), the loop would continue to allow recording on
top of previous recordings until the sound reached saturation level.
He'd stop at points, copy what he'd accumulated to a fresh tape, and
take the result to John or to an evening soirée at John Dunbar's flat
where it would be played as ambient music during a late-night smoking session.

Curious to discover hitherto unheard-of sounds, he experimented by stripping music down to its component parts before re-
configuring it in new and hopefully startling ways. Later in the year
he would tell Barry Miles, "With any kind of thing my aim seems
to be to distort it, to distort it from what we know it as—even with
music and visual things—and to change it from what it is to see what
it could be. To see the potential in it all. To take a note and wreck it
and see in that note what else there is in it, that a simple act like distorting it has caused. . . . It's all trying to create magic. It's all trying to
make things happen so that you don't know why they've happened."

Paul's auditory imagination had been affected by his drug
taking—both pot and LSD. He (along with the other Beatles) became
conscious of intricacies they would once have overlooked, and this
gave them the motivation to make music with sonic subtleties that
would engage others with a similarly heightened awareness. When
they were under the influence of drugs, small details took on great

significance, previously hidden patterns revealed themselves, and unconventional associations were made.

In *The Varieties of Psychedelic Experience* (1966), the first in-depth book about the effects of LSD, R. E. L. Masters and Jean Houston reported that the drug (along with peyote) was "a potent psychochemical that altered and expanded consciousness." Among the effects they noted were "changes in visual, auditory, tactile, olfactory, gustatory, and kinaesthetic perception; changes in experiencing time and space; changes in the rate and content of thought . . . depersonalization and ego dissolution . . . upsurge of unconscious materials . . . enhanced awareness of linguistic nuances . . . concern with philosophical, cosmological and religious questions and, in general, apprehension of a world that has slipped the chains of normal categorical ordering, leading to an intensified interest in self and world and also to a range of responses moving from extremes of anxiety to extremes of pleasure."

Although John wasn't involved in Paul's extracurricular activities at this point, the two men would share their discoveries with each other. There was no sense of one wanting to trump the other by going it alone. It helped that whatever either of them wrote would eventually be jointly credited. So Paul would excite John about Stockhausen or Berio, and John would introduce Paul to LPs of *musique concrète*. The point was that the results of their investigations would ultimately benefit the Beatles.

When John was interviewed for *NME* by Chris Hutchins in early March, the Beatles' next LP was uppermost in his mind. "We've got plenty to do writing songs, taping things and so on," he said. "Paul and I ought to get down to writing some songs for the new LP next week. . . . George thought we'd written them and were all ready—that's why he came back from his honeymoon and we hadn't got a thing ready. We'll have to get started. There's been too much messing around."

Queried about what direction the Beatles might take he said,

Literally anything. Electronic music, jokes . . . one thing's for sure—the next LP is going to be very different. We wanted to have it so that there was no space between the tracks—just continuous. But they wouldn't wear it. Paul and I are very keen on this electronic music. You just make it [by] clinking a couple of glasses together or with bleeps from the radio, then you loop the tape to repeat the noises at intervals. Some people build up [a] whole symphony from it. It would have been better than the background music we had for the last film! All those silly bands. Never again!

John complained that he was "fed up of doing nothing," but at the same time confessed that he often lacked motivation. "I just sort of stand there and let things happen to me," he admitted. He was due to complete a follow-up to *A Spaniard in the Works*, published in June 1965, but so far had only written a single page. "I thought, why should I break my back getting books out like records?" It was this lackadaisical attitude that would eventually allow Paul to dominate the group with his ideas.

John also felt cut off living in Weybridge. "I'm dying to move into town," he said. "I'm waiting to see how Paul gets on when he goes into his town house. If he gets by all right then I'll sell the place at Weybridge, probably to some American who'll pay a fortune for it. . . . I suppose I could have a flat in town but I don't want to spend another £20,000 just to have somewhere to stay overnight when I've had too much bevy [alcoholic beverage] to drive home."

The same day that Hutchins's feature was published in *NME*, March 11, 1966, Ringo's interview with Maureen Cleave appeared in the *Evening Standard*. A week after that, on March 18, George's interview was published. Paul had not yet met up with Cleave and had to squeeze in an appointment between arriving back from Klosters and starting work with John on songs for the new LP. He rendezvoused with her on the morning of March 21, arriving at a central London restaurant clutching a copy of *In the Bronx, and Other Stories* by Jack Micheline, a New York poet and fiction writer associated with the Beat generation.

Cleave observed Paul to be tall, agile, neatly dressed, and well organized. His hair always seemed to be the right length—never too long or too short—and he was never at a loss for words. He liked teasing and was a good mimic. He had wicked charm, a shriveling wit, a critical intelligence, and enormous talent. With Paul she never got away with an ill-considered remark or a hazy recollection. He was self-conscious, nervy, restless, and always on the go. Cleave thought that ultimately he would be the Beatle who would surprise everyone with his talent and durability.

The preoccupations he discussed this spring Monday were very similar to those recently shared with Alan Freeman—his music lessons (from "a composer," he boasted); his discovery of Jarry, Stockhausen, and Berio; his love of drama (he twice quoted Shakespeare and spoke of his love for British television drama); and his hunger for self-education. "I'm trying to cram everything in, all the things I've missed. People are saying things and painting things and writing things and composing things that are great, and I must know what people are doing."

Paul spoke of his national pride. He valued Britain's theatrical heritage and the standard of its broadcasting. He also liked the British penchant for preservation. Societies were set up to preserve everything from buildings and ancient customs to traditional beer brewing methods and endangered species. As an example of this spirit he mentioned the often-eccentric poet John Betjeman, who was well known as a fighter for the protection of Victorian architecture, old railway stations from the steam age, and medieval churches. Paul implied that Britishness was a key component of the radical nature of the Beatles. Speaking about teenagers on the other side of the Atlantic that he first encountered in 1964, he said, "There they were in

America, all getting house trained for adulthood with their indisputable principle of life: short hair equals men, long hair equals women. Well, we got rid of that small convention for them."

He told Cleave that he was about to drive down to Weybridge to write with John, his first such joint session for some time. By way of illustration he pulled an unfinished lyric from his jacket pocket and showed it to her. It was about loneliness and old age, a spinster and a priest, and a wedding. Even without the violins that would later accompany them, she found the words "heartrending." She asked him if it was based on anyone he had known. "I don't know whether poets think they have to experience things to write about them," Paul answered. "But I can tell you our songs are nearly all imagination—90 percent imagination."

Almost three months had elapsed since Paul started the song in the basement at Wimpole Street, and the music and words were sufficiently complete for him to have played it informally to friends in Klosters, but according to John's friend Pete Shotton the lyric still needed a resolution. In his memoir *John Lennon: In My Life* Shotton recalled a weekend dinner party at Weybridge attended by all four Beatles and their partners after which all the men retired to John's music room to work on the song. Paul played it on his guitar while the others chipped in with suggestions for how the story could progress. The first two verses introducing Eleanor Rigby and then Father McKenzie (originally Father McCartney) had been more or less finished, but Paul hadn't found a satisfactory way of having their lives intersect.

Shotton had called out, "Why don't you have Eleanor Rigby dying and have Father McKenzie doing the burial service for her? That way you'd have the two lonely people coming together in the end—but too late." John opposed the suggestion, saying, "I don't think you understand what we're trying to get at, Pete." John said it with such vehemence that the session ground to a halt and everyone returned to join the women. However, when Paul wrote the final verse, he ignored John's outburst and incorporated Shotton's suggested denouement.

John and Paul's writing stint was interrupted at the end of its first week by a round of interviews for broadcasters and print journalists from India, Canada, and Brazil; a special recording for a flexi disc; and a photo session with Robert Whitaker, all of which took place at Oluf Nissen's photographic studio at 1 The Vale, in Chelsea, which Whitaker had rented for the occasion because his own nearby studio was too small. The interviews would soon disappear into the mists of time, but the photo shoot would become legendary and, like the "Jesus" interview with Maureen Cleave, would mire the Beatles in controversy and tarnish their innocent image.

The photographer Robert Whitaker, British-born but transplanted to Australia at the age of twenty, had met the Beatles in June 1964 when they were playing in his adopted home city, Melbourne. Brian Epstein liked Whitaker's work so much that he invited him to London to be the "artistic adviser" to NEMS, a position that meant being an unsalaried house photographer. Epstein not only gave Whitaker unprecedented access to the Beatles but also encouraged his creative experiments and allowed him to retain copyright of his work.

The Beatles gelled with him. He was their age, had similar experimental ambitions, and felt a kinship with the same surrealists, Beats, and bohemians that inspired them. He liked messing with conventional portraiture as much as they liked messing with conventional pop. In 1965 he'd toured with them in America, visited the set of *Help!*, and took photos that captured not only the glory of being the Beatles in the mid-sixties but the frenzy, pressure, and boredom.

On this Friday they arrived wearing conventional modish clothes—four-buttoned single-breasted jackets, ribbed turtlenecks, and either lace-up shoes or boots. The choice reflected their habit of picking the latest lines from the new men's fashion boutiques springing up on Carnaby Street, a two-minute walk from the NEMS office on Argyll Street. They would window-shop in the early evening after the shops closed and the crowds dispersed and then send Tony Bramwell, Brian Epstein's assistant, to buy their choices the next day.

The Beatles never knew what Whitaker might demand of them, but they trusted his imaginative leaps. On his last studio shoot with them he'd had them wrap themselves in polyethylene and destroy blocks of polystyrene with their feet and fists on a set built with silver foil and mirrors. With Whitaker props were symbols, and he would constantly draw inspiration from sources as varied as Greek dramatist Euripides and Spanish surrealist Salvador Dali.

For the Chelsea session he unveiled even more unusual props—a canary cage, a bag of six-inch nails, a hammer, large cuts of fresh beef bought that morning from a butcher in Chiswick, cardboard boxes (some with writing on), and the component parts of a collection of baby dolls. His aim was to demythologize the Beatles.

His main inspiration this time was Hans Bellmer, a German artist who'd made life-sized dolls during the 1930s and photographed them in different stages of dismemberment—twisted, distorted, sexualized, brutalized, and hung in trees. Bellmer claimed that he was illustrating the destruction of innocence and was trying to shock the rising Nazis (including his father), who placed such a strong emphasis on purity, self-control, and moral rectitude. Some commentators think that Bellmer had mixed motives and that he was attracted to sexual perversity.

Although throughout his life Whitaker consistently said that the genesis of the idea for the images he shot that day came from what he saw on the 1965 American tour, he would give varied explanations of what the meat and the dolls represented. Sometimes he said that the plastic limbs and the raw meat were a warning of what the fans would reduce the Beatles to if they ever broke through security and got hold of them with their bare hands. At other times he said that these props were reminders that John, Paul, George, and Ringo were not gods to be worshiped but creatures of flesh and blood.

For the main portrait the Beatles donned white butcher coats and draped themselves with cuts of meat and the arms, legs, torsos, and heads of the dolls. It looked like a scene of carnage, especially when blood from the meat began to drip on their clothing. It would have led most viewers to think of massacres rather than taking it as a commentary on fame and idolatry. The Beatles never asked Whitaker what his aim was. They just enjoyed the fact that they were doing something that seemed so un-Beatle-like. Asked about it later, Paul said he thought it was a protest about Vietnam. John was hoping that it would help relieve them of their image as the happy-go-lucky boys from Liverpool. Asked by a journalist to explain the inspiration behind the picture, John said, "It was inspired by our boredom and resentment at having to do *another* photo session and *another* Beatles thing. We were sick to death of it. The combination produced that cover."

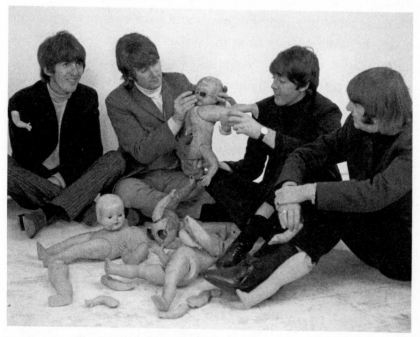

The Beatles with the dolls that would feature in the notorious "butcher" LP cover portrait.

Whitaker's full vision was never realized. Inspired by Russian church iconography, he had imagined a triptych. In the left panel would be a photo he took of the Beatles attached to a woman by an umbilical cord made from a string of sausages (birth). The right panel would be a photo of George apparently hammering nails into John's head (mortality). The butcher image would be in the central panel, but the background would be embossed with gold, and over the heads of John, Paul, George, and Ringo would float silver halos encrusted with jewels. He hadn't planned for any of the pictures to be used in their raw form on a record cover or in ads.

One of the interviews the Beatles gave while Whitaker was setting up was with Tom Lodge of pirate ship Radio Caroline. He was recording the interview for a free record to be given away with the first edition of *Disc and Music Echo,* a new amalgamation of two music weeklies in which Brian Epstein now had a financial stake, but also hoping to get some inserts for his breakfast show. The giveaway, being organized by Tony Barrow, would have interviews with contemporary stars ranging from the Walker Brothers and Cilla Black to the Beatles.

But despite their willingness to contribute, the Beatles treated the interview frivolously, and Lodge had problems eliciting any hard facts, let alone news. Spoken to alone, as could be seen from the Maureen Cleave interviews, the individual Beatles could be serious and reflective, but as a group they engaged in wordplay and nonsense, no one wanting to step out of line and become profound lest the others mock them. Lodge couldn't even get coherent plugs for Radio Caroline out of them or congratulatory messages for his fellow DJs. The whole episode degenerated into a none-too-successful absurdist play.

TL: Do you think, George, that Ugly Ray Teret is really ugly? [*"Ugly" Ray Teret was a Radio Caroline DJ.*]

GEORGE: Who? Ugly Red Terror?

TL: Ugly Ray Teret.

RINGO: Ray Teret?

PAUL: Who's he?

GEORGE: I don't know Ugly Ray Teret.

RINGO: No, Ray's okay.

TL: You know Ray, don't you?

RINGO: I know Ray. Good ol' Ray.

JOHN: Oh, Ray.

RINGO: Ray Terripp. Owes me two and six.

PAUL: Who's that?

TL: He's shaved his head off.

PAUL: Who is he?

TL: He's a disc jockey.

PAUL: Oh, yeah?

TL: Caroline North.

PAUL: Oh, of course!

RINGO: Of course!

PAUL: Of course, Eggley Ray—

JOHN: Ugly Ray Taylor!

PAUL: Eggley Wreck Tailor. Great!

GEORGE: Keep playin' em, Ugly!

Lodge would have liked them to talk about the music they were currently writing, but they avoided it. At one point John joked that Gershwin and Trotsky wrote the music for them, and Paul joined in with "And Lenin and Blavatsky are writing the lyrics." Asked if they were planning to make a new LP, George answered, "They [John and Paul] try and write a few songs and then we gather together and emerge with an LP. But we never sort of plan it saying 'This is what it's gonna be fellas!'"

On the same day, Paul's interview with Maureen Cleave was published in the *Evening Standard,* and, spurred on by its appearance and the fact that it was the last one with the Beatles to come out, Tony Barrow wrote to Art Unger, the influential editor of the American teen magazine *Datebook,* with a view to getting the series out in America. Brian Epstein loved the profiles, reading each one as it was published and writing to Cleave to tell her that he was "very satisfied with the outcome," adding that he thought the series "must rank among the best that's been done."

The next week Epstein flew to Memphis at the request of the Beatles to investigate the possibility of the group recording in the city. They were all huge fans of the "Stax sound"—records made at the Stax studio by artists associated with the Stax label or its subsidiary Volt—and it had influenced tracks such as "The Word" and "Drive My Car" on *Rubber Soul.* Ten of the forty tracks on George's home jukebox (see Appendix B) were from Stax.

In interviews the Beatles repeatedly praised Stax stars such as Wilson Pickett, Eddie Floyd, Otis Redding, and Booker T. and the M.G.'s. They loved the arrangements, the punchy raw sound, and the ambience derived from the fact that the studio had unusual acoustics because of its steeply sloping cinema floor. Paul had said to Alan Freeman, "The equipment in most British recording studios is much better than it is in the States. But there's some extra bit they get to the sound over there that we haven't quite got. You put a record of ours [on after] an American record and you'll find the American record is always a fraction louder and it has a lucid something I can't explain."

The Stones had recorded in America during 1965, both at Chess Studios in Chicago and RCA Studios in Hollywood, and the big result from this was "(I Can't Get No) Satisfaction," the group's first huge international hit. From then on Mick Jagger kept urging Paul to get the Beatles to cross the Atlantic to make a record, arguing that the session musicians were cooler and the ambience funkier.

The Beatles had specifically spoken about the possibility of leaving EMI Studios for Stax. To the *Beatles Book Monthly* George had said, "Some terrific records have been made. They get these great band sounds as well. Wilson Pickett, Otis Redding and lots of them record in Memphis. Even if we didn't use some local musicians on the actual sessions, there'd be this great atmosphere. They concentrate on rhythm & blues and rock in Memphis."

When interviewed in London by American journalist Michael Lydon for a *Newsweek* profile of the Beatles, Paul mentioned being a fan of Otis Redding, and John singled out Stax guitarist and writer Steve Cropper as an influence, adding that they "would like to have Cropper produce some recording sessions."

Cropper played with the studio house band at Stax, was a member of Booker T. and the M.G.'s, had produced Otis Redding, and was the cowriter of such classic songs as "In the Midnight Hour" (Wilson Pickett) and "Knock on Wood" (Eddie Floyd) as well as the instrumental tracks "Green Onions" and "Time Is Tight" (Booker T. and the M.G.'s). He was twenty-four years old, born in Missouri, and, in 1966, the epitome of all that was cool about the new American music.

To this day Cropper isn't sure exactly what the Beatles had in mind other than benefitting from the spirit of the famed studio and possibly getting technical help from him or studio owner Jim Stewart. "In those days there was not much mention of George Martin, at least in Memphis," Cropper told me. "We also didn't listen to much Beatle or pop music. Only what was played on radio.

"I just assumed from what I was told by Epstein that they wanted me to produce them. We never got far enough to discuss engineers or other musicians' involvement. Brian Epstein was around for a couple of days. He only came to the studio to discuss things so I didn't hang with him or anything. We talked a few times by phone when he returned to England." A start date (April 9) was put in the studio diary.

Epstein made a great fuss about privacy and security, something that Cropper found unusual at the time, because Stax had good connections with the Memphis Police Department and had never had any trouble protecting musicians. He also wasn't happy with the local hotels that he visited, but the manager of the Hilton offered the use of his own home on Central Avenue, and Elvis said the Beatles could stay at Graceland.

Stewart instructed staff not to talk about the upcoming visit, but word got out. On March 31, the local newspaper the *Memphis Press-Scimitar* ran a story announcing that the Beatles would be arriving in April for a two-week session at Stax. They cited Stewart as producer, Cropper as arranger, and engineer Tom Dowd of Atlantic Records as supervisor. Epstein hit the roof. All his worst fears about Memphis seemed to be confirmed. "He contacted me and asked if I would be willing to come to New York and record them at Atlantic's studio," Cropper says. "He felt the Beatles would be safer there. I told him I would be willing if that was what the band wanted. After a few weeks of hearing nothing he called me back and explained that the band had been working really hard and had most of the new album recorded and it might be better to wait until the next album to work with them. I said okay and life continued forward. I later spent time with George in LA and did sessions for Ringo and John but the subject was never brought up."

The reason the plan was so suddenly abandoned has never been adequately explained. To Cropper, Epstein stressed the issue of privacy, but whenever the Beatles were asked about it directly they mentioned money, implying that Stax had wanted to charge them too much. Paul commented:

> We were going to record in America, but they wanted a fantastic amount of money to use the facilities there. . . . When we finished *Revolver,* we realised that we had found a new

British sound almost by accident. I think there were only two tracks on the LP that would have sounded better if we'd cut them in America—"Taxman" and "Got to Get You Into My Life"—because they need that raw quality that you just can't get in this country for some reason. But "Eleanor Rigby" would have been worse, because the string players in America aren't so good.

The same theme appeared in a letter written by George in May 1966 to Atlanta DJ Paul Drew, in which he commented that the recording had "nearly" happened. According to him, the Beatles had all been in favor of the idea, but it fell through because too many people got "insane" about money as soon as the name of the Beatles was mentioned. At an August press conference in Memphis Paul would only say that they had intended to come, had wanted Cropper "to A&R the session," but "little things kept getting in the way."

In 1987, when I interviewed George Martin on the occasion of the twentieth anniversary of the release of *Sgt. Pepper's Lonely Hearts Club Band,* he offered another reason why the Beatles had never recorded in America. "There were problems with that," he told me. "Firstly, I didn't want to record in the States. Secondly, from EMI's point of view it wouldn't have made sense because every record would have had to bear the 1.5 percent AFM [American Federation of Musicians] levy. It wasn't feasible. Anyway, I had to do what EMI told me."

As the Stax story was breaking in the Memphis press, the British public was voting in a national election called because the ruling Labour Party needed a more significant majority in the House of Commons to govern effectively (it only had an overall majority of four seats).

The success of the Labour prime minister Harold Wilson coincided with that of the Beatles. He came to power in February 1963, four months after the release of "Love Me Do" and a month before

"Please Please Me." He was forty-five years old, from Huddersfield, Yorkshire, and smoked a pipe. He replaced Alec Douglas-Home, who was fifty-nine years old, born in Mayfair, and went on grouse shoots. Wilson was portrayed in the media as young, dynamic, and thrusting, an unpretentious working-class man who would shake up the establishment. In September 1963 he made a name for himself at the annual Labour Party Conference when he spoke passionately about the need for Britain to be at the center of innovations taking place in what he dramatically referred to as "the white heat of technology."

Commentators saw his ascendency as part of the same social upheaval that had created mods, rockers, Carnaby Street, David Bailey, Terry Stamp, Twiggy, and the Beatles. Appropriately, his parliamentary seat since 1950 had been Huyton, a district of Liverpool only four miles from John's Woolton home and six miles from Paul's council house in Allerton. Controversially, in May 1965, Wilson recommended the Beatles for MBEs (Most Excellent Order of the British Empire), which they received five months later at Buckingham Palace. They were the first pop stars ever to be given such an honor. Critics argued that Wilson had done it to ingratiate himself with the young and gain some reflected glory. Some who'd previously been awarded MBEs for military gallantry or other forms of service to the country returned their medals, saying that the honor had now been degraded.

On paper the Beatles and Wilson were a good fit. They were all from the north of England, came from Labour-supporting backgrounds, and disapproved of snobbery, privilege, and the class system. "In Harold Wilson, Downing Street sports a Yorkshire accent, a working-class attitude and a tolerance towards the young," trilled *Time* magazine in a paragraph that also mentioned Lennon and McCartney, Mary Quant, hairdresser Vidal Sassoon, and the Rolling Stones and used the adjectives "kinky" and "uninhibited." However, since they'd become wealthy the Beatles resented the huge sums they had to pay in taxes. The Labour government, under Wilson, had introduced a "supertax" of 96.25 percent for high earners. This meant that for every one million pounds the Beatles earned, they were only allowed to keep less than fifty thousand.

George in particular was angered by this imposition. He was not only the most financially concerned Beatle but also the most anti-war. It angered him that a percentage of his earnings would finance fighter planes and bombers. Paul thought that the leaders of the three main parties were equally unsavory: "The terrible thing," he said, "is seeing them going round adapting themselves, being friends with the people."

John was most vociferously against the political status quo, and the more secure he became in his position in society, the more emboldened he became in sharing his views. He was energized by the writings of Aldous Huxley, the British author (later a California resident) who'd developed an interest in hallucinogenic drugs and Eastern religion. After reading *The Doors of Perception* and *Brave New World,* John called him "the new guv'nor." Ray Coleman, twenty-eight, who had worked for *Melody Maker* between 1960 and 1965 and was now editor in chief of *Disc and Music Echo,* was a huge Lennon fan, an ardent socialist, and someone the group trusted. He encouraged John to be frank and controversial in their interviews.

At the end of March, on the eve of the election, Coleman got John talking at length about his evolving political views. "What I would really like to see is people generally getting more say in what goes on," he said.

> From what you hear, none of the politicians [of the three main British political parties] has any intention of giving ordinary people complete freedom.
>
> Just keep them down—that's what they really want. I'm not suggesting I know what the answer is—I just know there's something wrong with the present way of governing the country and the more people like us realise it at least we

are on the way to changing it. . . . What we need to change things is a bloody revolution.

The opinions of the Beatles were no different from those you might hear at any Liverpool pub, dock, or factory gate. What was unusual in 1966 was hearing these opinions, expressed in unvarnished Liverpool accents, in major media outlets. Most entertainers became more compliant as their audience grew. It was normal for stars to avoid expressing controversial opinions and to modify their regional accents into something "classless." When, in 1963, Edward Heath, then the Lord Privy Seal, complained that he couldn't understand what the Beatles said because they didn't seem to speak the Queen's English, John responded by saying that many people who had voted for Heath also didn't speak the Queen's English.

The Beatles resisted such pressure to conform, and in doing so allowed some of the grievances of working-class Britons to get a more public airing than they usually did. A lot of the group's perceived "rebellion" was simply that. They were representatives of a working-class culture that had acquired a better education than any of their forebears and was therefore better informed and more eloquent, and they also had the attention of a vast audience.

By the time the interview with John was published, Wilson was still in power. He decisively beat his Conservative Party opponent, Edward Heath, winning 364 seats to Heath's 253, increasing Labour's majority over the Conservatives and Liberals to 99.

APRIL

When something came out like *Revolver* there
was still an element of surprise. We didn't know
where it came from, and how it arrived.
-JOHN, 1969

On April 6, three days before what had been their scheduled date in
Memphis to record at Stax, the Beatles reassembled at EMI Studios
on Abbey Road with George Martin, balance engineer Geoff Emerick, and technical engineer Phil McDonald. Up to sixty other staff
members would also have been on the premises, ranging from studio
attendants (in brown coats) who moved chairs and equipment to a
chief engineer (in a white laboratory coat) who established the company's technical standards and made sure they were upheld.

There couldn't have been a greater difference than that between
Stax and EMI. Stax was in a converted movie theatre in downtown
Memphis surrounded by beer joints, barbershops, and beauticians.
Kids sang doo-wop on the sidewalks, neon lights shone, and the former concessions area of the building had been turned into a record
store. EMI was in an upscale tree-lined residential area of North London, housed in an early nineteenth-century Georgian mansion that
had once boasted nine bedrooms and bathrooms. The first record

made at Stax, in 1960, was "'Cause I Love You" by Rufus Thomas and his daughter Carla. The first record made at EMI, in 1931, was *Pomp and Circumstance* March No. 1 by the London Symphony Orchestra, conducted by the music's composer, Sir Edward Elgar.

Stax had one studio, and it was set up for small bands and singing groups. EMI had three studios, the largest of which was big enough to record a 110-person orchestra along with a 100-strong choir.

It can seem remarkable that the Beatles' innovations of 1966 took place in such august surroundings, yet they benefitted from the formality and rigor of the old institution. Technically it provided them with the best available equipment along with a team of on-site experts who knew everything there was to know about sound recording. Culturally, the uniforms, regulations, and decorum were a constant and useful reminder of the norms from which they wished to deviate, and accentuated their sense of rebelliousness and desire to do things differently. A less structured environment may have dulled their cutting edge by making them forget what they were up against. For similar reasons, the notoriously straightlaced BBC proved to be the perfect incubator for the anarchic humor of the Goons and, later, Monty Python.

The Beatles appear to have had around a third of the songs for a new LP in rough form when they returned to the studio after their winter break. Paul and John had finished "Eleanor Rigby," Paul had written "For No One" and "Got to Get You Into My Life," and George had written "Love You To." Yet what they would record this Wednesday night was something John had only sketched out in the past few days. It would be one of the most extraordinary songs of their career and, indeed, one of the most extraordinary songs in popular music so far. Just five months after their last session, when they'd recorded John's "Girl" and Paul's "You Won't See Me," they were about to record a track evoking the experience of an LSD trip, drawing indirectly on a text of Tibetan Buddhism, incorporating random tape recordings played backward, and distorting the vocal to sound like the chanting of an Eastern monk.

This was a leap and a bound from recent songs like "I Feel Fine" and "Day Tripper" and the material that made girls scream, faint, and throw jelly beans. In fact, one of the most notable differences about it was that it wasn't created either as a potential single or to be reproduced on stage in concert. What it had in common with the works of the electronic composers they'd recently been listening to was that it was a statement in sound at a particular moment with little likelihood of ever being performed live. This was a career-changing declaration of intent for a group that had established itself by playing crowd-pleasing songs with lyrics that were easy for adolescents to relate to.

The new song was initially referred to as "Mark 1" and then became "The Void," before getting the title under which it was released, "Tomorrow Never Knows." Like "It's been a hard day's night," this phrase was coined by Ringo. Interviewed on BBC TV on their return to London Airport after the group's first American dates in February 1964, Ringo was asked about an incident that had taken place at a British embassy reception in Washington when someone snipped a lock of his hair as a souvenir. "What happened, exactly?" asked the interviewer, David Coleman. "I don't know," answered Ringo. "I was just doing an interview. Like I am now! I was talking away and—there it goes! I looked round and there were about four hundred people, smiling. You can't blame anyone. I mean—what can you say?" John chimed in with "Well, what can you say?" to which Ringo responded by saying, "Tomorrow never knows." John, who was standing behind him, doubled over with laughter. It was a non sequitur he would remember, and he used it as the song's title to counteract what he would refer to as "the heavy, philosophical lyrics."

The track set the tone for an artistically bold LP that was informed by their drug-altered perceptions and only incidentally concerned with the familiar pop song subject matter of love and loss. It was to be a record that pushed the envelope of pop further than ever before.

During the previous week John and Paul had visited the Indica bookshop to pick up a fresh stock of books. John was still curious about religion and asked Barry Miles if there were any books by "Nits Ga." It took a second or two before Miles realized that he was refer-ring to the anti-Christian German philosopher and cultural com-mentator Friedrich Nietzsche, author of *The Twilight of the Gods* and *Thus Spake Zarathustra*. Miles found him a copy of Viking Press's *The Portable Nietzsche*.

Browsing the shelves, John then came across *The Psychedelic Experi-ence* (1964), written by Timothy Leary and two fellow academic psychol-ogists, Richard Alpert (later to adopt the name Ram Dass) and Ralph Metzner. He sat on a sofa in the middle of the shop floor and thumbed through its pages. Leary had encountered psychedelic drugs in 1960 when he was a lecturer in clinical psychology at Harvard. As a result of his experiences he became an advocate for what he believed was their potential for personal transformation. In 1963 he had his tenure at Har-vard terminated, purportedly for not delivering his required classes, but he believed it was because the university disapproved of his continued experimentation with the then-legal drug that he was convinced could change the treatment of people with psychological problems.

It was Leary more than any other individual who made com-parisons between the LSD experience and the feelings of transcen-dence reported by devotees of Hinduism and Buddhism through techniques such as fasting, sensory deprivation, and meditation. He often did this by appropriating religious language to describe and then reflect on LSD trips. In *The Psychedelic Experience* he specifically took texts from *The Tibetan Book of the Dead* (or, at least, from a 1927 English-language translation of it compiled and edited by the Ameri-can anthropologist Walter Evans-Wentz from an oral translation by a school teacher he met in Darjeeling called Lama Kazi Dawa Samdup) and reworked them for a contemporary acid-dropping readership at the suggestion of Aldous Huxley. Leary had a keen eye for public-ity, an appetite for controversy, and a knack of coining memorable phrases and slogans.

A UK edition of *The Psychedelic Experience*, Timothy Leary's paraphrase of texts from *The Tibetan Book of the Dead*.

The Tibetan Book of the Dead dated back to at least the fourteenth century and was originally known by its full title, *The Great Liberation upon Hearing in the Intermediate State*. Evans-Wetz came up with the shorter, snappier title by alluding to the Egyptian *Book of the Dead*. "What is translated *Book of the Dead* really means *Book of the Dying* or *Book of the Changing*," Leary told me in the 1990s. "It is your ego that is dying. The British translator took it literally, like a first aid kit or a guide for medical technicians."

The purpose of the original Buddhist text was to prepare devotees for the stages of dying, passing beyond death to what was thought to be the truly real, and then onward to eventual rebirth. The words were intended for reading out to the terminally ill in order to guide and encourage them. In accordance with Buddhist teaching, those close to death were urged to let go of life and what they thought of as "reality" lest their rebirth be hindered. In the hands of Leary and his colleagues the text became a map for those who were tripping, urging them to lose their egos and dispense with the illusory world that was really no more than a mind game. It was, in the words of Ralph Metzner, "a paradigm for a spiritually-oriented psychedelic experience."

One of the most significant experiences of the LSD trip was the sense of ego loss resulting in the feeling of being part of the dance of atoms that makes up the universe. Leary saw that the temporary elimination of the user's sense of self had obvious parallels with the experience of death itself. This was why the words of *The Tibetan Book of the Dead* had such resonance with trippers as they encountered the "void" that opened up when the psyche's traditional supports were removed. He also knew that good trips benefitted from taking place in appropriate settings using art, music, and text to provide guiderails for the tripper so that they didn't experience complete psychic disintegration. The biggest fear of these early experimenters with LSD was the "bum trip" that turned the user into an "acid casualty"—someone who could no longer function in the normal world because of an inability to distinguish between real and unreal.

In a recent essay, "A New Look at the Psychedelic Tibetan Book of the Dead" (2015), Metzner wrote: "With appropriate preparation and orientation, so we proposed, psychedelic travelers could be guided, or guide themselves, to release their ego-attachments and illusory self-images, the way a Tibetan Buddhist lama would guide a person who was actually dying to relinquish their attachment while noting the physical signs of bodily death."

Cyndy Bury *(left)*, the girlfriend, then wife, of cosmetic dentist John Riley *(right)*, who slipped LSD into the coffees of John, Cynthia, George, and Pattie in 1965.

John became a regular user of the drug after having it slipped into his coffee by George and Pattie's private dentist, John Riley, at a dinner party in April 1965 held in the apartment of Riley's fiancée, Cyndy Bury. The experience initially terrified him, as he had received no preparation or guidance. He was in an elevator on his way up to the Ad Lib nightclub near Leicester Square and became convinced the building was on fire at a moment when, according to Leary, he should have been surrounded by nurturing sounds and familiar objects.

"It was done without our knowledge so we didn't know how to handle it," Cynthia Lennon explained to me in 2005. "We didn't know the effect it was going to have on us. It was like sitting in this room and it suddenly became like the Albert Hall. Pattie and George were opposite, John was beside me, and they started disappearing in the distance. I wondered what on earth was happening. We just had to get out."

Pattie Boyd remembers, "I didn't know what was happening to me. It was more frightening than anything I'd ever experienced. I thought I would be like this for the rest of my life. John Riley said that we shouldn't leave the house because he'd given us LSD but we thought 'So? What's that?' It was a totally irresponsible thing to have done."

The next song John wrote was "Help!" where the "mind" that he referred to as changing was most likely a reference to what William James in his classic study *The Varieties of Religious Experience* (1902) referred to as "normal waking consciousness," and the "door" that he'd "opened" was one of the doors of perception as described by Aldous Huxley in his novel of that title. So changing his mind was not simply altering his opinion (although it involved that) but enlarging his consciousness and having a fresh set of heightened perceptions. At the same time, the song implied, his life had been turned upside down. His independence (his view of himself as a distinct and separate entity) had "vanished in the haze." That sounds like an accurate description of an ego being dissolved.

John next tripped at a rented house in Benedict Canyon, Los Angeles, in August 1965 during the Beatles' US tour, in the company of George, Ringo, and the Byrds' David Crosby and Roger McGuinn. The actor Peter Fonda and *Daily Mirror* journalist Don Short were also present (although Short wasn't indulging and was regarded suspiciously by John, who feared he might report on their activities). By early 1966 John was regularly tripping, usually at home. It fitted his sedentary lifestyle to have a drug that filled his mind with powerful impressions without him having to even leave his house.

Because the Beatles mentioned the source of the lyric as being *The Tibetan Book of the Dead*, it is frequently assumed that John simply took a chunk of *The Tibetan Book of the Dead* and set it to music. This was not so. For a start, *The Psychedelic Experience* was, as its subtitle says, "a manual *based on* the Tibetan Book of the Dead" (emphasis added) rather than a strict translation. It was divided into four sections: an introduction, a description of an acid trip incorporating the stages described in the Buddhist text, practical suggestions for conducting a trip, and instructive passages from a text within the book known as the Bardo Thodol. Only a small part of Leary's book comes directly from *The Tibetan Book of the Dead*, and even this is a loose paraphrase of the Evans-Wentz translation.

The introduction, which sounds like the writing of the media-savvy Leary, provided the first line of the song. "Trust your divinity, trust your brain, trust your companions," says *The Psychedelic Experience*. "Whenever in doubt, turn off your mind, relax, float downstream." This gave John his starting point. It not only suggested the point of view—that of the instructor or guide—but the tone and the rhythm of the lyric. (This was the first Beatles song not to employ the normal verse-chorus structure and a strict end-line rhyme scheme, and to have a title composed of words not appearing in the lyric. In these respects it was closer to the jazz-poetry experiments that had started in America in the 1950s than it was to a conventional pop song.)

The next lines from "Tomorrow Never Knows" were not actual reproductions of Leary's text but were inspired by a paragraph he wrote: "The light is the life energy. Do not fear it. Surrender to it. Join it. It is part of you. You are part of it. Remember also: beyond the restless flowing electricity of life is the ultimate reality—The Void." The Void is described in the book as "unobstructed, shining."

Other lines written by John containing the phrases "the meaning of within," "love is all," and "the color of your dream" don't appear in *The Psychedelic Experience,* although there is plenty in the book about meaning, love, and colors. The confusing phrase of John's about "ignorance and haste" sounds like the King James translation of Psalms 19:2: "Also, that the soul be without knowledge, it is not good; and he that hasteth with his feet sinneth."

John's penultimate line, referring to "the game existence," comes from Leary's final paragraph, headed "Instructions for Choosing the Post-Session Personality": "Whatever you choose, choose impartially, without attraction or repulsion. Enter into game-existence with good grace. Voluntarily and freely. Remain calm. Remember the teachings." The acid tripper returns to the world, now having been revealed as illusory, and regards its participants as acting out a series of games. The advantage is that the tripper—the acidhead—knows that it's a game (or a "play," as Paul would later put it in "Penny Lane") and takes on the role knowingly.

John played his new song to Paul and George Martin at a planning meeting for the new LP at Brian Epstein's home in Belgravia. What surprised them both was that the song appeared to use only one chord and that the lyrics were profoundly philosophical, unlike anything the Beatles had tackled before. Paul had spoken for some time about writing songs with as few chords as possible, but his model had been Little Richard, not the harmonic drone of a tambura. Paul remembers that Martin was not at all fazed by the unconventional composition. He just nodded his head and said, "Very interesting, John. Very interesting."

At the start John knew more about how he wanted his voice treated than how he wanted the music recorded. As George Martin told me in 1987: "John always found it very difficult to express what he wanted. He was the least articulate of the three writers. I would have to dig deep into his brain to find out what I had to do with his songs whereas Paul was much more demonstrative. Paul would sit down and say 'This is the kind of thing I'm thinking of.' John would describe it in not very accurate clinical terms."

In this instance he said he envisaged a sound like that of someone participating in a Tibetan Buddhist ritual. In the studio he regularly asked for his voice to be doctored, as he was self-conscious about its limitations and aspired to sound like someone other than himself. According to George Martin, for "Tomorrow Never Knows" John wanted to sound "like a Dalai Lama singing from the top of a mountain." It was the words rather than John Lennon he wanted to be heard. At one point he even suggested being swung from a rope suspended above the microphone so that the clarity and volume of his voice would increase and decrease as his body came in and out of range.

Allen Ginsberg, Timothy Leary, and Ralph Metzner at *The Illumination of the Buddha: A Psychedelic Celebration*, Village Theater, New York, December 1966.

The idea was indicative of how far beyond normal recording practices the Beatles were beginning to conceptualize. Although they weren't trying to sound like Stockhausen and Berio, their exposure to these composers had increased their expectations of what could be achieved in the studio. They were no longer limiting themselves to what had been done by early heroes like Chuck Berry, Elvis Presley, or Smokey Robinson and the Miracles. "The important thing in all recording," said George, "is that you take something from other people, but give back more in return to the listeners."

John would ultimately not be suspended from the ceiling of EMI Studios. The effect he was striving for was achieved less dramatically and dangerously, by passing his voice through a Leslie speaker. Developed in the 1930s, the Leslie speaker was traditionally used in conjunction with a Hammond organ. It was a cabinet housing an amplifier and two small mounted loudspeakers that could be rotated so that the sound oscillated rapidly, gaining and losing intensity as the front of the speaker pointed directly at or away from the listener (or microphone). Until this session no one had thought of using it to treat the human voice.

During a tea break Martin assigned engineer Geoff Emerick the task of finding alternatives for vocal distortion. None of the options available seemed to create the difference that John was asking for. Emerick asked technical engineer Ken Townsend to rewire a Leslie speaker so that it transmitted vocals rather than a Hammond organ, and then placed two microphones in front to pick up the sound. John was called in to sing with the Leslie speakers projecting and spinning his voice. This was added to a basic backing track of bass, drums, and a slowed-down tape loop of a Leslie-treated guitar, a fuzz guitar, and tom toms. The result, when mixed, sounded close to the song he'd imagined—especially the voice.

On April 7, Martin did more work on the track, rerecording John's vocal (in the finished version the voice is heard double-tracked for half the song and "Leslied" for the rest) but adding a new backing track. This was a symphony of tape loops Paul had made on his home tape recorder and a new rhythm track by Paul and Ringo. The musical bedding was now as discordant and puzzling as the voice and combined to suggest an altered mental state.

The loops had been inspired both by Stockhausen and the experimental "cut-up" work of William Burroughs and his Tangiers-based writer-artist colleague, Brion Gysin. Starting in the 1950s Burroughs and Gysin had been randomly chopping up texts from books and newspapers and reassembling the pieces to create new and unexpected meanings. The same procedure was then used with tape recordings of radio broadcasts and the two reading their own work.

Burroughs said of the technique, "When you cut into the present, the future leaks out."

Paul and George Martin had reviewed the loops and selected the five most likely to work on "Tomorrow Never Knows." These were threaded into five available tape machines in different rooms at EMI, where technical staff maintained the tension in the loops manually with pencils. In the mixing room, to which the output from all the machines was fed, faders were used to bring the sounds of the different loops in and out of the mix.

Whether it was intentional or not, the selection from the tape loops, along with the bass and the heavy thudding pattern of Ringo's drums, created a pop music equivalent to the sounds trippers experience, according to Leary in his book. These were the sounds of a human body: the clicking, thudding, clashing, ringing, tapping, moaning, and whistling of bones, teeth, heart, arteries, throat, stomach, and limbs.

Leary reckoned that the primal music Tibetan lamas used in their rituals approximated such amplified body noises: "Although the combined sounds of these instruments are far from being melodious," he wrote,

> the lamas maintain that they psychically produce in the devotee an attitude of deep veneration and faith, because they are the counterparts of the natural sounds which one's own body is heard producing when the fingers are put in the ears to shut out external sounds.
>
> Stopping the ears thus, there are heard a thudding sound, like that of a big drum being beaten; a clashing sound, as of cymbals; a soughing sound, as of a wind moving through a forest—as when a conch-shell is blown a ringing as of bells; a sharp tapping sound, as when a timbrel is used; a moaning sound, like that of a clarinet; a bass moaning sound, as if made with a big trumpet; and a shriller sound, as of a thigh-bone trumpet.

No one at the time noted the sources of the sounds that ended up in the final mix of "Tomorrow Never Knows," but recently digital technology has enabled researchers to isolate the sounds and reverse or change their speed. According to Kevin Ryan and Brian Kehew in their book *Recording the Beatles,* the five sources were a B-flat major chord struck by an orchestra (dubbed from an unknown record) and (all played at double speed) a reversed sitar phrase, a mandolin or acoustic guitar with tape echo, a reversed scalar sitar line, and a laughing male voice. Two weeks after this initial mix George added tambura and a reversed guitar, while John again rerecorded his voice (still sticking to the split between double-tracking and the Leslie treatment).

Speaking about the tracks six months later George said, "This is easily the most amazing new thing we've ever come up with. Some people might say it sounds like a terrible mess of a sound. It's because of the electronics, which might throw you at first. . . . But the song ought to be looked on as interesting—*if* people listen to it with open ears. It's like the Indian stuff. You mustn't listen to eastern music with a Western ear. You must listen to it with wide-open feelings and just take it in. And this goes for 'Tomorrow Never Knows.' It's a sound. It's not to be pigeon-holed as Beatles, Beach Boys, or anything else."

The next recording couldn't have been more different. The change was like going from Stockhausen to the Supremes and illustrated the extent of their musical palette. However, the subject was similar. The song was "Got to Get You Into My Life," Paul's paean to LSD written after his experience with Tara Browne and Viv Prince. Whereas John had composed a piece intended to evoke the experience itself, Paul had chosen a jaunty, upbeat approach influenced by the pop singles being produced by Motown, Stax, and Atlantic, and had written a love song inviting the drug into his life just as poets such as Shelley and Pablo Neruda had written love poems to wine. The title may have been derived from Solomon Burke's No. 1 R & B hit from 1965, "Got to Get You Off My Mind," which had been pro-duced by Jerry Wexler and released on Atlantic.

Starting at 8:15 p.m., they worked for five and a quarter hours on the song, completing five takes before deciding the last take was the best. It was a slower version than the one released, with a single organ chord played by George Martin used as a place-holder during parts that would eventually be filled with brass. It ended with Paul singing a 1920s-style outro ("Got to get you into my life / Oh ho ho") and John messing around with a "dee dee dee." On April 8 they attacked the song again, slowing it down, and finally arriving at a version (take 8) that they were happy with.

Being a love song to LSD, it was naturally a hymn to expanded consciousness. Just as "Tomorrow Never Knows" had praised the shin-ing void, so "Got to Get You Into My Life" celebrated "another kind of mind." It was fitting that the day recording began on the song *Time* magazine published its arresting "Is God Dead?" cover story, which suggested that "the new approaches to the problem of God may lead to a realistic, and somewhat more abstract, conception of God."

After a weekend break the Beatles returned to start work on George's first song for the LP, "Love You To"—provisionally known as "Granny Smith," because George (typically) couldn't come up with a title. Like "Tomorrow Never Knows," this was another song unlikely ever to be played in one of their concerts, this time because it used Indian instruments along with the more familiar sounds of guitars and a tambourine.

Although George had added sitar to John's "Norwegian Wood" in October 1965 he was an inexperienced player back then, and his contribution was basic and tentative. He'd since been practicing daily, and "Love You To" was the first song he'd specifically composed on the sitar, and probably the first song in Western pop to be written in emulation of the North Indian music rather than as a parody.

The words, scant as they were, bemoaned the fleeting passage of time and the inevitability of death, with the conclusion that we (or

APRIL 8, 1966

TIME
THE WEEKLY NEWSMAGAZINE

Is God Dead?

This was the first time in *Time* magazine's history that the front cover was type-only.

at least he) should grasp love while it's available and enjoy it fully. When he sang of each day going by "so fast," the observation had particular poignancy for him as a Beatle caught up in such a whirlwind of activity that there was so little time available even to digest all the experiences he was having. He'd already written the song by February when Maureen Cleave interviewed him. She had reported, "He wishes he could write fine songs as Lennon and McCartney do, but he has difficulty with the words. 'Pattie keeps asking me to write more beautiful words,' he said. He played his newest composition. His own voice came over on the tape singing: 'Love me while you can;

before I'm a dead old man.' George was aware that these words were not beautiful."

George Martin contacted Ayana Angadi of the Asian Music Circle to find a tabla player to perform on the track late that afternoon. Angadi recommended Anil Bhagwat, who he'd heard playing for dancer Sunita Golwala. Bhagwat, then a twenty-five-year-old electrical engineering student paying his way through university with the money earned from sessions, was at that moment rehearsing with a sitar player but jumped at the opportunity to earn thirty-five pounds. It was only when a chauffeur-driven Rolls-Royce came to collect him that he realized he would be working with someone important.

When he arrived at EMI Studios, Paul and Ringo were playing chess and John was nowhere to be seen, but George welcomed him, offered him a drink, and spoke to him about the track he wanted him to work on. At this stage George and Paul had made a basic version of the song with George's voice and guitar along with backing vocals. George told Bhagwat that he wanted the sort of sound that Ravi Shankar and his tabla player Alla Rakha had achieved on a specific album track. "Yes, I know that piece. That's sixteen beats," said Bhagwat. "Then," responded George, "that's what I'd like you to play, please."

They sat on the studio floor facing each other. Geoff Emerick placed high-performance ribbon mics close to George's sitar and Bhagwat's tabla to give what he would later describe as an "in your face" sound. They both listened to the basic track on their headphones and then played along to it. It was strange music for Bhagwat to be playing, because there was no space in which to improvise and there were stops and starts that he identified as typical of "Beatles music" but which had no equivalent in the musical traditions of India. "If you go on the Internet there are a lot of questions asked about 'Love You To,'" Bhagwat told me. "They say, 'It's not George playing the sitar.' I can tell you here and now—100 percent it was George on sitar throughout. There were no other musicians involved. It was just me and him."

Tabla player Anil Bhagwat accompanied George on the track "Love You To."

Ayana and Patricia Angadi came to watch, and Patricia made a sketch (since lost) of the two musicians playing. The song was rehearsed a dozen times before they were ready to do a take. When the session was completed, a car collected Bhagwat and dropped him off at his flat in Earls Court. He would be mentioned on the back cover of *Revolver*, one of only two occasions when the Beatles credited a session musician on an LP.

There hadn't been a new Beatles single since "We Can Work It Out" / "Day Tripper" in December 1965, and Capitol Records, who would typically put out a new American single every two to three months, had released "Nowhere Man" from *Rubber Soul* in February to fill the gap. EMI was pressuring Brian Epstein and George Martin to supply a new single as soon as possible to maintain the momentum they'd had in the United States for over two years. The problem was that the tracks already in progress, like "Tomorrow Never Knows," "Love You To," and "Got to Get You Into My Life" (in its present form), were not obvious singles. They were challenging and innovative but not the sort of songs to do battle with the likes of the Walker Brothers, the Hollies, the Kinks, the Spencer Davis Group, and Dave Dee, Dozy, Beaky, Mick, and Tich in the UK or the Lovin' Spoonful, the Mamas and the Papas, and Simon and Garfunkel in America.

John and Paul always responded well to challenges and deadlines. Possibly on April 12, when they were not needed at the studio, they met at John's house to write a song that could be a single. During the hour-long drive from St John's Wood to Weybridge, Paul toyed with a song idea about a desperate would-be novelist begging to be published. Paul loved the beat of the words "paperback writer" (the sound of language often inspired him more than ideas or insights), and his Aunt Millie had challenged him about his subject matter. "My Aunt Mill said, 'Why do you write songs about love all the time? Can you ever write about a horse or the summit conference or something interesting?' So I thought, 'All right, Aunt Mill. I'll show you.'"

The lyric, as he imagined it, took the form of a letter. He and John had seen enough begging letters from aspiring musicians to know the general gist, and Paul had written his own share to promoters when the Beatles were starting out, usually exaggerating the number of songs they had composed and the group's accomplishments so far.

On arrival at Kenwood Paul had the title, theme, and format, but no actual lyric or tune. Over a cup of tea he talked it through with John and began writing out the words in the shape of a letter rather than a song, starting with the greeting "Dear Sir or Madam," as if writing a formal letter to an unknown person and signing it "Yours sincerely, Ian Iachimoe" (the sound of his name when reversed on a tape). As he spoke the lines John nodded in assent, and then they went together to John's music room to compose the tune.

As they had dealt with the spiritual in their songs so far, "Paperback Writer" reflected on the material realm. This was the age of a buoyant British economy, the rise of the so-called meritocracy, and vigorous popular arts. The new color supplements and glossy magazines were full of stories of the sons and daughters of factory workers and waitresses who'd experienced meteoric rises to fame without the advantages of further education because of their skill at photography, design, modeling, or some other glamorous occupation.

Running alongside the sixties of Timothy Leary, Alan Watts, and Allen Ginsberg, where states of transcendence and the renunciation of materialism were emphasized, there was the sixties of David Bailey, Batman, James Bond, Vidal Sassoon, Twiggy, the Avengers, and *Playboy*, where style, wealth, and glamor reigned supreme. It was during this week in mid-April, coincidentally, that *Time* magazine published its iconic cover story "London: The Swinging City," which cemented the concept of "Swinging London" and gave the capital a much needed rebranding. London was now not merely the city of Beefeaters, bearskins, bankers, and bowlers but of dolly birds, boutiques, bistros, and Beatles. The city "steeped in tradition" had been "seized by change" and "liberated by affluence." *Time* concluded that London "has burst into bloom. It swings; it is the scene."

The story, contributed to by seven staff writers at the London bureau but written by Piri Halasz, quoted Robert Fraser, actor Terry Stamp, TV personality Cathy McGowan (mod cohost of the weekly TV music show *Ready, Steady, Go!*), playwright John Osborne, and aristocrat Jane Ormsby-Gore. The writers dashed from art galleries and nightclubs to boutiques and theatres in an attempt to capture the effervescent scene. The recurring words and phrases in the report were those that could have been used to describe the Beatles' current music: "refreshing," "vital," "experimental," "new," and "passionate for change."

"Paperback Writer," in its own way, distilled the same moment. This was a time when it seemed as though almost anyone, however humble their background, could break into the big time. All it took was a

"London: The Swinging City," the *Time* magazine cover story
that spawned the idea of "Swinging London."

strong idea, good contacts, and chutzpah. The precise nature of the
paperback under discussion was unclear (a novel based on a novel? A
novel about a *Daily Mail* journalist who wants to be a novelist?), but
the spirit of the author's quest wasn't. This was a writer so desperate
that he would compromise his text in any way that was deemed necessary just to get it in print. It was an approach to work diametrically
opposed to that of the Beatles.

Fiction writing was an unusual topic for a pop song of the time,
especially for a pop song by the Beatles. Paul was aware that he was
venturing into new lyrical territory. A journalist from the *Beatles Book
Monthly* who was at the session asked him what he was trying to do

with "Paperback Writer." "Have you heard the lyrics?" Paul asked. The writer had and told him that they seemed "very unusual." Paul explained: "The trouble is that we've done everything we can do with four people, so it's always a problem to ring the changes and make the sound different." To *Melody Maker* he would later say, "We always try to do something different and this idea is different."

The other contender as a single was "Rain," which started out as John's idea, to which Paul believed he made a 30 percent contribution. As far as Paul was concerned, it was about the pleasurable side of rain: "Songs have traditionally treated rain as a bad thing and what we got on to was that it's no bad thing. There's no greater feeling than the rain dripping down your back."

"Rain" was more than that, though. It was philosophical rather than meteorological. John was again tackling the issue of consciousness and the need to expand or alter it. A rainstorm, he argued in the song, is neither good nor bad. Our "state of mind" is what determines how we feel about getting showered on. Restructure the mind, and negative experiences can be eliminated. As Hamlet said, "For there is nothing either good or bad, but thinking makes it so."

His use of the phrases "I can show you" and "Can you hear me?" positioned him as a spiritual leader, just as he had been in "The Word" ("I'm here to show everybody the light") and "Tomorrow Never Knows" ("Turn off your mind") and would be in "Strawberry Fields Forever" ("Let me take you down"). The message of "Rain" was another lesson absorbed from *The Psychedelic Experience* where Leary advised, "Whether you experience heaven or hell, remember that it is your mind which creates them. Avoid grasping the one or fleeing the other. Avoid imposing the ego game on the experience."

"Paperback Writer" was recorded on April 13. To distinguish it, Paul wanted the sound of his bass guitar to feature more prominently in the mix. He was taking a cue from the way that Motown featured its session bassist James Jamerson and Stax used the playing of Donald "Duck" Dunn. Recent British singles such as "My Generation" and "Substitute" by the Who and "Keep on Running" and "Somebody Help Me" by the Spencer Davis Group also had turned up the bass.

In August 1965, while in America, Paul had been given a custom-made left-handed Rickenbacker 4001S bass guitar and used it on *Rubber Soul,* finding that its directness and clarity fit with the new fluidity he was aiming for in his playing. He continued using his trademark Hofner violin bass on stage, because it was lighter and better suited for live performance.

He asked Geoff Emerick to enhance the sound of the Ricken-backer so that it could function as a lead instrument rather than being buried. Emerick devised another unique solution. Rather than putting a normal microphone in front of the bass speaker, as was cus-tomary when recording, he rewired a loudspeaker so that it became a microphone. The extra-large surface taking in the bass boosted its sound to unprecedented levels.

The result was so powerful that it exceeded the limits decreed by the EMI rule books. This was because high-volume recordings could cause styli to jump out of the grooves of vinyl records. However, the Beatles were by now such a valuable act for EMI that allowances were made for them. In this case the disc cutter, Tony Clarke, was an ally of Emerick's, and so he didn't interfere with the mix by toning down the bass.

"Rain," recorded in five takes the next day, also used the heavy bass sound, but its most memorable innovation was the final back-ward chorus. The story as John always told it was that he took home a rough mono mix, but when he played it he was so stoned that he threaded the tape wrong and the track came out backward. In his drugged state of mind this sounded revelatory, so the next day he asked George Martin to splice a backward section of the song to the end of the tape.

"He didn't do that," Martin told me when I quoted John's dis-covery story. "I can tell you—I created that. I actually suggested we

Paul with his Rickenbacker bass guitar the day he
recorded "Paperback Writer" at EMI Studios.

try to turn this round and when he was out I actually lifted off the
voice track, turned it back, slid it around until I found a good spot,
and played it to him when he came back. He fell over the floor. He
thought it was great." Martin pointed out to me that he'd "been experimenting with tapes for years before the Beatles ever came along,"
citing his 1962 single "Time Beat," which he recorded with the BBC
Radiophonic Workshop under the name Ray Cathode.

The thirty-second section turned backward for "Rain" (actually only one line of the lyric plus the elongated chorus of the word
"rain") was duly tagged on, and its distorted and vaguely Eastern
sound supported the psychedelic vision of the lyric. When released as

the B-side of "Paperback Writer," it was the public's first inkling that something unusual was coming out of the Beatles' sessions for their new LP. This wasn't just the advancement of pop due to improvements in recording. This was a new way of seeing things.

"DOCTOR ROBERT," WRITTEN BY JOHN, WAS ANOTHER SONG that wouldn't have emerged without the group's experience with drugs and drug culture. Recorded on April 17, it told the story of a doctor dispensing drugs to those "in need"—that is, to those wanting a boost. Paul revealed in 1967 that it was about one of the notorious New York physicians who dispensed "shots" to affluent revelers wanting to live a twenty-four-hour party lifestyle. "It was a big racket," he said. "The song was a joke about this fellow who cured everyone of everything with all these pills and tranquilizers. He just kept New York high."

This was the era not only of hallucinogens and cosmic consciousness but of pep pills and the long weekend. The Beatles had used amphetamine since their days playing in Hamburg, when it was the drug of choice for musicians having to stay awake at all-night clubs. It was already widely used by jazz and country musicians, many of whom regularly traveled through the night between gigs and shared driving duties.

London mods popularized the "purple heart" (amphetamine with barbiturate) as a recreational drug in the early 1960s, finding it particularly useful for their ideal weekend, which would start on Friday night with dancing, continue the next day with shopping, and end with an all-night session at a basement club in Soho on Saturday night and Sunday morning. The Who had caused consternation by admitting to using pills (as Pete Townshend had done in January on *A Whole Scene Going*), and Roger Daltrey's stuttering on "My Generation" was generally assumed by mods to be a knowing simulation of the "blocked up" state. The Rolling Stones' new album, *Aftermath*, released just two days before "Doctor Robert" was recorded, led with

"Mother's Little Helper," a song about the tranquilizer diazepam, which was being routinely prescribed for housewives suffering from stress (or boredom). Mick Jagger had visited the Beatles in the studio on April 14, as they recorded "Paperback Writer," and had no doubt shared his new material with them. John may also have known Donovan's affectionate song about a drug dealer, "Candy Man," which had been an LP track in 1965.

As Paul indicated, John's song was about a specific physician who he'd heard of (and possibly visited). This was almost certainly Dr. Robert Freymann, who had a clinic on East Seventy-Eighth Street. At the time it was still legal to supply amphetamine in this way, and Freymann, who'd treated the jazz musicians Charlie Parker and Thelonious Monk, was an apologist for the drug cocktails. High-profile customers would often collect drugs from two or three doctors like him and treat these clinics like bars to be dropped into for refreshment. "It sounds like my father," Sarah Jane Freymann told me in 1994. "He treated one of the Beatles. I think it was John. He was a general practitioner but had a real feel for artists and he wasn't judgmental about their lifestyles."

Movie director Joel Schumacher was caught up in the sixties drug doctor scene in New York and explained to me how it worked: "The tragedy is that none of these shots were said to be speed. They were said to be 'vitamin injections.' Nobody knew that much about drugs then. At first people thought this was a magic formula but it was really liquid amphetamine that shook you up higher than a kite and made you feel like God."

Although Dr. Robert Freymann may have been the inspiration for "Doctor Robert," the fictional Dr. Robert supplied psychedelics as well. He was part speed doctor (picking you up when you're down) and part acid dealer (offering you his "special cup"). The former made you feel fine, but the latter did much more. He could transform your mind, help you to "understand" and "see yourself," and ultimately make you "a new and better man."

So Dr. Robert was the archetypal dope contact (some in the Beatles' circle thought Dr. Robert was a reference to Robert Fraser, who was always a reliable source of pot and cocaine for London's hip set) as well as the archetypal medicine man. The three authors of *The Psychedelic Experience* were all doctors (of psychology)—Dr. Timothy Leary, Dr. Richard Alpert, and Dr. Ralph Metzner. John certainly thought he had drunk from their recommended special cup.

Unlike "Rain" and "Tomorrow Never Knows," "Doctor Robert" was brief and punchy without any attempted musical simulations of the drugged state. The only studio trick was the use of what was known as ADT (automatic double-tracking, or artificial double-tracking) on John's vocal. This technique, which later became a standard recording practice, was developed by EMI engineer Ken Townsend during the sessions for this LP specifically in response to John's requests to sound different. In contrast to double-tracking, where singers sing along to their own voice, ADT allowed exactly the same vocal to be doubled up but very slightly out of sync. This altered the sound of the voice by thickening it, as demonstrated on the first part of "Tomorrow Never Knows."

The next song tackled was John's "And Your Bird Can Sing," the lyric of which remains a puzzle. It became one of the rare compositions that John never fully explained. In 1971 he brusquely dismissed it as "a horror," and in 1980 as "another of my throwaways." Marianne Faithfull has speculated that the person being addressed was Mick Jagger and that she was the "bird" (British slang for a girl) who could sing, but she must be mistaken, because at the time the song was written she wasn't Jagger's partner. Paul told me in 2009 that he thought it was just John doing his "Jabberwocky thing" but the lyric doesn't fit comfortably into the nonsense poetry genre either.

"And Your Bird Can Sing" may not have been directed at a known individual but at a type of person (just as Dylan's "Ballad of a Thin Man" had targeted the culturally unaware person in the form of a Mr. Jones). The theme is one that would reappear in John's songs and interviews. It's an attack on someone he doesn't feel is hip enough to get him.

Since childhood he had believed that he was different and that he'd been gifted with special insight. LSD accentuated this feeling. This was what gave him the confidence to use his songs to guide people. The person addressed in "And Your Bird Can Sing" has material wealth ("prized possessions") but not enlightenment. This person doesn't understand John. This person neither truly "sees" nor "hears" him.

The recording was started on April 20, but the two versions taped that day were nothing like the eventual release. Jangling guitars emulated the sound of the Byrds, and eventually the session drew to a close as John and Paul collapsed in fits of laughter. They moved on to a song that George had written in response to the result of the recent British election. "Taxman" was a protest about the so-called super-tax that George was particularly angry about. Speaking to Maureen Cleave in February, he had said that he regarded Harold Wilson, the prime minister of England, as the sheriff of Nottingham as depicted in the legend of Robin Hood. "There he goes," George said. "Taking all the money and then moaning about deficits here, deficits there—always moaning about deficits."

During the interview with Tom Lodge of Radio Caroline at the Chelsea photo shoot, George had been the most vocal Beatle when it came to discussion of taxation.

TL: Do you—do you have any ideas of—you like to change this country in any way?

JOHN: Yes, like to change it a lot.

TL: In what way?

JOHN: Well, the tax problem.

TL: What would you do with the tax?

JOHN: Well, I'd reduce it drastically.

TL: That's if your—you were Chancellor of the Exchequer.

JOHN: No—if I was anybody. I'd reduce it. Drastically.

PAUL: Give the pop stars a fairer share of the country's wealth!

TL: That—if you were in—in politics, that's what you would do.

PAUL: Yes, and any boy that can swim like that ought to be in England's team.

TL: What would you do if you were in politics, to help the country?

RINGO: Oh, I don't know.

JOHN: Go on, tell 'em, Ringo. You know what you'd do.

RINGO: I don't know, no!

PAUL: You've got a plan!

GEORGE: But they can't—they can't pull the—take the taxes down, 'cause they haven't got enough money. And, uh, they'll never have enough money while they're buying all that crap like F-111s [a newly developed tactical fighter-bomber]. Harold! Which—they've proved they're no use whatsoever 'cause we're not all—y'know, what good's all that? So if they pay off a few of the bloody debts—

RINGO:—steel industry—

GEORGE:—then maybe they'd be able to cut the tax down a little, Harold?

"Taxman" became a smart little pop art song with references to Harold Wilson and Edward Heath (leader of the opposition Conservative Party) and a chorus inspired by the theme song from the newly launched *Batman* TV series, starring Adam West as Batman and Burt

Ward as Robin. *Batman* had yet to be screened in Britain (it had premiered in American on January 12), but George (along with the other Beatles) had been sent the single "Batman Theme" as covered by the Marketts, and it was already on his home jukebox.

"Taxman" would be the first song by the Beatles to address anything political, encouraged by the recent popularity of so-called protest music. In the wake of songs by Bob Dylan and Curtis Mayfield on civil rights issues, protest songs became a short-lived vogue starting in 1965, yielding such songs as Barry McGuire's "Eve of Destruction" (written by P. F. Sloane), Buffy Sainte-Marie's "Universal Soldier," and even the British hit "Good News Week" by Hedgehoppers Anonymous (written by Jonathan King). Although they liked Dylan, they thought a lot of the imitations lacked genuine feeling or commitment. "The 'protest' label means absolutely nothing," said John. "It's just something that the press has latched on and, as usual, has flogged to death."

Although "Taxman" was credited exclusively to George, a few of its high points came from other Beatles. Paul played a blistering guitar solo in the middle that he would come to regard as one of his best (it was copied and repeated in the fade-out), and John, in his own words, "threw in a few one-liners to help the song along, because that's what [George] asked for."

John was annoyed when George's autobiography *I, Me, Mine* (1980) made no mention of his contribution.

The draft version of the song that George reproduced in his book had little of the wit of the finished version. The lines were limp and the rhymes forced. The sarcasm that eventually elevated the lyric all came from John.

Eleven takes of "Taxman" were completed in just under ten and a half hours. The next day a cowbell was added, and on May 16, as an afterthought, a fake 1–2–3–4 count-in, mirroring the one Paul had done on the very first track of their first album, "I Saw Her Standing There," but with less urgency in the voice. In 1963 the count sounded as though it could have come from a Sergeant Major on a parade ground. In 1966 it sounded more like the chilled advice of a stoner lying on a waterbed in Kathmandu. The Beatles were counting in a new stage in their career.

"And Your Bird Can Sing" was rerecorded on April 26, and the next day work started on John's "I'm Only Sleeping," a song he'd only recently composed on the back of a General Post Office reminder advising him that he owed twelve pounds, three shilling for an unpaid radio telephone bill. Like so many of the songs on this record, "I'm Only Sleeping" had a possible innocent explanation (it's about sleeping at night or napping during the day) and a possible deviant explanation (it's about a drug reverie). Just as "dancing" and "holding tight" in early Beatles songs were euphemisms for sex, so "dreaming" and "floating" became their euphemisms for drugs.

Friends and colleagues knew of John's love for his bed; Maureen Cleave had called him "possibly the laziest man in Britain," and John admitted to her that he was physically lazy. "I don't mind writing or reading or watching or speaking, but sex is the only physical thing I can be bothered with any more." In February 1964 he had told *Rave* magazine, "The trouble is, I'm dead lazy. You need discipline to write, and I'm too easily side-tracked."

"I'm Only Sleeping" was at least partly about such indolence. He was often still in bed when Paul arrived for their songwriting sessions. Paul was the well-organized craftsman ready to get down to work, whereas John was the casual bohemian who preferred to write only when inspiration struck. "Everybody seems to think I'm lazy / I don't mind; I think they're crazy." But the language also borrowed from *The Psychedelic Experience*—its reference to floating downstream now altered to floating upstream. This could be a song about not wanting to be interrupted while tripping or relaxing with a joint.

John's rationale for dropping out in this way was that the world outside—the world that condemned him for being lazy—was madly rushing about in pursuit of—what? Maybe they were mad and he was sane. This theme was present in "Nowhere Man," where the people hurrying and worrying were the nowhere people, and "Rain," where those who ran in and out of the showers were portrayed as having the wrong state of mind. John was practicing the art of detachment by "lying there and staring at the ceiling" rather than getting tangled in the games of life. At this stage the track had only acoustic guitar and John's voice. The experimental work would take place next month.

On Thursday, April 28, attention turned to "Eleanor Rigby," the music of which would be scored by George Martin based on a Vivaldi-like arrangement suggested by Paul and inspired, in Martin's case, by composer Bernard Herrmann's staccato sounds on the soundtrack of Alfred Hitchcock's film *Psycho* (1960). The few composition lessons Paul had from a teacher at the Guildhall School of Music had spurred him on to be more ambitious. (The teacher in question apparently didn't think much of the tune of "Eleanor Rigby" when Paul played it for him on the piano.)

Paul had started the song while still at the Asher home, on a piano they kept in the basement music room. Vamping on an E-minor chord, he had found the tune and then overlaid it with a second melody. At this stage he thought the music sounded almost Indian. Somewhat incongruously, he recorded the earliest demos of it in the presence of William Burroughs at the small studio in Montagu Square. "I saw Paul several times," Burroughs recalled years later. "The three of us [Burroughs, his boyfriend Ian Sommerville, and Paul] talked about the possibilities of the tape recorder. He'd just come in and work on his 'Eleanor Rigby.' Ian recorded his rehearsals. I saw the song taking shape. Once again, not knowing much about music, I could see that he knew what he was doing. He was very pleasant and very prepossessing. Nice-looking young man, hardworking."

Through Laurie Gold, the session organizer for EMI, George Martin booked eight of the top chamber musicians working in London—violists John Underwood (Delme Quartet) and Steve Shingles (Hirsch Quartet), cellists Derek Simpson (Aeolian

The sheet music for "Eleanor Rigby," with a cover design by
Klaus Voormann.

Quartet) and Norman Jones (Element Quartet), and violinists Jurgen Hess (Delme Quartet), Tony Gilbert (Landsdowne Quartet and
a fixer of session musicians for *Top of the Pops*), John Sharpe (ATV
Orchestra), and Sid Sax (National Philharmonic Orchestra). In 1965
Gilbert and Sax had played on "Yesterday."

For these accomplished musicians, the youngest of whom was
in his thirties, it was no big deal to be playing on a Beatles recording.
Their focus was classical music, and they spent little time listening
to pop or rock. John Underwood, then thirty-four, didn't even know
who the recording was to be with when he was booked. All he knew
was that it was for George Martin and that Martin, with his classical
training, was well respected by all the musicians.

The only Beatle present was Paul. The musicians sat near each other, as they would have done for a concert, read the music that was on their music stands (and which didn't seem exceptional to them), and played when asked to. They weren't prepared by listening to a demo tape beforehand, and although they were always welcome to go to the control room, none of them were sufficiently interested to stay on to hear a playback.

The session lasted just under three hours, during which time they performed fourteen takes. Between the first and second take there was talk about whether they should play with or without vibrato, and they decided to go without it, even though after playing it both ways Paul couldn't tell the difference. The lack of reverb and the compression of sound gave the music a stark, urgent sound. On the final recording day of the month, April 29, Paul added his vocals with help from John and George on refrains, although it would all be stripped later off and replaced.

IT SEEMS TO HAVE BEEN IN APRIL (CERTAINLY IT WAS IN 1966) that Paul went to Paris with Robert Fraser and returned with two oil paintings by René Magritte. This was the start of a lifelong appreciation of the work of the Belgian surrealist. Long after the artist's death in 1967 Paul would acquire his easel, spectacles, and palette. A painting of Magritte's would inspire the logo for Apple Records.

Magritte was unusual in that he was an apparently very ordinary man who dressed in pinstripe suits and wore a bowler hat but who saw the world in a very extraordinary way. On April 22 he had been the subject of a four-page spread in *Life* magazine headlined "The Enigmatic Visions of René Magritte" that was prompted by a touring exhibition of his work in America. In the feature he was quoted as saying, "I want to show reality in such a way that it evokes the mystery"; "I look for poetry in the world of familiar objects"; and "The past and present are united in the imagination. But who can explain such a poetic moment?"

His obsession was mystery, the unknowable, and the hidden. He asked questions about our grasp of reality that chimed with the questions of the psychedelic culture. He said, "If the dream is a translation of waking life, waking life is also the translation of the dream." This sounded like something that could have been said by Timothy Leary or Swami Vivekananda—or John Lennon.

His art was gently disturbing. He painted a man looking in a mirror who sees only the back of his head reflected. He painted people whose faces were removed or obscured by apples, oranges, or cloth wrappings. He famously painted a pipe (*The Treachery of Images*) with the accompanying statement: "Ceci n'est pas une pipe."

PAUL LOVED PARIS BECAUSE IT ALWAYS REMINDED HIM OF his teenage bohemian dreams. Being in the city with Fraser, who had such impeccable connections, heightened his appreciation. The two of them went to a dinner party hosted by the celebrated art dealer Alexandre Iolas over his gallery on the Boulevard Saint-Germain. Iolas was a living connection with twentieth-century art history. Born in Greece in the early years of the century, he had become a dancer and moved to Paris from Berlin after the rise of the Nazi Party. In Paris he became friendly with the great artists of the time, including Cocteau, Braque, Ernst, Magritte, and Picasso. In 1944 he gave up dance and entered the world of art as a dealer, collector, patron, and gallery owner. In 1952 he mounted Andy Warhol's first solo exhibition and went on to have galleries in Paris, New York, Milan, Geneva, Madrid, Rome, and Athens. He was flamboyant, gay, rich, and influential.

After the meal Iolas took Paul downstairs to the gallery to show him a wealth of Magritte paintings. Paul was wide-eyed and picked two to buy for his new home—a medium-sized (65 cm x 81 cm) painting titled *Gloria!* that he has since described as "like a big hooded figure with one eye but when you look at it the other way it's carp, it's a fish, in the shadows inside a castle keep and outside is the sky and clouds where we all want to be" and a smaller painting (45 cm x 55 cm) titled *La Comtesse de Monte Cristo,* which showed a collection of wine bottles, one of which was painted as the body of a woman.

It's easy to see how Paul would have identified with Magritte— the decent, straight-seeming man who surprised people with his apparently skewed vision. The new recordings he was working on would try to unite past and present (and future), look for poetry in the world of the familiar, and seek the boundaries between reality and illusion.

WITH HALF THE LP AND BOTH SIDES OF A NEW SINGLE RE-corded, the feeling was building that the Beatles were making break-throughs and that more were to come. "Musically we're only just starting," said George at this point. "We've realized for ourselves that as far as recording is concerned most of the things that recording men have said were impossible for 39 years are in fact very possible.

"In the past, we've thought that the recording people knew what they were talking about. We believed them when they said we couldn't do this, or we couldn't do that. Now we know we can, and it's opening up a wide new field for us."

MAY

They are purposely composed to sound unusual.
They are sounds that nobody else has done yet.
I mean, nobody . . . ever.
-PAUL, 1966

The Empire Pool at Wembley in North London was built in 1934 for
the British Empire Games but hadn't been used for swimming since
1948. Instead, it had become one of the country's largest indoor arenas, seating ten thousand people. It was the regular venue for the
NME Poll Winners' Concert, a prestigious show that would feature
what the paper's readers considered the best of the established acts
around and the brightest hopes for the future.

Toward the end of each year an entry form would be printed,
and readers would vote in categories ranging from Best Vocal Group
to Best British Disc. The winning musicians would then be invited
to appear at a concert in April or May where they would each have
a short performance spot and then be presented with their awards.
Popular radio DJs would host the evening.

The Beatles had appeared every year since 1963, although the fit
was looking increasingly uneasy. The concert had the format of the
popular package tours of the time where many acts appeared on a

single show, each performing only two or three songs. These were an inheritance of the old variety circuit, where ventriloquists and gymnasts shared bills with dance bands and opera singers in fast-moving shows.

The bill for Sunday, May 1, included the Seekers, the Walker Brothers, the Yardbirds, the Small Faces, the Who, the Stones, Cliff Richard and the Shadows, and Roy Orbison. The Beatles arrived at a service entrance at the venue dressed as chefs in white aprons and toques, each holding a tray of food. It successfully fooled the fans, but once they were in the kitchen Ringo slipped on the greasy floor, and his tray of goodies landed in the path of his fellow Beatles.

The show was already in progress when they arrived at their dressing room, and the Beatles hoped to be able to get ready, go to the stage, perform, and leave swiftly in their escape vehicle. However, when they arrived in the huge holding area backstage, the Stones were performing "The Last Time," with "Play with Fire" and "Satisfaction" to come. Then there would be the award ceremony. When *NME* publisher Maurice Kinn told John that the group wasn't needed for at least another twenty-five minutes, John exploded. He wanted to trump the Stones by following them immediately before the applause died down. "We're not waiting," he announced. "We're going on now." Kinn took John into a corridor and explained that he couldn't renege on the agreement with Andrew Oldham. John insisted that the alternative was that they wouldn't play at all.

Kinn tried to reason with Brian Epstein, who suddenly seemed less powerful than he usually appeared. He took the attitude that "the boys" were beyond his control. Kinn put to Epstein what he saw as the stark alternatives. Either the Beatles played immediately after the awards, as they had agreed, or DJ Jimmy Savile would be sent out to announce that the Beatles were on site but refusing to appear. The results of the latter course, Kinn warned Epstein, would be ten thousand fans rioting and causing damage that NEMS would have to pay for and *NME* suing Epstein for breach of contract.

Epstein ruefully gave in to Kinn's demands but refused to sign an agreement with ABC-TV, the company filming the event. All they would be allowed to cover of the Beatles' appearance was the group members receiving their awards.

John didn't like seeing the Stones get their own way. He cornered Kinn and screamed at him. Kinn would later describe it as "abuse like you have never heard in the whole of your life" and said that everyone in the backstage area could hear the shouting. "You can't do this to us," exclaimed John. "We will never appear on one of your shows ever again."

Oldham, who had worked as a publicist for the Beatles when they first arrived in London, later saw it as evidence of Epstein losing his grip. The group was no longer automatically bowing to his wisdom and accepting all his judgments. During their time off the road, when they didn't see him on a day-to-day basis, they had grown in independence.

The backstage dispute didn't affect their show. After the general awards had been handed out by American actor Clint Walker, from the TV western series *Cheyenne*, they bounded on stage dressed in dark suits and black turtlenecks and played "I Feel Fine," "Nowhere Man," "Day Tripper," "If I Needed Someone," and "I'm Down" during a powerful fifteen-minute set. The fans screamed as they had been doing for the past three years, but John's threat never to play for Maurice Kinn again proved true. Not only did the Beatles never play an *NME* Poll Winners' Concert again, they never played a concert in Britain again.

On Monday afternoon, the Beatles were taken to the Playhouse Theatre on Northumberland Avenue to prerecord interviews with radio host Brian Matthew. Matthew had been fronting *Saturday Club* on what was then known as the BBC Light Programme since 1957, when the show was started as *Saturday Skiffle Club* and John was in the Quarrymen. It had turned into a rare oasis of pop, rock 'n' roll, R & B, and jazz on BBC radio. Each program played a limited num-

The Beatles receiving their NME Poll Winners' awards from actor Clint Walker (of the TV show *Cheyenne*), with NME publisher Maurice Kinn (*right*) looking on, May 1, 1966.

ber of records because of restrictions on "needle time" imposed by the Musicians' Union, which was keen to protect the livelihoods of its members but had several live performers, news, and guest interviews and became vital listening for British teenagers eager to keep up with what was going on in the world of pop.

The Beatles had a good relationship with Matthew, who at thirty-seven was old enough to earn their respect but young enough for them to tease and joke with. When interviewed as a group, they rarely gave the information that journalists needed to write their stories, but on the radio their flip comments and verbal shrugs became part of the informality and irreverence that their audience loved. It felt as though they'd been hauled into the principal's office and were being quizzed about their work, but all they wanted to do was chew gum, giggle, and distract whoever was speaking.

This recording, due for transmission on June 4, was to mark the four hundredth edition of *Saturday Club*, and Matthew's angle was the group's recent low profile. Since the end of 1965 there'd been no touring, no TV, and very little radio. Were they quietly trying to retire? Why was it taking them so long to record an album?

"We spend more time on recording now, because we prefer recording," said George. John commented on the as-yet untitled LP everyone knew they were working on. "We've done half an LP in the time we'd take to do a whole LP and a couple of singles. We can't do it all y'know. But we like recording." He pointed out that the new record was "all our own compositions," another reason it took so long. This was an odd defense, because *A Hard Day's Night* and *Rubber Soul* had also both been self-written. One of the main differences between the way they worked on the earlier recordings and the way they'd worked over last month was that in the past the group didn't stay around for the mixing process. That was considered to be the domain of the producer and engineers. They just played their music and left.

Matthew spoke alone with Ringo, who extolled the virtues of being able to just sit at home and do nothing. "We used to work every night, practically. We were always tired—and hungry. Now we have plenty of time off." He didn't appear to be highly motivated, confessed to having a short attention span, and admitted that he was in danger of turning into a blob if work didn't propel him into action. The best thing about his life now was that he had no worries.

Following Ringo, Matthew spoke to Paul, who was becoming the spokesman for the Beatles—the one most conscious of the information journalists and broadcasters needed and most aware of the group's public image. When interviewed with John, he was caught between his natural instinct to be gracious, polite, and cooperative and the peer pressure to be cool, offhand, and mysterious. Spoken to alone, he would be charming and communicative.

After talking briefly about the loss of privacy that came with fame, he settled on his favorite topic of 1966—the expansion of his cultural experiences. He regretted the attitude he'd grown up with, which was that music forms from other cultures or periods were de facto "boring," as were art forms like theatre. He now realized that in writing them off before knowing enough to understand he had been narrow-minded.

"When I was in Liverpool I went once or twice to the Liverpool Playhouse, a repertory theatre there, and I wasn't very keen on it. I used to go to see if I liked going to these plays, you know? I just never went back again. But I went when I came down to London. I went to something that wasn't like the plays they did in repertory. So, you see some great actors acting in a great play and you think, 'Wow! That is good.' I was wrong to say that theatre is just rubbish."

Matthew probed him to see if he was considering either producing or directing plays. Paul said that he couldn't do either without being taught, and he didn't have a strong enough desire to learn a whole new craft. However, he confessed to having a new interest in filmmaking. By this he didn't mean commercial films with actors and screenplays but experimental home movies, or, as he called them, "films that you sort of just make because you fancy making a film."

He was encouraged in this pursuit by Robert Fraser, who had regular showings of art films at his apartment on Mount Street to which he invited all the bright young things from fashion, music, photography, and the aristocracy. Fraser showed shorts from independent directors like Kenneth Anger, Stan Brakhage, Bruce Conner, and Andy Warhol, which gave Paul an appetite to create nonnarrative films to which he could add appropriate soundtracks. Just as the work of Berio and Cage had showed him that music didn't have to be governed by strict rules of rhythm and melody, so the work of people like Conner and Brakhage opened him up to the idea that film didn't have to involve character development, linear storytelling, or even dialogue.

Italian director Michelangelo Antonioni had recently come to London to film *Blow Up*, which tried to distill the essence of the swinging city into a drama about a young fashion photographer based on David Bailey and played by David Hemmings. For some time Antonioni had been discreetly hanging around the most happening restaurants, cafés, and clubs to imbibe the feel of the city now regarded as being as much at the center of cultural change as Paris and New York.

He arrived at one of Robert Fraser's soirees on a night when Paul happened to be showing some of his shorts, using a slow-moving projector. "We'd play sitar music or Beethoven or Albert Ayler, who was a great favourite," Paul later told Barry Miles. "It was very, very slow but it created a hypnotic mantra kind of effect. I showed Antonioni these movies and he was quite interested. They lasted about a quarter of an hour. It was really a five-minute flick but we showed it so slow."

Two of his shorts, *The Defeat of the Dog* and *The Next Spring Then*, were mentioned in *Punch* in 1966, where they were described as "not like ordinary people's home movies" and as consisting of "over-exposures, double-exposures, blinding orange lights, quick cuts from professional wrestling to a crowded car park to a close-up of a television weather map."

After the Brian Matthew interview at the BBC, Paul and John went to the nightclub Dolly's at 57–58 Jermyn Street, accompanied by Neil Aspinall and Rolling Stones Keith Richards and Brian Jones. Already at the club was Bob Dylan, who'd arrived that afternoon from Copenhagen for a European tour that would start in Dublin on May 5. Later in the night all six men returned to Dylan's suite at the Mayfair Hotel, where Paul and Dylan played pressings of their latest songs. The ace in Paul's pack was "Tomorrow Never Knows," proof, he thought, that the Beatles were at the experimental cutting edge of pop. Dylan didn't show any emotion and then turned to him and said, "Oh, I get it. You don't want to be cute anymore."

This was a typical Dylan put-down of the period, implying that "cute" was all the Beatles had ever been and suggesting that "Tomorrow Never Knows" was a mere exercise in confounding expectations rather than a substantial change in their art. One of the few people to observe the dynamic in the relationship between the two musicians was director D. A. Pennebaker, who was filming the tour in the same way he'd filmed Dylan's last UK tour for the documentary *Don't Look Back*. In Pennebaker's view Dylan didn't really connect with Paul. Even though the two of them were talking in the same room, Dylan's thoughts were always elsewhere.

Dylan then played some of his own tracks, almost all of which had been recorded in Nashville during February and March and were to be released two months later as *Blonde on Blonde*. Like *Pet Sounds* and *Revolver*, it would be one of the year's seminal records—a fourteen-track double LP that broke new ground with its mash of symbolist poetry and hard electric blues. The cover, which had no title or name printed on it, consisted of an out of focus portrait of

While visiting London, Bob Dylan played Paul tracks from his forthcoming LP, *Blonde on Blonde*.

the spiral-haired singer that echoed the doped vision of the curved photo of the Beatles used on *Rubber Soul*.

DESPITE DYLAN'S WITHERING COMMENT, HE KNEW THAT HE and the Beatles were exploring similar territory, albeit in different ways. They were more overtly enthusiastic about the mystical potential of drugs, whereas Dylan tended to write about the paranoia of having a strangled-up mind or the ecstasy of getting stoned (as in "Rainy Day Women # 12 & 35.") He expressed the experience of distortion through surrealistic scenarios in the lyrics while the music remained straight, but the Beatles wanted to distort the music as well.

John admired Dylan but thought that his much-respected lyrics were phony. They were difficult to fathom, he surmised, not because they were deep but because Dylan used literary trickery to dazzle his listeners. John didn't believe that the madmen, judges, jugglers, and thieves that thronged Dylan's songs were anything other than nice sounding words to sing and exotic images for fans to puzzle over. He felt the enigmatic lines that often sounded like proverbs had no real wisdom at their core.

(Interviewed in 2007 by *Rolling Stone*, Dylan was far more charitable to Paul than he had been in 1966, saying that he was "in awe" of him and that his talent was all-embracing. "He's got the gift for melody, he's got the gift for rhythm, he can play any instrument. He can scream and shout as good as anyone, and he can sing a ballad as good as anyone. And his melodies are effortless, that's what you have to be in awe of. . . . He's just so damn effortless.")

"I'm Only Sleeping," the song that the Beatles returned to three days later, was typical of John's approach of using simple statements embedded in unusual musical environments. It was a dreamy-sounding track about being lost in a dream. The session was a long one, as George spent five and a half hours mastering the backward-solo sound. In order to make a well-constructed solo rather than random swishes as in "Tomorrow Never Knows," he first had to plan the order of notes, painstakingly work out how to play them in reverse order, record them, do the same with a second guitar using a fuzz-box, and finally play these tapes backward. For the outro to the song Paul and George combined for a duet of backward-sounding guitars. The session didn't finish until three the next morning, and they returned later in the day to add vocal harmonies.

The following Monday, May 9, Paul recorded "For No One," the song he'd written in Switzerland. The only other Beatle involved was Ringo, on drums, cymbals, and maracas. Paul played piano throughout and then added clavichord. It was a short song—less than two minutes—yet packed with drama. The next week Alan Civil, soon to be the principal horn player with the BBC Symphony Orchestra, added an obbligato on French horn.

For Civil, like many of the other classical musicians used on the album, this was just another session—the third he would do on that day—and the Beatles were nothing exceptional. His musical colleagues would be more impressed to hear that he'd toured America with Herbert von Karajan or worked with Sir Thomas Beecham than that he'd played on a Beatles track. He found the song to be in "rather a bad musical style" because the tuning on the guitars was neither B-flat nor B-major but somewhere in the middle. It was what he termed "in the cracks" and it created difficulties when it came to choosing a key for his instrument.

Paul had long loved the sound of the horn and communicated what he wanted to George Martin by humming the type of break he wanted to hear while Martin drew up a score. What he wanted went higher than the normal register of a French horn. Martin duly added in the extra leap. Civil was able to make it, but not without difficulty. He later commented, "I think they had a method of raising or lowering the pitch in this case, but it made the horn part for me a very, very awkward key, purely because these fellows just tuned their instruments to themselves and not to an A on the piano."

Having been given "Paperback Writer" as the next single, Capitol now requested some of the tracks from the current sessions to be advanced to them for use on an interim LP that would also include songs from the UK versions of the *Help!* and *Rubber Soul* LPs that had not yet been released in America. The fact that the American LPs differed from those released in Britain irked the Beatles. Somewhat reluctantly, mono mixes were made of "Doctor Robert," "I'm Only Sleeping," and "And Your Bird Can Sing" on May 12 and shipped to Los Angeles.

The next day the group returned to the unfinished "Got to Get You Into My Life," to add the brass that would give it the feeling of a track recorded at Stax in Memphis or Motown in Detroit. Five of the best brass players in London had been recruited for the session: Jamaican Eddie "Tan Tan" Thornton (sax) and Peter Coe (tenor sax) from Georgie Fame's backing group, the Blue Flames, and jazz musicians Ian Hamer (trumpet), Les Condon (trumpet), and Alan Branscombe (tenor sax).

Paul wanted the brass to sound huge, so Emerick poked the microphones inside the bells of each instrument rather than a yard away as per the EMI rulebook, which warned that if the air pressure was too great, it could damage the diaphragms of the microphones. The other Beatles had nothing more to do with the track. George had lost interest, and Ringo and John played chess.

There was no written score. Paul vocally imitated the breaks he wanted the players to embellish, and they then each wrote out their musical parts. During the mixing Paul felt the sound was too weak, and so Emerick fattened it up by dubbing the track onto two-track tape and playing it back alongside the multitrack recording but slightly out of sync. This had the effect of making it sound like the work of ten horn players. Paul then added a new and inspired vocal.

Three days later Bruce Johnston of the Beach Boys arrived in London to talk up the group's latest LP, which had just been released in America. He was taking advantage of the interest stirred by

"Sloop John B," a single from the LP that was currently at No. 3 on the UK charts behind Manfred Mann's "Pretty Flamingo" and "Daydream" by the Lovin' Spoonful. Johnston had joined the Beach Boys in April 1965 after Brian Wilson gave up doing live shows following a breakdown. Foreshadowing what would happen to the Beatles, Wilson decided to channel all his creative energy into writing and recording.

While in London Johnston fortuitously befriended Keith Moon after being introduced to him by Tony Rivers of the harmony group Tony Rivers and the Castaways. Through Moon he met a wide range of British rock aristocracy (including Mick Jagger), was interviewed by the main music weeklies, and appeared on the TV show *Ready, Steady, Go!*

At the Scotch of St. James Moon introduced him to John and Paul in what would be the ultimate PR coup for Johnston. This led to the two Beatles being invited to a farewell party in Johnston's suite at the Waldorf Astoria in the Aldwych on May 19, where they joined eccentric producer Kim Fowley (an old school friend of Johnston's brought in to whip up interest in the forthcoming release), drummer Dave Clark of the Dave Clark Five, Billy Kinsley and Tony Crane of the Merseys (fresh from a live appearance on *Top of the Pops*), Marianne Faithful, and organizers from the Beach Boys' UK fan club.

On a mono record player sent up to the suite by the concierge Johnston played a copy of *Pet Sounds*, the LP that was two months away from its UK release. According to Fowley, John and Paul silently played canasta with the fan club girls as the record was played twice and then immediately went to a piano they'd asked to be brought in for them and began playing chords and discussing a song with each other in a whispered conversation.

Pet Sounds was a Beach Boys LP in name only. It was a Brian Wilson LP featuring twenty-seven different types of instrument and fifty-nine session musicians. The Beach Boys merely held it together with their vocal harmonies. Daring as it was, it caused consternation within Capitol Records (and among the other Beach Boys) because it broke with the group's past as a surf group writing songs for the teenage market.

Departing from the predominant trends of the time, it was multitextured, drawing from jazz, doo-wop, folk, spirituals, classical, pop, choral, and avant-garde music and using instruments (glockenspiel, Theremin, ukulele, harpsichord, accordion) not usually used in either pop or rock 'n' roll.

For John and Paul *Pet Sounds* endorsed their own recording adventure and inspired them to reach even higher. They identified with Wilson's vision of transforming the LP into a cohesive unit and admired his writing, instrumentation, and vocal arrangements. Fowley later said, "They weren't there to pay tribute to Brian Wilson or Bruce Johnston; they were there to see what the competition was. They were there to take the best of *Pet Sounds* and apply it to *Revolver*. . . . They didn't steal lyrics, or notes, or chords. They stole emotional impact and pathos."

Paul was particularly impressed with the melodic bass lines that set up tension by emphasizing notes that were not the roots of the chords. (Even though bass was Wilson's instrument, most of the lines he scored were played by legendary session bassist Carol Kaye.) Paul would later say that hearing *Pet Sounds* "blew [him] out of the water." John liked it so much that he called Wilson to tell him that it was the greatest LP he had ever heard.

Johnston's self-funded trip to London was remarkably successful in making *Pet Sounds* a talking point and raising interest in the Beach Boys' fall tour of Britain. The record was openly endorsed by John and Paul and then by Andrew Oldham, who called it "the most progressive album of the year . . . a complete exercise in pop music." EMI brought forward its UK release, and by the year's end the Beach Boys were the bestselling artists in the country for both singles and LPs. Audiences in Great Britain and elsewhere in Europe were far more welcoming of the changes that Wilson was introducing than those in America, where the sales of *Pet Sounds* were less than half that of previous LPs by the Beach Boys.

The Beatles didn't need to spread the word by arranging listening sessions with influential contemporaries. The world's attention was already on them, and the longer the sessions for the new LP went on, the greater was the sense of anticipation. However, this didn't mean that they could release a single with no fanfare. They still relied on print advertising, interviews with key publications, and appearances on TV and radio.

Performing live on TV was becoming more onerous for them. Interviews could be slotted in during breaks in recording, but performances required rehearsals, run-throughs, and travel to television studios. There was no way they could satisfy the continual flow of requests to appear on shows as far away from home as Tokyo, Sydney, New York, and Los Angeles.

Beginning in 1965 they had satisfied the demand by having themselves filmed playing new singles and selling each clip for up to $20,000 to TV stations around the world. This not only gave them international exposure on a variety of shows but also gave them control over the way they appeared.

For the first UK single of 1966 they brought in Michael Lindsay-Hogg, the director of the cutting-edge weekly pop show *Ready, Steady, Go!,* to film them at EMI Studios. Over two days, with Brian Epstein's assistant Tony Bramwell producing, they shot several versions of "Paperback Writer" and "Rain" in both black and white and color. There was no acting or storytelling, props or costumes. They just played the songs to camera.

After the first day of filming, which was done directly to video, Epstein was concerned that the color material had only been reviewed on a black-and-white monitor. This included a special personal greeting from the Beatles to Ed Sullivan, who was due to screen the songs on his show. What if the color balance was faulty or, worse still, the filming hadn't been captured in color at all?

Epstein asked a runner from InterTel, the company supplying the cameras and crew, to reconnoiter an outdoor location so that they could shoot both songs again in color as an insurance policy. His only specifications were that it should be somewhere beautiful, within London, and surrounded by trees.

The runner duly found a suitable place—Chiswick House in West London, an eighteenth-century neo-Palladian villa only seven miles from Abbey Road with beautifully landscaped gardens featuring trees, hedges, shrubs, flowers, and garden ornaments. None of the Beatles (or Brian Epstein) had been there before, but it sounded ideal.

The Beatles arrived on location early on the morning of May 20, along with driver Alf Bicknell, Neil Aspinall, Brian Epstein, Tony Barrow, Mal Evans, photographer Robert Whitaker, producer Tony Bramwell, and journalist Sue Mautner from the *Beatles Book Monthly*. "Paperback Writer" was filmed partly in an area of the gardens enclosed by yew hedges and lined with statues and giant stone urns and partly in the eighteenth-century glass conservatory. "Rain" was filmed in the conservatory, as well as beside a cedar tree with children playing on its low hanging branches. Reflective cutaway shots were taken of each of the Beatles framed by green leaves and red camellias.

On both days of filming the Beatles were wearing clothes recently bought at boutiques emerging in Chelsea rather than their normal Carnaby Street mod outfits. At EMI Studios John had worn a patterned shirt with a long floppy collar from Granny Takes a Trip and George had on a velvet Hung On You jacket with wide lapels. For the outdoor shoot John wore a black jacket with silk-faced lapels, also from Hung On You.

Nigel Waymouth and John Pearse from Granny Takes a Trip and Hung On You's Michael Rainey were influenced in their design choices by acid trips, Victoriana, fin de siècle decadence, military uniforms, and art nouveau. Just as the Beatles were pushing the boundaries of pop sounds, they were pushing the boundaries of fashion with

Filming promotional clips of "Rain" and "Paperback Writer" at Chiswick House, London, under the direction of Michael Lindsay-Hogg, May 20, 1966.

satin shirts, crushed velvet trousers, brocade jackets, Indian-print scarves, kipper ties, and sheepskin jackets from Afghanistan. There was a blurring of cultures, periods, styles, and genders.

King's Road in Chelsea had long been the stomping ground of younger members of the aristocracy and the nouveau riche. Michael Rainey was married to Jane Ormsby-Gore, the daughter of Lord Harlech. Old Etonian antiques dealer Christopher Gibbs, who played a central role in importing Moroccan style to London and was close to the Stones, influenced their tastes. Nigel Waymouth, who like Rainey had been born in India during the time of the British Raj, had studied economics at University College London.

The boutiques they created were novel at the time. They sold clothes for both men and women, painted giant murals on their front windows to prevent passersby peering in, and had staff who would sit looking immaculately cool rather than walk around asking browsers if they needed help. Hung On You was named after a 1965 track by the Righteous Brothers (the B side of "Unchained Melody"), and Granny Takes a Trip, which sounded like a band from San Francisco, alluded to both antique clothing and LSD.

John and Paul were the first of the Beatles to visit these shops. When it became difficult for them to shop in person, they had new collections brought over to them to peruse or sent Mal Evans to buy four of each of the latest shirts. It was the beginning of the Beatles still dressing similarly yet with an individual stamp. For example, in Robert Whitaker's photos taken during the filming at EMI, they all wore sunglasses (the new cool accessory), but each pair was different; John's lenses were wire-framed and oblong, Ringo's were oval, those of Paul and George had black plastic frames.

The day of the Chiswick Park filming an interview with Ringo appeared in *NME*. In it he briefly discussed the LP currently under construction. "I think this will definitely go down as one of the longest sessions ever," he said, "but we're trying to produce a really musical LP, not just a record by 'those four boys on guitars and drums'! We're using strings this time, and even a trumpet on one track."

Asked if he would be doing his traditional vocal track, he said he would. "We haven't done it yet," he clarified. "John and Paul have written a song which they think is for me but if I mess it up then we might have to find another country-and-western song off somebody else's LP. It all depends."

The song in question was "Yellow Submarine," as unusual a track for the Beatles to record at that time as "Tomorrow Never Knows" had been. It was a children's song with a story, a central character, and a sing-along chorus that Paul had woken up with playing in his mind. It shared some similarities with Bob Dylan's "Rainy Day Women # 12 & 35," which was currently at No. 10 on the UK singles charts. The Beatles spent six hours rehearsing and recording a basic rhythm track for it on May 26, to which Ringo then added his vocals.

George Martin was off sick with food poisoning, and so Geoff Emerick took charge.

In a 1967 interview Paul implied that the colored submarine idea had its genesis during a Greek vacation he'd taken in 1963 when he had been introduced to the "spoon sweet" known locally as vanilla submarine (or strawberry submarine if red), where mastic resin mixed with sugar is submerged in a glass of icy water and hardened, then chewed or sucked like a popsicle. "It's like a sweet," Paul had said. "It's called submarine."

Paul had grown up during the golden era of children's music, when songs ranging from Henry Blair's "Sparky's Magic Piano" (which he specifically mentioned in relation to "Yellow Submarine" in a later press conference in America) to "The Little Red Monkey" by Joy Nichols, Jimmy Edwards, and Dick Bentley were heard regularly on the radio. It was assumed that children were too young to appreciate adult pop, and so special songs that were innocent and playful were written for the juvenile market. From 1952 onward the BBC Light Programme had an hour-long record show for children at 9:00 a.m. each Saturday hosted by Uncle Mac (Derek McCulloch).

In true BBC fashion Uncle Mac saw his job as being not only to entertain children but also to inform and educate them. Between novelty songs such as "Nellie the Elephant" by Mandy Miller (produced by George Martin) and Charles Penrose's ever-popular "The Laughing Policeman," he would slip in some classical music, light opera, folk songs, hymns, or Danny Kaye's musical retellings of such fables as "The Ugly Duckling" and "The Emperor's New Clothes."

Children's records could be highly innovative. They had fun with tape speeds, sound effects, and vocal treatments. "Beep Beep" by the Playmates described the race between a Cadillac and a Nash Rambler, and as the cars in the song were driven faster, the song speeded up. "The Typewriter," written by Leroy Anderson, embedded the clacking of a typewriter into an instrumental by the Boston Pops. The Chipmunks used sped-up voices. In these records imaginations were allowed to run wild.

The psychedelic experience often prompted a reevaluation of childhood. Dr. Robin Carhart-Harris, who directed research into LSD using neuroimaging at Imperial College, London, said after the report of his team's findings was published in the journal *Proceedings of the National Academy of Sciences* (vol. 113, no. 17, April 26, 2016), "In many ways, the brain in the LSD state resembles the state our brains were in when we were infants; free and unconstrained."

For the frequent tripper in the 1960s childhood was no longer a period of life to grow out of, but a state of mind to aspire to. (In "My Back Pages" Bob Dylan boasted that in the past he'd been "so much older" but he was younger now.) The child's view was looked upon as more "real" because it hadn't been tainted by pain, evil, and disappointment, and children were capable of wonder, whereas adults naturally became more blasé and harder to amaze. It was common for trippers to revisit childhood memories and to feel that they had recaptured a sense of childlike awe where all the senses were intensified.

One result of this was a fresh appreciation of children's literature (*The Hobbit; The Lion, the Witch and the Wardrobe*), fairy tales, playground rhymes, animated films (*Fantasia*), and Romantic poetry such as William Blake's *Songs of Innocence and Experience*. The shop fronts of Granny Takes a Trip and Hung On You, with their giant painted images, the "baby doll" image for girls, and the medieval pageboy look for boys, were all a part of this regression to infancy.

George had expressed this new attitude in his interview with Maureen Cleave when he said, "Babies, when they are born, are pure. Gradually they get more impure with all the rubbish being pumped into them by society and television and that; till gradually they're dying off, full of everything." Cleave accurately commented that his view had a lot in common with that of poet William Wordsworth, who regarded childhood as divine and the then-modern world of industrialization as corrupt and dehumanizing. In his poem "Ode: Intimations of Immortality from Recollections of Early Childhood" Wordsworth wrote,

But trailing clouds of glory do we come
From God, who is our home:
Heaven lies about us in our infancy!
Shades of the prison-house begin to close
Upon the growing Boy,
But he beholds the light, and whence it flows,
He sees it in his joy.

These were some of the reasons why an apparently lightweight song about a submariner who sailed the world didn't seem out of place in the repertoire of a group at the forefront of pop music in 1966 and why its nursery-rhyme quality fitted the mood of the times. "There isn't a single big word," said Paul. "Kids will understand it easier than adults."

After recording the basic track with Emerick, the Beatles returned a week later with George Martin to overlay it with a selection of sound effects—chains, bells, hooters, and tubs of water to create a nautical atmosphere and chinking glasses, whistles, and whoops for the party spirit. Brian Jones, Pattie Harrison, and Marianne Faithfull were among those who joined in the sing-along and added celebratory shouts.

The final week of May was dominated by Dylan's return to London after having played around Britain with the Hawks (referred to in *Melody Maker* at the time as "the Group" and later to become known as the Band). In Liverpool, Dylan had posed for photographer Barry Feinstein near some warehouse buildings on Dublin Street exactly where the Beatles had been photographed in 1962. In Manchester a vocal member of the audience notoriously called him "Judas" for performing his music with an electric guitar and backing group.

Along with the Rolling Stones, Dylan was part of the Holy Trinity of white pop acts with huge cultural clout. Musicians looked to them for clues as to where music was likely to go next, and young people were guided by their fashion choices, opinions, and beliefs.

Recording *Revolver* at EMI Studios.

They impacted each other as well. Dylan introduced the Beatles to pot during their 1964 tour of America but had already affected their music by challenging them (by example) to write lyrics that were more substantial and self-revelatory. "Paul asked Mal Evans to follow him around the night they took pot and write down everything he said," the journalist Al Aronowitz (who arranged the meeting and supplied the grass) told me in 1987. "He felt as though he was really talking for the first time. That's what happens."

The Beatles had been shown the LP *The Freewheelin' Bob Dylan* while in Paris in 1964, which made them relatively late converts. However, once converted, they became passionate. During their stay in France they bought this and his 1962 debut LP *Bob Dylan* and played them endlessly in their spare time. The effect of his influence was particularly noticeable the next year in the folkish sound of "You've Got to Hide Your Love Away," the surrealism of "Norwegian Wood," and the introspection of "In My Life."

Conversely, it's hard to cite examples of Dylan music clearly influenced by the Beatles, other than two songs that parodied or mocked their work ("4th Time Around" being based on the tune of "Norwegian Wood" and "I Want to Be Your Lover" sending up the simplicity of "I Wanna Be Your Man"). British Invasion groups in general opened his eyes to see that the kind of folk he enjoyed could be electrified and reach more people. He'd perked up when he heard "I Want to Hold Your Hand" in 1964. "They were doing things nobody was doing," he said of the Beatles. "Their chords were outrageous. . . . It was obvious to me that they had staying power. I knew they were pointing the direction where music had to go."

But he was more directly inspired by the Animals, who in July 1964 had a No. 1 American hit with "The House of the Rising Sun," a traditional song Dylan had recorded on his debut album in 1962 after hearing it played in New York clubs by Dave Van Ronk. The Animals' record revealed to him the potential for taking a song with folk roots and transforming it into a hit by giving it a pop-beat treatment.

So whereas Dylan admired the Beatles and had initially been motivated by many of the same musicians that had inspired them (Buddy Holly, Little Richard, Elvis), his roots were in blues, gospel, country, and folk, along with the poetry of writers like Walt Whitman, Allen Ginsberg, William Blake, and Arthur Rimbaud. He had never written music to get girls screaming or lyrics about adolescent anguish and puppy love.

"The Beatles looked on Dylan as [providing] a kind of intellectual input," says director Pennebaker. "He kind of looked on them as popularizers. It interested him that they had such a wide following. Albert Grossman knew that Dylan was going up and he protected him very carefully. When we were with the Beatles we never saw their manager. Albert was with Dylan all the time. That was interesting to the Beatles—that Albert took such a close interest in what Dylan did and where he went. I think they missed that in their own operation."

Although John had unashamedly benefited from listening to

Dylan's first four LPs, he claimed only to have heard "Highway 61 Revisited" in 1965 because George made him. In his view, the more obscure lyrics were "artsy fartsy" and designed to impress more than to communicate. In 1980 he would tell *Playboy*, "Dylan got away with murder. I thought 'Well, I can write this crap too.' You know, you just stick a few images together, thread them together, and you call it poetry." His imitation of this kind of Dylan song was "I Am the Walrus." Fooling around on a tape at home in New York in the 1970s he parodied Dylan's "Stuck Inside of Mobile" by singing "Stuck Inside of Lexicon with the Roget's Thesaurus Blues Again."

In 1978, Dylan was more charitable regarding John's songwriting with the Beatles, saying, "John has taken poetics pretty far in popular music. A lot of his work is overlooked, but if you examine it, you'll find key expressions that have never been said before to push across his point of view. Things that are symbolic of some inner reality and probably will never be said again." In 2005 he praised John's vocals, saying, "To this day it's hard to find a singer better than Lennon was." (On his 2012 album *Tempest* Dylan would record an affectionate tribute to his peer titled "Roll on John.")

It seemed to be a given that the two writers would gel. They were both bookish, enjoyed poetry, specialized in witty put-downs, and were determinedly nonconformist. Yet they were never relaxed in each other's company. According to friends they were both too conscious of having to be smart, mysterious, and aware, and this meant they were continually on guard. Unusually, it was George, the least lyrically fluent of the songwriting Beatles, who was most galvanized by Dylan's songs and who would form the strongest bond with him. This then rankled with John, who felt overlooked.

D. A. Pennebaker captured the machinations of the two icons in half an hour of film shot in the back of a car going through London to the Mayfair Hotel on the morning of May 27. Both men were the worse for drink or drugs, but whereas this made John subdued, Dylan became rowdy and spewed out reams of nonsensical comments and non sequiturs. Instead of an illuminating summit between two of the most creative songwriters of the era, it became a game of jibes and ripostes. In 1968, John confessed to a writer that he and Dylan were "uptight" around each other. Speaking to *Rolling Stone* editor Jann Wenner two years later he said, "We were both in shades and both on fucking junk. . . . I was nervous as shit. I was on his territory, that's why I was so nervous."

"They were both off their heads and it was one of those awful meetings where Dylan was embarrassed about John and John was embarrassed about Dylan," says Tony Bramwell. "I think John was a bit in awe of Dylan because he was mysterious and Dylan was in awe of John because he was John Lennon. Neither of them were really open people or immediately cuddly. They just didn't strike it off together."

The previous night Dylan had played the first of two shows at the Royal Albert Hall. Afterward, Johnny Cash, who'd seen an earlier Dylan concert in Cardiff, had returned to the Mayfair with him, where Dylan sat at a piano and played his version of Cash's hit "I Still Miss Someone." This scene was also captured in Pennebaker's film, although the finished product, provisionally titled *Eat the Document*, would never receive an official release.

In the car conversation turned to Cash:

DYLAN: I have Johnny Cash in my film. Are you gonna shit yourself when you see it. You won't believe it.

JOHN: Hey! John's gonna shit again!

DYLAN: He doesn't know. You know what he looks like, right, Johnny Cash? Have you spent much time around him? He moves great. He moves like that [*makes sloth-type gesture*]. [*To Pennebaker*] You gotta cut that part of the film, man, 'cause I really like him. He moves like all good people. Like prize fighters.

JOHN: Johnny! "Big River"! "Big River"!

PENNEBAKER: [*Putting head around camera and beaming*] That's for Johnny, too!

DYLAN: Yeah, he's on film too. He's incredible.

JOHN: Quite a guy, huh?

DYLAN: Quite a guy, John. Oh man, you shoulda been around last night, John. Today's a drag.

JOHN: Oh really, Bob?

DYLAN: Haha! I wish I could talk English, man.

JOHN: Me too, Bobby.

In the afternoon, Pennebaker arranged a private showing of *Don't Look Back*, the startling black-and-white documentary he'd shot on Dylan's previous British tour. He had an answer print with him hoping to be able to show it at the Festival de Cannes. Subsequently deemed a classic of its genre and a penetrating portrait of Dylan at his most powerful and enigmatic, it had not yet been seen by the public and wouldn't be released for another year. In a screening room in the bowels of the Mayfair Hotel the four Beatles watched the ninety-six-minute film.

According to Pennebaker, the black-and-white film—shot with handheld cameras, that had no narration, and where the director was merely a fly on the wall—confused John and Paul. Because of their own experience with film they were expecting something more slick, linear, and smartly packaged. "They thought of it as Dylan's home movie," Pennebaker recalls. "I don't think they took it very seriously." George, on the other hand, was totally impressed and told the director that he understood what he was doing. He said, "That's a real movie, isn't it?" Pennebaker agreed with him. "No," George continued, "I mean that's a movie that could be shown in theatres, right?" Pennebaker said, "Well, I hope so. It hasn't happened yet but that's the idea."

Road fever was affecting Dylan, just as it had affected John, but whereas the expectations foisted on the Beatles were dispersed among four people, Dylan had to take the full weight of his alone. He coped by taking drugs, cutting himself off from those not his immediate family or entourage, and traveling with Bobby Neuwirth, who acted as his companion, protector, and court jester. Significantly, the second Albert Hall concert would be Dylan's last tour date for eight years. Like Brian Wilson before him and the Beatles after, he would leave the stage to focus on the business of making and recording songs.

The Beatles were at his final date, along with Cynthia, Jane, Pattie, Maureen, Tony Bramwell, and friends, all of them occupying one of the venue's prestigious private boxes. Dylan was at his glorious height as a Byronic rock poet—his skinny body wrapped in the latest mod clothes, his hair billowing out in a mass of curls, and an electric guitar in his hands. Yet, despite having reached this peak, his performance was still mired in controversy. The fans who had discovered him as a scrawny folkie singing starkly realistic songs in defense of the poor, oppressed, and forgotten people of America were perplexed by his adoption of what they thought of as rock 'n' roll–style music and lyrics as obscure as those of T. S. Eliot or the nineteenth-century French symbolist poets. He was now loud *and* difficult.

The first half of the show was played acoustically, and his hardcore fans approved. He played "4th Time Around" from the upcoming *Blonde on Blonde*, and John was left uncertain as to whether it was meant as an affectionate tribute or a vicious parody. The punch line about not asking for anyone's "crutch" sounded to some like a dig, implying that John was getting support by imitating Dylan's style of writing. "I didn't like it," John commented in 1968 to *Rolling Stone* writer Jonathan Cott when asked what he felt when he first heard the song. "I was very paranoid. I just didn't like what I felt I was feeling. I thought it was an out-and-out skit, but it wasn't. It was great. I mean, he wasn't playing any tricks on me."

When Dylan returned after the intermission accompanied by

Robbie Robertson on electric guitar, Rick Danko on bass, Richard Manuel on piano, Garth Hudson on organ, and Mickey Jones on drums, there were boos, heckles, and walk-outs. His devotees thought he had betrayed them by abandoning a standard of authenticity that they had bought into. Rock 'n' roll still had the stigma of being "commercial" music aimed at nonreflective teenagers. Dylan, understandably, felt dispirited and weary at this reaction. If his own devotees couldn't understand his choices, who could?

After the concert the four Beatles and their partners along with Tony Bramwell accompanied Dylan to the Mayfair Hotel, where he talked with them all night in his suite. Bob Johnston, who had produced *Blonde on Blonde,* believed that it was a significant moment for the group. He would say, "When the Beatles left his room, they weren't the Beatles anymore. They were John Lennon, George Harrison, Paul McCartney and Ringo Starr, in terms of how they thought about themselves. They were different people. It went on from there."

To D. A. Pennebaker, though, it was an awkward encounter, not much of an advance on Paul's earlier meeting. The Beatles, he felt, were easy to talk to individually, but together they relied on a style of banter built up over years of being in close proximity to each other that was superficial yet powerful enough to keep outsiders at a distance. "When all four of them were together they had this conversational attack mode that they used on anyone who was not part of that group," Pennebaker told me. "It wasn't very interesting conversation and Dylan watched it but was not drawn into it much."

Later in the year John spoke about Dylan's Albert Hall show in an unpublished interview with *Datebook* editor Art Unger as they flew between concerts in America. "They wrote about it the next day saying they were all booing [Dylan]," he said.

Well, about four people booed when the group came on. He shut them up quick enough and the rest of the audience was saying "shut up," too.

He just said, "This is American music. Some of you may have heard it before." He just told them what he was doing and it was a great concert. He went down great. They just wrote rubbish because he won't see the press. He's fed up with being asked the same [questions]. He doesn't have to answer those inane questions. . . . He doesn't want to, and he never will.

Overhearing the conversation, George chimed in: "Dylan is so good that the average listener doesn't get it because he goes right over their heads, and they put it down. They don't realise that he's going over their heads so they think he's writing rubbish and sending them up. But he's not. Bob Dylan just says more things in one song than I could say in ten years."

JUNE

This year we've got more boys in the audience
which is good because usually girls start the
crazes.
–RINGO, 1966

It had been just over a year since George first picked up a sitar on the set of *Help!,* and during that period his interest in the instrument had steadily grown. He listened to ragas at home, had been taught the rudiments of playing by a teacher in London, and was now aware that a full appreciation of the music of India would only come when he'd learned the fundamentals of the Hindu religion.

At first George knew only of sitar music in general. It was David Crosby of the Byrds who in the summer of 1965 introduced him to Shankar's music in particular. Crosby had been given a Shankar LP by Jim Dickson, manager of the Byrds, who had previously worked as a producer for World-Pacific Records in Hollywood, a small label that specialized in albums for connoisseurs of all things hip. World-Pacific recorded not only jazz musicians such as Chet Baker, Art Pepper, Gerry Mulligan, and Gil Evans but also the blues singers Sonny Terry and Brownie McGhee and the eccentric monologist Lord Buckley. In 1959, the company put out the first LP Shankar recorded in America and later followed it up with two more.

Crosby played the LPs for George when the Beatles hung out with him and fellow Byrd Roger McGuinn while in Los Angeles. George told Maureen Cleave that he'd become so enamored of the music that before going to sleep at night he fantasized about what it would be like to actually be inside one of Shankar's sitars.

Early in June 1966 he finally met his new hero. Shankar had been appearing regularly in Britain for the past decade. He had played to a full house at the Royal Festival Hall in 1958 with Alla Rakha on tabla and Prodyot Sen on tambura and five years later had been a sensation at the Edinburgh Festival. George had first seen him in London on November 7, 1965, just two weeks after recording "Norwegian Wood" and meeting the Angadis for the first time. This time Shankar was in England to appear with violinist Yehudi Menuhin at the Bath Musical Festival for an experimental concert combining the classical music of East and West.

Prior to this, on June 1, he returned to the Royal Festival Hall accompanied by Alla Rakha, and George and Pattie went to see him. The Angadis then invited the Harrisons to a meal at their house, where George met the sitarist for the first time. "I was there when they met," says the Angadis' daughter Chandrika. "George was a bit awkward and was resting his foot on the sitar case. Ravi Shankar said the first lesson was to take his foot off. They then both played a little in our sitting room."

Shankar had heard of the Beatles but knew nothing of their music. "I'd vaguely heard the name of Beatles but I didn't know what it stood for or what was their popularity," he told me in 1982. "I hadn't heard a single LP or song. But it was nice to see George's humility and to know that he wanted to learn. I said he should come to India, and eventually he did."

When journalists asked him what he thought about the Beatles' use of Indian instruments, he would only say that if they were serious about it, they should make sure they learned to play them properly. This had been interpreted as a criticism, but he had meant only that anyone attempting to master the sitar needed to invest the necessary time. It wasn't an instrument to be toyed with.

George was aware of his inadequacies. He'd only had a handful of lessons, from a student of one of Shankar's students. He was now embarrassed at the rudimentary nature of his playing on "Norwegian Wood" but had an appetite to learn more. He was willing to put aside time for practice and also wanted to learn more about Indian culture and beliefs.

Shankar found him a "sweet, straightforward young man" and was impressed by his questions. He told him that learning the sitar was like learning classical music on the violin or cello. It wasn't simply a matter of how to hold the instrument and play a few chords. It wasn't as easy as knowing enough about a guitar to master a few rock 'n' roll songs.

"It's not only the technical mastery of the sitar," said Shankar. "You have to learn the whole complex system of music properly and get deeply into it. Moreover, it's not just fixed pieces that you play— there is improvisation. And those improvisations are not just 'letting yourself go,' as in jazz—you have to adhere to the discipline of the ragas and the talas without any notation in front of you. Being an oral tradition, it takes more years."

George was in awe of Shankar. As a Beatle he'd met many famous, powerful, and influential people, but he was aware of depths of creativity and spirituality in this musician that he'd never come across before. "He was the first person who impressed me in a way that was beyond just being a famous celebrity," he later said. "Ravi was my link to the Vedic world. Ravi plugged me into the whole of reality. Elvis impressed me when I was a kid, and impressed me when I met him . . . but you couldn't later on go round to him and say, 'Elvis. What's happening with the universe?'"

More than anything, George wanted Shankar to become his

mentor. Shankar must have been aware of this, which is why he stressed the toil and commitment required. He asked George if he could give "time and total energy" to work hard on it. Mindful of the Beatles' calendar, George could only say he would try his best.

During this stay in England Shankar recorded the album *West Meets East* with Yehudi Menuhin (at EMI), visited George and Pattie at home in Esher, and gave George lessons at the South Kensington apartment of folksinger and artist Rory McEwen. He showed George how to hold the sitar and told him the traditional names of the various notes, and George made a promise to spend extended time with him in India as soon as he was free of Beatles commitments.

Shankar was a cultured man who, besides having an extensive knowledge of his own country's culture, had been exposed to the best of Western classical music, dance, film, painting, and theatre. He was also open to cross-fertilization that didn't compromise the purity of sitar music. Yet despite mixing with the bohemian and avant-garde of Europe and America, Shankar didn't approve of drug use. He resisted the overtures of those who thought he'd be an even greater musician if he took LSD and complained about cannabis use when his UK promoter, Basil Douglas, booked him into folk clubs. It particularly irked him that some longhairs would trip out at his concerts as if there was some connection between Eastern classical music and hallucinogens. He found this disrespectful to the music.

The Beatles helped make sitar music voguish in pop circles, but it had already been popular among Beats in the 1950s and was now with hippies. Allen Ginsberg had traveled to India in 1962 and came back chanting the Hare Krishna mantra. Hip musicians like folkie Davey Graham incorporated Eastern scales into their guitar playing. The London-based Indian violinist John Mayer had formed a group called Indo-Jazz Fusions with Jamaican sax player Joe Harriott. The "hippie trail" favored by seekers of enlightenment from North America and Europe went overland to India. There were hippie hangouts in places like Rishikesh, Goa, Puri, and Benares (now Varanasi).

The week that Shankar arrived in London the Rolling Stones were poised to take the top spot on the singles charts with "Paint It Black," on which Brian Jones played sitar, and the Yardbirds had entered the charts with "Over Under Sideways Down," a track on which Jeff Beck used eastern modes of tuning for his guitar. *Melody Maker* had recently run a feature titled "How About a Tune on the Old Sitar?" that investigated the trend with a lot of information gleaned from guitarist (and sitar owner) Jimmy Page.

On June 8, Shankar played a short raga on BBC TV's new weekly pop magazine show *A Whole Scene Going* and then answered questions from studio guests, including members of the Yardbirds. Singer Keith Relf asked him what he thought of English and American pop groups using sitars. "Well, I'm afraid this sudden interest might go away suddenly," Shankar told him. "But on the other hand it will make me very happy if I see that some people take true interest and learn properly because after playing the sitar for thirty-six years I have seen that one has to give some time to it." Someone else asked how long he thought the "gimmick" would last. "It has always been the case with pop that new sounds come and go," he said. "It could be the Japanese koto tomorrow."

The same day that George went to the Ravi Shankar concert at the Royal Festival Hall, *NME* ran a back page ad for "Paperback Writer" and "Rain" that used a black-and-white copy of Robert Whitaker's "butcher" photographs. There was no clue as to what connection—if any—there was between the image of the Beatles with huge cuts of meat and the songs. The only information was that the single was to be released on June 10. On June 11 *Disc and Music Echo* used a color photo from the same session on its front cover under the headline "Beatles; What a Carve-Up!"

Meanwhile, in America, the image was being used for *Yesterday and Today*, the filler LP with tracks from *Help!*, *Rubber Soul*, and the current sessions that was being prepared for June 15 release. Capitol's art director George Osaki liked the butcher shot, and so the

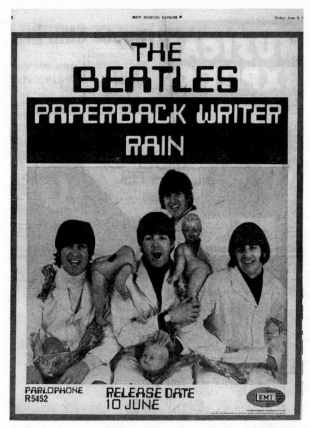

A UK advertisement for the single "Paperback Writer" on the back cover of *NME*, June 3, 1966.

sleeves went into production for a run of a million copies for the mono format and two hundred thousand for the stereo. Sixty thousand advance copies were shipped to newspapers, magazines, radio, TV, and Capitol Records' promotional teams, who in turn were presenting the new product to key retailers. Alan Livingston, then president of Capitol, had blanched when he first saw the chosen image and called Brian Epstein, but was told that the Beatles were insistent that it be used.

Then the retailers refused to handle it. They found it brutal and offensive, even though the bloodstains on the Beatles' coats had been airbrushed out. Livingston got back to Epstein, who, after pressure, allowed Capitol to use an earlier photo by Whitaker taken at the NEMS office showing the group posed inoffensively around a steamer trunk. By now so many copies of the album with the butcher photograph had been pressed that the only way of salvaging the existing copies was to keep the vinyl but destroy the cardboard and wait for new covers to be printed. Operation Retrieve—which would cost Capitol over two hundred thousand dollars—started on June 10 with the pressing plants recalling all copies. Workers in New York spent a weekend stripping ninety thousand discs out of their sleeves. Queens Litho, where printing took place, destroyed a hundred thousand unused copies. At the Scranton and Los Angeles facilities they found a way of cutting costs by pasting the newly approved image over the old one. In future years when careful collectors were able to steam off the replacement image, these preserved "butcher covers" would become valuable items on the pop memorabilia market.

A release was put out by Capitol press officer Ron Tepper telling reviewers about the new cover and asking them to disregard their "butcher" copies (and, if possible, return them). Livingston was quoted as saying, "The original cover, created in England, was intended as 'pop art' satire. However, a sampling of public opinion in the United States indicates that the cover design is subject to misinterpretation. For this reason, and to avoid any possible controversy or undeserved harm to the Beatles' image or reputation, Capitol has chosen to withdraw the LP and substitute a more generally acceptable design."

But for the Beatles the only LP occupying their attention was the one they were making. George's "I Want to Tell You" was recorded on June 2, Paul's vocal was added to "Eleanor Rigby" on the sixth, and on the eighth they started on the newly written "Good Day Sunshine," a typically buoyant and optimistic song written mainly by Paul on one of his writing visits to Weybridge. Although ostensibly about the joys of good weather, it had all the hallmarks of being as much about the benefits of sunlight as "I'm Only Sleeping" is about restorative rest. In the context of June 1966 it sounded like a song about being mellowed out on dope and the resultant feeling of well-being.

An immediate source of musical inspiration was "Daydream" by the Lovin' Spoonful, then at No. 15 on the Top 20, a carefree song about walking in the sun and falling about on a new-mown lawn. Paul, John, and George had seen the Lovin' Spoonful perform at the Marquee Club in London seven weeks earlier and enjoyed their gentle electrified folk. Another inspiration could have been "Sunny Afternoon" by the Kinks, which had just charted.

The next song that Paul wrote at John's house was "Here, There and Everywhere," the recording of which started on June 14. It was in part influenced by the recent exposure to *Pet Sounds*, as Paul explained to American writer David Leaf in 1990.

> It's actually just the introduction that's influenced [by the Beach Boys]. John and I used to be interested in what the old fashioned writers used to call the verse, which we nowadays would call the intro . . . this whole preamble to a song, and I wanted to have one of those on the front of "Here, There and Everywhere." John and I were quite into those from the old-fashioned songs that used to have them, and in putting that [sings "To lead a better life"] on the front of "Here, There and Everywhere," we were doing harmonies, and the inspiration for that was the Beach Boys. We had that in our minds during the introduction to "Here, There and Everywhere."

The day after starting "Here, There and Everywhere" John went to Dolly's in the evening with Mick Jagger and his girlfriend, Chrissie Shrimpton. Later the trio was joined by John Phillips and Denny Doherty from the Mamas and the Papas, who were in London to promote their new single "Monday Monday." Like the Byrds, the members of the Mamas and the Papas had been part of the American

The Mamas and the Papas: Denny Doherty, John Phillips, Michelle Phillips, Cass Elliot.

folk scene until the music of the Beatles transformed their vision. As a group they felt the kinship between folk melodies and the tunes from Liverpool and switched to a louder sound and electric guitars, scoring a huge hit with "California Dreamin'."

They were identified with the emerging counterculture that had developed out of California's 1950s hipster culture. Beat generation writers, comedians from the satire boom, civil rights, pot, LSD, and the peace movement had affected them. The Papas wore facial hair and suede boots. The Mamas wore kaftans and skinny jeans. (A year later Phillips would cowrite "San Francisco [Be Sure to Wear Flowers in Your Hair]" with his friend Scott McKenzie, who would go on to have a huge international hit with the song. It was designed to publicize the imminent Monterey International Pop Music Festival, the first of the iconic open-air music festivals.)

Phillips asked John where he and Doherty could get marijuana. John made a call, and half an hour later Paul came down from St John's Wood with a small bag of grass. They spoke openly to Phillips about being introduced to the drug Eskatrol while in America in 1964. This was an amphetamine-based weight-loss drug manufactured by SmithKline and French in America but unavailable in the UK. John claimed that he and Paul had been writing songs while high on it ever since. Phillips admitted to the same practice.

Cass Elliot had stayed behind in the Montagu Square apartment that the group was renting, but, knowing that she was such a huge Lennon fan, Phillips invited John and Paul back to meet her when they left the club in the early hours of June 16. When they reached the apartment, Cass was asleep and was awoken by John leaning over and kissing her gently on the cheek. She sat up, got out of bed, and danced around the room with him out of sheer joy.

John and Paul stayed up all night listening to music, playing songs on the apartment's out-of-tune grand piano, and smoking dope. They didn't leave until eight in the morning. "[John] was charming, courteous and intelligent," Cass told a journalist later that day. "He was witty, amusing and entertaining. It was like everything had been motivating towards that meeting last week." She invited the Beatles to stay at her home next time they were in LA.

The final track of the album was John's "She Said She Said," recorded on June 21. It was at the last stage that the group realized that the record was much too short. The last three LPs were on average around thirty-four minutes in length. This LP, so far, ran to only just over thirty-two minutes. "Paperback Writer" and "Rain" could have added bulk, but including them went against their principle of not adding previously released singles to their UK LPs. Five days previously John had remarked to a journalist, "I've got something going [for the LP's final number]. About three lines so far."

He was referring to "She Said She Said," a song based on John's 1965 LSD trip in the company of George, Roger McGuinn, David Crosby, and actor Peter Fonda at the Beatles' rented home in Benedict Canyon, Los Angeles. Both John and George were hoping for a better experience than they'd had with the dentist in London now that they knew more about the drug and were taking it voluntarily. However, early on in his trip George developed a fear that he was dying, and Fonda attempted to calm him down. He did so by recounting the story of how he had accidentally shot himself in the stomach as a ten-year-old and how his heart had stopped three times while in the operating room because of the severe loss of blood. He drove home what he hoped would be a reassuring message by saying, "It's all right, George. I know what it's like to be dead." John overheard the remarks and became upset. In his altered state he didn't want to hear about guns, bullets, blood, and death. "You're making me feel I've never been born," he told Fonda.

This bizarre drug-induced conversation became the foundation of a song that John put to the side as not going anywhere but then salvaged by joining to another abandoned lyric exploring the joys of childhood innocence. "When I was a boy," he wrote, "everything was right." This wasn't just nostalgia. He believed the mind of a child to be more aware and less corrupted than that of an adult. He also claimed to have had uninvited experiences of rapture at an early age that he hadn't understood at the time but which he later recognized in the writings of men like Thomas De Quincey (*Confessions of an English Opium-Eater*) and Lewis Carroll (*Alice's Adventures in Wonderland*). Through poetry anthologies that Aunt Mimi collected he may have been aware of the popular Victorian poem "I Remember, I Remember" by the English poet Thomas Hood, which recounted pleasant childhood memories before concluding:

It was a childish ignorance
But now 'tis little joy
To know I'm farther off from Heaven
Than when I was a boy.

The splicing of separate unfinished songs in this way was a new departure that echoed the practice of electronic composers who connected material from previously unrelated sources to create new work. It was something the Beatles would pursue in later songs such as "Baby You're a Rich Man," "A Day in the Life," "Happiness Is a Warm Gun," and the medley on *Abbey Road*, which often blended a fragment of a song started by John with a fragment of something started by Paul.

"She Said She Said" was recorded and mixed in nine hours, the only song on the LP to be completed in a single session. It appears that George played the bass after Paul stormed out following an argument with John. "I think it was one of the only Beatle records I never played on," said Paul. "I think we'd had a barney [a noisy quarrel] or something." John saw the incident as giving him the opportunity to complete the track in the way he saw fit without Paul's suggestions. In January 1969, when recording the *Let It Be* LP, John was again at loggerheads with Paul, who he accused of taking over the project. In one revealing exchange, captured by the film team covering the whole event on their soundtrack, John said that he'd found that the only way to record something to his satisfaction was to do it alone. Speaking to Paul, he then referred back to this session in 1966, saying, "The only regret I have about past numbers is because I've allowed you to take it somewhere I didn't want it to go. Then my only chance was to let George take over because I knew he'd take it. Like on 'She Said She Said.'"

During the recent recording musician and artist Klaus Voormann had been preparing an album cover, the Beatles having rejected a montage of black-and-white images put together by Robert Freeman, who'd done all their UK LP covers since *With the Beatles* in 1963. They were looking for something different and more in keeping with their new music. Voormann had met the Beatles in Hamburg in 1960 when he was studying to be a commercial artist and they were struggling musicians playing in clubs. He, his girlfriend Astrid Kirchherr, and photographer Jurgen Vollmer were an important link between the Beatles and European culture. Up to this point they had mostly been influenced by British and American culture, but now, through recommendations from these young "exis" (existentialists), they connected with postwar French and German photography, films, art, clothing, and literature. The Beatles copied the long swept-forward hairstyle of Vollmer and Voormann and also their black turtlenecks, and out of this developed the early Beatles style as captured on the cover of their second UK LP, *With the Beatles*.

Voormann had left Germany for Britain, where he played bass in Paddy, Klaus, and Gibson alongside two Liverpool musicians (Paddy Chambers and Gibson Kemp) he'd met in Hamburg. Initially managed by Tony Stratton-Smith (who later founded the independent record label Charisma), the trio then became part of Epstein's roster. When John approached Voormann about the cover design, he had just quit the group and was about to replace Jack Bruce in Manfred Mann. (Bruce was forming Cream with drummer Ginger Baker and guitarist Eric Clapton.) Because of this transition he almost passed on the offer but eventually accepted.

Voormann went to EMI Studios, where the Beatles played him some already mixed tracks, including "Tomorrow Never Knows," and he was so impressed with the direction they were going in that he determined to produce a design that was as adventurous pictorially as this track was musically. All he asked of them was that they collect some old images of themselves that he could incorporate into his artwork.

While Voormann worked on his preliminary drawings John, Paul, and Pete Shotton trawled through a pile of photographs, the majority of which happened to be images from 1964 and 1965 by the recently rejected Robert Freeman, and snipped out images that they then glued onto a paper sheet. Voormann transferred these pictures to four heads he had drawn of the Beatles so that the photos appeared to be emerging from the heads and crawling out of the hair.

Voormann's style of black-ink line drawing that contrasted fine detail (the strands of hair) with white space (the faces) was strongly

One of Klaus Voormann's preliminary sketches for what would become the cover art of *Revolver.*

influenced by the Victorian artist Aubrey Beardsley, who was associated with fin de siècle decadence, aestheticism, and art nouveau. King's Road boutique designers were enamored of Beardsley's erotic illustrations and doomed romanticism (he died at twenty-five), and the most comprehensive exhibition of his work ever mounted opened on May 20 at the Victoria and Albert Museum, where it would run for four months. (A portrait of Beardsley would turn up in 1967 on the cover of *Sgt. Pepper's Lonely Hearts Club Band,* and Paul collected some of his original work.)

It was very different than any other LP cover on the pop market at the time. The Beatles didn't look pretty, and there were virtually no smiles. The eyes were expressionless. The name of the group appeared on the spine and the back, but not on the front. Like Goya's eighteenth-century illustration *The Sleep of Reason Produces Monsters,* it was as though John, Paul, George, and Ringo were in another state of consciousness that was causing these earlier versions of them to escape. (Peter Blake's cover art for *Sgt. Pepper* would also contrast old and new Beatles by standing them next to wax models of themselves as they were in 1964 from Madame Tussauds.)

Voormann took the completed art to a meeting at EMI with George Martin and Judy Lockhart-Smith (now engaged to Martin following his divorce from his first wife in February), Brian Epstein, and the four Beatles. He stood the page on top of a steel filing cabinet and awaited their response. Initially there was a silence that for a moment he feared was a mixture of shock and disapproval, but then the plaudits started coming. They all felt it was a perfect visual complement to the music, even though he hadn't been given a title to work with. Brian Epstein even cried, perhaps out of relief after the debacle of the "butcher" cover. "Klaus, this is exactly what we needed," he said. "I was worried that this whole thing might not work. But now I know that his cover, this LP, will work. Thank you."

Over the past few months Epstein had been preoccupied not only with ensuring that the single and LP were prepared and on schedule but also with arranging the concerts in Germany, Japan, the Philippines, and America (the Philippines having being added at a late stage). On June 16 the Beatles had the necessary inoculations for travel and then performed on BBC TV's *Top of the Pops* in what would be their last live TV appearance other than the satellite linkup for "All You Need Is Love" in 1967.

During a break at the BBC Television Centre in White City, London, *NME*'s Alan Smith had a chance to interview Paul, albeit in a restroom, the only place where they could be sure to be safe from the fans. He spoke about the new LP: "I suppose there are some who won't like it," he admitted, "but if we tried to please everyone we'd never get started. As it is, we try to be as varied as possible."

"There's no real weird stuff. . . . Anyway, I've stopped regarding things as way-out any more. There'll always be people around like that Andy Warhol in the States, the bloke who makes great long films of people just sleeping. Nothing is weird any more. We sit down and write, or go into the recording studios, and we just see what comes up. I'm learning all the time. You do, if you keep your eyes open. I find life is an education."

He then spoke about "Tomorrow Never Knows," claiming responsibility for the "electronic effects." "We did it because I, for one, am sick of doing sounds that people can claim to have heard before. Anyway, we played it to the Stones and The Who, and they visibly sat up and were interested. We also played it to Cilla [Black]—who just laughed!"

The same day, in the same place, Alan Walsh from *Melody Maker* managed to corner George, who told Walsh how much he'd been changing since 1964. "I've increasingly become aware that there are other things in life than being a Beatle," he said. "I'm not fed up at being a Beatle, far from it, but I am fed up with all the trivial things that go with it. For instance, at one time you could never go to the pictures or out for a meal without some idiot taking a photograph of you. I suppose I have consciously been backing away from this side of Beatle life. In fact, it wouldn't worry me at all if nobody ever took my photograph again."

He wanted to talk about music and the progress they were making.

In the Beatles, we're fortunate because each of us has something different going. I've been going for the Indian thing in a big way, John and Paul have their own thing going, and there are also things Ringo likes. Paul likes classical music— at least, I think he does from what I've been able to make out watching him—and he contributes the things like "Yesterday," and "Michelle," while John does things like "Norwegian Wood." This means there's no single influence, such as there is with Brian Wilson in the Beach Boys. We have a wide range of things available to us, which makes us so exciting.

Although they'd appeared on *Top of the Pops* before, their performances had always been prerecorded. This was the first, and last, time that they would appear in person on the TV show that was integral to the life of every British pop fan, with its latest news of what was climbing or slipping on the charts, what was tipped for the top, and, most of all, what had reached No. 1. The Beatles, wearing dark suits over open-necked white shirts, mimed along to "Paperback Writer" and "Rain." Their co-performers on the show were Gene Pitney, Herman's Hermits, and the Hollies. Previous appearances by the Yardbirds ("Over Under Sideways Down"), the Kinks ("Sunny Afternoon"), and Cilla Black ("Don't Answer Me") were replayed, along with a video the Beach Boys had made to accompany "Sloop John B" and a troupe called the Gojos dancing to Frank Sinatra's latest hit, "Strangers in the Night." The hosts were Samantha Juste, who later married Monkees drummer Mickey Dolenz, and DJ Pete Murray.

It was a shock when "Paperback Writer" didn't immediately take the top spot on the charts. It was held off by Sinatra's single and had to wait until the following week to make it to No. 1. This would have been a supreme accomplishment for anyone else, but the Beatles weren't expected to have to wait, and No. 2 on the charts wasn't good enough. Again questions were being asked in the press. Was their immersion in more serious art forms taking the pop out of their music? Had "Paperback Writer" been a slower seller because it wasn't about love? Patrick Doncaster, the show business correspondent for the *Daily Mirror,* commented that neither "Paperback Writer" nor "Rain" had "any romance about them. Gone, gone, gone are the days of luv, luv, luv." When Doncaster quizzed Paul about the new direction, Paul stuck to his convictions. "It's not our best single by any means," he said, "but we're very satisfied with it. We are experimenting all the time with our songs. We cannot stay in the same rut. We have got to move forward. . . . Our new LP is going to shock a lot of people."

June 17 was the day that Paul closed the deal on the 183-acre High Park Farm on the Scottish peninsula of Kintyre that would become his beloved getaway when times got tough. He had bought it on the recommendation of his accountant, who told him that he needed to invest some of his wealth. It was remote, unmodernized, and exposed to the winds and rains that whipped across the Irish Sea. He'd always been a nature lover, and so he liked the fact that the surrounding fields had sheep and deer, while the hedgerows and trees were home to thirty-seven different types of birds. The next year, when visiting with Jane for a weekend, he told a photographer who tracked them down, "This is one of the quietest places on earth. The scenery is wonderful. We can relax and get away from it all."

On June 21, the group attended a "pre-opening celebration" at the latest London discotheque, Sibylla's, on Swallow Street, close to Piccadilly Circus, in which George had a 10 percent shareholder stake (he hadn't invested money but was given the shares because of the obvious publicity value he brought to the venture). Other shareholders included photographer and advertising man Terry Howard, copywriter Kevin Macdonald (a grandnephew of *Daily Mail* owner Lord Northcliffe), DJ Alan Freeman, champion National Hunt jockey Sir William Pigott-Brown, and property developer Bruce Higham. The interiors were created by soon-to-be fashionable designer David Mlinaric, and the guest list, which also included Mick Jagger, Keith Richards, Brian Jones, Julie Christie, Michael Caine, David Bailey, Michael Rainey, Mary Quant, Celia Hammond, Jacqueline Bissett, John Barry, Jane Birkin, and Jane Ormsby-Gore, epitomized the cool scene so perfectly that it was later published in *Queen* magazine under the heading "How Many Swinging Londoners Do You Know?"

There were also connections with the darker side of London's nightlife. The club's manager, Laurie O'Leary, was a friend of the notorious Kray twins, Reggie and Ronnie (he'd previously run their club Esmerelda's in Knightsbridge for them), and groups hired to play at Sibylla's were contracted by an agency run by their elder brother, Charlie Kray. All three Krays ran a gang based in London's East End that earned money through robberies, hijackings, and protection rackets, but, partly because of their connections with show business, they were glamorized and were regarded as being as much a part of the swinging scene as pop stars, models, and the aristocracy. They were photographed by David Bailey and feted by members of the House of Lords, and they socialized with movie stars and stage entertainers. In his autobiography, Ronnie Kray, eventually sent away for killing fellow gangster George Cornell at the Blind Beggar pub in March 1966, wrote, "They were the best years of our lives. They called them the swinging sixties. The Beatles and the Rolling Stones were rulers of pop, Carnaby Street ruled the fashion world . . . and me and my brother ruled London. We were fucking untouchable."

Thus it was that gangland characters and gay hustlers mingled in the new "classless" society with pop stars, photographers, disc jockeys, wealthy aristocrats, and ruthless landlords. Sibylla's was named after former debutante Sibylla Edmonstone, raised at Duntreath Castle in Scotland as the daughter of a baronet, yet Kray associate Freddie Foreman could say of it in his autobiography, *Brown Bread Fred,* "Although [Sibylla's] was an exclusive club with a restricted membership of only 800, I was always welcome at the club."

When shareholder Kevin Macdonald was interviewed by Jonathan Aitken in 1966 for his book *The New Meteors,* he said,

Sibylla's is the meeting ground for the new aristocracy of Britain, and by the new aristocracy I mean the current young meritocracy of style, taste and sensitivity. We've got everyone here: the top creative people; the top exporters; the top brains; the top artists; the top social people. And we've got the best of the PYPs [pretty young people]. We're completely classless. We are completely integrated. We dig the spades man. . . . We've married up the hairy brigade—that's the East End kids like photographers and artists—with the smooth brigade, the debs, the aristos, the Guards officers. The result is just fantastic. It's the greatest, happiest, most swinging ball of the century, and I started it!

Writing in the *Daily Express* earlier in the year, the Scottish aristocrat Robin Douglas-Home had argued that swinging Londoners were rapidly becoming Britain's new cultural elite. "The 'privileged class' today consists of actors, pop singers, hairdressers, and models," he wrote. "Look what happens when Richard Burton and Elizabeth Taylor arrive at London Airport or when the Beatles leave London airport. They get special treatment of the kind that would never be granted to, for instance, the Duke of Marlborough, whose main privilege nowadays is that he has to pay more taxes than most. If a 14th Earl with a grouse moor and George Harrison with Patti [*sic*] Boyd walked together into a restaurant and there was only one table left, who would be given the table? Well—if the head waiter had any sense—obviously George and Patti."

The morning after the party at Sibylla's, the Beatles took an 11:05 BEA flight from London to Munich on the first leg of their world tour. It was the first time they'd played in the country since 1963 and their first tour date since Cardiff in December 1965. The tour was organized by Karl Buchmann Productions in conjunction with the German teenage magazine *Bravo*. Because the Beatles didn't want to appear in massive arenas, they were booked into venues with capacities of fewer than eight thousand seats, and it was accepted from the start that *Bravo* would be subsidizing the tour rather than making money, because the income from 34,200 tickets (the total sold) didn't cover the cost of mounting the tour.

After arriving at just before 1:00 p.m. the Beatles were picked up in a white Mercedes and taken to the 125-year-old Hotel Bayerischer Hof on Promenadeplatz, where in their fifth-floor suite they immediately set about thinking of a title for the new LP with Brian Epstein, Neil Aspinall, Mal Evans, and Tony Barrow. The tracks were played on a small reel-to-reel tape recorder that George had brought with him. "Magic Circle" suggested Paul. "Four Sides to the Circle" responded John. Ringo humorously suggested "After Geography," a play on the Stones' recent LP title *Aftermath*. Nothing was decided.

At 4:10 on their way down to the hotel's nightclub the elevator stuck between floors, making them late for their press conference, which didn't start until 4:20. Journalists treated them as if they were still children. Did they like Munich? Did they speak German? What sport would they choose if they could participate in the recently announced 1972 Olympic Games in Munich?

The two concerts, held the next day at the 3,500-seat Circus Krone at 5:15 and 9:00, consisted of eleven songs, none of them from the forthcoming LP. The only difference from the set list of their winter tour of the UK in 1965 was the replacing of "Act Naturally" with "I Wanna Be Your Man," "We Can Work It Out" with "Paperback Writer," and "Help!" with Chuck Berry's "Rock and Roll Music." Instead of dark suits over black turtlenecks they were now all wearing the Hung On You bottle-green suits with silk faced lapels and high-collared crepe shirts in lime and yellow. Their supporting acts were the German group the Rattles, Peter and Gordon, and London R & B group Cliff Bennett and the Rebel Rousers.

Their performances weren't great. They were underrehearsed and often out of tune, and occasionally forgot the lyrics. Not that any of this mattered, because they were competing against a wall of sound that was louder than anything they could generate. What was important to the fans wasn't what they sang, or how they sang it, but that they were there in the flesh. The opening chords of each song announced what was about to be played, and then the screaming started and lasted until the song ended.

The difference on this tour was that the ferocity of the fans was met with equal ferocity from the police. For the first time the Beatles and their entourage witnessed fans being manhandled and beaten by men in trench coats carrying long clubs. They didn't like what they saw but were powerless to intervene.

Sean O'Mahony, publisher and editor (as "Johnny Dean") of the *Beatles Book Monthly,* asked Paul if he felt that playing so many old songs rather than the ones they'd just completed was a retrograde step. "They're a step back in time," he agreed. "As for performing [the new material] on stage—I don't think our audience would like it. That, of course, depends on where we're playing. Germany cried out for the old hits." They were still playing primarily old hits and tracks from *With the Beatles, Beatles For Sale,* and *Help!* There was one track ("Nowhere Man") from *Rubber Soul.* "I can't play any of *Rubber Soul,*" John explained. "It's so unrehearsed. The only time I played any of the numbers on it was when I recorded it. I forget about songs. They're only valid for a certain time."

After the two shows there was a party to which a number of high-class escorts from the area were invited. Sue Mautner, from the *Beatles Book Monthly,* was the only journalist present. The girls seemed so beautiful to her that she assumed they were models, and she couldn't understand why they all disappeared at midnight. When she asked George, he just laughed. "The hotel doesn't allow those sorts of girls in guests' rooms after midnight," he explained to her.

On June 25 the Beatles were transported the four hundred miles from Munich to Essen in northern Germany by a chartered train with carriages that had been designed for use by visiting heads of state (including Queen Elizabeth and Prince Philip in May 1965). Each Beatle had his own compartment with a marble bath and bed, and there was a central dining carriage offering such lunchtime delicacies as clear oxtail soup with vintage sherry, artichokes with Hollandaise sauce, and medallions of Hawaiian veal.

At Essen they played two concerts at the Grugahalle, between which they conducted a press conference. Again the questions were banal. What did they think of Essen? What did they think of the noise made by the crowds at beat music concerts? Did they play for love or money? What did they think of the Rhine River? The Beatles were clearly disgruntled with not being asked anything serious or anything about their musical or lyrical contributions. No one asked about the LP they'd just finished.

Q: What do you think about people who have written about you? Do you think they have intelligence or not?

GEORGE: We don't think . . .

JOHN: Some are intelligent, some are stupid. Some are silly, some are stupid. [It's] the same in any crowd. They're not all the same. Ein is clever. Ein is soft . . . [*Laughter*]

Q: What do you think of the questions you are getting asked here?

JOHN: They're a bit stupid. [*Laughter, applause, end of press conference*]

The concerts were memorable for the riotous behavior of the fans and the militaristic way in which the security police dealt with them. "Essen was frightening," recalls Sue Mautner. "Peter Brown saved me from being trampled to death. There was a stampede like I'd never seen. The police were like Nazis with long greatcoats and they used tear gas and vicious guard dogs. It was awful. People were trying to get away from them. They left their shoes behind in the panic."

After the second concert a limousine took the Beatles straight from the concert hall to the station, where they reboarded the train, which was now bound for Hamburg, an overnight journey of 230 miles. John was reading *A Thurber Carnival,* a collection of humorous pieces from the *New Yorker* by James Thurber, and nursing a sore throat by drinking lemon tea and sucking lozenges. Paul came up with another suggestion for the album title—"Pendulum"—and then, when no one responded positively to this, facetiously suggested "Rock 'n' Roll Hits of '66."

Their arrival in Hamburg was highly anticipated. It was the German audiences in Hamburg who'd spotted the group's potential and had nurtured their development from callow adolescent hobbyists to battle-hardened professionals. It was the Hamburg audiences' demand to be entertained, calmed down, excited, amused, and surprised that had forced John, Paul, George, Stuart Sutcliffe, and Pete Best to learn how to orchestrate a set and taught them what worked from a vast catalogue of rock 'n' roll standards, show tunes, ballads, and, eventually, their own self-written songs.

They arrived at Hamburg's main rail station at 6:00 a.m. on June 26 and were given a police escort to the Hotel Schloss in Tremsbüttel, a converted nineteenth-century palace eighteen miles north of the city. Once settled in, the group rested until their 2:45 pickup, again with a police escort, which got them to the Ernst-Merck-Halle at 3:45.

There were many old friends in the audience for the shows: Astrid Kirchherr, Stuart Sutcliffe's old girlfriend, who'd taken the first artistic portraits of the Beatles, with her boyfriend, Gibson Kemp; Bettina "Betty" Derlien, a waitress from the Star Club who'd been particularly close to John; Katharina "Kathia" Berger, an artist who met them at the Top Ten Club; the actress Evelyn Hamann; and Bert Kaempfert, the composer, producer, and arranger who'd first recorded the Beatles as the backing group for guitarist/vocalist Tony Sheridan in Hamburg in 1961. Coincidentally, Kaempfert was also the composer of "Strangers in the Night," the Frank Sinatra hit that had prevented "Paperback Writer" going straight to No. 1 on the UK charts. John greeted Kaempfert by singing him the opening lines of the Sinatra song.

Most of these old friends hadn't seen the Beatles perform since their last Hamburg club dates. Now they were on stage before 5,600 screaming fans with riot police on hand. Kirchherr handed John a collection of the letters he'd written to Stuart Sutcliffe after the Beatles returned to England. "A lot of ghosts materialised out of the woodwork," said George of the date, which seemed to stir as many bad memories for the Beatles as good ones. "There were people you didn't necessarily want to see again who had been your best friend one drunken Preludin [stimulant tablets] night back in 1960."

Between the two shows there was the last German press conference, one that clearly frustrated the group because of its banality.

Q: What do you think about your fans in Germany?

RINGO: They're good, you know. They're the same as everywhere else, only there's more boys in Germany.

Q: Do you believe your book [*A Spaniard in the Works*] is literature, or do you believe just for fun?

JOHN: It's both, isn't it? I mean, it doesn't have to be one or the other.

Q: Do you think it's GREAT literature like James Joyce?

JOHN: It's nothing to do with James Joyce, you know. I mean, you've been reading the wrong books and magazines. It's nothing to do with it. It's just a book, you know.

Q: Would Paul make music to go with your books?

JOHN: Well, I'll make it meself, if anybody's gonna do it.

PAUL: You're not really writing songs.

Q: What do you dream of when you sleep?

PAUL: The same as anyone dreams of. Standing in my underpants.

JOHN: What do you think we are? What do you dream of? [*Under his breath*] Fucking hell!

PAUL: We dream about the same things as everyone.

Q: Ringo, what do you dream?

RINGO: I just dream of everything like you do, you know. It's all the same.

JOHN: We're only the same as you, man, only we're rich. [*Laughter*]

While in the dressing room at Hamburg between shows a telegram was delivered to the Beatles that said PLEASE DO NOT FLY TO TOKYO. YOUR CAREER IS IN DANGER. It wasn't signed. Was it a friendly warning from someone who knew of a plot or a sinister threat from a plotter? Paul and Ringo shrugged it off. They were used to the behavior of cranks. But George took it more seriously. "It makes you think," he said after reading it. "We've got a lot of enemies as well as friends."

After the second show there had been a plan for the Beatles to visit their old haunts in the St. Pauli district, but it was deemed too risky in light of the fan mania in Germany. There was no way they could go alone without protection, and yet if they'd gone with security guards, it would have only drawn more attention. In the end, Sue Mautner went to investigate with *Daily Mirror* journalist Don Short. They visited one club on Grosse Freiheitstrasse, where the owner exploded when he heard that they were part of the Beatles' tour entourage, because he claimed that Paul had gotten his daughter pregnant. (This case lingered on until 2007, when DNA tests proved that Paul was not the father of Erika Hubers's daughter Bettina, who had been born in December 1962.)

On June 27, they left Hamburg for the grueling journey to Tokyo. It should have been a sixteen-hour and thirty-five-minute flight, including an hour of refueling in Anchorage, Alaska, on what JAL proudly referred to as one of their "Polar couriers." But on arriving in Anchorage the pilot was told to delay his departure, because Japan was being battered by Typhoon Kit, one of the most intense cyclones on record, with winds of up to 195 mph.

Brian Epstein was concerned about the Beatles being confined on the plane with no announced departure time, so he arranged with local ground staff to allow them to disembark and camp out in relative comfort at a nearby hotel. After the relevant paperwork was signed, a shuttle bus took them to the Westward Hotel, only a ten-minute drive from the airport. Here they were ushered in through a back entrance and taken up to suite 1050.

By the time they arrived at the hotel, word was already out that the Beatles were in Anchorage. For local teenagers who heard the news on the radio this sounded unbelievable. The city had a population of less than fifty thousand, was one of the most remote locations in the United States, and was certainly not on the regular tour circuit for pop groups. Rapidly fans made their way to the alley behind the Westward Hotel, hoping for a glimpse of the most famous pop group in the world, looking up to the tenth floor and singing "We love you, Beatles" to the tune of "Bye Bye Birdie."

For the Beatles it was a day of frustration. They were tired. Their clothes were wrinkled. The view from the window was of a large construction site, a few scattered buildings, and a distant mountain range. George called the local gentlemen's haberdashers, Seidenverg and Kay's, and requested that two shirts and a hat be delivered to him. Room service sent up hamburgers and king crabs while three police officers stood guard in the hallway.

Robert Whitaker photographed them looking listless and bored as they waited. Ringo had a cassette recorder that he was using to tape an oral documentary of the tour; George was playing with a large Polaroid camera; and Brian Epstein was in another room of the suite conducting business by phone. Neither John nor Paul had brought anything with them to read.

The teenagers moved away from the hotel when a 10:00 p.m. curfew was enforced, and two hours later the Beatles were told that their flight would be leaving shortly for Tokyo. At 1:00 a.m. local time on June 28 they finally lifted off from Anchorage.

Assigned to look after them in first class on this leg of the journey was Satoko Kawasaki, one of the most English-proficient stewardesses employed by JAL. As a Beatles fan she had pitched for the job when she first heard of their booking, and the company's PR chief had given it to her on the understanding that she could secure a publicity scoop by getting John, Paul, George, and Ringo to wear happi coats bearing the JAL logo. Photos of the Beatles in these silk jackets would be priceless in advertising the airline.

Paul, George, and Ringo with Brian Epstein in an Anchorage hotel room en route from Germany to Japan. They had to wait until a typhoon in Tokyo died down before they could complete their journey.

John approached her to ask if she could iron his now crumpled jacket and trousers. She convinced him that the best solution was to slip on a happi coat that would hide all the wrinkles. As can be seen from Whitaker's in-flight photos, that's exactly what happened. Each of the Beatles slipped them on, and when they arrived at Haneda Airport at 3:39 a.m. on June 29 (they lost a day when crossing the International Date Line), they stood on the gangway blinking in the glare of flashbulbs, each wearing a happi coat, the JAL initials prominent.

The Beatles all piled into one vehicle while a dozen police cars, sirens wailing, rode in front and behind them on their way to the hotel. Security was exceptionally tight because of threats from a right-wing nationalist group that was outraged that these decadent Westerners were being allowed to perform at the Budokan, an arena built principally for martial arts contests in an effort to preserve Japanese culture. There was also dissension from educational groups who'd been leafleting high school pupils with the message that the music of the Beatles was synonymous with juvenile delinquency.

Japan was looking for its place in the postwar world. The nuclear destruction of Nagasaki and Hiroshima followed by the humiliating surrender to the Allies had happened less than twenty-one years before. Was the way forward to become more resolutely Japanese or to partner with Britain and America, openly exchanging influences? For those favoring the former course the Beatles personified a threat to their children. Not only were they seen as effeminate and non-deferential, but they also played American-influenced music that appeared to cause teenagers to lose their self-control.

The prime minister of Japan, Eisaku Sato, was opposed to their visit. Influential journalist Hosokawa Ryugen was outspoken in condemning it, and Matsutaro Shoriki, proprietor of the *Yomiuri Shimbun*, the newspaper financially backing the concerts, began to waver. Eventually, Yomiuri published a letter from the chairman of Budokan's executive board explaining that the Beatles were reputable people who had recently been decorated by the Queen of the United Kingdom. They would not be desecrating the arena.

While there was concern over the visit in some quarters, others believed that a visit from the Beatles would mark Japan as modern, affluent, and forward-looking. There had already been great strides taken in putting the country back among the leading nations. The bullet train between Tokyo and Osaka, the world's fastest, more than halved the traveling time. Then came the 1964 Tokyo Olympics, for which the Nippon Budokan was built to house the judo events, the first time that any martial art had become an Olympic sport. In four years' time Osaka would host the World's Fair.

The Beatles were controversial in Japan because on the one hand they were prosperous and had good business sense, things that Japanese elders admired, but on the other hand they represented antiauthoritarianism and individualism, things that the elders feared. The concerts were therefore divisive and had become an issue. In May, the newspaper *Yomiuri Shimbun* had reported, "Regardless of whether one likes it or not, the interest of the public is now focussed on the problem of the Beatles' visit to Japan. . . . [It is] the biggest topic of discussion since the Tokyo Olympics."

They were given the Presidential Suite at the Hilton, room 1005, which consisted of a large living room with sofas, an office desk, and a dining table with eight chairs and two bedrooms both with two single beds. Policemen were stationed outside the door, along the corridor, in every second room on the tenth floor, and elsewhere throughout the hotel. Brian Epstein and Peter Brown were down the hall in the equally ostentatious Imperial Suite. All entrances and exits to the building were under twenty-four-hour surveillance. The Beatles were kept in a virtual lockdown. They were not allowed to leave their rooms until the precise time when they needed to be escorted to the car that would take them to the concert.

At 2:30 they gave an hour-long press conference and photo op in the hotel's Red Pearl Ballroom for the Japanese press and foreign correspondents. Before they'd even gotten into the elevator, they had to do a brief interview with E. H. Eric (actor Taibi Okada), the MC in charge of their concerts.

Q: Did you have a good sleep?

A: Yes.

Q: Did you have any knowledge of Japan before coming?

A: A little bit. Not much.

Q: How are the Japanese fans?

A: Great. They seem very great.

Q: I understand you have met your Queen. What was your impression?

A: She's OK. One of the best.

Q: How did you feel when you received your medals?

A: It was nice.

Q: Which composer do you admire the most?

A: John Lennon.

Q: And, Paul's marriage . . .

A: It's not true. It's wrong.

Q: How many times do you wash your hair in a week?

A: About once. It depends how dirty it gets.

They seemed emotionally drained and desperate to get away. John, who contributed the least, was making faces, dancing, and talking to other members of the Beatles retinue. Paul was doing his best to be diplomatic. Ringo was expressing concern that the beefed-up security might end up hurting the fans.

The mood continued into the press conference. Ringo and Paul smoked throughout. John had his elbow on the table and his head resting on his hand. Proceedings were slower than normal, because everything that was said had to be translated.

Q: You have attained sufficient honor and wealth. Are you happy?

JOHN: Yes.

Q: And what do you seek next?

JOHN: Peace. [*Laughter*]

PAUL AND JOHN: Peace.

PAUL: Ban the bomb.

JOHN: Ban the bomb, yeah.

TONY BARROW: There are three questions submitted to us

from the Foreign Correspondents' Association of Japan, I believe. And Mr Ken Gary of *Reuters* will represent the group in asking those questions.

KEN GARY: What do you think the differences are between Japanese fans of yours, and teenagers elsewhere in the world?

PAUL: I think the only difference with fans anywhere is that they speak different languages. That's all. That's the only difference. And they're smaller here.

KEN GARY: Some Japanese say that your performances will violate the Budokan which is devoted to traditional Japanese martial arts, and you set a bad example for Japanese youth by leading them astray from traditional Japanese values. What do you think of all that?

PAUL: The thing is that if somebody from Japan—If a dancing troupe from Japan goes to Britain, nobody tries to say in Britain that they're violating the traditional laws, you know, or that they're trying to spoil anything. All we're doing is coming here and singing because we've been asked to.

JOHN: Better to watch singing than wrestling, anyway.

PAUL: Yeah. We're not trying to violate anything. Umm, we're just as traditional, anyway.

KEN GARY: Why do you think that you are popular not only in western countries, but in Asian countries like Japan?

JOHN: It's the same answer as before about the fans. They're international. The only difference is the language. That's why, you know, all different kinds of people like us.

RINGO: And also because the east is becoming so westernized in clothes, it's doing the same with music, you know. It's just happening that . . . Pretty soon we'll all be the same.

Most of the questions, as usual, were about trivial issues from journalists hoping for a catchy headline. What was the origin of their haircuts? Would they pay to see themselves play? Why were they so successful? But at times, when asked about plans for the new record or to analyze the reasons for their success, they gave more thoughtful and prolonged answers.

The fact was that they didn't plan their LPs ahead of time and had no idea why their music had made such an impact around the world. They knew they were good (although during this press conference Paul would say they were only "adequate" as musicians), but they also knew that merely being good was no guarantee of acceptance by the public.

Time magazine had recently published a feature in which it was suggested that "Norwegian Wood" was about an affair with a lesbian and "Day Tripper" was about discovering a girlfriend was a prostitute. The Beatles saw the issue in their suite at the Hilton and were amazed by this conclusion. "Psychologists have tried to analyze our music," said John after reading it. "I don't know why. There's no hidden meaning in our lyrics. . . . We just write music."

KEN GARY: But why is it you think that there is such fantastic response to your music? Is there something in it that people find in you a handy opportunity to let off steam?

JOHN: There's no excuses or reasons for seeing us. People keep asking questions about why they come and see us. They come and see us because they like us. That's all. There's nothing else to it, you know. And they don't have to let off steam at our concerts—they can go and let off steam anywhere.

PAUL: It's the equivalent of a sort of football match for a girl, you know.

KEN GARY: Do you think that the response that people give, which sometimes gets violent and hysterical, do you think this is a good thing? Are you happy to see people behaving in this rather extravagant way?

PAUL: It doesn't normally get violent, actually. You know, it may get hysterical. But it only gets as hysterical as men do at a football match. It's no more hysterical than that. Nobody's really trying to hurt each other. The thing is that obviously when you get a lot of people together, whatever they're doing, there's always a risk of that. But that's what we were saying about security before. It's always best if you can keep it so that it never gets out of hand. And it doesn't very often get out of hand. In fact there are far more, I imagine, injuries at football matches all over the world than there are at our concerts.

JOHN: And less violence too.

KEN GARY: Would you then be disappointed if in fact you didn't have this kind of response?

PAUL: No, you know. We'd just . . . If we didn't have this kind of response, or we didn't have this kind of life, you know . . . It's no use really asking us what we'd do if we didn't have it, 'cos if we didn't have it we'd just do something else and we'd adapt to that. There's no sort of great thing behind all of this. There's no big message or anything, you know. We just get up and we sing, and people happen to like it, and we happen to like being liked. And that's all there is to it, you know.

KEN GARY: You've been tremendously successful for a very long time now. Do you think this will continue?

PAUL: Do YOU think it will?

GEORGE: We don't think anything. We think very little at

all. You know . . . we just do it. And if the time comes when
we don't have an audience, then we'll think then about it.
But now we don't think.

This was also the first press conference where the Beatles commented specifically about the war in Vietnam. They were asked how
much interest they took in the situation. "Well, we think about it
every day, and we don't agree with it and we think it's wrong," said
John. "That's how much interest we take. That's all we can do about
it . . . and say that we don't like it." This provided an anxious moment
for Brian Epstein, conscious that they were about to tour America,
where this sort of comment could be inflammatory. He had advised
them to steer clear of such controversial subjects and knew that Paul
would have been much more diplomatic if he'd taken the question.

On the hot issues of the day—Vietnam, nuclear armaments,
apartheid, civil rights—the Beatles took a liberal view but rarely
stated it emphatically and had never hitched their wagon to a particular cause. In January Paul had been asked by *Melody Maker* what
"Vietnam" suggested to him. "Bombs and shooting and killing and
people doing things they shouldn't," he said.

The Tokyo dates introduced new elements to the Beatles' story.
Until now the police had been involved to control audiences and protect the group from overexuberant fans. Now the police were being
used to foil potential acts of terrorism and violence. Likewise, political involvement had meant those in power acknowledging the
Beatles' positive spirit and giving them awards for their economic
contribution. Now politicians in some parts of the world were denouncing them as morally degenerate and a threat to youth. This
made touring feel increasingly dangerous as the music they'd created for pleasure seemed to fuel the fight between conservatives and
liberals.

Tokyo had become such a battleground. For the visit 8,370 police officers ranging from plainclothes detectives to snipers had been

involved in one of the biggest security operations ever mounted in the country. Additionally, the Kojimachi Fire Department was involved. Some Japanese commentators believed that the true total of personnel involved in crowd control and group protection was closer to thirty-five thousand.

The power of the Beatles phenomenon was becoming harder to fathom. What had happened so far in Britain, Europe, and America could be understood only through comparisons with Elvis, Johnny Ray, Frank Sinatra, and even Bing Crosby. It was the same youthful reaction but more intense and more widespread. What was astonishing was that young people in Tokyo, whose cultural educations had been so different, were responding in the same way as their counterparts in Tooting and Toronto. Also astonishing was the fact that the Beatles found themselves in the eye of a cultural storm as the postwar world adapted to new realities. Even two years before it would have been unthinkable that the Beatles' presence—merely appearing on a stage and singing eleven songs, none of them with controversial content—would have vexed senior politicians, cultural commentators, radical political groups, Shinto priests, community leaders, and educators.

Dudley Cheke, the chargé d'affaires at the British embassy, saw the arrival of the "four young 'pop' singers from Liverpool" (as he described them in an internal memorandum later circulated in Whitehall) as a huge boost for the image of Britain in Japan. He wrote, "In sober truth, no recent event connected with the United Kingdom, with the sole exception of the British Exhibition in 1965, has made a comparable impact in Tokyo."

He realized that the Beatles conveyed the impression of a forward-looking, exciting, irreverent, colorful, cheeky, relaxed, and experimental Britain rather than a fusty, dull, serious, and inhibited one. It was good for business; it exposed British culture and creativity to the world, and, on a personal note, Cheke wrote, "The Beatles' visit enabled my wife and me to harvest goodwill among various highly-placed Japanese and foreign personalities who had seen in us the only hope of obtaining tickets for themselves or their offspring."

The Beatles initially anticipated being able to go shopping and sightseeing the next day, but their police guards were insistent that they stay in their suite. The right-wing protestors were patrolling the streets in black and white trucks waving flags and playing martial music through loudspeakers, some of them holding banners saying GO HOME BEATLES. Extra police had been drafted in over the weekend, and there were forty armored personnel carriers on standby in case serious trouble broke out. They didn't want to contemplate what could happen if an easily identifiable Beatle went wandering the streets without security.

John was the first to make a break. He put on a hat and sunglasses, borrowed Robert Whitaker's press pass and camera, and slipped out of the hotel with Neil Aspinall. Together they walked down Omotesando, an avenue lined with zelkova trees, to the Oriental Bazaar, one of the best souvenir shops in Tokyo, where he picked up a china *fukusuke* figure (a man kneeling *seiza*-style with a large head and topknot) that he would later use on the cover of *Sgt. Pepper's Lonely Hearts Club Band,* a small "god of fortune," and a nineteenth-century snuff box for which he paid the equivalent of a thousand dollars. Then they went to the Azabu district, where John bought a pair of glasses. (It was in Azabu that Yoko Ono, his future wife, had taken refuge in an air raid shelter during the allied bombing of 1945.)

Paul was stopped by the police, as expected, when he tried to leave the Hilton, but, after a period of haggling, they agreed to let him out if he and Mal Evans would travel in a car packed with plain-clothes detectives. They were given a tour of the Meiji Jingu Shrine and part of the grounds of the Imperial Palace before being spotted by photographers and bundled back into the car.

For the one concert on June 30 they stuck to the same set they'd used in Germany. They were wearing the same dark green Hung On You suits but with wine-colored shirts with long collars. The crowds

The Beatles ascending to the stage of the Budokan in Tokyo.

screamed, but less volubly than was usual at a Beatles concert. This wasn't from lack of enthusiasm—it was wild by Japanese standards—but because of the heavy police presence and the warnings issued against anyone standing, dancing, or leaving their seats. Uniformed officers took up the first few rows in each section, and in the balconies were agents with binoculars looking out for potential snipers.

Musically, the group was creaky. Often the harmonies were off-key, and "Paperback Writer," which they'd only played live six times before, sounded flat because it had been recorded using both ADT and double-tracking. When John introduced songs, he frequently couldn't recall if they'd been singles or LP tracks and, if from LPs, which ones. They'd learned that when they came to a difficult part in a song—something underrehearsed or impossible to recreate in a live situation—all they needed to do was wiggle their heads and the crowd's screams would disguise the fault.

The concert was a success, not least because the agitators hadn't won the day. The protests had been quelled, the armored vehicles hadn't been needed, and no one had kidnapped a Beatle and forced him to undergo an involuntary haircut (as was threatened).

The effect on those who saw them was profound, and the ripples would spread out. Reviewer Shuji Terayama wrote, "It was a celebration which came close to spontaneous human combustion. The energy of the fans will change Japanese history."

JULY

We never expect to be knocked because we
feel harmless. We don't want to offend but we
can't please everybody.
-PAUL, 1966

The Beatles whiled away their time in their Tokyo hotel suite before
the two daily shows on July 1 and 2 by painting and buying goods
from local tradesmen who they called in. They had bought paint sets
designed for Japanese brush painting, and for two mornings the four
Beatles sat at the dining table with a thirty-by-forty-inch canvas in
front of them, each diligently decorating his own corner in his own
style. While working they listened to the fourteen songs they'd just
recorded back in London to help them decide on the sequence in
which the tracks would appear on the still-unnamed LP. In the center of the canvas stood a table lamp, leaving a blank circle that they
would later use for their autographs.

John and Paul were at one side of the table, George and Ringo at
the other. Their contributions were all different (Paul's looked like
a rainbow-colored uterus; Ringo's carefully outlined shapes were
reminiscent of Joan Miró) but had in common the feel of abstract
expressionism mixed with contemporary psychedelic painting. Once

they started it they became preoccupied, anxious to return to it after performing, and it provided them with a collaborative escape from the surrounding demands. Robert Whitaker later said of the exercise, "Other than their music this painting was the only creative enterprise I saw the Beatles undertake as a group. I had never seen them so happy—no drink, no drugs, no girls—just working together with no distractions."

They donated the completed work to Tetsusaburo Shimoyama, their local fan club president, who would eventually sell it to a collector. In 2012, it was sold at auction in America for $155,250. Cleaners found other small drawings and paintings in the trash bins. A cartoon by John featured a man with nine strands of hair, one of which dangled to street level and had a dog attached to it.

The traders who showed off their wares provided the other distraction. From them the Beatles bought kimonos, jade, Noh masks, netsuke, incense holders, carvings, kites, gold lacquer boxes, sun-

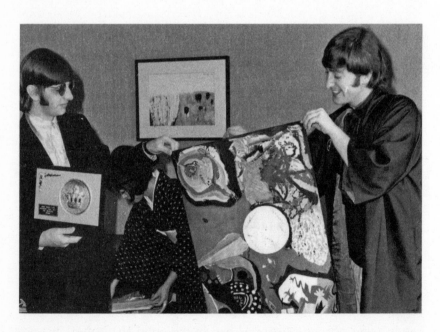

Ringo and John with the painting all four Beatles created while confined to their hotel suite in Tokyo.

glasses, and electronic goods. Sushi chefs brought in trays of fresh fish, and geisha girls offered their services. Tats Nagashima, known for his generosity toward acts he promoted, bought each of them an expensive Nikon camera and gave movie cameras to Mal Evans and Neil Aspinall.

The matinee concert on July 1 was at two o'clock, and the opening half featured local acts each playing one or two numbers of a uniquely Japanese take on Western rock. Drummer Jackey Yoshikawi appeared with his group, the Blue Comets; the singer Isao Bito performed Cliff Richard's hit single "Dynamite"; and Yuya Achido, who would go on to become friends with John, opened the show with a specially written song called "Welcome the Beatles."

The Beatles, wearing gray suits with thin orange stripes from Hung On You, were filmed by Nippon TV, as they had been the day before, for a quickly edited show transmitted that night on NTV Channel 4 as *The Beatles Recital: From Nippon Budokan, Tokyo*, while they were back on stage for their second show. Some fans complained that at half an hour the set was far too short for the price charged (tickets were the equivalent of $16 for the "cheap" seats and $24 for the rest).

The final concerts were on July 2, and between the two shows they continued to ponder the LP title. New suggestions included "Abracadabra" (Paul still pursuing the theme of magic), "Beatles on Safari" (a nod to the Beach Boys), and "Freewheelin' Beatles" (a tribute to Dylan), but again nothing was settled.

Until "Revolver," suggested by Paul. It was a succinct but playful title. A revolver was a handgun with a rotating bullet chamber, but it could also be another word for anything else that rotated, like a record. An LP was a revolving disc. Asked about the title, John denied that there was a special significance to the name yet at the same time implied that it could have multiple meanings. He said, "It's just a name for an LP, and there's no meaning to it. Why does everyone want a reason every time you move? It means Revolver. It's all the things that Revolver means, because that's what it means to us, Revolver and all the things we could think of to go with it."

Some of the things that "go with" the word "revolver" are "revolution," "evolve," and "evolution"—words that have roots in the Latin *volvere*, which means to roll (and eventually lent its name to rolled parchments—*volumen*—and left us with the word "volume" for books). The album certainly announced both a revolution, in sound as well as attitude, and an evolution of their art. In 1968 John would say, "The Beatles were part of the revolution, which is really an evolution, and is continuing." From the Hilton they sent a telegram to EMI in London announcing *Revolver* as the title of their next LP.

THE BEATLES WERE CERTAINLY REVOLUTIONARY FOR JAPAnese youth. Their appearances in Tokyo signposted a new way of living that was less reflexively reverent of tradition, self-restraint, and formality. Literature professor Toshinobu Fukuya has since written, "In their three days of concerts in Tokyo, the Beatles demonstrated to Japanese youth that one did not always have to obediently follow arrangements prescribed by adults; it was possible to follow one's own path and still be socially and financially successful in life."

On July 3 they took a flight out of Haneda Airport bound for Manila via Hong Kong, where they deplaned for seventy minutes. During the stopover they visited the VIP lounge of Kai Tak Airport, where John and George did interviews with local radio reporters. The rest of the journey, with Cathay Pacific, was on a narrow-body Convair 800, and everyone on board was made aware of the VIPs in first class. The Philippine promoters, Cavalcade International Productions, had endorsed Cathay as the official incoming carrier on their posters and tickets, and Cathay had issued all passengers with a souvenir folder including a four-by-five-inch glossy black-and-white photo of the group (some of which John defaced with a pen while feeling bored on the flight).

There had been no death threats from Manila and no suggestion that the Beatles were a challenge to political stability. The Philippines was proud of its European heritage and its current ties with America. Yet after they landed at 4:30, the Beatles' party sensed an air of tension and barely concealed disdain. It was routine that the group and their team would disembark from an airport terminal and be whisked away in limousines to avoid press attention and fan mania. Their equipment would clear customs separately, with Mal Evans in attendance, where personal bags were treated as diplomatic pouches and therefore immune from scrutiny. These bags were where they would hide their illegal substances.

At Manila they left the plane in the normal way and their bags were placed on the runway, but before they could collect them the group was roughly bundled into the back seat of a waiting car, and the driver pulled away, leaving behind the bags as well as Neil Aspinall and Brian Epstein. Customs collector Salvador Mascardo was insistent that carry-on luggage had to be inspected. They didn't know why they'd been separated from their possessions. Would their pot stash be discovered?

They were driven ten miles to the Philippine Navy Headquarters on Dewey Boulevard, overlooking the city's marina. Here they were they were interrogated by forty journalists in the appropriately named War Room. They were in a more frivolous mood than in Japan or Germany, giving answers that were as inane as the questions. When did they last cut their hair? "Nineteen thirty-three," said John. What was their favorite song? "God Save the Queen." What was their second favorite song? "God Save the King." Their unease about the earlier treatment at the airport surfaced when they were asked what they'd be telling the soon-to-be-touring Rolling Stones about the Philippines. "We'll *warn* them." What was the title of their next song? "Philippine Blues."

Security in the city was as intense as it had been when US president Dwight Eisenhower visited in 1960. Police officers, motorcycle cops, armored cars, fire trucks, riot squad jeeps, and police prowl cars controlled the ten thousand fans that turned up at the airport. The army was on red alert. "Is there a war in the Philippines?" an unidentified Beatle was quoted as saying shortly after arrival. "Why is everybody armed?"

Following the press conference John, Paul, George, and Ringo were briskly ushered out of the back entrance of the building to an awaiting yacht, the *Marima*. Photographers gathered on the water's edge and begged the Beatles to line up and peer out of a cabin window. They seemed willing, but the newly arrived Brian Epstein didn't want them manipulated in this way. He was already furious at being forced to pay a bond on the band's equipment to the airport customs agents.

The craft belonged to Don Manolo Elizalde, one of the founders of the Manila Broadcasting Company, who'd made his fortune from steel, hemp, paint, and wine, and was a friend of promoter Ramon Ramos as well as President Ferdinand Marcos. But the host for the evening was his twenty-four-year-old son, Fred, who'd recently graduated magna cum laude from Harvard. With him were his sister; his girlfriend, Josine Loinaz (Miss Manila 1966); and a handful of employees from Cavalcade International. Epstein ordered two TV men from Channel 11 (owned by Elizalde Sr.) to leave the boat, unaware that they had been promised an exclusive interview as payback for the group's use of the yacht.

As the *Marima* pulled out into Manila Bay, the Beatles began to relax. They were away from the bustle, the guns, and the fans. They sunbathed on the deck wearing rubber sandals, listened to tapes of Ravi Shankar, and drank whiskey and Cokes. Loinaz and Fred Elizalde found them charming. The Beatles lit up and openly shared their dope with Elizalde and some of his male friends. Epstein, however, was still frantic. Not for the first time he felt that events were slipping out of his control. He'd just learned that the plan, approved by NEMS's Far East booking agent, Vic Lewis, who had been the one to negotiate directly

From top: The *Marima*. Brian Epstein, George, John, and Paul on board the *Marima*. Paul, George, and John.

with Ramos and establish the itinerary, was for the Beatles to stay on the boat rather than at the hotel for security reasons. They could easily protect and police a yacht, but not a city-center hotel.

As the evening drew on, food was served—consommé, fried chicken, filet mignon, mashed potatoes, carrots, and sweet peas—but then one of Elizalde's brothers arrived on a launch with eighteen of his friends, and Epstein declared it all over. The Beatles, who'd just started their consommé, would return to the yacht basin and be transferred to the luxurious turn-of-the-century Manila Hotel on Rizal Park, where the rest of the team was staying. Because the hotel was fully booked, rooms had to be swapped to create space, and they weren't finally checked in until four in the morning.

What they weren't aware of at this point was that the day's issue of the *Manila Times* had announced that at eleven o'clock the Beatles would be visiting the presidential palace, Malacañan, as special guests of President Ferdinand Marcos and his wife, Imelda, who had invited three hundred children and young people to meet the group. All that was mentioned in the itinerary was that at 3:00 p.m. they might "call in on the first lady . . . before proceeding on from the Malacañan Palace directly to the stadium." Phrased in this way it appeared to be a casual suggestion, but even so the time was wrong, and in the confusion over the accommodations, the arrangement hadn't been discussed with Epstein or the Beatles.

It appears that Ramos had been told by the palace to deliver the Beatles, but, knowing that their likely response was to decline, he had stalled by burying the invitation in the small print, hoping for a compromise on the day. Imelda Marcos was a formidable woman who expected her requests to be fulfilled, but Brian Epstein and the Beatles were equally stubborn. Ramos was caught in the middle.

The Beatles routinely turned down invitations to such official events around the world ever since the hair-snipping incident at the Washington, DC, embassy reception. They didn't want to be treated as playthings or figures of amusement by people of privilege and power. Besides, in practical terms, the hours before a concert were always a time of relaxation and preparation.

Ferdinand Marcos had won the presidential election in November 1965 and was enjoying his honeymoon period. He was not yet regarded as a dictator and had broad popular support. He shared his birth year with John Kennedy, as Imelda did with Jackie Kennedy, and they tried to replicate the sheen of the Kennedys' Camelot, hoping that it would result in a similar love affair between people and power in their country.

Paul got up first on the morning of July 4, which was the day of their two concerts, blissfully unaware of the 11:00 engagement, and went with Neil Aspinall to Makati, the financial district of the city, and then to an adjacent shanty town settled by squatters where he bought a couple of paintings as souvenirs. After this the two of them went to the beach, where they smoked a joint.

Chaos was ensuing at the hotel by the time they got back. A reception team from the palace dressed in military uniforms had banged on the door of Vic Lewis's room to tell him that the Beatles were expected at the palace by eleven and that everyone was waiting. As he'd been the one to deal with Ramon Ramos and Cavalcade, Lewis was deemed personally responsible for getting the group there on time. "This is not a request," they told him. "We have our orders." He in turn found Epstein, who was in the restaurant eating breakfast, and tried to persuade him to at least have the Beatles drop in to avoid a huge controversy, but Epstein was adamant that they would do no such thing. "I'm not going to ask the Beatles about this," he said dismissively. "Go back and tell the generals we're not coming."

Ramon Ramos, Colonel Morales of the Manila Police District, and Colonel Flores of the Philippine Constabulary came to the fourth-floor suite to persuade the Beatles in person to honor the appointment, but the more the Filipinos argued their case, the more contrary the Beatles became. Over the years they had grown to dislike hobnobbing with dignitaries and their offspring. This was not their natural audience, and often these people didn't personally like the Beatles' music but used the occasion to boost their own standing. "If they want to see the Beatles, let them come here," said John. Morales explained to him that the "they" included Ferdinand Marcos. "Who's he?" asked John.

Even Dudley Cheke in Tokyo hadn't been able to interest the Beatles in a cocktail party or reception in their honor. "This was only because they felt unable to accept our invitations," he informed his superiors in London. "Their manager had been at pains to explain to me in correspondence which we exchanged before their arrival that they had decided after experiences in Washington, not to go to any more Embassy parties."

British diplomatic pleading didn't help in Manila either. The Beatles had a northern working-class suspicion of officialdom. The British ambassador, John Addis, was away on

A souvenir program for the two concerts the Beatles gave in Manila, July 4, 1966.

business, and so it was left to his chargé d'affaires, Leslie Minford, to explain that Filipinos were proud of their hospitality and that it was considered very impolite to refuse it. To invite someone into your house was the supreme gesture of friendship. He also pointed out that all the personal security the Beatles were enjoying came courtesy of the palace and could be withdrawn on short notice if they appeared to be ungrateful.

The children who'd gathered in expectation were either related to high-ranking government officials or friends of five-year-old Irene, eight-year-old Bongbong, and ten-year-old Imee, the offspring of the president. At noon Imelda gave up. Many of the children stayed, but eventually they all left, and Irene, Bongbong, and Imee tore up their concert tickets in disgust. (Imee said that the only Beatles track she'd ever liked was "Run for Your Life.") The big story now was that the Beatles, the longhaired lads from Liverpool, had publicly rejected the president, the first lady, and a few hundred Filipino children and were not going to apologize.

The shows were at 4:00 and 8:30 at the Rizal Memorial Football Stadium. The stage was small, wire fencing had been erected in front of it to prevent any mobbing, and blocks of seats had been reserved for dignitaries who now refused to come. The six Filipino opening acts (whose combined performance lasted twice as long as the Beatles' set) were the same acts who'd recently supported Peter and Gordon in Manila, and they performed the same songs and told the same jokes.

The Beatles were hard to hear and even harder for most of the crowd of thirty thousand to see. Many people thought they seemed to be merely going through the motions. Between shows they stayed with each other in a specially constructed dressing room on the field behind the stage. For the second show the organizers had improved the sound a little, but the lighting shone too brightly in the eyes of the group.

The Filipino novelist and historian Nick Joaquin (also known as Quijano de Manila), who reviewed the show for a Manila newspaper, wrote,

So alive, original and imaginative were their two films one expected a live show of theirs to be just as different and inventive. Alas, they performed like any local combo, only not so spiritedly. There was no style, no verve, no poetry to their performance. They stood before mikes and opened their mouths, that was all. It was a one-two-three, "Now we'll do this song." They sang. "Now we'll do this next song." They sang. And so on, until they had sung, very listlessly, all the ten songs they had to sing [they had dropped "Nowhere Man" for this show]. Then they bowed out. Who would have cared for an encore? Even the periodic squealing of girls seemed mechanical, not rapture but exhibitionism. The audience was too vexed over the poor sound, if they could hear at all, and the languor on stage, if they could see at all. Those who couldn't see or hear didn't miss anything.

Between shows, back at the hotel, Epstein, Tony Barrow, and Vic Lewis had watched the TV news, which was dominated by the story of how the Beatles had stood up the first lady. It showed the forlorn faces of the children and the place cards of John, Paul, George, and Ringo being removed after the group's nonappearance. "This was the most noteworthy East-West mix-up in Manila for many years," intoned the announcer.

Barrow thought the best immediate fix was to have Epstein make a public statement. He composed a brief speech and invited Channel 5, the government-sponsored TV channel, to come to Epstein's suite, where he would make an announcement. The offer was accepted, and Epstein explained that he and the Beatles were unaware of the invitation. "The first we knew of the hundreds of children waiting to meet the Beatles at the palace was when we watched television earlier this evening."

This statement was partly true. They hadn't known the extent of the welcoming party until they saw the images, but of course they had known about the invitation since early morning. What he wasn't going to say in the broadcast was what he later admitted on reflection, "Even if we had [received the invitation] we'd have turned it down. I'd much rather the boys met 300 average children in India than 300 kids who happened to be at the palace because their parents knew somebody."

When Epstein's statement was broadcast, as part of a late-night news bulletin, the sound was distorted, although it seemed to be fine during the rest of the transmission. Before midnight Vic Lewis was taken to a police station where he was interrogated for three hours. "Why did you snub our country?" he was asked. "You represent the Beatles. You did not bring them to the palace today."

Lewis contacted the British embassy to let them know what was happening, but no report of this intimidation or the death threats that Barrow was told had been received by embassy officials was reported in written exchanges between chargé d'affaires Minford and London. Minford sent a telegram to the Foreign Office explaining the situation so far, but appeared unruffled and his tone was matter-of-fact. The Beatles had failed to keep an appointment with the first lady, and it had been "treated as a snub," but he didn't think it had been intended as one. However, he wrote, "There is a possibility that a technical hitch over payment of Philippine income tax may delay their departure." But not to worry; he had been "in touch with Philippine authorities to smooth out local difficulties."

Lest London should think that he or the ambassador had been lax in their duties, he made the point that "at no time and at no stage was I or the Embassy consulted about the arrangements of the Beatles' visit to Manila." He had been in touch with Imelda Marcos "to express regret that there should have been any discourtesy which I have been assured by the Beatles was in no way their intention."

On July 5, the Beatles were ready to fly to Delhi, India, for an overnight stay en route to London. It was George's big dream to visit the country of gurus, meditation, yoga, sitars, and Ravi Shankar, and he had persuaded Neil Aspinall to join him and was hopeful that the rest of the group would also come. They packed their bags early and nervously paced around their suite. They'd been shown copies of Manila's morning papers, where the headlines were all about the failed meeting at the palace. The *Manila Chronicle* was typical. In bold letters at the top of the front page it said FUROR OVER BEATLES "SNUB" MARS SHOW.

It soon became clear that part of their punishment was to have special treatment and privileges removed. The hotel reception turned frosty, security was withdrawn, and no cars arrived to take them to the airport. At shortly after 8:00 a.m. a representative of the Bureau of Internal Revenue visited Vic Lewis in his room with a tax bill. Lewis explained that Cavalcade had agreed to pay all local taxes. "Your fee is taxed as earnings," said the impassive official. "This is regardless of any other contracts." The regime was coming down hard.

At the airport, the porters refused to carry the Beatles' luggage, leaving them struggling to get through the crowds. When they entered the terminal, the escalator to take them to the first-floor check-in was turned off. They then made the mistake of making a dash for the desks, thinking that by cutting down on time they'd make themselves less vulnerable. However, the sight of four fleeing Beatles drew even more attention, and soon they found people chasing after them who didn't know what the pursuit was about.

Fights broke out. Citizens loyal to Marcos (or possibly under-cover agents) were determined to show their displeasure by roughing up the Beatles. Ringo and John were apparently both punched. Brian Epstein was knocked to the ground, and Mal Evans was kicked so hard his leg bled. This had all been orchestrated by the airport manager, Willy Jurado, who himself joined in the melee in the belief that to protect the honor of the Marcos family was to protect the honor of the Filipino people. In 1984, now living in San Francisco, Jurado was happy to boast of his activities. "I beat up the Beatles," he told Bob Secter of the *Los Angeles Times,* who was researching a story on the Marcos regime. "I really thumped them. First I socked Epstein and he went down. . . . Then I socked Lennon and Ringo in the face. I was kicking them. They were pleading like frightened chickens. That's what happens when you insult the First Lady."

After playing the bad cop, Jurado then played the good cop by waving off fellow attackers and getting the Beatles to a desk for their papers to be sorted. He asked for a gangway to be created to expe-

Neil Aspinall (*left*) under attack at the Manila airport while John and Brian Epstein's assistant, Peter Brown (*far right*), look on with concern. Mal Evans has his back to the camera.

dite them, but as they headed for the plane there was more cuffing, pushing, and spitting. When some fans of the group started crying because of the mistreatment of their heroes, the rest of the crowd turned on them as if they were traitors.

Once on the plane they thought their ordeal over. The Beatles kissed their seats out of sheer joy. But before takeoff officials boarded and demanded that Mal Evans and Tony Barrow accompany them back to the terminal, as their papers weren't in order. According to their records, the two men had never entered the Philippines, and there were no appropriate stamps in their passports. As Evans walked down the aisle, he asked George to tell his wife, Lil, that he loved her. He was seriously concerned that he was about to be imprisoned. After an anxious forty minutes Barrow and Evans were allowed back on the plane.

Epstein was sweating in his seat. He felt that he had let the Beatles down, especially by not having paid more attention to the itin-

erary submitted by Ramon Ramos. Now his fellow passengers were
furious with him for delaying their flight. Vic Lewis lost his temper
with Epstein over the tax issue, and Epstein accused Lewis of only
being concerned about money. It took Peter Brown's intervention to
stop the spat from turning physically violent. Epstein now looked
ill rather than merely dejected. Finally, at 4:45 p.m., KLM flight 862
took off for its three-thousand-mile journey to India.

Back at the British Embassy chargé d'affaires Minford prepared
his second and final communiqué on the incident. He told the Foreign Office in London that "a few persons at the airport showed unnecessary zeal in being unpleasant to them during the departure
formalities." But he assured his bosses that it had all been settled by
the intervention of Mrs. Marcos's brother Benjamin Romualdez.

President Marcos then took the unusual step of issuing a press
statement, saying that he'd ordered the controversial tax and customs claims to be lifted. He spoke of his regret that the affair had
happened and referred to it as a "misunderstanding."

"The incidents at the airport shouldn't have happened since
they were a breach of Filipino hospitality and totally disproportion-
ate to the triviality of the whole matter. The president and Mrs. Marcos, unlike the reaction elsewhere in Manila, were not at all ruffled
by the non-appearance of the Beatles at the palace and were in fact
surprised at the high feelings engendered in other sections of the
community."

The facts of what happened that day are still not clear. Were the
Beatles ever paid for their two appearances in Manila? Did Epstein
finally pay the $17,000 tax demand? In 1971, when trying to clear
up Apple's finances, Peter Brown wrote to John asking if he could recall being paid or seeing Epstein hand over money to the authorities
while on the grounded plane. John replied that he thought Epstein
gave the money demanded but couldn't be sure. All he knew for certain was that the Beatles didn't receive their fee and that the flight
wasn't delayed because of alleged unpaid taxes or unstamped pass-

ports but because the authorities wanted to frighten them.

Nick Joaquin, who'd already been perceptive in his review of the concert, made an astute assessment of the whole fiasco in an article published in Manila two weeks later. In his estimation, the issue was not a simple one of a political leader being rebuffed. It was a deeper matter of official culture fearing the challenge posed by change and punishing the Beatles because they represented a free spirit that ran counter to the Philippine ideals of order and formality. As in Japan, the controlling powers wanted to benefit by hitching themselves to the creativity, popularity, and commerciality of the Beatles without comprehending what they represented at a deeper level and what it was about them that tapped into the zeitgeist.

"Because the Beatles are supposed to be very 'in,' we had to make all that fuss over them to prove that we, too, are 'in'—but do we ever ponder why the Beatles are so 'in' with Westerners?"

He suggested that Filipinos tended to overlook the essence of the Beatles, which was "the delight in doing what everybody else is not doing, or the irreverence for mores and manners, or the urge to be singular, spontaneous, original, new, or the courage to be unconventional, unpleasant, outside, not with it," and argued these were "the very qualities we need to get us moving."

He saw the Beatles as an affirmative voice in the world—a "Yeah, Yeah, Yeah" at a time when there was too much "No, No, No." He quoted John as saying, "The Bomb? Nuclear disarmament? Well, like everybody else I don't want to end up a festering heap, but I don't stay up nights worrying. I'm preoccupied with Life, not Death."

Ultimately Joaquin felt the Beatles had "failed" in the Philippines in the sense that even though the country liked their veneer and wanted to emulate the long hair and the guitar sounds, it was resistant to their implicit call for change. "How could they not flop in a land which only wants not to be disturbed, not to change, not to be shocked?" he asked. "Having made a career of outrageousness, they have taken for granted that any audience that asks for them is asking to be outraged. If they made a mistake in Manila, the mistake is flattering to us: they assumed we were in the same league. But they were Batman in Thebes."

When the Beatles touched down in Delhi late at night, they thought they were entering a country where they were unknown and where they would therefore be left alone, but there were over five hundred fans to greet them at the airport, and an impromptu press conference had to be organized to satisfy a contingent of journalists. They were then driven to the Oberoi Intercontinental on Wellesley Road, their home for the next two nights.

It was while at the Oberoi that discussion turned for the first time to the future of the group. Epstein's anxiety, which at first had seemed to be a result of the strain experienced in Manila, was more serious. He had developed a fever and had to remain in his room, which left John, Paul, George, Ringo, and Neil Aspinall with time alone to talk to each other. There was a consensus that Epstein was losing his grip because the job had grown too big for him. A year before, overexcited fans breaking through barriers outside a provincial English cinema where the group were about to perform would have been the worst thing that could happen. Now it was mob revolt, violence, political backlash, and threats of assassination.

Aspinall told them that Epstein was already planning tours for 1967. George wanted to know whether these were going to become an annual event. "Nobody can hear a bloody note anyway," said John. "No more for me. I say we stop touring."

George had persuaded the others to join him on this Indian detour, but during the flight they changed their minds (they were tired of travel and wanted to get home). By then KLM had sold the Delhi-to-London section of the flight, so John, Paul, and Ringo had to honor their original bookings.

On their first day they shopped for musical instruments, visiting the Lahore Music House and then the Rikhi Ram Musical Instrument Manufacturing Company at Marina Arcade on Con-

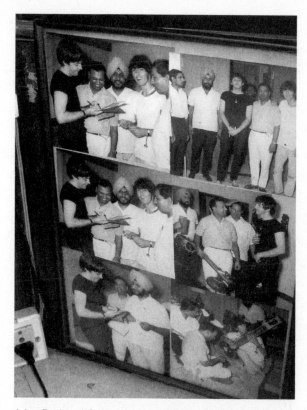

John, Paul, and George receiving basic instruction in tuning
their newly purchased Indian instruments, July 1966 (photos
on display at the Rikhi Ram music store in New Delhi).

naught Place. The Rikhi Ram store was small, and within minutes
fans were clustered outside on the street. Bishan Dass Sharma, the
son of the late founder, arranged for a selection of instruments (a
tambura, sitar, tabla, and sarod) to be taken to the Oberoi later in the
day along with instructors to give the Beatles basic lessons in tuning.

In the afternoon they were given a tour of Delhi before being
driven to villages outside the city. Decoy limousines were used at the
main entrance of the Oberoi to distract the crowd of fans and journalists that had gathered while the Beatles were whisked out of an
underground garage in black Cadillacs driven by Sikh chauffeurs in
blue turbans.

Tipped off by his driver that the Beatles were going to be leaving from a back exit, the local bureau chief for the Associated Press (AP), Joe McGowan, broke from the press pack and gave chase in the bureau car. A wild drive ensued, and when all three cars got to the city outskirts, the Cadillacs carrying the Beatles stopped, and Paul and John got out to confront McGowan, who explained to them that he was from the AP, the world's largest news agency, and just needed a couple of quotes. Paul told him about the problems in Manila and offered apologies to Imelda Marcos. McGowan was happy with his haul and left them to continue their trip unmolested.

The Beatles were surprised at the contrast between the wide avenues that the British had lined with their administrative buildings and executive bungalows and the narrow streets choked with cattle, people, and cars that spread out through the rest of the city. They were even more surprised by the primitive conditions in the outlying villages, where camels were still used to hoist up water buckets from wells and the children gathered around to beg for money, or "baksheesh." They visited the famous Red Fort and were taken to Qutub Minar Park, where, at the summit of a flight of steps, there was an iron post that it was customary to back up to and wrap your arms around in order to bring good luck. At night, according to a letter written by George, the traveling party availed themselves of "hookers etc.," and Neil Aspinall paid the price by getting "Oriental Crabs."

The visit was fleeting yet significant. It was the Beatles' introduction to Indian culture—something they'd explore more fully when returning in 1968 to study meditation in Rishikesh—and also their first experience of real poverty. George said it was "quite an eye-opener" for him when he realized his camera was worth more than some of the villagers he photographed would earn in a lifetime. Ringo commented, "India was the first foreign country I ever went to. I never felt Denmark or Holland or France were foreign, just that the language was different."

They flew from Delhi to London with BOAC on the night of July 7. Either on the flight or earlier in the day while still at the Oberoi the Beatles announced to Brian Epstein that they planned to stop touring after fulfilling their commitments in America. The pressures were too great, the dangers too real, the expectations too high, and the rewards for playing too low. They felt that they had outgrown that stage of their career and looked forward to concentrating on the part of their work that they found most fulfilling—writing and recording.

Epstein took the news badly. During the flight he broke out in a rash and felt so ill that the pilot radioed ahead for an ambulance to meet the plane in London. Before landing Epstein turned to his NEMS colleague Peter Brown and asked, "What will I do if they stop touring? What will be left for me?" Brown tried to console him. "Don't be ridiculous," Brown said. "There's lots for you to do."

On their arrival on the morning of July 8 the Beatles were greeted by screaming fans, as they had been after every overseas tour since Beatlemania took hold in 1963, and then they headed straight to a business lounge for brief press interviews where the journalists were eager to hear exactly what had happen to them in Manila.

> **Q:** At the airport, did they come up and start physically threatening you?
>
> **PAUL:** We got to the airport and our road managers had a lot of trouble trying to get the equipment in because the escalators had been turned off, and things. So we got there, and we got put into the transit lounge. And we got pushed around from one corner of the lounge to another, you know.
>
> **JOHN:** [*impersonating and demonstrating by shoving Paul repeatedly in the shoulder*] "You're treated like ordinary passenger!! Ordinary passenger!!" . . . Ordinary passenger, what, he doesn't get kicked, does he? [*Beatles laugh*]
>
> **PAUL:** [*laughs*] And so they started knocking over our road

managers and things, and everyone was falling all over the place.

Q: That started worrying you, when the road manager got knocked over.

PAUL: Yeah, and I swear there were thirty of 'em.

Q: [*turning back to John*] What do you say there were?

JOHN: Well, I saw sort of five in sort of outfits, you know, that were doing the actual kicking and booing and shouting.

Q: Did you get kicked any?

JOHN: [*giggling*] No, I was very delicate and moved every time they touched me. [*Beatles laugh*]

JOHN: But I was petrified. . . . I could have been kicked and not known it, you know. We'll just never go to any nuthouses again.

Q: Would you go to Manila again, George?

GEORGE: No, I didn't even want to go that time.

JOHN: Me too.

GEORGE: Because we'd heard that it was a terrible place anyway, and when we got there . . . it was proved.

Asked again whether they would ever return to the Philippines, John muttered under his breath, "We should have taken over Manila in the war," then commented in his normal voice, "No plane's going to go through there with me on. I won't even fly over it."

Brian Epstein went directly home to his sickbed and was later diagnosed with glandular fever (infectious mononucleosis). He canceled a trip to America set up for him to do advance preparation for the upcoming tour. His doctor, Norman Cowan, recommended taking time off work and getting out of London if possible. At the end

Brian Epstein came to recuperate at Portmeirion in Wales after the Far East tour.

of the month Epstein chose to go to Portmeirion in North Wales, a tourist village on the sea built entirely in an Italianate style starting in the 1920s, where he rented the gatehouse that straddled the main entrance to the village.

Few places could seem further removed from the center of the cultural hurricane of the Beatles than Portmeirion. After the high security of Tokyo, the violence of Manila, and the dust and dirt of Delhi, he was safely ensconced in a fairytale village full of classical sculptures, trees, gardens, lawns, narrow streets, and colorfully painted buildings. Seagulls wheeled overhead, fresh air blew in from the sea, and there was a large deserted beach on which to take walks.

THREE DAYS BEFORE EPSTEIN LEFT FOR WALES *NME* PREviewed *Revolver* ahead of its British release. The reviewer was Allen Evans, and it was written in his typical fusty style. "Taxman" was "a fast rocking song with twangy guitar," "Eleanor Rigby" was a "folksy ballad," "Love You To" was "an Oriental-sounding piece," and "Doctor Robert" was "John Lennon's tribute to the medical profession about a doctor who does well for everyone." "Tomorrow Never Knows" clearly floored Evans. It was John telling you to turn off your mind and relax, but, Evans worried, "How can you relax with the electronic, outerspace noises, often sounding like seagulls?"

Older writers like Evans could describe the songs in a cack-handed way but were not yet able to successfully evaluate them or comprehend music that didn't fit into the preordained categories of rocker, ballad, catchy, slow, fast, or lyrical. Presented with an LP that would go on to be critically regarded as one of the greatest recordings of the twentieth century, all Evans could conclude was, "The latest Beatles' album, *Revolver*, certainly has new sounds and new ideas. You'll soon all be singing 'Yellow Submarine.'"

Disc and Music Echo gave the LP to Ray Davies of the Kinks for a track-by-track appraisal, and he was surprisingly mean-spirited about it. "Taxman" was "a bit limited," "Eleanor Rigby" sounded as though it had been written "to please music teachers in primary schools," "Love You To" was "the sort of song I was doing two years ago," "Yellow Submarine" was "a load of rubbish," "And Your Bird Can Sing" was "too predictable," and "I Want to Tell You" was "not up to Beatles standard." The only tracks he mustered enthusiasm for were "Good Day Sunshine," "I'm Only Sleeping," and "Here, There and Everywhere." His overall verdict was that it wasn't as good as *Rubber Soul.*

There had been bad blood between the Kinks and the Beatles since they played together on the same bill in 1964. John upset Davies backstage by saying, "We've lost our set-list, lads. Can we borrow yours?" implying that the Kinks, who had only released two singles at that point, were mere imitators. Paul was more respectful. When the Kinks released "See My Friends" in 1965, a track now widely regarded as one of the first pop songs to use Eastern scales, Paul played it over and over at the apartment of John Dunbar and Marianne

Faithfull, and when he saw Ray's brother Dave at the Scotch, he reputedly joked, "That 'See My Friend.' I really like that. I should have written it," to which Dave retorted, "Well, you didn't. You can't do everything." Ray Davies later commented, "Paul McCartney was one of the most competitive people I've ever met. Lennon wasn't. He just thought everyone else was shit."

The Kinks often didn't get the recognition they deserved, and the Beatles didn't lavish praise on them in interviews in the same way that they did when speaking of the Lovin' Spoonful, the Who, the Beach Boys, and the Byrds. The only complimentary mention of them I could find by the Beatles was when George said, "I think Ray Davies and the Beatles have plenty in common." The Kinks had pioneered the use not only of the drone-like sound in pop but also of the distorted guitar ("You Really Got Me") and social satire (in "Dedicated Follow of Fashion" and "A Well Respected Man") that paved the way for songs like "Doctor Robert." Ray Davies was sporting a mustache in April 1966, a good half year before the Beatles appeared to start the trend. Interviewed in 1988 Davies was asked what it was like being in a group in the 1960s. "It was incredible," he said. "The Beatles were waiting for the next Kinks album while the Who were waiting for the next Beatles record."

Melody Maker was far more positive and understanding of the LP and noted that "only a handful of the 14 tracks are really Beatle tracks. Most are Paul tracks, John tracks, George tracks, or in the case of 'Yellow Submarine,' Ringo's track." The review struggled to find appropriate critical language—"I'm Only Sleeping" was "mid-tempo with intriguing harmonies," "And Your Bird Can Sing" was "beaty mid-tempo with another fine Lennon lead," and "I Want to Tell You" was "a touch of the bitonalities with a piano figure which resolves into tune for nicely spread harmonies"—but it acknowledged that huge steps had been taken and that pop would never be quite the same again.

The review concluded, "*Rubber Soul* showed that the Beatles were bursting the bounds of the three-guitar-drums instrumentation, a formula which was, for the purposes of accompaniment and projection of their songs, almost spent. *Revolver* is confirmation of this. They'll never be able to copy this. Neither will the Beatles be able to reproduce a tenth of this material on a live performance. But who cares? Let John, Paul, George and Ringo worry about that when the time comes. Meanwhile it is a brilliant album which underlines once and for all that the Beatles have definitely broken the bounds of what we used to call pop."

Perhaps the most sympathetic review in Britain was published in the *Gramophone,* a serious monthly magazine largely devoted to classical music. Peter Clayton, a thirty-nine-year-old jazz critic, wrote,

This really is an astonishing collection, and listening to it you realise that the distance the four odd young men have travelled since "Love Me Do" in 1962 is musically even greater than it is materially. It isn't easy to describe what's here, since much of it involves things that are either new to pop music or which are being properly applied for the first time, and which can't be helpfully compared with anything. In fact, the impression you get is not of any one sound or flavour, but simply of smoking hot newness with plenty of flaws and imperfections but *fresh.* . . . [I]f there's anything wrong with the record at all it is that such a diet of newness might give the ordinary pop-picker indigestion.

The younger American writers that *Crawdaddy* had anticipated got it immediately, even though the Capitol version lacked "Doctor Robert," "And Your Bird Can Sing," and "I'm Only Sleeping," which had come out earlier on *Yesterday and Today*. Jules Siegel, a Hunter College graduate in philosophy and English, compared the Beatles to John Donne, Milton, and Shakespeare and said their fate was now "in the hands of those who someday will prepare the poetry textbooks of the future, in which songs of unrequited love and psychedelic phi-losophy will appear stripped of their music, raw material for doctoral dissertations." Richard Goldstein, a recent graduate of the Columbia School of Journalism in New York who thought *Revolver* was "revolu-tionary" astutely observed in the *Village Voice* that "it seems now that we will view this album in retrospect as a key work in the develop-ment of rock 'n' roll into an artistic pursuit."

Just as Epstein settled into his vacation home in Wales, events were taking place in America that would profoundly affect his own future and that of the Beatles. The edition of *Datebook* containing the

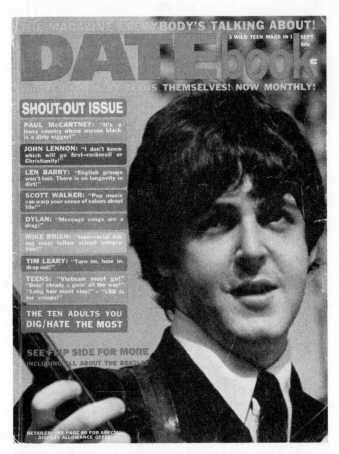

John's comments on Jesus and Christianity were featured in the September 1966 issue of *Datebook*.

interviews with John and Paul that Maureen Cleave had carried out earlier in the year had now been printed. The theme of the "shout-out" issue was controversial statements on hot issues such as interracial dating, long hair, drugs, sex, and the war in Vietnam. The only alteration to the text as it had appeared in the *Evening Standard* was the excision of most of the first two paragraphs of preamble in order to lead with the punchier opening of "When John Lennon's Rolls Royce, with its black wheels and its black windows, goes past, people say: 'It's the Queen,' or 'It's the Beatles.'" A color photo of Paul was on the cover next to two quotes from the interviews that editor Art Unger thought were sufficiently controversial: "PAUL MC-CARTNEY: It's a lousy country where anyone black is a dirty nigger." "JOHN LENNON: I don't know which will go first—rocknroll or Christianity." John's quote was used again in the feature's headline. A photo of him on a yacht shielding his eyes from the sun and gazing toward the horizon was prophetically captioned "John Lennon sights controversy and sets sail directly towards it. That's the way he likes to live!"

Unger wanted the stories to stir up some trouble, and so ahead of the August date when the publications were due out on the newsstands, he mailed copies to some of the most outspoken DJs in the South hoping to get an incensed reaction. In an unpublished memoir he wrote that he did it "figuring that if one story didn't catch their eyes, the other would." It had the desired effect. Tommy Charles and Doug Layton, two DJs from Birmingham, Alabama, were aroused enough to begin berating the Beatles on air for their arrogance.

It wasn't Paul's critical comment about racism in America that drew their ire but John's comparison of rock 'n' roll with Christianity and his claim that that Beatles were now more popular than Jesus. Neither Charles nor Layton was particularly religious ("We went to church but not with any degree of regularity," Layton later admitted to me), but they knew the sort of issues that stirred listeners and got the station phones ringing. Charles in particular had a reputation

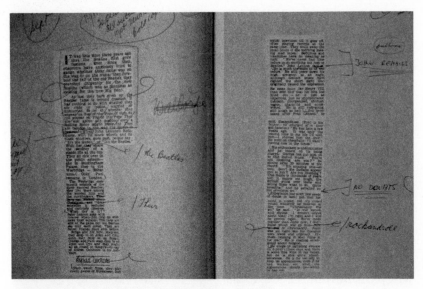

Art Unger's edit of Maureen Cleave's *Evening Standard* interview with John Lennon.

for lighting the blue touchpaper and then standing back to watch the explosion, although usually it was over local politics, and so the biggest target in view was City Hall.

There was a mood building among conservative Americans that the Beatles had been in the spotlight too long, and they were longing for their predicted decline in popularity. They were just waiting for them to make a wrong move or be pushed out of the way by a newer phenomenon. At this stage the public didn't know about the group's fornicating, swearing, and drug taking and not much about their working-class socialist views, but nevertheless there was a strong suspicion that they were a threat to decent values and were leading a generation astray.

When the Beatles had appeared on the Ed Sullivan Show two years previously, the evangelist Billy Graham had said, based on hope rather than hard evidence, that they were likely to be a short-lived craze. Youth preacher David A. Noebel had made a name for himself by writing books and pamphlets with titles such as *Communism, Hypnotism & the Beatles* (1965) and *Rhythm, Riots and Revolution* (1966) where he portrayed the Beatles as destroying the morals of the young and thus preparing the West for a Marxist takeover orchestrated by Moscow.

Layton and Charles had a daily breakfast show on WAQY in Birmingham, and on Friday, July 29, they started discussing what John had said, trying to ignite a debate. According to Layton, it was Charles who picked up the magazine

Preacher David Noebel saw rock 'n' roll as part of a communist plot to undermine the morality of Western youth.

and said something like "Did you hear what John Lennon said?" Layton hadn't, and so Charles obligingly read out the quotes from *Datebook* and added, "That's it for me. I'm not going to play the Beatles anymore." It was an off-the-cuff remark. Nothing had been planned, but Charles knew that it would play to the prejudices of the Bible Belt audience that listened to morning radio between six and nine.

Although *Datebook* wasn't even on the stands yet, the comments triggered an unprecedented number of calls, alerting the DJs to the fact that they'd touched a nerve. They took a snap poll of their listeners and found 99 percent of them shared their disapproval of John's apparent arrogance. They then suggested it would be a good idea if fans brought in their unwanted Beatles records so that WAQY could organize a huge bonfire when the Beatles next came to the area. As it happened, they weren't due to play Birmingham on the next American tour but were scheduled to play 240 miles away in Memphis on August 19. What had started as no more than a rash statement to goad listeners was turning into a campaign with its own uncontrollable momentum.

The program director, Frank Giardina (who was also an announcer under the name Frank Lewis), was horrified at what he was hearing. He knew that the records of the Beatles played a vital role in attracting a valuable teenage audience. WAQY was, after all, in the business of Top 40 radio, and as a thousand-watt station up against two far more powerful local stations it could ill afford to lose young fans that tuned in while dressing, having breakfast, and being driven to school. But as Layton and Charles also owned the station, Giardina had little influence in the matter.

These events would probably have remained in Birmingham if twenty-six-year-old Al Benn, the Birmingham bureau manager of United Press International (UPI), hadn't been driving in the city that morning with his car radio on. The DJs he was listening to were well known to him, and his reporter's instinct told him that this threat to make a bonfire of the Beatles records was a story in the making. If he filed it to UPI, it would almost certainly get picked up by papers in Atlanta and, soon after, by New York. Little did he know that this would turn into the scoop of his lifetime, a story that immediately ran around the world and later became so much a part of history that people would need only to hear the phrase "more popular than Jesus" to be reminded of the story.

In an article titled "Birmingham Disc Jockeys to Hold Beatles Burning," UPI reported: "Two local disc jockeys, angered at recent disparaging remarks about Christianity by the 'Beatles,' Saturday announced their plans to hold a 'Beatle burning.' Tommy Charles and Doug Layton of WAQY said they have asked listeners to send in

Beatle records, pictures and clothing for a Beatle bonfire in a couple of weeks." Charles thought the ban on the Beatles he had introduced two days ago might show the British group that they were "not the godlike creatures" they appeared to think they were. "It's a shame because they're talented boys," he was quoted as saying. "They are as good as or better than any group today but we think it's time somebody stood up to them and told them to shut up."

The story ran in papers on Sunday, July 31. When Art Unger heard about it, he immediately called Brian Epstein in Portmeirion to say, "This is getting a little out of hand here. They're planning to burn Beatles' records." Initially, Epstein wasn't bothered. "Arthur," he said, "if they burn Beatles records, they've got to buy them first."

But Epstein had seriously underestimated both the instinct of the religious to protect what they consider sacred and the power of the media to stir up controversy and then feed on its own frenzy.

AUGUST

I think that everybody is entitled to an opinion, including entertainers. Entertainers most of all.
–JOHN, 1966

For a few days the Beatles and Brian Epstein remained unconcerned about the hostility building in America. Epstein was still recuperating in the sea air with George Martin as his houseguest; George and Pattie had driven down to Stoodleigh in Devon to stay with Pattie's mother, Diana, on her farm; and John and Ringo were spending time with their families in Weybridge. On July 30, at Wembley Stadium in London, England's soccer team had dramatically triumphed over West Germany in extra time to win the FIFA World Cup for the first (and so far only) time, unleashing a booster dose of good feelings in a nation that was just getting used to being vital, trendy, and swinging. "Good Day Sunshine" captured the mood of the day, and the best of the British summer still lay ahead.

On August 1, Paul went to BBC's Broadcasting House to be interviewed for David Frost's new radio series *David Frost at the Phonograph*. It was a fairly light conversation, but an interesting exchange took place when Paul spoke of the creative restlessness that always kept him searching for the next breakthrough. Frost asked him if

he was ever completely satisfied with a Beatles record once it had
been made. "No, that's the trouble. Immediately we've done an LP,
we want to do a new one, because we're a bit fed up. And the time it
takes a record company to get it out, by the time it's out, we really
hate most of the tracks. That's the way it is." Frost wanted to know in
that case whether any Beatles record still felt satisfying to him. "No.
I go off records because . . . we're developing," he said, adding that
two years ago their songs were in his opinion "a bit cornier," and, for
that reason, "I suppose I go off records a bit quicker than anyone else
would."

The same day, in a follow-up story titled "Hot Time Is Scheduled
for Beatles," Al Benn revealed that the threatened bonfire of Beatles
paraphernalia was scheduled for mid-August in Birmingham, Alabama. From August 2 onward, at the top of every hour, Layton and
Charles made spot announcements advertising the planned im-
molation and listing collection points where fans could bring their
records, posters, pictures, and books. WAQY would arrange for the
materials to be collected and stored, ready for the day of destruction.

Other news agencies, notably the Associated Press, had now
picked up on the story, and, as it spread, radio stations around the
country began to echo the rabble-rousing rhetoric of Layton and
Charles. By August 4, "Lennon Says Beatles More Popular Than
Jesus" had become a nationwide story. An AP release that day bore the
headline "Broadcasters Hit Beatles" and reported on more planned
record burnings. It repeated John's statement and then quoted
Tommy Charles: "We just felt it was so absurd and sacrilegious that
something ought to be done to show them they cannot get away with
this sort of thing."

Only a small number of stations had issued outright bans so
far—maybe as few as forty—all of them inspired by what had happened in Birmingham, and many of them not stations that normally
played a lot of Beatles music anyway. The Maureen Cleave interviews
with all four Beatles (worked together as a single piece over five pages)

'Ban the Beatles' Campaign Growing

Birmingham Beatle Boycott Spreads Across Four States

BIRMINGHAM, Ala. (UPI)—across the nation.

Beatle Hit Below the Bible Belt

The Beatles is dead, insists Birmingham, Ala., radio station manager Tommy Charles.

Charles, of WAQY, has organized a "Ban the Beatles" campaign because of an article he read in a teenagers' magazine called "Datebook."

The story quotes John Lennon, the literary Beatle, as saying that the British foursome is more popular than J——

"Christianity will go," the article quoted Lenn...

"Jesus Remark"

Boston Snubs The Beatles

BOSTON UPI - Boston teenagers virtually ignored the Beatles Thursday when the mop topped

Apologizes

Teenagers at a 'Beatles Burning' staged by WAYX radio station

Beatles Flying into Religious Storm

LONDON (AP) — The Beatles took off for the United States today to face what could be the first real challenge to their popularity since becoming worldwide show business sensations.

As they winged toward Boston, a small section of the big crowd of hysterical girl teenage fans chanted:

"John not Jesus . . . John not Jesus."

In Chicago tomorrow, the Beatles open their third tour of American cities. One, Memphis, has suggested through its City Council that the two scheduled perform-

ances in the Tennessee city be cancelled.

This followed a ban by a number of radio stations on the playing of quartet's records after Beatle John Lennon was quoted as saying that he and the other three mop-headed musicians, Paul McCartney, George Harrison and Ringo Starr, are more popular than Jesus.

Before the Beatles plane took off, Lennon told newsmen:

"I am worried about what's been going on, but I'm not worried about this tour."

Asked if he was worried

about the Beatles' American reception McCartney replied: "No. No. No."

A few hours before the Beatles boarded their plane, Harrison backed up Lennon's explosive remark.

bigger than Jesus

Boycott ban Burn

jesus lennon

I'm sorry about quote, Beatle says

BY NORMAN GLUBOK
CHICAGO, Aug. 12 —(CDN)—Beatle John Lennon wants the world to know he's sorry he ever said that the Beatles are more popular than Jesus.

"I'm sorry I said it for the mess it's made," Lennon said.

"But I never meant it as a lousy or anti-religious thing or anything."

"From what I have read of Christianity and from what I have observed it just seems to be shrinking.

Beatles Manager Here to Quell Storm Over Remark on Jesus

SATURDAY, AUGUST 6, 1966.

GERALD SCARFE IN PRIVATE EYE (LONDON)

John's casual comment about Jesus heightened security fears when the Beatles toured America.

had already appeared in the *New York Times Magazine* on July 3 under the title "Old Beatles—A Study in Paradox" and even though John's soon-to-be controversial quote had been included, it hadn't provoked comment. It even had an additional quote—"Show business belongs to the Jews. It belongs to their religion"—that likewise failed to draw any indignation. *Newsweek* (circulation two million) had used John's words in its March 21 issue, and in May the interview had appeared in *Detroit* magazine. Again, no records were burned as a result, and John's comment didn't even become a talking point.

Although the record-burning, Beatle-banning campaign was an exercise in manipulation by the media and much of the outrage was either exaggerated or fake, it had real-life consequences. *Datebook* became inundated with calls—from fans wanting to know whether John had really said what he was quoted as saying, from radio stations requesting quotes from editor Art Unger, and from magazines like *Newsweek* requesting advance copies. Fred Forest of WMOC in Chattanooga called to get John's comments clarified, and when *Datebook*'s message taker asked him to describe the reaction in Tennessee, Forest responded, "The Beatles better watch out when they hit the Southern States." The message taker added a personal note: "Forest is apparently not a Bible thumper. He was just quoting from general public reaction." Christie Barter, a press officer from Capitol Records overseeing the East Coast, called to express concern that sales of Beatles records could be affected if DJs continued to announce bans.

Nat Weiss, Epstein's business partner in New York; Sid Bernstein of the booking agency General Artists Corporation; and Epstein's American entertainment attorney Walter Hofer phoned Epstein in Portmeirion to update him about the buildup in America, recommending that, despite his illness, he fly to America as soon as possible to organize some damage control. In his view, if John didn't explain himself to the satisfaction of the Christian constituency in the South, the danger was that some promoters might cancel their concerts out of fear of violence either toward themselves or toward the Beatles. Brian suggested John should go to the studio with George Martin to record an apology scripted by former journalist Derek Taylor (ghost writer of Epstein's autobiography *A Cellarful of*

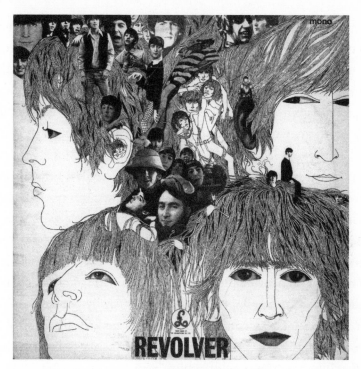

The cover of *Revolver* as released in Britain, August 1966.

Noise and now West Coast PR man for the Byrds and the Beach Boys) that could be released to US radio stations.

Epstein was driven from Portmeirion to Chester, where he took a chartered four-seater Cessna plane to London and then a scheduled Pan Am flight on to New York. Weiss met him at the airport. That day's papers carried the news that the satirical comic Lenny Bruce—the man famous for lines such as "People are straying away from the church and going back to God"—had died in his Hollywood home of a heroin overdose. The next morning (August 5, the day of *Revolver*'s release in the UK) Epstein woke up to find the John and Jesus story on the front page of the *New York Times*. A press conference was hurriedly arranged for that afternoon at the Americana Hotel on Seventh Avenue.

The *New York Times* splash was a UPI story about the continuing wave of Beatles record bans with a quote from Maureen Cleave that was typically intelligent and succinct. "[John] was simply observing that so weak was the state of Christianity that the Beatles were, to many people, better known than Jesus," she said. "He was deploring rather than approving this. He said things had reached a ridiculous state of affairs when human beings could be worshiped in this extraordinary way."

In another interview, with DJ Clark Race of KDKA (Pittsburgh), Cleave said that the comments had been "taken out of context and did not accurately reflect the article or the subject as it was discussed." She said that John's intention was to say that "the power of Christianity was on the decline in the modern world and that things had reached such a ridiculous state that human beings (such as the Beatles) could be worshipped more religiously by people than their own religion." These comments were scooped up by Capitol and used as the basis of a press release headed "Author of Beatles Article Denies Quote Attributed to Lennon."

Epstein arrived at the Americana looking subdued, wearing a dark suit with an appropriately dark tie. Two further stories had appeared in print that day which made matters worse, and he was not happy that Maureen Cleave was sharing her thoughts with other news outlets. An extract from Paul's interview with David Frost had been released ahead of its transmission. In it Paul had said that Americans "seem to believe that money is everything. This applies especially to the sort of people that we meet—agents and corporation people. You get the feeling that everybody's after money, and it's frightening." George had also been outspoken. Speaking to *Disc and Music Echo* shortly after getting back from the Far East and before the Jesus controversy had blown up, he made the comment, "We'll take a couple of weeks to recuperate before we go and get beaten up by the Americans."

Epstein was furious. Although these statements were not as controversial as what John had said, it wasn't good at this time for any of the Beatles to appear to be anti-American as well as anti-Christian. Epstein immediately sent a telegram to his assistant Wendy Hanson in London instructing her to clamp down on any loose talk. "Please advise Beatles to continue not to speak to the press under any circumstances," he wrote. "Also, it is not necessary for John to make the [apology] tape with Martin. Please advise Maureen Cleave."

When Epstein stood up before the gathered journalists and photographers at the Americana, he spoke clearly and assuredly but was conscious that he had to choose his words carefully, because the wrong verb or adjective could overheat an already tense situation. He stepped up before the phalanx of microphones, adjusted his papers, and then delivered his prepared statement on behalf of John.

The only reason I'm here, actually, is in an attempt to clarify the situation, the general furor that has arisen here, and I have prepared a statement which I will read which has had John Lennon's absolute approval this afternoon with myself by telephone. This is as follows: The quote which John Lennon made to a London columnist more than three months ago has been quoted and represented entirely out of context. Lennon is deeply interested in religion and was, at the time, having serious talks with Maureen Cleave, who is both a friend of the Beatles and a representative for the London *Evening Standard*. Their talks were concerning religion.

What he said, and meant, was that he was astonished that in the last 50 years the church in England, and therefore Christ, had suffered a decline in interest. He did not mean to boast about the Beatles' fame. He meant to point out that the Beatles' effect appeared to him to be a more immediate one upon, certainly, the younger generation. The article, which in depth was highly complimentary to Lennon as a person, was understood by him and myself to be exclusive to the *Evening Standard*. It was not anticipated that it would be

The back cover of *Revolver* as released in Britain, showing the track listing and a photo of the Beatles taken while filming promotional sequences for "Paperback Writer" and "Rain" at EMI Studios.

displayed out of context and in such a manner as it was in an American teen-age magazine.

In the circumstances, John is deeply concerned, and regrets that people with certain religious beliefs should have been offended in any way whatsoever.

What Epstein did not appear to have been aware of—or chose to ignore—was that his employee Tony Barrow had offered the interview to *Datebook* on March 5 (the day after it was first published) in a letter that Art Unger kept in his files. Written on NEMS Enterprises Ltd. letterhead stationery and sent to Unger at *Datebook*'s office at 71 Washington Place in New York, it read:

Dear Art,

I haven't any positive information for you just yet regarding your proposed visit to London. In the meantime, I think you might be more than interested in a series of "in-depth" pieces which Maureen Cleave is doing on each Beatle for the London Evening Standard. I'm enclosing a clipping showing her piece on John Lennon. I think the style and content is very much in line with the sort of thing DATEBOOK likes to use.

I have told Maureen I am writing to you on this and, in fact, I think she would be quite willing to do a re-write job on the full series specifically for DATEBOOK.

Perhaps you could get together with her when you're in London. If you have more urgent interest in the material I'll ask her to drop you a line in the meantime. Let me know.

With good wishes,
Yours sincerely,
for NEMS ENTERPRISES LTD

TONY BARROW
Senior Press and Publicity Officer.

Beginning March 10, Unger and Cleave exchanged correspondence that resulted in *Datebook* buying rights from the United Feature Syndicate on March 31. Unger confirmed the purchase with Barrow on April 4 and asked whether "you or the boys felt there was any distortion in the material since there is still time to cut or correct in case of factual error etc." Barrow responded on April 14 saying, "I am glad to hear that you managed to secure the magazine rights for the Maureen Cleave series." He didn't take up the invitation to make any changes.

After his speech, Epstein opened himself up to questions. A lot of the writers pursued rumors that the American concerts were not selling as well as expected. There was speculation that this apparent flagging interest might signal the beginning of the end. "This is the third time that the Beatles have been to the United States and quite obviously they're not the novelty they were in the first place," Epstein conceded.

Someone wanted to know how they felt having gone from being objects of adulation to objects of resentment, hostility, and derision. "They feel absolutely terrible," he admitted, adding that it was worrying for them to be pushed around and face antagonism. "The business of coming out of Manila was something that they and I will never forget. It was very unpleasant."

Another journalist asked if any tour dates would be altered to avoid the Bible Belt cities where protests were taking place. "This is highly unlikely," Epstein said. "I've spoken to many of the promoters this morning and when I leave here I have a meeting with several of the promoters who are anxious that none of the concerts should be cancelled. Actually, if any of the promoters were so concerned and it was their wish that a concert should be cancelled I wouldn't in fact stand in their way. As a matter of fact, the Memphis concert which is nearest to the place where this broke out apparently sold more tickets yesterday than they had done up until that day."

The issue of sluggish sales resurfaced. "This has been exaggerated because I've been through the figures for many of the concerts and they are good as could possibly have been expected. In fact, in many areas they are complete sell-outs and you must remember that the Beatles are not doing ordinary concerts. They are playing in enormous auditoriums and stadiums."

At this point Art Unger stood up to defend the integrity of *Datebook*. "I believe John had a perfect right to say what he did say and I think that it's objectionable to deny him the right to say what he believes," he said. "However, that has nothing to do with the fact that the story that Maureen Cleave wrote appeared not out of context in *Datebook*. All of the quotes are there. The entire story is there."

Epstein looked slightly taken aback. "It did appear out of context," he asserted. "This was taken as the predominant part of the article, which it wasn't. Anyway, I could go on discussing that with you at great length. It is very definitely my view, and practically everybody else's view, that it was out of context."

It was unclear whether Epstein thought the whole article was out of context by being placed in *Datebook* (having initially been produced for an adult readership in London) or whether he thought that the quote on Christianity was out of context on the front cover. It's true it wasn't representative of the entire interview, but no single quote would have been. In America, it was certainly the one thing he said most likely to gain traction.

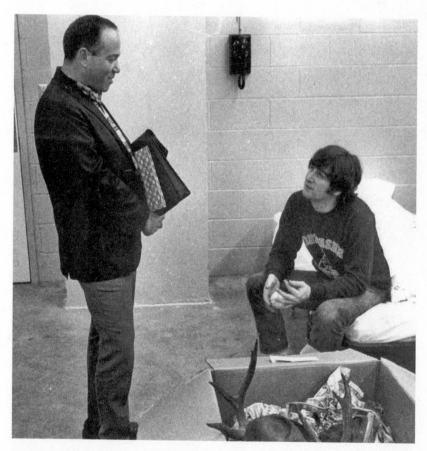

During the Beatles' 1965 tour of America, John spent time backstage with *Datebook* editor Art Unger.

"What about future interviews?" someone asked. "Will the Beatles be a bit more careful or a bit more selective in who they do stuff with?" Epstein thought carefully before saying, "The Beatles are basically very honest people. Naturally as one goes on in this business one learns and it is unfortunate that this quote and this article appeared in a teen-age magazine and was open to so much misinterpretation. When it originally appeared in the *Evening Standard* in London nothing happened at all. As a matter of fact, there were four articles, one on each of the boys, and they were all thought to be of the very best and highest standard. Maureen Cleave is an excellent columnist."

Q: What is Mr. Lennon's reaction to the furor?

EPSTEIN: He is very genuinely and truly concerned.

Q: Do any of the Beatles have any formal religious affiliation?

EPSTEIN: No.

Q: Mr. Epstein, could you say that this was implicitly a criticism of the Church of England since that is the official state church in England.

EPSTEIN: No. It's not an official criticism of any kind. It was a comment that was incidental.

Q: Are they definitely still coming to the States?

EPSTEIN: They will arrive in Chicago on August 11—where the concerts are sold out. I believe there are about 100 seats to go.

Q: Brian. Are you worried in any way what might happen to the Beatles when they arrive?

EPSTEIN: Yes. I am concerned.

Q: What about?

EPSTEIN: Security.

Q: What do you propose to do?

EPSTEIN: There is very little that you can do because they have always enjoyed maximum security in this country and the tours have been exceptionally well arranged and one just hopes for the best.

Q: Are you worried because of things that have happened in places like Austin and Chicago? [This was a reference to Richard Speck's knifing of eight student nurses in Chicago on July 14 and Charles Whitman's shooting spree from the University of Texas tower in Austin, where he hit forty-three people, killing thirteen of them, the first mass murder in a public place that America had ever experienced.]

EPSTEIN: Not specifically, because this sort of thing has happened before previous tours.

Q: Are you taking any special precautions?

EPSTEIN: No. But I shall watch the security personally, very much.

The Beatles left London Airport on August 11 on a Pan Am flight bound for Boston. On arrival they were greeted by up to six hundred screaming fans. A connecting flight took them to Chicago, where they disembarked ahead of the rest of the passengers close to a hangar away from the main terminal. From here they were driven straight to the Astor Tower Hotel, which was two blocks from Lake Michigan. Tony Barrow had arranged a press conference in his suite on the twenty-seventh floor for local and national journalists at which he hoped the Beatles, and John in particular, would explain themselves sufficiently well to defuse the situation.

Art Unger had a private meeting with Brian Epstein in his penthouse suite. The Beatles' manager appeared to be in a good mood.

He was dressed in tight white corduroy trousers and a flowing lavender shirt, and he offered Unger a drink. But his mood soon changed. Unger was an accredited member of the press corps that would be following the Beatles to every venue, attending every concert, taking part in conferences and round table interviews, and flying on the group's chartered planes and buses. Epstein wanted him to "voluntarily" surrender his pass. He thought that being a visible presence on the tour might lead some critics to suspect that the whole controversy had been a publicity stunt engineered by *Datebook* and NEMS to put the tour on the front pages and sell tickets.

"It was a bad idea for you to run those interviews in the first place," he told him. "But if you agree to cancel your participation, there are many other things I could do for you. We could make a great publishing team." In his private notes Unger recorded, "I resisted the temptation to tell him that his own publicist had sent me the stories in the first place. I never revealed that to anybody because I didn't want to place the burden on a nice guy who had only been doing his job."

He was angry that Epstein was trying to bribe him, although he didn't believe he would actually go as far as to have him banned. "Brian," he said. "I came here to cover the tour and I'm going to cover it. If you don't want me to come you'll have to throw me out of the press corps and you know how the other press people will react." Unger left the room but remained on the tour. When he told John what had taken place, John was angry. "Don't you worry," he said. "You're coming with us. I'll tell Brian that if you don't go, I won't go."

There was a select group of journalists and DJs with the precious red passes that allowed them total tour access as well as seats on the buses and charter planes that ferried the Beatles between cities. Besides Unger there was Judith Sims, founding editor of *TeenSet*, English journalist Bess Coleman from *Teen Life*, Marilyn Doerfler from Hearst Newspapers, and the DJs Ken Douglas (WKLO Louisiana), Jerry Ghan (WKYC Cleveland), Paul Drew (WQXI Atlanta),

Jim Stagg (WCFL Chicago), Scott Regan (WKNR Detroit), George Klein (WHBQ Memphis), Tim Hudson (KFWB Los Angeles), Kenny Everett (Radio London), Ron O'Quinn (Radio England), and Jerry Leighton (Radio Caroline North). Other writers and DJs joined the tour only for one or two dates, usually concerts immediately preceding ones in their home city.

Before going into the suite for the press conference, Epstein and Barrow took John aside and briefed him. They again explained that he needed to reassure the Americans that he was neither attacking Christianity nor suggesting that the Beatles were divine. He had simply meant to compare the passion and interest surrounding the group with the same generation's apparent loss of interest in formal religion.

John was torn. One the one hand he didn't want to risk wrecking the popularity of the Beatles and everything he had ever worked for, but on the other he didn't want to be insincere or water down his opinions. People valued the Beatles' irreverence, honesty, and challenging comments. He didn't want to compromise his views and turn into the sort of bland entertainer he had so often derided as being "soft." During the 1965 tour of America he had told a reporter from *Datebook,* "I've reached the point in my life when I can only say what I feel is honest. I can't say something just because it's what some people want to hear. I couldn't live with myself."

"He was terrified," Cynthia Lennon told me in 2005. "What he'd said had affected the whole group. Their popularity was under the microscope but he was the one who had opened his mouth and put his foot in it. I didn't go on the tour with him but I know he was very frightened."

John knew that there had been letters from anonymous sources threatening violence, and there were worries that white supremacists in the South could plant a sniper at one of the concerts. It upset him that something he had said could make his best friends Paul, George, and Ringo vulnerable to an attack. After listening to the options of what he could say and do he put his head in his hands and began weeping in front of Epstein, Barrow, and photographer Harry Benson. None of them had ever seen him so broken. "He was trying, but not actually succeeding, in hiding it from us," Tony Barrow told me. "It was so uncharacteristic of the guy."

The main room of Barrow's suite was a small space for such a major press conference. So many journalists were squeezed in that the Beatles were clustered together with their backs against a wall. To reassure outraged America that they were reasonable and responsible they wore the dark suits, white shirts, and neckties they'd worn on previous tours rather than the cool Chelsea fashions. John was chewing gum to calm his nerves.

The first questioner asked John to clarify the *Datebook* remarks. "If I had said 'television' is more popular than Jesus, I might have got away with it," he answered. "But as I just happened to be talking to a friend, I used the word 'Beatles' as a remote thing—not as what *I* think of as Beatles—as those other Beatles like other people see us. I just said 'they' are having more influence on kids and things than anything else, including Jesus. But I said it in that way, which is the wrong way."

What did he think when he heard that some teenagers agreed with him—that they did love the Beatles more than Jesus? "Well, originally I was pointing out that fact in reference to England—that we meant more to kids than Jesus did, or religion, at that time. I wasn't knocking it or putting it down, I was just saying it as a fact. It is true, especially more for England than here. I'm not saying that we're better, or greater, or comparing us with Jesus Christ as a person or God as a thing or whatever it is. I just said what I said and it was wrong, or was taken wrong. And now it's all this."

He admitted that the burnings and the bans bothered him, but he was pressed further to make a statement as to whether he felt any regret over having made the comment. "I am. Yes, you know. Even though I never meant what people think I meant by it, I'm still sorry I opened my mouth."

Some journalists seemed to think that this fell short of a full apology. One asked, "Did you mean that the Beatles are more popular than Christ?" John sighed before answering, rattled that after all he'd said through Brian and now in person the discussion hadn't moved on: "When I was talking about it, it was very close and intimate with this person that I know who happens to be a reporter. And I was using expressions on things that I'd just read and derived about Christianity. Only I was saying it in the simplest form that I know, which is the natural way I talk. But she took them, and people that know me took them exactly as it was—because they know that's how I talk."

The conversation then turned to the music. Writers found it difficult to reconcile the mop tops of "I Want to Hold Your Hand" with the serious-minded musicians behind "Eleanor Rigby" and "Tomorrow Never Knows." Paul picked up the question, relieved that the conversation appeared to have moved away from the controversy. "The thing is," he said, "we're just trying to move it in a forward direction. And this is why we're getting in all these messes with saying things—because we're just trying to move forwards. People seem to be trying to sort of hold us back and not want us to say anything that's vaguely inflammatory. I mean, if people don't want that, then we won't do it. We'll just sort of do it privately. But I think it's better for everyone if we're just honest about the whole thing."

This was Paul doing what he did best—ameliorating potentially explosive confrontations. He was eager on the one hand to assert the group's commitment to progressive art and attitudes but concerned on the other not to cause unnecessary offense. He implied that the Beatles' only motivation was honesty but offered to compromise by only being honest "privately" if that's what it took to avoid causing upset. Thus, in the most charming way possible, he placed the Beatles on the higher moral ground without accusing or denigrating their antagonists.

The next day the group faced another press interrogation, this

Maureen Cleave's interview with John as it appeared in *Datebook*.

time from DJs and some accredited journalists on part of the tour. John repeated his position on the *Datebook* affair but went into more depth: "My views on Christianity," he explained, "are directly influenced by *The Passover Plot* by Hugh J. Schonfield. The premise is that Jesus' message had been garbled by his disciples and twisted for a variety of self-serving reasons by those who followed, to the point where it has lost validity for many in the modern age. The passage that caused all the trouble was part of a long profile Maureen Cleave was doing for the London *Evening Standard*. Then, the mere fact that it was in *Datebook* changed its meaning that much more."

Asked what his religious background was, he explained,

Normal Church of England—Sunday school, and church. But there was actually nothing going on in the church I went to. Nothing really touched us. . . . By the time I was nineteen, I was cynical about religion and never even considered the goings-on in Christianity. It's only the last two years that I, all the Beatles, have started looking for something else. We live in a moving hothouse. We've been mushroom-grown, forced to grow up a bit quick, like having thirty- to forty-year-old heads in twenty-year-old bodies. We had to develop more sides, more attitudes. If you're a bus man, you usually have a bus man's attitude. But we had to be more than four mopheads up there on stage. We had to grow up or we'd be swamped.

Q: "Mr. Lennon, do you believe in God?

JOHN: I believe in God, but not as one thing, not as an old man in the sky. I believe what people call God is something in all of us. I believe that what Jesus, Mohammed, Buddha, and all the rest said was right. It's just the translations have gone wrong.

As with the first conference, there were questions about whether the Beatles' popularity was slipping. A UPI story had mentioned that shares of Northern Songs (the publisher of the Beatles' songs) had dropped from $1.64 to $1.36 since the scandal. The latest single, "Eleanor Rigby" / "Yellow Submarine" (like "Paperback Writer" before it), had not gone straight to No. 1 in the United Kingdom. "Love Letters" (Elvis Presley), "Mama" (Dave Berry), "God Only Knows" (Beach Boys), "Black Is Black" (Los Bravos), "The More I See You" (Chris Montez), "Out of Time" (Chris Farlowe), and "With a Girl Like You" (The Troggs) had held it back from the top spot. Unbelievably, there were still tickets available for the American tour.

Q: Do you feel you are slipping?

JOHN: We don't feel we're slipping. Our music's better, our sales might be less, so in our view we're not slipping, you know.

Q: How many years do you think you can go on? Have you thought about that?

GEORGE: It doesn't matter, you know.

PAUL: We just try and go forward.

GEORGE: The thing is, if we do slip it doesn't matter. You know, I mean, so what—we slip and so we're not popular anymore so we'll be unpopular, won't we? You know, we'll be like we were before, maybe.

JOHN: And we can't invent a new gimmick to keep us going like people imagine we do.

Q: Do you think this current controversy is hurting your career?

JOHN: It's not helping it. I don't know about hurting it. You can't tell if a thing's hurt a career or something until months after, really.

For the two shows (3:00, 7:30) at the International Amphitheatre on South Halsted in Chicago the Beatles stuck to the eleven-song set they'd used in Germany, Tokyo, and Manila with the exception of performing Little Richard's "Long Tall Sally" as the closer rather than "I'm Down." They played nothing from the newly released *Revolver*, because so many of the songs depended on other instruments ("Got to Get You Into My Life," "Eleanor Rigby," "Love You To," "For No One") or studio trickery ("Tomorrow Never Knows," "I'm Only Sleeping," "And Your Bird Can Sing," "She Said She Said"). The equipment of the day didn't permit them to do it.

The same four American acts supported them during the whole tour: black R & B singer Bobby Hebb, who'd had a recent hit with the single "Sunny"; East Coast girl group the Ronettes (with Ronnie Spector temporarily replaced by her cousin Elaine Mayes because her husband, Phil Spector, didn't trust her on the road with the Beatles);

Boston garage band the Remains (who did their own set but also played behind Hebb and the Ronettes); and the Cyrkle, a Pennsylvania band managed by Epstein and Nat Weiss.

Chicago didn't sell out in the way that Epstein had predicted (although there were around twelve thousand fans for each concert), but at least there had been no trouble. Fans waved supportive banners declaring SAY WHAT YOU THINK JOHN and WE LUV YOU MORE THAN EVER. The next morning the Beatles flew into Detroit for another two shows, again not sold out, at the Olympia Stadium on Grand River Avenue. This time a sole protester was spotted carrying a placard that said LIMEY GO HOME.

Few people bothered to ask Ringo for his opinions. He wasn't a composer, didn't need to fret about the group's direction, and was a relative latecomer to the lineup (he joined in 1962), but when journalists engaged him, he gave long and thoughtful answers. Asked by one writer whether he'd seen any change in teenagers over the years, he said, "Yes. I think they're getting a bigger chance to express themselves than ever before, which is good. This has been helped by the likes of Dylan and us. All the stars of the 1920s were men, you know? There were no teenagers. You had to be over 30 before anyone took any notice of you. It's only over the last ten years or so that anyone under the age of 20 has got anywhere."

Asked if the Beatles had ever wanted to record soul music, he answered, "We feel the urge but we've wised up. We've realized that we are white and haven't got what they've got. We haven't got that thing, so therefore that's why we called the LP *Rubber Soul*. In Britain all these groups are playing soul music that has as much soul in it as this tape recorder. No soul at all. And, really, we haven't got the soul that they have."

Between the afternoon and evening show in Detroit three journalists were allowed to interview the Beatles in a private office behind the stage. One of them was Loraine Alterman, who wrote a teen column for the *Detroit Free Press* and would go on to write for

Rolling Stone and have John Lennon as best man at her 1977 wedding to actor Peter Boyle. Alterman was a smart and understanding woman who the group found refreshing to talk to after the press conferences, where, as usual, everything but the music was discussed. In her published story she said of the Beatles, "They showed people that pop music can have meaning and its creators can be intelligent, talented artists."

George, wearing a black shirt and black trousers, sat on a table with his legs tucked under him as he talked to Alterman. "The main hang-up for me is Indian music," he told her.

> Really groovy—to pardon the expression, as opposed to the hip things in Western music which are opposed to Western classical music. Indian music is hip, yet 8,000 years old.
>
> I find it hard to get much of a kick out of Western music—even a lot of Western music I used to be interested in a year ago. Most music is still only surface, not very subtle compared to Indian music. Music in general, including ours, is still on the surface.
>
> We were right for the time when we came out. The pop scene five years ago was definitely looked upon by "musicians" as a dirty word. Pop was just something crummy. Now I think a lot of things in the pop field have more to them. We're very influenced by others in pop music and others are influenced by us. That's good. That's the way life is. You've got to be influenced and you try to be influenced by the best.

His growing dissatisfaction with the superficialities of pop was apparent, as was his desire to delve deeper both into the music and the spirituality of India. "I'm far from the goal I want to achieve," he said. "It will take me 40 years to get there. I'd like to be able to play Indian music as Indian music instead of using Indian music in pop. It takes years of studying, but I'm willing to do that."

Alterman was worried about talking to John, having heard of his intolerance toward poorly thought-out questions and his wounding wit, but he put her at ease. Regarding the "more popular than Jesus" issue he confessed: "I was shocked out of me mind. I couldn't believe it. I'm more religious now, and more interested in religion, than I ever was."

He was vague about his creative process, saying that he just made things up and that "some of it is just whatever comes into my head." Significantly, he felt that the Beatles had developed from a group that imitated rock 'n' roll heroes to one with a sound that was distinctively theirs. "It has progressed and gotten more like Beatle music," he said. "Before, it was more of anyone else's music. . . . We worked hard [on *Revolver*] because we wanted everything so perfect. On the *Rubber Soul* album we found out a lot technically. Things have come into focus. From there we could evolve into *Revolver*."

Paul, who Alterman regarded as "the handsomest Beatle of all," was charming and flirtatious, rubbing his knees against hers and joking with her that she could now sell them to collectors. He explained how his songs (he cited "Eleanor Rigby" and "Yellow Submarine") tended to come directly from his imagination and were not necessarily based on personal experience or intense feelings. They arose from concepts, words, or characters that entered his mind and seemed to demand investigation by being turned into art. She asked him what he thought the Beatles had done for contemporary pop music. "Given it a bit of common sense," he said. "A lot of it was just insincere, I think. Five years ago you'd find men of forty recording things without meaning just to make a hit. Most recording artists today really like what they're doing, and I think you can feel it on the records."

Another of the three journalists granted time in Detroit was Leroy Aarons of the *Washington Post*. Aarons, who had covered the Beatles in Washington, DC, in 1964, had been dispatched by his city editor to get something more in depth than was coming out of the press conferences. He was scheduled to do ten minutes with John, but the interview went so well it ended up lasting forty minutes, and he was invited to join the tour until the August 15 date in DC.

Aarons figured that he'd get more out of John by treating him as a serious thinker rather than a mouthy pop star. He talked to him about the recent *Time* magazine "Is God Dead?" cover story, and John opened up with thoughts about religion, his conventional Anglican upbringing, and the problems of pursuing truth in an industry designed to trade in fantasy. "That's the trouble with being truthful," he said. "You try to apply truth talk, although you have to be false sometimes because the whole thing is false in a way, like a game. But you hope sometime that if you're truthful with somebody they'll stop all the plastic reaction and be truthful back, and it'll be worth it but everybody is playing the game and sometimes I'm left naked and truthful with everybody biting me. It's disappointing."

Perceptively, Aarons could see that John's questioning of the faith handed down to him at Sunday school in Woolton, Liverpool, was all part of the adventurous, challenging, and experimental approach that was currently enlivening their music. What he had said to Maureen Cleave was no more than a provisional opinion but emerged from a serious search. "I can't express myself very well," John confessed. "That's my whole trouble."

When John left to go on stage, Aarons found a desk and composed his story. After the show he joined the Beatles on the bus that took them 170 miles to Cleveland, Ohio, where they were due to give a single concert at the Cleveland Municipal Stadium. They stayed at the thousand-room Sheraton Cleveland and scheduled a press conference for 5:45 in the hotel's Empire Room.

Aarons had handed them his story to look over—not usual *Washington Post* practice, but, hey, this was the Beatles—and in the afternoon was summoned to their suite. Tony Barrow told him they were all pleased with the story, but there was one thing they wanted changed. Aarons had commented that the latest single had slipped on the charts, but it hadn't.

He may have been referring to "Paperback Writer," which had reached No. 1 on the US charts but was now tumbling down, as would be expected ten weeks after its release, or he may have been talking about "Yellow Submarine," which was what DJs would call "a slow climber." It wasn't slipping down, but neither was it racing up. This sing-along single was a far cry from what young fans expected from the world's premier rock band. Released on August 8, it was only at 52 on the *Billboard* charts of August 20, rose to 8 the next week, then 5, then 3, before reaching its highest position of 2 in September.

But 1966 was a year of exceptional pop singles. Records later to be regarded as classics crammed the charts every week. In August alone the following singles were among those in *Billboard*'s Top Twenty: "Wild Thing" by the Troggs, "Summer in the City" by the Lovin' Spoonful, "Sunny" by Bobby Hebb, "Over Under Sideways Down" by the Yardbirds, "I Want You" by Bob Dylan, "Mother's Little Helper" by the Rolling Stones, "Summertime" by Billy Stewart, "Working in the Coal Mine" by Lee Dorsey, "Land of 1000 Dances" by Wilson Pickett, "You Can't Hurry Love" by the Supremes, and "Wouldn't It Be Nice" by the Beach Boys. The competition was tough.

Cleveland was the first concert where fans got out of hand. Four songs into the set, Paul mistakenly introduced a song by saying "For our next and final song." Fans, thinking the group was about to disappear, crashed through the wall separating them from the stage and began clambering up, breaking through the police cordon. The group had to be rushed to safety by helmeted riot officers, and the show was stopped for half an hour until order was restored.

The next afternoon they flew to Washington, DC, where six limousines were waiting at the airport to take them to the Shoreham Hotel on Calvert Street. The *Washington Post* had Leroy Aarons's story on its front cover—"'Can't Express Myself Very Well': Beatle Apologizes for Remarks." At the press conference the group was asked whether the Jesus comments had been made in order to sell seats. "That's not a publicity stunt," said John. "We don't need that publicity. Not like that."

At the DC Stadium on East Capitol Street they played one show for over thirty-two thousand fans before reboarding the bus and driving to Philadelphia. The incidents that they feared might take place hadn't occurred, and there was no serious opposition from right-wing political groups or religious fundamentalists other than five costumed members of the KKK who paraded incongruously outside the stadium in Washington. After the repeated explanations and apologies from John, the record bans were being lifted. Even the Birmingham burning was called off, leaving WAQY with a basement full of unwanted Beatles paraphernalia that it would have great difficulty in destroying.

American newspapers in 1966 didn't publish reviews of the concerts in their arts sections but reported on them as news. There was never any mention of the songs that were played or the quality of the performance. The journalists were interested only in the volume of the screams, the views of the teenagers, the size of the audience, and the takings at the box office.

Many of them clearly thought the Beatles were participants in a cynical moneymaking exercise, which is why they couldn't understand the artistic developments on *Revolver*. As they saw it, the point of show business, like any other business, was to give people more of what they wanted. The Beatles' hair and clothes were regarded as gimmicks designed to draw attention.

In some coverage there was disdain for John, who was regarded as someone trying to be too smart for a pop star. He was repeatedly referred to as "the brainy Beatle" or "the literary Beatle," as though it was unnatural for someone to try to be successful in more than one medium or as though it was improper for someone of intelligence to make a career out of writing and performing pop songs.

On tour the Beatles were trapped, in hotel rooms where the corridors were patrolled by security guards or on buses, planes, limousines, press conferences, airports, and stages surrounded by fences. They could circle the world but saw very little of it. They could talk freely, but had to weigh the consequences of every statement. Donovan, who had contributed a couple of lines to "Yellow Submarine" ("Sky of blue and sea of green"), concluded that the song was indirectly about the shared life of the Beatles—four guys trapped in a constricted space who sang songs to keep up their spirits.

After Philadelphia there were concerts in Toronto (August 17) and Boston (August 18) before the Beatles flew down to Memphis for potentially the most dangerous date of the tour, the first of only two appearances in the South, the region that had been most vociferous in denouncing John for his *Datebook* comment. Although they weren't going to be staying overnight (they would fly directly to Cincinnati in the early hours of the next morning), they were assigned eighty-six police officers and twenty private guards. Jerry Foley, the local promoter, had built a seven-foot-high stage at the Mid-South Coliseum with a five-foot wall in front to protect it from invasion.

Ticket sales had dipped in the wake of the protests in early August but picked up afterward. Over twenty-two thousand fans, out of a potential twenty-six thousand, would see the two shows. For the Beatles these were the tensest of all the concerts. Earlier in the day there had been a message that one of them would be assassinated on stage. In the afternoon there were half a dozen members of the Ku Klux Klan parading in their robes outside the venue. Elsewhere in the city, at the Ellis Auditorium, there was a Christian revivalist meeting planned in the hopes that the turnout (estimated at eight thousand) would disprove John's point about the decline of Christianity among the younger generation.

The Beatles were filmed between shows by a British news team preparing the thirty-minute documentary *The Beatles Across America* for the ITN program *Reporting 66*. Host Richard Lindley had inter-

viewed Tommy Charles in Birmingham and Imperial Wizard Robert
Shelton of the KKK faction the United Klans of America in Tusca-
loosa, had filmed a record burning in Georgia, and was going to the
youth revival meeting booked to clash with that night's concert.

Q: What difference has all this row made to this tour, do
you think? Any at all?

PAUL: Umm, I don't think it's made much. It's made it more
hectic. It's made all the press conferences mean a bit more.
People said to us last time we came, all our answers were a
bit flippant, and they said, "Why isn't it this time?" And the
thing is the questions are a bit more serious this time. It
hasn't affected any of the bookings. The people coming to
the concerts have been the same, except for the first show
in Memphis, which was a bit down, you know. But, uhh, so
what?

Q: The disc jockey, Tommy Charles, who started this row
off, has said that he won't play your records until you've
grown up a little. How do you feel about that?

JOHN: Well, I don't mind if he never plays them again, you
know.

PAUL: See, this is the thing. Everyone seems to think that
when they hear us say things like this that we're childish.
You can't say things like that unless you're a silly little child.

GEORGE: And if he [Charles] was grown up, he wouldn't
have done the thing 'cuz he only did it for a stunt, anyway.
So I mean, who is he to say about growing up? Who is he?

JOHN: [*demandingly*] Who!!

PAUL: [*jokingly to George*] Who is this guy?

JOHN: [*smiling*] Other than that, it's great.

PAUL: Quite a swinging tour.

Q: Do you feel that Americans are out to get you . . . that this is all developing into something of a witch hunt?

PAUL: No. We thought it might be that kind of thing. I think a lot of people in England did, because there's this thing about, you know, when America gets violent and gets very hung-up on a thing, it tends to have this sort of "Ku Klux Klan" thing around it.

Q: It seems to me that you've always been successful *because* you've been outspoken, direct, and forthright, and all this sort of thing. Does it seem a bit hard to you that people are now knocking you for this very thing?

JOHN AND PAUL: [*smiling and nodding with comic exaggeration*] Yes!!

JOHN: It seems VERY hard.

They dealt with the tension in the air by joking with each other as they prepared for the day's final show. "Send John out. He's the one they want," said George. "Maybe we should just wear targets on our chests," Paul suggested.

The audience was enthusiastic and screamed throughout. Three songs into their set, as the group was performing George's "If I Needed Someone," a firecracker hurled on stage from the balcony made a sizeable explosion at the foot of Ringo's drum kit. For a few seconds, on the final verse of the song, the screams turned into a collective gasp of shock. The Beatles themselves quickly looked around at each other to see which one of them had been shot but resolutely played on to the end. A young man (some newspaper reports said three young men) was seized by police and ushered out of a side exit. "They didn't miss a note," one pleasantly surprised audience member told the *New York Times*.

The August 20 show in Cincinnati had to be postponed because of torrential rain and was rescheduled for the next day. The Beatles were already playing an evening show in Saint Louis, Missouri, so they had to do Cincinnati at noon, then travel to Saint Louis for the evening concert. It was while standing out on the covered stage in Saint Louis as a storm broke over them that Paul finally decided that, like George and John, he no longer wanted to tour in this way. After the concert they flew to New York and checked into the Warwick Hotel at Fifty-Fourth Street and Sixth Avenue, ready for their return to Shea Stadium in Queens on August 23.

On August 22 they gave two press conferences at the Warwick. The first was for journalists and followed the by-now-predictable pattern. There was only one question about the Jesus comment (which John batted away by saying he'd already dealt with it), but there were several that circled around the suggestion that the Beatles' days as a performing group might be nearing their end. Was the low turnout of fans at the airport when they flew in an indication of declining popularity? (No.) Would John and Paul consider retiring from the stage and becoming the new Rodgers and Hammerstein? (No.) Had they ever considered individual recording careers? (No.)

On August 3, during the early days of the controversy, NEMS had announced that John was to star in a film to be directed by Richard Lester (director of *A Hard Day's Night* and *Help!*) called *How I Won the War*. This fueled rumors that each Beatle was going his own separate way, but John took great pains to explain that he'd only taken on the role at Lester's invitation—he wasn't seeking a film career—and filming would take place during a period when the Beatles weren't scheduled to be working.

Someone asked if they were doing "a Bob Dylan in reverse." He had started by doing folk songs and had moved toward rock 'n' roll. They had started by doing rock 'n' roll and had moved toward folk-rock. "That thing about Bob Dylan is probably right," Paul agreed, "because we're now getting more interested in the content of the songs whereas Bob Dylan is getting more interested in rock 'n' roll. It's just that we're both going towards the same thing. I think."

The other press conference was for a selection of young fans and was a Beatles initiative. Both the New York Top 40 radio station WMCA and the Official Beatles Fan Club of America asked fans to send in postcards with their details, and seventy-five fans from each group would be picked to attend the Junior Press Conference. The belief was that the questions of teenagers passionate about the music of the Beatles might be more refreshing than those of jaded journalists, many of whom didn't necessarily like the group or know much about their music. WMCA alone received forty-eight thousand cards.

It was a more light-hearted affair than the grown-ups' conference but yielded no big revelations. Many of the questions started "Is it true that . . . ?" and then cited a news report. Others were about the songs. Fans wanted to know whether they were about real events or real people. Apparently a story had circulated that there was an actual Eleanor Rigby who hung out with the Beatles.

During the day two teenage girls from Staten Island—Carol Hopkins and Susan Richmond—failing to gain entry to the Warwick, where the press conferences were taking place, had climbed out onto a narrow ledge on the twenty-second floor of the nearby Americana (where Epstein had made his initial defense of John's statement earlier in the month) and threatened to throw themselves off the building unless they could meet John and Paul. The police set up barriers to clear the sidewalks and spent twenty minutes coaxing the girls back to safety.

The Shea Stadium concert became an anticlimax. Almost exactly a year before the Beatles had played the same venue to a sellout audience of 55,600. It was the biggest crowd they had ever played to and set a world record for attendance at a pop concert and also for box office takings. This time there were eleven thousand empty seats despite tickets having been on sale for over two months. This led to fresh media speculation that the Beatles had already reached their peak. (Timothy Leary's eighteen-year-old daughter, Susie, was among those who attended.)

The latest *Newsweek* on the stands in Manhattan had a story titled "Blues for the Beatles" that focused on what it saw as the group's inevitable decline. The low turnout at Shea "suggested that the Beatles' era of sure-fire sell-outs had passed." The group members were now "married, rich and rococo." They were out of touch with their audience. "Their music, now baroque and folk, has cooled off many who used to pack the palladiums," it announced.

Astonishingly, although the Beatles had conquered New York, they had never really seen it, because they were cosseted by security and restricted by schedules. Only George had ever hit the tourist trail, and that was because he'd made a solo visit in 1963 when the group was not known in America. Asked to compare New York to London, John was forced to admit, "I just don't know. I haven't really seen enough. I'd like to but, you know, unless they blow it up I'll come and see it. It'll still be here."

After the concert they flew directly to Los Angeles, boarding the first-class section of their plane while it was in a hangar to avoid detection by the fans. While on the flight across America Art Unger from *Datebook* spent around five hours talking with George ("It's unusable, of course," Unger confided in notes he recorded immediately afterward; "it's about life and LSD etc. etc."), before briefly talking to Ringo, who was the first of the Beatles to openly admit the possibility of the four of them going their separate ways. The worst thing about this was that, he confessed, "I couldn't stand never seeing the lads again."

Acknowledging that each Beatle was looking for new projects to get involved in, he explained that he was still considering opening a hairdressing salon or a club. He was the most content but the least secure of the group. He was not a composer or a singer of note, and had no substantial publishing royalties to fall back on, having only had one partial writing credit thus far. "I've always

A fan's-eye view of the Curson Terrace property rented by the Beatles in West Hollywood for their dates in Seattle, Los Angeles, and San Francisco.

been short and small and all the other guys seem to get along but I'm not sure that I can [make a solo career out of music] because all I do is sit there and play the drums. I don't even like the way I sound when I sing. I'm not a millionaire. I am the poorest of the four. George and I are the poorest, although George has a bit more since he wrote a few songs."

The Beatles liked Unger. Not only was he a vital connection between the group and its base audience of nine- to fifteen-year-olds, he also was a sophisticated and intelligent man whose interests ranged from Broadway musicals to the Mayan civilization. As a gay man in New York he was knowledgeable about some of the city's fringe scenes, and they were interested in hearing his stories about theatre, art, and literature.

Timothy Leary had introduced Sanford Unger, Art's brother, to LSD. He was now a prominent psychologist researching the potential benefits of treating neurosis sufferers with hallucinogenic drugs. One of his most cited academic papers was "Mescaline, LSD, Psilocybin and Personality Change," published in the journal *Psychiatry* in May 1963. In 1965, he had been featured in a major CBS documentary, *LSD: The Spring Grove Experiment.*

Datebook, despite its young readership, had already tackled the topic of hallucinogens in a double-page spread, "LSD: Newest Teen Kick," in which Art Unger had balanced differing views on the still-legal drug. "The librarian in your local library may be able to help you track down exciting reading matter on the subject. Read up on LSD now—you can still be in the forefront of those with any real knowledge about what may be a revolutionary development in man's ability to appreciate himself."

Unger had yet to experience the drug, but his brother had offered to administer it to him under clinical conditions and guide him through the trip. Paul, in particular, thought this was a good and sensible offer and encouraged him to accept. He would do so in October and write to Paul with a detailed description of a trip that he considered "an ecstatic experience filled with wild, soaring, multiple perspectives."

Although the flight arrived in LA in the early hours of the morning, there were around four hundred fans awaiting them. The Beatles were driven to a gated compound with an eighteen-room house at 7655 Curson Terrace in West Hollywood that Brian Epstein had rented for the rest of their tour. Before leaving England George had told a journalist, "I'm not looking forward to [the tour] much, except for California, which comes at the end. There at least we can swim and get a bite to eat."

On August 24, their supposed day off, the Beatles relaxed around the pool with Joan Baez, David Crosby, Art Unger, Atlanta DJ Paul Drew of WQXI, and Ray Morgan of KLIV in San Francisco; they played billiards in the game room, swam, and played with a large plastic yellow submarine given to them by a fan. Late in the afternoon they were driven to the landmark Capitol Records Building at Hollywood and Vine, where, at six o'clock, they gave a press conference and also met with Robert Vaughn from the popular TV espionage series *The Man from U.N.C.L.E.*

The press conference revealed little that wasn't already known. This wasn't entirely the fault of the journalists. The Beatles had perfected the art of nonchalance in the face of inquisition. What was their most memorable occasion? "No idea." How does filming compare with recording? "We don't compare it much, you know." Would they prefer to play the Hollywood Bowl rather than Dodger Stadium? "We don't mind." What was the meaning of the butcher album cover? "We never really asked." How much had they made on the tour? "We don't know about that." Would they be touring America again in 1967? "Ask Brian."

The one potentially interesting line of investigation wasn't pursued. A journalist asked whether they would ever consider recording in America. The question appeared to take them by surprise, but once Paul had started talking he had to carry on:

PAUL: We tried actually, but it was a financial matter. Mmm, mmm! A bit of trouble over that one. No, we tried but—it didn't come off.

GEORGE: Internal politics.

PAUL: Hush hush.

RINGO: No dice.

JOHN: No comment.

No one followed up to find out when, where, and with whom this happened. Paul's "Hush hush" and John's "No comment" suggest either that the subject was off-limits or that if they told the truth, it would stir controversy. The conference ended with the Beatles being awarded a set of branding irons by Debbie Pinter, Yolanda Hernandez, and Stephanie Pinter of the Dallas Beatles Fan Club Charter. Two years before in Dallas the girls had given them ten-gallon hats they then wore on a photo shoot at a local farm.

When the conference was over, they hung out with David Crosby and Mama Cass and the next day flew to Seattle for two concerts. A rumor had swept Seattle that Jane Asher was flying in and that Paul was going to marry her there and then. At an afternoon press conference at the Edgewater Inn Paul was asked to confirm this story:

PAUL: It's tonight, yeah.

Q: What time and where?

PAUL: Tonight—I can't tell you that, now can I? It's a secret.

GEORGE: We don't want all the people there, do we?

Q: You are confirming the report?

PAUL: No, not really. It was . . . it's a joke. Who started this? Anyone know? Does anyone know? I just got in today and found out I was getting married tonight. No, she is not coming in tonight as far as I know.

GEORGE: And if she does, we are going out tonight anyway . . . so we'll miss her.

Jane was actually in Scotland. At a lunch in Edinburgh with the omnipresent Don Short, she laughed off the rumors of an imminent marriage to Paul. "We're perfectly happy as we are," she told him. "We may not marry for some time, quite possibly for years. I just can't say."

Speaking to Unger for *Datebook*, Paul was equally noncommittal. Asked how he felt about Jane's plan to tour America with the Old Vic next year, he said. "I won't try and stop her. It's a drag. I'd rather she didn't or I'd rather we were together for the four months." What does a boy of twenty-four do when his girl goes away? Does he wait, or date? "He has no idea what he does" was Paul's answer. "It hasn't happened to him yet. He hasn't got a clue. Anything could happen. It depends, you know, as everything depends. It's all relative."

In the past, male pop stars had risked destroying their appeal to a female audience by going steady or marrying. Even John had initially concealed his marriage to Cynthia. "Some pop musicians don't even associate with women because they believe they're not allowed to once they've become stars," Paul admitted. "They believe that they're wrecking their lives for their sake of their careers. That kind of thing is no longer important to me. You reach a point where you realize that the most important thing is to sort your own life out, and then possibly start indulging yourself and catering for other people."

It was also still risqué for stars to give the impression that they were sexually involved with partners they weren't married to. The year before Ringo had been asked in an interview, "Do you think a pop star could live in sin today without damaging his career?" and he had answered, "I don't really know. But I'm sure the mums and dads would hate him because they are trying to bring their kids up right." When Paul was living with the Ashers, he always made it clear that he had his own room and even when he moved to Cavendish Avenue spoke of Jane as a girlfriend who visited rather than a cohabitant. When Hunter Davies interviewed Paul at home in 1966, he reported in the *Sunday Times* that he "lives alone."

It was harder to pretend that they slept separately when they vacationed together. "Going on holiday with Jane? That doesn't bother me at all, because I know in my mind that there is nothing wrong with it. To people who want to 'keep television clean' and don't like miniskirts it would be scandalous. They'd love to think we were chaperoned everywhere but I'm afraid that doesn't fit in with what I believe. It would be hypocritical of me to pander to their tastes rather than my own."

AFTER THE SECOND CONCERT IN SEATTLE THE BEATLES FLEW back down to Los Angeles to stay at their Hollywood home. The next two days were for rest and relaxation. On one of them Derek Taylor invited Paul and George over to his home in Nichols Canyon to meet Brian Wilson and his brother Carl. On being introduced Paul broke the ice by saying "Well, you're Brian Wilson and I'm Paul McCartney so let's get that out of the way and have a good time."

The lights were turned down low, the Glenn Miller Orchestra played on the turntable, and the four musicians talked together for two hours. During the evening David Crosby joined them and Brian Wilson previewed a new Beach Boys track that he'd been working on for eight months. It was the most complex and labor-intensive single ever recorded. Wilson had used four studios, and his master version of the song, "Good Vibrations," was compiled from the most outstanding sections of over ninety hours of tape. The recording of this one song had already cost more than the whole of the *Pet Sounds* LP.

Wilson's meticulous method of assembling sounds and his decision to compose, arrange, and record rather than play on stage accorded with the growing feelings of the Beatles about their own future. The concert at Dodger Stadium in LA on August 28 illustrated the problems they now faced when giving a performance. The private security team hired to protect the group, US Guards Co., was stretched to the limit in shielding them from ravenous fans. Around seven thousand of the forty-five thousand in attendance broke through the fencing designed to separate them from the stage and tried to storm it once the show was over. The Beatles had to be taken to a safe room in the stadium until the crowd was under control and then were rushed away in an armored car. Over a hundred fans who had found where the Beatles were staying traveled to the compound, where police had to disperse them.

It was clear to everyone concerned that the Beatles couldn't continue to perform in such circumstances. It was not only physically dangerous but also artistically unfulfilling. They were no longer the group that teenage girls imagined they were when screaming and professing undying devotion. Ivor Davis, New York bureau chief for London's *Daily Express,* had been on the whole tour and on August 27 published a story titled "Could This Be the End of the Beatles Saga?" He quoted George saying, "Some nights I'm standing in front of the mike opening my mouth and I'm not even sure myself if anything is coming out." Paul told him, "When we started at the Cavern people listened and we were able to develop, to grow, to create. But when the screaming started the first casualty was the humour we put into our performances. Now of course we are prisoners, with 50 per cent of our act taken over by the audience."

It wasn't only the Beatles who felt the pressure. As much as he delighted in the touring side of the Beatles' career, Brian Epstein was finding it hard to maintain control as everything grew bigger and fraught with unprecedented problems. He sought relief in drugs and transient relationships with (usually) highly unsuitable young men who often took advantage of him both physically and financially.

While in Los Angeles he was paid a visit by "Diz" Gillespie, an aspiring actor from Ohio whom he'd hooked up with during the 1964 tour of America and subsequently brought to England to manage. There had been a dramatic falling out in London in 1965 involving threats, blackmail, and violence. Gillespie was now back, saying that he'd changed, and the gullible Epstein believed him, inviting him to share a meal with Epstein and Nat Weiss at the Beverly Hills Hotel. After Gillespie left the table at the end of the meal, Epstein realized that both his and Weiss's attaché cases were missing from their rooms.

Epstein panicked. Among his papers were contracts, letters, barbiturate tablets, intimate Polaroids, and twenty thousand dollars in cash. There was enough to destroy him if it was either found by the police or turned over to a newspaper. Gillespie knew the precise fears that would be running through Epstein's mind. He made an approach to Weiss demanding payment in exchange for the cases. Aware that he couldn't involve the LAPD, Weiss hired a private detective, who was able to entrap Gillespie's runner at the agreed drop-off point behind Union Station and have the case (minus the drugs, photos, letters, and eight thousand dollars of the cash) returned to its owner. Epstein was left humiliated. Weiss later spoke of it as the beginning of the serious depression that would create the circumstances leading to his early death.

The incident with the case was the reason why Epstein wasn't around for the last concert on the tour in San Francisco, the city that, for those interested in the twists and turns of youth culture, was now competing with London as the hot place to be. The soon-to-be legendary Trips Festival, where LSD taking was blended with loud music and mesmerizing light shows, had taken place in January at the Longshoreman's Hall near Fisherman's Wharf. Bands that played at this event included Big Brother and the Holding Company and the Grateful Dead. The local scene was exploding with musicians exploring the potential of rock music that could change consciousness—bands with long and surreal names whose members had hair longer than the Beatles'.

New venues were catering to audiences that wanted to walk around or dance rather than sit and scream. The weekend before the Beatles arrived, promoter Bill Graham had presented the Thirteenth Floor Elevators, the Great Society, and Sopwith Camel at the Fillmore Auditorium, and Chet Helms' Family Dog Productions had featured the Charlatans and Captain Beefheart and his Magic Band at the Avalon Ballroom. These were the new sounds for the older, tripped-out kids.

The musical outlook of these groups corresponded with that of the Beatles, particularly as showcased on *Revolver*, but because the Beatles flew in and out and didn't come into the heart of the city, they didn't visit Haight-Ashbury, where they would have seen the psychedelic street art, head shops, and impromptu concerts at the Panhandle east of Golden Gate Park.

Some of these innovators would see the show, including Marty Balin of Jefferson Airplane and Bob Weir of the Grateful Dead. "[The Beatles] were important to everybody," said the Grateful Dead's Jerry Garcia. "They were a little model. . . . It was like saying 'You can be young, you can be far-out, and you can still make it.'" The poster for the show was the work of Wes Wilson, one of the Bay Area's foremost designers of psychedelic posters for concerts at the Fillmore and Avalon (as well as an op-art poster for the Trips Festival), commissioned by Tom Donahue, a DJ at KYA, the station promoting the event. It featured a yin/yang circle enclosing the Stars and Stripes and Union Jack and a photo of the Beatles on a background of red and blue dots. "Our common English-language culture and basic humanistic zeitgeist was contained in this symbolic sharing," Wilson told me. "The British and American flags were united."

The concert on August 29, held at the Candlestick Park baseball stadium, has become legendary as the Beatles' final concert performance, but no one, neither the group nor the audience, knew at the time that this was the case. The Beatles flew up from Los Angeles in the afternoon, and the show was not notable for any other reason. Around

The last Beatles concert, Candlestick Park, San Francisco, August 29, 1966.

a quarter of the thirty-two thousand available seats remained unsold; the organizers, Tempo Productions Inc., lost money as they'd guaranteed the Beatles a fifty-thousand-dollar fee (and had to pay a standby orchestra because of local musician union rules); and a cold wind was blowing across San Francisco Bay. Unusually, Paul asked Tony Barrow to record the sound using a cassette recorder. The Beatles themselves had preserved no other concert on the tour in this way.

Backstage (in the visiting-team clubhouse converted into a dressing room) they were visited by Joan Baez and her sister Mimi Fariña (whose novelist/poet/songwriter/performer husband, Richard Fariña, had been killed in a motorcycle accident four months earlier) and spent time talking to Ralph Gleason, an influential cultural critic contributing to the *San Francisco Chronicle* who would go on to found *Rolling Stone* magazine in November 1967 with the much younger Jann Wenner. As they talked each Beatle did drawings on the paper tablecloths with colored Pentel crayons at the request of the catering company, who wanted to display them in their shop. John did a huge yellow sun, Paul a psychedelic flower, George a psyche-delic face, and Ringo a tiny comical face. Two days later there was a break-in at the catering company, and the cloth was stolen.

The UPI report of the concert concentrated on how much the Beatles would earn per minute for a thirty-minute performance and the behavior of fans that were kept in check by two hundred private security guards. It made no mention of music. The story concluded, "After the performance, the Beatles jumped into a waiting armored car and were driven off the field before anyone could get near to them."

Tony Barrow told me: "It was probably one of the most aver-age and ordinary concerts the Beatles had ever given. It lasted thirty minutes and musically was far from being the best. It was the end of a very tiring tour."

The last number they performed was "Long Tall Sally," the Little Richard song from 1956 that had been in the Beatles' repertoire since their formation. It always became a standout performance for Paul. After its final chords had died away John wished the crowd good night and added, "See you again next year." They flew back to LA on a chartered American Airlines plane. Once on board and at cruising altitude George turned to Tony Barrow and announced, "That's it. I'm not a Beatle anymore." Later he expanded on what he had meant. "We knew—this is it. We're not going to do this again. We'd done about 1,400 live shows and I certainly felt that was it."

John was sitting at the back of the plane as Art Unger approached him with a copy of the controversial issue of *Datebook* to ask for his signature. "Is this for you, or for the magazine?" John asked. Unger said it was for his own scrapbook. John took a pen and wrote "To Art with love from John C. Lennon." "The 'C,'" he told him, "stands for Christ."

He invited Unger to take the seat next to him while the in-flight meal was served. They talked about everything from LSD and music to archaeology and anthropology, and Unger was left with the impression that John was lost and without direction. He repeatedly said that he would like to pursue certain activities based on his personal interests but each time would conclude that because of his position it would be impossible. In his notes Unger observed, "He was very depressed about everything. He felt there was no point in doing anything since it wouldn't last very long anyway."

One comment John made was so poignant that Unger scribbled it down. "There is so much I would like to do, but there is no time," he said. "In ten years, I'll either be broke or crazy. Or the world will be blown up."

Reviewing the show in the *San Francisco Chronicle* (August 31, 1966) Ralph Gleason concluded with this prescient comment, "Is it all worth it? As a spectacle it is not without sociological interest, of course. As a performance it is, like John Lennon says, a puppet show. It can hardly continue to be attractive to four such rational, intelligent and talented human beings."

SEPTEMBER

The urge to be something more than a mere
Beatle provoked me to come to India. By
learning to play the sitar, I can give Beatle fans
a little more.
–GEORGE, 1966

On the last day of August the Beatles arrived at London Airport on a flight from Los Angeles. They emerged from the plane onto the tarmac wearing wide-lapelled jackets and long-collared shirts. This was the last time they would fly back home together and be greeted by screaming fans. The next day, at eleven o'clock, their journalist friend Maureen Cleave, whose interview with John had caused so much controversy, married her fiancée, Francis Nichols, at St Anne's Church, Knocknarea, in County Sligo, Ireland, and bade farewell to her stint as the *Evening Standard*'s pop music correspondent. "I've never played a pop record from 1966 to this day," she told me in 1994. "I never saw them again."

No official announcement had been made about the future of the Beatles, but it was becoming clear that they each wanted time to pursue their own interests outside of the group confines. They also each needed privacy after the intensity of the tour and the day-by-day scrutiny of the media. John had already committed to filming *How I Won the War* just to see how he fared as an actor; Paul had let it be known that he wanted to compose for a film soundtrack; and George couldn't wait to study the sitar and yoga.

They needed time apart for self-discovery and to establish pursuits previously crowded out by the business of the group. George was now following car racing and had attended this year's Grand Prix in Monaco with Scottish Formula One driver Jim Clark. Ringo had started a construction company (Bricky Builders) and was interested in gardening. "It was like guys returning from Vietnam," explained Neil Aspinall. "When they get back one lives in Brooklyn and the other lives in the Bronx, but they rarely socialise. Why? Because they were very different people to begin with, but they were obliged to stay together for a long time."

It was unclear whether these individual pursuits would precipitate the breakup of the group or simply open up more lines of inspiration and therefore enrich the Beatles. It was hard to think of them splitting, if only because there was no precedent for a group at the top of its game just stopping because it didn't think there was anywhere left to go. In the *Daily Express* of September 20 pop columnist Judith Simons articulated the fears of many fans: "Teenagers may be dismayed at the way the Beatles are splitting off in all directions in pursuit of their separate careers."

Brian Epstein had similar fears, but for different reasons. If the Beatles disintegrated, he would no longer be needed. Even if they remained together, but only as recording artists, his role would be severely diminished. The end of touring would mean that he would be reduced to negotiating their contracts and liaising with EMI.

He coped by throwing himself into work with his other artists (Gerry and the Pacemakers, Cilla Black, Sounds Incorporated, the Fourmost, Billy J. Kramer and the Dakotas), taking more drugs (mainly stimulants, sleeping pills, and marijuana but also some LSD), and living more dangerously in the homosexual *demimonde* that he inhabited when out of the public eye. He even took on the management of a handsome Colombian-born bullfighter, Henry Higgins, who had a British father and a Mexican-Irish mother but was known to Spanish fans as "El Ingles" (the Englishman).

At this stage, not surprisingly, the Beatles were more assured about what they didn't want to do than what they did. They knew that they didn't want to continue playing their songs to audiences that couldn't really hear them, to have their lives threatened because of their honest opinions, to play the game according to conventional show business rules, to be confined to writing songs that worked as either three-minute hit singles or crowd-rousing performances, or to have to humor dignitaries in every city they visited. (In 1971, in a letter to Eric Clapton, John referred to his touring days with the Beatles as "night after night of torture.")

Because they'd been so successful as writers and performers, they were at times tempted to think that their talent could be easily transferred to other art forms. John had already proved to be a successful comic poet, artist, and humorist. There was foolish talk of them writing a screenplay until John discovered that "writing movie scripts is much more difficult than you think." Other projects speculated upon included a Lennon-McCartney musical, the production of a West End play, and a film that they would direct.

The Beatles themselves were more realistic in their ambitions. They wanted to stretch in order to discover the boundaries of their skills but not to overextend themselves. Paul was curious to find out whether he could write instrumental music for film, George was challenged by the possibility of composing within the Indian tradition (rather than a pop version of it), and John wanted to know if he could act the part of anyone other than John Lennon. Nothing would be lost if they failed in these side projects, and the chances were that they would learn something new that could later be put to good use in the context of the Beatles.

"I feel I want to be them all—painter, writer, actor, singer, player, musician," John told Leonard Gross of *Look* magazine. "I want to try them all, and I'm lucky enough to be able to. I want to see which one turns me on. This is for me, this film, because apart from wanting to do it because of what it stands for, I want to see what I'll be like when I've done it."

He'd been talking like this as early as February 1964, when he told *Rave,* "Sometimes I feel I'd like to try something completely different like film directing, for instance. I don't know whether I'd be any good, but it appeals to me—moulding a lot of different things into a complete entertainment. There'd be less of the limelight, but I wouldn't mind."

To Maureen Cleave, in a quote not used in the *Evening Standard* profile, he had said,

> We can't go on holding hands forever. We have been Beatles as best we ever will be—those four jolly lads. But we're not those people any more. We are old men. We can't go on hopping on *Top of the Pops* forever. We still enjoy it but sometimes we feel silly.
>
> We can't develop the singing because none of us can sing in tune. We've got to find something else to do. Paul says it's like leaving school and finding a job. It's just like school, actually, because you have the group to lean on, and then suddenly you find you're on your own.
>
> What we've got to do is find something we can put the same energy into as we did into being Beatles. That's why I go around taping and writing and painting and that because it may be one of them.

John was the first to engage in non-Beatles work following the end of the tour. On September 5 he flew to Hanover, Germany, to play the part of Second World War soldier Musketeer Gripweed alongside established British actors such as Michael Crawford and

Roy Kinnear. The production was set to start on the NATO tank range Bergen-Hohne Training Area on Lüneburg Heath near Celle, a town twenty-seven miles from Hanover.

John knew in advance that he would need shorter hair for the role. He couldn't wear a 1960s Beatles hairstyle in a film set in the early 1940s. His appointment with the scissors took place in the breakfast room of Celle's Inn on the Heath. Barber Klaus Baruck, a twenty-eight-year-old from Hamburg, did the cutting—trimming the back and sides, combing the front away from John's forehead, and shaving off his sideburns. The discarded hair was incinerated despite an earlier plan to distribute it as prizes for a competition to be run by German teen magazine *Bravo*. "I was there when it was burnt," announced Neil Aspinall, although fifty years later a lock sold in auction for $35,000.

There hadn't been a more famous loss of pop locks since Elvis Presley's GI crew cut in 1958. It became a huge story, picked up by newspapers around the world—"Shorn Lennon," "Beatle Severs Mop," "Top Chopped," "Lennon Acts without Locks," "Hair Today Gone Tomorrow"—alongside photos of John looking more like a meek bank accountant or a geography teacher from the 1950s than the Voice of the Generation.

Although it was a role requirement, the haircut had huge symbolic value, because the distinctive Beatles hair was the most instantly recognizable aspect of their appearance and what identified them as being different not only from their rock 'n' roll predecessors but from the generation of their fathers. In 1966, long hair for men was a gesture of defiance. In 1967, Jimi Hendrix would write about waving his "freak flag" high in "If 6 Was 9," as though his Afro was a symbol of protest against the world of "the white-collared conservative."

For John it was an interesting experiment to live without something that had been vital to his identity. Ever since his mid-teens his hair—from Tony Curtis quiff to mop-top—had been central to how he saw himself and how, in turn, others saw him. "I'm really quite

glad to get it cut," he admitted. "I've got a new face now." (In another unused comment given to Maureen Cleave in February, John
had said, "If I had enough money I could retire and wear a beard
and comb my hair back forever and not worry about flashing my ego
about.")

The new image was completed with a pair of Windsor spectacles of the sort that men would have worn in the 1940s. With frames
made of steel, they had round lenses, a saddle bridge rather than
nose-pads, and temples that wrapped around the ears. John had always been shortsighted but wore contact lenses in public because the
glasses he wore at home didn't fit with his image as a tough rocker.
Even though his Gripweed spectacles only had plain glass for lenses,
he started wearing them on and off set because the props department only had twenty pairs, and he was in the habit of mislaying
them if he took them off. Eventually, they became so integral to his
image that they became known as "John Lennon glasses" and started
a revolution in eyewear.

He wasn't the first well-known person to wear the Windsor style.
Ernest Hemingway, Groucho Marx, Theodore Roosevelt, and Joseph
Stalin had all worn similar round lenses. In music, jug-band player
Fritz Richmond, an influential figure on the American folk scene,
was the key innovator. He had worn a pair (sometimes with tinted
lenses) since at least 1963 and is said to have influenced other musicians such as Janis Joplin, Jerry Garcia (Grateful Dead), and John
Sebastian (Lovin' Spoonful). Roger McGuinn of the Byrds wore sunglasses with rectangular wire frames in 1965.

Although John's name brought attention to *How I Won the War*,
his role was small and his lines few. A YouTube compilation of his
appearances lasts less than eight minutes. The action filmed in Germany only amounted to two scenes, and yet he turned up every day
regardless of whether or not he was needed. He believed there was
always something to be learned and enjoyed the novelty of being an
ordinary member of a team lining up for tea just like everyone else.

At almost twenty-six he had very little experience of life as a normal adult.

"I was just a bundle of nerves the first day," he later admitted. "I couldn't hardly speak I was so nervous. My first speech was in a forest, on patrol. I was supposed to say, 'My heart's not in it any more' and it wasn't. I went home and said to myself, 'Either you're not going to be like that, or you're going to give up.' I don't mind talking to the camera—it's people that throw me."

IRONICALLY, WHILE JOHN WAS LEARNING TO BE SOMEONE else in front of Richard Lester's camera, the Monkees were imitating Lester's zany style for an American TV series launched on September 12. The timing couldn't have been more propitious. Just as the Beatles stopped being overly teen-friendly, along came a group— albeit a fictional one created for television—that was willing to do all the madcap things that John, Paul, George, and Ringo had grown tired of.

The producers selected members of the Monkees for their ability as musicians and actors. They also each replicated aspects of the Beatles, and the thirty-minute programs were indebted to Lester's style of filming, with lots of "crazy" action, sharp-witted comments, jump cuts, unusual angles, and sped-up sequences.

The group's debut single, "Last Train to Clarksville," written by Tommy Boyce and Bobby Hart, had been directly inspired by hearing "Paperback Writer" on the radio (Boyce heard the end of the song and thought Paul was singing "Take the last train" rather than "paperback writer") and was recorded using similar chord structures, jangly guitars, and harmonies.

In a further irony, the manufactured group would become a real recording and touring unit that during 1966 and 1967 would sell more records in America than the Beatles. Yet the two groups were trying to achieve such different things during those years that there was never the bitter rivalry that there had been between the Beatles and the Kinks or the invigorating competition that there was between the Beatles and the Beach Boys. They became friends. Micky Dolenz visited Paul at home in London and at EMI Studios, and Mike Nesmith visited John in Weybridge.

As John settled into his film routine in Germany, George was preparing to travel to Bombay with Pattie. On September 13, the day before departure, he visited Sibylla's for a drink. Being a shareholder, he didn't think he had to pay for the privilege, but his fellow director Terry Howard forwarded him a bill. Clearly offended, George responded with a sarcastic letter that said he was sorry he hadn't been able to force himself to spend on his own drinks at the club but couldn't Howard find a way of chalking it up to a publicity expense?

In order to be as anonymous as possible for his new venture George grew a mustache and, like John, had his hair cut short. "Try to disguise yourself," Ravi Shankar had advised him in a letter. At the Taj Mahal Palace, a grand turn-of-the-century hotel on the Bombay waterfront, he and Pattie checked into their top floor suite as Mr. and Mrs. Sam Wells. They both wore Indian kurtas, George wore wire-rimmed sunglasses, and initially they found that they could leave the hotel and walk the streets without being recognized. "It was," he later said, "the first feeling I had ever had of being liberated from being a Beatle."

Following their first meeting in London, Shankar had given George a copy of *Autobiography of a Yogi* by Paramahansa Yogananda, a book first published in 1950. George was intrigued by the stories of miracles told by the founder of the Self-Realization Fellowship, and they left him with a yearning to learn more about yoga and meditation. The cover photo of the guru as a young man also captivated him. He felt Yogananda's eyes were boring right into him with a compelling understanding.

He knew from what Shankar had told him that in order to master the music of the sitar it was important to learn the yogic disciplines of controlling the body and the mind. In India, music and religion were woven into the fabric of life and couldn't be teased apart. Raised as a Catholic in Liverpool, George had experienced religion only as something detached from daily life that people "did" on a Sunday morning. It didn't impinge on their ethics, food, leisure, work, or music. He wanted a form of spirituality that he could integrate into his everyday life, especially into his writing and playing. At the press conference before the concert at Shea Stadium he was pressed to say what was the most important thing in life. "Love," he had answered. Then he was asked, "What is your personal goal?" and without hesitation he had said, "To do as well as I can at whatever I attempt and, someday, to die with a peaceful mind."

Ravi came to the Taj Mahal hotel to tutor George, beginning with two hour-long sessions so that he was not overwhelmed with information. It began with basics—the names of the strings, the scales of the raga, and discussion about the interplay between sitar, tabla, and tambura. Shambhu Das, an advanced student of Shankar's who had been with him since 1959, took over when Shankar had other work, and a yoga teacher taught exercises that George needed to practice to become flexible enough to play in the traditional half-lotus posture. At the same time the teacher introduced him to the spiritual principles behind the Vedic tradition of meditation.

After only five days of such blissful anonymity, a young elevator operator at the hotel, who happened to be an amateur musician, realized the identity of the short-haired stranger from England, and word quickly spread. Fans, journalists, and photographers arrived at the Taj Mahal. The headline in a local English-language newspaper read "By George—A Beatle Is in Town." On September 19, George was forced to give a press conference and appeared with Pattie and Shankar at his side. "I am here not as a Beatle," he explained to his inquisitors. "I have come as plain George Harrison to learn the sitar and something of Indian classical music. I have what may be termed a Beatle's life, and a private life. It isn't

George and Pattie at the Taj Mahal hotel in Bombay, India.

always easy to separate the two. My growing interest in the culture of the East belongs to the latter."

The next day he gave an in-depth interview to Donald Milner, a radio correspondent for the BBC World Service. "The religions they have in India, I just believe in them much more than anything I learned from Christianity," George told him. "It may sound strange to some of the listeners because they will be Christians, or some of them will be, but the thing is the difference over here is that their religion is every second and every minute of their lives and it *is* them—how they act, and how they conduct themselves and how they think."

Of the music he was in the process of learning about, he said,

The thing is, being in the Beatles we've come across so much music during the last five years. So, naturally, we want to listen to better music all the time. And now I've reached the point where I think personally that this music is the greatest music I've ever heard. As far as I'm concerned it surpasses Western classical music. It just leaves it miles behind.

The other members of the Beatles are all equally as keen on Indian music and realize, the same as I do, how great it is. The thing is, we've already used sitar and a few things just [as] an effect. On our last LP I used sitar and I had an Indian fellow playing tabla. . . . But ["Love You To" is] a Beatles song and it's very Western in some respects.

In an unused section of the interview Milner asked him if he believed his primary interests were shifting from the material to the spiritual. "Yes, very much so," said George. "In fact, I have considered giving up all my money and all my cars and all things like that. But, you see, that probably wouldn't work. What could I do? But by keeping my position in the Beatles there will be a lot of people who like us and are influenced by us so in a small way I may be able to influence them in another direction."

Although this convergence of East and West was something new for rock music, there was nothing new about British fascination with Indian culture. Throughout the era of the Raj (1858–1947) many Britons studied the Bhagavad Gita and the Upanishads and became enamored of yoga. British Indologists translated the Vedic scriptures into English and extolled the virtues of Indian music, art, and architecture.

The Hindu monk Swami Vivekananda, who had a mission to evangelize the West, came to Britain in the 1890s and found a ready audience among socialites, the aristocracy, the intelligentsia, and the spiritually curious. He was feted and given accommodation while lecturing in educational institutions, art galleries, and drawing rooms. To late Victorians in London he appeared exotic, and he gave them hope with a religion that was light on doctrine but heavy on experience, in contrast to the often dull formalism of the Church of England. The guru from India viewed these people who welcomed him as opinion leaders who could help spread his message. "The British Empire with all its evil is the greatest machine that ever existed for the dissemination of ideas," he wrote to a friend in India at the time. "I mean to put my ideas in the centre of this machine, and it will spread them all over the world."

Another significant teacher, Paramahansa Yogananda, followed a similar route in the 1930s, capturing the support of public figures ranging from Sir Francis Younghusband, who was a soldier, explorer, and mountaineer, to Scottish music hall artist Harry Lauder. Like Vivekananda before him, he found England, "receptive to the timeless yoga message." Reporters and cameramen swarmed over his lodgings at Grosvenor House in London, and his meetings at Caxton Hall were packed to overflowing. His yoga classes became so popular that they had to be moved to larger premises.

For earlier generations the connection with India often came through a curiosity about nations of the British Empire and disillusionment with Christianity, but the new wave of interest was different. Its origin was in the mystical-like experiences engendered by LSD and other hallucinogens. Encouraged by writers like Allen Ginsberg and Timothy Leary, trippers began to look into Hinduism to find an explanation for what had happened to them as well as to find natural ways of attaining higher levels of consciousness. Without the use of LSD it's unlikely that a former electrician from a Liverpool council estate would have connected so enthusiastically and wholeheartedly with the teachings of Paramahansa Yogananda or Swami Vivekananda.

George had been reading the work of men like Leary, Alan Watts, and Aldous Huxley, all of whom were sympathetic to Eastern religions, had taken LSD, and believed that what they encountered while on drugs was best explained in the mystical language of Hinduism and Buddhism. Leary described LSD as "Western yoga" and said, "Our religious philosophy, or our philosophy about the meaning of

LSD, comes closer to Hinduism that any other [religion]." Huxley coined the phrase "biochemical mysticism." Watts said that his second LSD trip produced "an experience of cosmic consciousness; this sense of complete, fundamental, total unity forever and ever with the whole universe."

"Acid was the big psychological reaction," George admitted of his own journey from flippant atheism to a belief in a higher power. "It's really only after acid that it pushes home to you that you're only little, really. And there's all that infinity out there and there's something doing it, you know?" He described the drug as "a key that opened the door and showed a lot of things on the other side."

He specifically linked the arousal of his interest in India to LSD. "After I had taken LSD a lingering thought stayed with me and that thought was 'the yogis of the Himalayas,'" he said. "I don't know why it stuck. I had never thought about them before, but suddenly this thought was at the back of my consciousness. It was as if someone was whispering to me 'yogis of the Himalayas.' That was part of the reason I went to India. Ravi and the sitar were excuses. Although they were a very important part of it, it was a search for a spiritual connection." As he once put it in more poetic language, "I was awakened by the sound of Krishna's flute."

By the fall of 1966 George had renounced the drug, seeing it as a step on the way to enlightenment but not the final destination, "LSD isn't a real answer. It doesn't give you anything. It enables you to see a lot of possibilities that you may not have noticed before but it isn't the answer." Shankar consistently refused to believe that chemicals could bring about the states of mind that sadhus spent decades acquiring through strenuous discipline, regular rituals, and the mortification of the flesh.

With George's Sam Wells cover now blown and photos of him newly shorn and mustached published in newspapers, he had to escape from Bombay if he was to continue under Shankar's tutelage. With Pattie, Shankar, Shambhu Das, and singer and tambura player

Kamala Chakravarty he traveled 1,700 miles to Kashmir in the far north of India, where together they rented houseboats on beautiful Dal Lake.

The cross-country trip gave Shankar the opportunity to introduce George to Indian culture through its landscapes, temples, memorials, festivals, rituals, and holy men. He would tell him that Hinduism wasn't a religion of doctrine, like Christianity, but a religion of story, poetry, music, and art that permeated all aspects of life. From Bombay they drove up to the archeological site of Ellora, where they visited the caves of Ajanta cut into the side of a volcanic cliff by Buddhist monks for use as temples and monasteries. The nearby Kalaisa Temple was similarly carved out of a mountain, this time by Hindus.

Further north, at the holy city of Benares (birthplace of both Shankar and Das, and the center of Hindustani classical music), they visited ghats on the Ganges where bodies were being burned on funeral pyres so that the ashes could be scattered on the sacred river. Devotees who died and were cremated in Benares were believed to exit the otherwise endless cycle of life, death, and rebirth. (Both George and Shankar would eventually die in California but have their ashes flown here for immersion in the Ganges.)

Their arrival coincided with Ramlila, a huge festival where the life of Rama, an avatar of the god Vishnu, was reenacted. Rama was considered to be the Lord of Virtue, the perfect man, and his wife, Sita, was the epitome of womanhood. Thousands of pilgrims had descended on the city, and George sat with the group in a compound as part of Rama's story was illustrated with gigantic painted effigies mounted on wheels. The local maharaja arrived on the back of an elephant. Both George and Pattie felt that they had been lifted out of the twentieth century and transported to another age.

In the nearby town of Maihar they called on Baba Allauddin Khan, Shankar's 104-year-old guru, who was a Bengali multi-

Pattie and George in India with Ravi Shankar (*front right*) and friends.

instrumentalist living in a house with his young students. Khan had been a disciple of the poet, musician, and photographer Wazir Khan, the chief musician of Rampur State, who was born in 1851. George realized for the first time the illustrious heritage that he was being invited to join by being a pupil of Ravi Shankar.

Baba Allauddin Khan was the first person to impress on George the principle of karma—the theory that the morality of our actions affects our chances of spiritual realization. Acting wrongly incurs bad karma and therefore hinders our prospects of escaping the karmic cycle. This rang true to George's experience of life. As he put it:

> The whole thing of life, and all the answers to everything, are in one divine law—karma action and reaction. . . . With every action you do, there's a reaction to it. If you want a good reaction then you have to do a good action. If you want a bad

one, then you punch somebody. But that's where it's at, just that one thing. That's why there is the whole scene of heaven and hell. Heaven and hell is right now, right at this moment. You make it heaven or you make it hell by your actions. It's just obvious, isn't it?

During the trip Shankar played two engagements already on his schedule—one a performance in a public concert hall and the other in a private home. George was impressed with the preparation Shankar put into these events—carefully washing his body, putting on fresh new clothes, and burning incense. There were no hotels in the small towns that they traveled through, and so they had to be put up in "rest houses" where the owners would awaken them in the morning bearing trays with pots of hot tea. India was not yet set up for modern tourism.

The final destination was Naseem Bagh, on Dal Lake, near Srinagar, where they stayed on houseboats owned and run by an illustrious Kashmiri handicraft businessman named Gulam Muhammad Butt, who had been given eight hotel barges by Reginald Foster, the English tea planter who owned them. Foster had to leave India hurriedly in 1947 during the partition of the country, and he gave the boats to Butt because he'd been a good business contact for the Englishman. Foster's ancestral home was Clermont Hall in Norfolk, England, so the boats had been known as Foster's Clermont Houseboats. When they changed hands they were renamed Butt's Clermont Houseboats.

The vessel that George and Pattie stayed on—Clermont One—had palatial interiors with molded ceilings, chandeliers, stained glass door panes, ornately carved furniture, embroidered rugs, and cedar-paneled walls. Apple wood burned in stoves, hot water bottles were used to warm the beds at night, and fruit juice was served in crystal goblets. From the veranda there was nothing to see but the still-

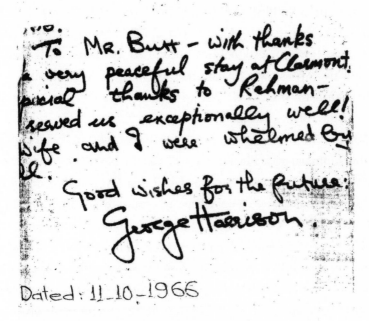

To Mr. Butt – with thanks
… very peaceful stay at Clermont.
… thanks to Rehman –
… served us exceptionally well!
… wife and I were whelmed by
… .
Good wishes for the future:
George Harrison.

Dated: 11_10_1965

The visitor's book from Butt's Clermont Houseboats on Dal Lake in Kashmir, India, where George and Pattie stayed with Ravi Shankar.

ness of the lake stretching ahead and the snowcapped Himalayas in the distance. The peace, coming after the frenetic bustle of Bombay, Benares, and Agra, was a dramatic contrast.

George was deeply immersed in reading books given to him by Ravi and his brother Raju, including the I Ching, and Raja Yoga by Swami Vivekananda. A quote from Vivekananda's writing struck home and became an article of his newfound faith: "Each soul is potentially divine. The goal is to manifest that divinity. Do this through work and yoga and prayer, one or all of these means, and be free. Churches, temples, rituals and dogmas are but secondary details."

Next to the boat was a Mughal garden with four-hundred-year-old chinar trees. George and Ravi would sit under the spreading branches of the ancient trees in the afternoon practicing scales and learning yoga as kingfishers fluttered in the air before diving into the water and returning with captured trout. When George left to return to Bombay, he wrote in the guestbook, "To Mr. Butt—with thanks for a very peaceful stay at Clermont. Special thanks to Rehman—who served us exceptionally well! My wife and I were whelmed by it all. Good wishes for the future."

Back in the UK *Revolver* was now at the top of the LP charts, and "Yellow Submarine" / "Eleanor Rigby" was the No. 1 single (with "All Or Nothing" by the Small Faces at No. 2 and "God Only Knows" by the Beach Boys at No. 3). The American version of *Revolver* had three fewer tracks ("I'm Only Sleeping," "And Your Bird Can Sing," and "Doctor Robert" having already been released on *Yesterday and Today*) but had likewise become the bestselling LP in the country. The experimentation and hard work of the Beatles had been justly rewarded.

Paul was returning to the London underground scene after his long summer absence. His literary friend Barry Miles was setting up an alternative newspaper called *International Times* that he intended to provide a focus for various liberal, experimental, and bohemian groups in the way that the *East Village Other* and the *Village Voice* had done for New York and the *San Francisco Oracle* and *Berkeley Barb* for the San Francisco area.

The plan was to publish challenging coverage of music, politics, art, drugs, sex, and protest that wouldn't get printed elsewhere in Britain. It would write about things that the mainstream media was either not yet aware of, or was aware of but disdained, often using words and images that flouted current censorship laws. In doing so it would bring together like-minded people who'd previously existed in isolated pockets—avant-garde artists, recreational drug users, anarchists, old bohemians, New Left political activists, beatniks, Campaign for Nuclear Disarmament campaigners, satirists, feminists, New Age believers, alterative therapists, mind expansionists, vegetarians. What united these people was a general belief in freedom, peace, love, diversity, and

tolerance, along with an irritation with conformity, dullness, authority, dead tradition, meaningless routine, and fear of experiment.

Paul was a supporter from earlier in the year when the idea was
first tried as a fourteen-page mimeographed-and-stapled magazine
sold for a shilling to protestors on the annual Easter "ban the bomb"
march from Aldermaston to London. Paul had even designed a film
competition for the only issue of the *Global Moon Edition Longhair
Times* and put up a prize of twenty guineas. Under the guise of Ian
Iachimoe, "the Polish 'new wave' film director," he presented an unfinished synopsis that entrants had to complete. (No one involved
remembers whether anyone responded or whether the prize was
awarded.)

Alternative newspapers were covering the often hidden culture
that was now of interest to Paul. In an appeal for submissions to
the *Global Moon Edition Longhair Times* Miles had listed its concerns as
global politics, the CIA, avant-garde jazz, free schools and universi-
ties, pot, LSD, happenings, censorship, love, and the fuzz (police).
"Pipe dreams need no longer be only dreams," announced the editorial. "Let's make this thing HAPPEN so all may SEE & Hear."

On September 15, Paul went with Miles to a performance by
the experimental improvisational group AMM, which met regularly
in a basement of the Royal College of Art in Knightsbridge. AMM
was formed by jazz players wanting to test boundaries; there were no
musical rules, and members contributed only when, or if, they felt
inspired. Even the boundary between performers and listeners was
questioned. The audience, perhaps only twenty strong, was invited to
join in. In the spirit of the event Paul scraped a coin along the ridges
of an old-fashioned steel radiator. His verdict was: "You don't have to
like something to be inspired by it."

The next day Paul went with his secret lover Maggie McGivern
and Brian Epstein to Paris, where they rendezvoused with John, who
had just finished his German location work. Before leaving Germany

John stayed overnight in Hamburg, where he was able to visit old haunts in the St. Pauli district before taking the train to France with Neil Aspinall. In Paris, with his new short hair, John was able to travel on buses and walk around a flea market without being recognized.

The five of them stayed at the Hotel Athénée on the Avenue Montaigne and spent time together in restaurants and cafes. When John noticed that Parisians were staring at Maggie McGivern rather than him or Paul, he made her walk a few steps ahead of the men when they were out in order to deflect attention. One night Paul and Maggie went out alone to Chez Castel, the fashionable nightclub on the Rue Princesse opened by Jean Castel in 1962 and frequented by Serge Gainsbourg.

On Sunday the eighteenth John and Neil left France for Spain, where the filming of *How I Won the War* was continuing in the rugged, dry landscape around Almeria that doubled for the North African desert. They were living in a building near the city's El Zapillo beach. Owned by an Irish landlord named Baron Alexander Gillinson (Baron was his first name, not a title, and his friends called him Barry), it had been a temporary home to other actors, including Clint Eastwood and Eli Wallach.

While at this apartment John started work on what would become his most ambitious song yet, "Strawberry Fields Forever." Separated from both his family and the Beatles for the first time in years, he became reflective and analytical. If the group stopped touring, in what way would they each remain Beatles? If he wasn't a Beatle, what was he, and what would he do with the rest of his working life? Traditionally, pop stars "diversified" in order to capture a less fickle, family-oriented audience. Elvis went first into movies, and then to Las Vegas as a resident performer. This was not a path that John wanted to pursue, because he thought it inimical to the spirit of his art. "That's when I really started considering life without the Beatles," he explained. "What would it be? And I spent that six weeks thinking about that."

John composing in the apartment he rented upon arriving in Almeria, Spain.

"Strawberry Fields Forever" was a product of this period of uncertainty and self-examination. He later referred to it as "psychoanalysis set to music." It didn't start out as a particularly ambitious song, but rather as a simple meditation on the trials of being misunderstood. The original opening line was "No one is on my wavelength," which led into a lyric about the isolation that came from being someone who few were able to "tune into." His acute perceptions and ability to see through things were great gifts but also great burdens. There was the hint of a resolution in the last of the five lines of the first draft ("I mean, it's not too bad"), which supplied the song with its provisional title—"Not Too Bad."

As he put working versions of the song on tape, he altered "wavelength" to "my tree" on the third take, which meant that the words "high" and "low" now referred to branches rather than frequencies. He made the change because he was afraid that saying no one was on his wavelength might sound arrogant. "Nobody seems to be as hip as me is what I was saying," he explained in 1980. "Therefore, I must be crazy or a genius." However, he still kept the earlier reference to tuning in, which was confusing now that he'd shifted from sound waves to trees but didn't really matter, because the song was a description of confusion that effectively used disjointed thinking to make its point.

He hacked away at this verse, recording his efforts on a cassette tape recorder, hoping that the more he sang, the more the rest of the song would emerge. He was coaxing it out into the open, unsure of what would be revealed about his inner life. At this stage there was no mention of Strawberry Fields in either the title or the lyric.

Fellow actors on *How I Won the War* saw John on the El Zapillo beach working on the song, but none of them took note of any of the particulars. Canadian photographer Douglas Kirkland photographed him at his apartment sitting on his bed with an acoustic guitar, a cassette recorder by his side. "It took me six weeks to write the song," John said. "I was writing it all the time I was making the film and, as anybody knows about film work, there's a lot of hanging around."

He was reading *Report to Greco,* an autobiographical novel by Nikos Kazantzakis (author of *Zorba the Greek*), recently translated into English. It's easy to see what attracted John to this book. It tells the story of a writer searching for spiritual meaning. "In these pages," Kazantzakis wrote in the introduction,

> you will find the red track made by drops of my blood, the track which marks my journey among men, passions, and ideas. Every man worthy of being called a son of man bears his cross and mounts his Golgotha. Many, indeed most, reach the first or second step, collapse pantingly in the middle of the journey, and do not attain the summit of Golgotha, in other words the summit of their duty: to be crucified, resurrected, and to save their souls. Afraid of crucifixion, they grow fainthearted; they do not know that the cross is the only path to resurrection. There is no other path.

Leonard Gross, European editor for *Look* magazine, interviewed John on set for a cover story that would run in December. He concluded that John was now a compulsive seeker of truth—about himself and about the world—but that he wasn't the cynic that people assumed him to be. "I'm not a cynic. They're getting my character out of some things I write or say. They can't do that. I hate tags. I'm slightly cynical, but I'm not a cynic. One can be wry one day and cynical the next and ironic the next. I'm a cynic about most things that are taken for granted. I'm cynical about society, politics, newspapers, government. But I'm not cynical about life, love, goodness, death. That's why I really don't want to be labelled a cynic."

Back in London Paul and Jane Asher, although often separated by work, interests, and friends, had settled into Cavendish Avenue. When Paul was alone at home he would invite Maggie McGivern to visit, but Jane was never discussed. Jane was a fiercely independent woman who was not about to sacrifice her career to be a pop star's "other half." During August she had been acting in *The Trojan Women* and *A Winter's Tale* at the Edinburgh Festival, and now the company was preparing *A Winter's Tale* (with the same cast) for a run at the Cambridge Theatre in London opening on September 30, followed by its filming in November at Wembley Studios.

Paul commissioned the design company of Binder, Edwards & Vaughan to paint the small Alfred E. Knight piano in his music room. The trio (Binder and Edwards being the designers and painters and Vaughan the manager and frontman) had transformed Tara Browne's AC Cobra into a work of art, the likes of which had never been seen in London. The whole exterior was painted in a British fairground style with flashes of yellow, blue, purple, red, and orange until it looked more like a bumper car than a top-of-the-range two-seater sports car. Paul wanted a similar effect on his piano, and so Binder and Edwards took the piano to their studio, where they transformed it into a work of art.

Although it was often referred to by commentators as a "psychedelic" piano, the aim of the artists was to make something joyful rather than hallucinatory, and their inspirations were early rock 'n'

Artist Dudley Edwards painting Paul's home piano "in a colorful way."

roll, British teddy boys, and the traveling fairs of the 1950s when they were one of the few places where rock 'n' roll records could be played at full volume.

They started with a few coats of gesso that they sanded down until it was almost glasslike, and then applied vibrant colors in household gloss and Flamboyant enamel (a popular fairground paint). The back of the piano featured what looked like a series of lightning bolts in sophisticated color combinations that reflected their interest in art deco, geometrical shapes, and primitive folk art. Paul would go on to create some of his best-known songs on what he called his "magic piano."

On September 30, while the piano was still being painted, the first report emerged in an American newspaper that the Beatles would no longer be touring and that their summer tour had been their last. It quoted John as saying: "We can get $500,000 for a TV special. Why go through the terrible trial of being badgered by kids and never seeing any part of the ruddy country we're traveling through?"

The same day there were news stories in England that Brian Epstein had been released from "a Putney hospital" where he'd been taken for "an investigation following glandular fever." A spokesman for NEMS explained that Epstein had been "feeling tired recently." The truth was that he'd attempted suicide by overdosing on pills. He was discovered by his assistant, Peter Brown, and rushed to a private hospital in Richmond to have his stomach pumped. From there he was taken to the Priory in Roehampton, a private hospital specializing in "the management and treatment of mental health problems including addictions and eating disorders." Later, a suicide note was found beside his bed. "This is all too much," it read. "I can't take it any more."

For the Beatles the conclusion of their life as a touring group was the end of the beginning. For Epstein it signaled the beginning of the end.

OCTOBER

Our whole outlook on life is changing
because our circumstances have changed our
surroundings. But this has not done anything
to disunite the Beatles. We are going to keep
on making better tracks and become better
entertainers—as the Beatles.
–PAUL, 1966

The Tabernas Desert in Spain had become a convenient European location for Hollywood directors who wanted the look of North Africa or the Middle East but with all the infrastructure of the modern world, as well as having Paris, Rome, Madrid, and London within easy reach. Recent films shot in these arid badlands included *King of Kings*, *Lawrence of Arabia*, and *Cleopatra*. It had also doubled for Mexico in *A Fistful of Dollars* and *For a Few Dollars More* and the Wild West in *The Good, the Bad and the Ugly*.

John's fifty-two days in the wilderness may have been good for cleansing his soul, but he started to miss the comforts of his normal life. "It's like a dump really," he told journalist Fred Robbins, who turned up on set to interview him for the American radio program *Assignment: Hollywood*. "It's like the moon—just desert and sand and hills and mountains. It's not very nice to look at, but the weather's OK."

To make things easier for him he had his chauffeur, Les Anthony, bring his black Rolls-Royce Phantom V down to Almeria so that he could be driven to work each day in style. He'd had the car fitted with internal speakers to listen to music and also external speakers with which to prank passing strangers with bursts of loud noise. There was a floating record player that stayed level even when the car hit bumps, a fridge, a telephone, and a TV. Then Cynthia arrived with Julian, and on October 5 Ringo and Maureen came to watch some of the filming and celebrate John's twenty-sixth birthday on October 9.

There wasn't much to do in Almeria during the evenings, so John passed the time watching TV, playing board games like Monopoly and Risk with fellow actor Michael Crawford, eating out, reading, and rehearsing the next day's lines with Neil Aspinall (who had a nonspeaking role as a private). Richard Lester would frequently change the script during shooting, so John was needed on set, dressed and ready each day lest he be required to make an unscheduled appearance.

The hanging around bored him, and he found the heat oppressive. The only relief came in the form of playing impromptu cricket games with real bats and balls but improvised stumps, relaxing in the back of the Rolls, which locals nicknamed El Funebre (the hearse), or smoking the grass that had been delivered to him from London concealed inside boxes of candy.

On October 7, John was visited by photojournalist Zdenko Hirschler, who, besides getting some exclusive shots of him cricketing and picking up his lunch of stew and rice pudding from the catering caravan, managed to draw him out on the state of the Beatles. "For the last six years I have been a Beatle," he told Hirschler. "It's been a jolly good life and we've had a good many laughs, but it can't go on forever."

Hirschler asked him whether he'd taken on the film because he was fed up with being a Beatle. "Oh no," he said.

It's not that. It's something else. It's like a finishing school in a way. It's a problem for all of us. George is now in India, nosing around and shopping and taking sitar lessons. Paul has brought a new house in North London . . . [and] is so busy decorating it that he's finding little time to do anything else, although I hear he is writing the music for Hayley Mills' new picture. Ringo is spending a week or so in Spain to watch me act. Each one of us has more or less the same dilemma—what to do in the future.

John still sounded unenthusiastic about his film experience. He had taken on *How I Won the War* because it offered the challenge of portraying someone other than himself, but this was the very thing he found most difficult. All his life he had found it hard to play a role, whether it was the obedient schoolboy or the cheerful, compliant celebrity. Even in his songwriting he couldn't, like Paul, take on the voice and outlook of someone else. He rarely wrote about experiences that were not his own. His great skill was in discovering, and then being, himself.

"Some of [the acting in the film] is natural but the most unnatural bits are hard," he had told Fred Robbins. "[It's hard] when it's really out of character for me. . . . I am limited in what I can do. It's all right, but it's not the be-all and end-all." He also confessed to feeling inhibited acting in front of the assembled crewmembers. Despite his years on stage as part of a group, he was self-conscious performing alone.

Ringo wanted to be with John, because he was missing the camaraderie of having the "lads" around and knew that John was lonely. He was also interested to find out more about what it took to be an actor, because if the Beatles were to break up, that seemed to be his only other option in the world of entertainment besides the unappealing prospect of starting all over again as a drummer with a new group.

John and Ringo on the set of *How I Won the War* in Spain.

He had confided to Art Unger that he wanted to act but wasn't sure he'd be any good at it. Both his roles so far had only required him to be Ringo. He'd met Charlie Chaplin earlier in the year when the veteran actor and comedian was in London doing postproduction work on *A Countess from Hong Kong*, and he also expressed interest in meeting the British actor and raconteur Peter Ustinov. "He'd tell me whether I'm any good or not, and he'd tell me where I could improve and how to do it."

While Ringo was spending time with John, Cynthia and Maureen searched for bigger and better accommodations than the down-at-the-heels property at the beach. Together they found a thirteen-bedroom luxury villa called Santa Isabel on Camino de Romero with an overgrown garden, tall steel gates, and a swimming pool. Built in the nineteenth century on the site of a convent, it was an oasis of calm and greenery in an otherwise dry and rather drab landscape. Film director David Lean, actor Peter O'Toole, and producer Sam Spiegel had used it while on location. Cynthia became convinced that it was haunted. The electricity supply was inexplicably cut off, and Maureen complained that the ribbon in her nightdress had been tied in a knot while she slept.

In order to "shock the spooks" (as she put it) Cynthia threw a party for the actors and crew. Again the house was plunged into darkness. To restore the light she spread candles throughout the huge hall. According to her, the atmosphere changed immediately. She later wrote:

> At this point I was convinced beyond all doubt that the villa houses many beautiful spirits. . . . The glowing warmth lit up the faces of the guests in an almost religious light and, as if the whole episode had been rehearsed, we all dotted ourselves around the hall in orderly groups and, without hesitation, began singing. It was a matter of seconds before the air was stilled and the most beautiful singing you ever heard filled the hall. . . . It was an incredibly magical experience which lasted for about half an hour by which time, as if an unseen force had snapped its fingers, the lights went on again breaking the spell for one and all. I firmly believe our voices and bodies during that time were instruments and outlets for the nuns' spirits.

This villa was the place where "Not Too Bad" was to grow into "Strawberry Fields Forever." John's sixth take of the song was the longest yet, and recording in a larger room gave the sound the benefit of an echo. It felt as though two different works had been brought together in rather the same way that he'd connected two partially written songs in "She Said She Said."

In the first song John addressed his uncertainty and did it brilliantly through incorporating his hesitant thinking into the structure of sentences that were full of self-corrections, pauses, rephrases,

The villa known as Santa Isabel, which John and Cynthia rented in Almeria. This photo was taken in the 1930s. The building was rediscovered in 1988 by Spanish journalist Aldolfo Iglesias and is now a museum.

and fillers. It describes a state of being where he is caught in the tension between opposites—between all right and not too bad, high and low, always and sometimes. "I'm expressing it haltingly," he explained, "because I'm not sure what I'm feeling."

The second song is about going back to Strawberry Field—an actual place but in John's lyric a symbol of paradise. Strawberry Field, we are led to believe, offers relief from the confusion just described. In the last song he had completed—"She Said She Said"—he had spoken of everything having been right "when I was a boy," and four months later he had picked up the same theme, this time telling us a bit more about what made it so idyllic.

Strawberry Field (John added the s because it sounded better in the song) was a Salvation Army orphanage in Woolton that made a big impression on him as a young boy. The gothic building was large and foreboding, but the gardens were magical. He and his friends would gain entry by climbing over its walls, finding among the trees and flowers a timeless kingdom of nature and adventure where he felt liberated from school, home, and city.

When the Salvation Army purchased Strawberry Field in 1935, its magazine, *The Deliverer,* described it as the "most imposing of any of our Children's Homes in Britain." It was a "stately gabled building" from which the top of Mount Snowdon in Wales could be seen on a clear day from one side and, from another, the spires of Chester Cathedral. "Of the six acres on which it stands, nearly three are garden and lawn. A graceful, white stone lady stands amidst the rosary; beyond is a glorious playing field. Woolton quarries (a stone's throw away) produce the hardest stone in the world, and the house, built on this same solid red rock, should surely be as dry and healthy a home as it is possible to imagine."

John's childhood friend David Ashton told me the grounds appeared to be magical to them as children. "Strawberry Field was rhododendrons, brambles, cypress trees and beautiful exotic plants. There was a high sandstone wall around it but you could get up it. It

Strawberry Field, the orphanage in Woolton, Liverpool, that exercised such a powerful pull on John's imagination.

was about fifteen feet tall with a peak on it. To grow up in Woolton was a near-religious experience because there was so many beautiful things—beautiful houses, beautiful sculptures, a cuckoo clock in Woolton Woods, walled gardens, flowers, Calderstone Park with its druid stones, the rose garden in Reynolds Park . . ."

John's line "nothing is real" suggested to some people that Strawberry Fields was merely a hallucination, but it's more likely that he was embracing the Hindu concept of maya—the belief that the world of opposites is illusory. He said that he was reading Hindu philosophy in Spain, and he may have been referring to Yogananda's *Autobiography of a Yogi*, recommended to him by George.

Yogananda said, "To rise above the duality of creation and perceive the unity of the Creator is conceived of as man's highest goal. Those who cling to the cosmic illusion must accept its essential law of polarity: flow and ebb, rise and fall, day and night, pleasure and pain, good and evil, birth and death. This cyclic pattern assumes a certain anguishing monotony, after man has gone through a few thousand human births; he begins then to cast a hopeful eye beyond the compulsions of *maya*. To tear the veil of *maya* is to pierce the secret of creation."

John could have linked the ideas in the two songs, but it was more powerful simply to juxtapose them and allow the listener to make the journey from one to the other; from the place where it's hard to be someone to the place where there's nothing to get hung about. The technique was reminiscent of what William Burroughs called the "mosaic of juxtaposition," where the truth is arrived at through nonsequential associations rather than linear logic.

While in Almeria, John was visited by Juan Carrión Gañán, a forty-one-year-old teacher of English from Cartagena who regularly used Beatles lyrics in his lessons for university students. Since first hearing "Love Me Do" on Radio Luxemburg he had painstakingly written out the words to each song. However, the Beatles had recently been using less familiar language, and his notebooks were showing more gaps, guesses, and question marks.

Top: Pages from notebooks held by Juan Carrion Gañán with corrections made by John to the lyrics of "Yellow Submarine," "Good Day Sunshine," and "She Said She Said." Students in Gañán's English class transcribed the songs but didn't correctly identify all the words.
Right: The front of one student's notebook inscribed with John's good wishes.

Hearing that John was in his country filming, he determined to meet him to ask him to clarify the words of the songs. He took the bus from Cartagena to Almeria and managed to find John on the beach playing a ball game with Michael Crawford and showed him his notebook and those of his students. John graciously filled in the spaces and corrected words that he'd misheard. For the lyrics to "Yellow Submarine" John took appropriately colored pens to inscribe the words "yellow," "blue," and "green." For "Eleanor Rigby" he wrote out key lines in red pen and underlined words such as "dirt" and "darning" that Gañán had been unable to distinguish. In an asterisked footnote he explained that the "jar" kept by the door was a "pot." He said he thought it was a great idea to teach the English language through the songs of the Beatles and autographed the notebook to Gañán with the message "Good luck with the English." (A fictionalized version of this incident would provide the basis of the 2013 film *Living Is Easy with Eyes Closed,* directed by David Trueba.)

With John, George, and Ringo out of England, it was left to Paul to keep up with cultural events in London. He played tambourine with and virtually coproduced the Escorts (guitarist Paddy Chambers knew Paul from Liverpool) when they covered the Miracles' song "That Magic Feeling," and he was at the studio when Donovan recorded his single "Mellow Yellow." At the Robert Fraser Gallery he attended the launch of an exhibition by British pop artist Richard Hamilton (later responsible for designing the cover of the White Album).

On October 14 the first issue of *International Times* was published. The twelve-page newspaper could only be bought at twenty outlets in London—mostly bookshops, hip fashion stores, arts centers, and fringe theatres. The editorial promised that the paper would succeed by exemplifying the sort of changes it advocated rather than making grand statements. The issue also carried a poem by Adrian Mitchell, an appraisal of the recently deceased surrealist and anarchist Andre Breton by Jean-Jacques Lebel, ads, reports from major European and American cities, a review of the recent Destruction in Arts Symposium, pop news, and a cartoon strip.

In its pages a new alternative arts scene was coming to light that would soon transform not only the culture of Britain but the culture of the world. On page three there was news of an upcoming art show. "At Indica Gallery from November 9th to 22nd there will be a one-man show of Instructional Painting by Yoko Ono, photographed above performing her Cut Piece in the Destruction of Art Symposium. This will be the first show of these works outside of the USA and Japan and the first one-man show in which the audience will be directly responsible for the construction of the paintings."

The day after publication there was a launch party at the Roundhouse in Chalk Farm, North London. Paul went dressed in an Arab costume and Marianne Faithfull in a nun's habit. Film director Michelangelo Antonioni was there with his star (and lover) of the moment, thirty-five-year-old Monica Vitti. Also in the 2,500 person crowd was theatre director Peter Brook, rock group manager Tony Secunda (Procol Harum, the Move), Mick Jagger, and acclaimed San Francisco poet Kenneth Rexroth, a participant in the earliest experiments that combined poetry with jazz.

Designed by Robert Dockray in 1847 and commissioned by the celebrated engineer Robert Stephenson, the Roundhouse was built as a maintenance and storage shed for rail engines but had fallen into disuse over the years. Like the old theatres and ballrooms in San Francisco, it proved an ideal space for the new kind of rock show that involved standing or dancing audiences, loud music, screens, and lights. It would be Paul's first taste of the new immersive experience of rock.

On stage that night were two unknown British bands pioneering rock influenced by avant-garde art, drugs, music experimentation, and jazz. They were the Soft Machine (a name taken from the title of a 1961 novel by William Burroughs, where it referred to the human body), who brought a motorcycle onto the stage to use the sound of its engine as an additional instrument, and Pink Floyd (a name taken from two blues singers—Pink Anderson and Floyd Council), who'd been inspired by the LA band Love (at least as described to them by their manager Peter Jenner) and the type of music they imagined would be played by psychedelic groups in San Francisco who were either as yet unrecorded or whose records weren't available in the UK.

The *Sunday Times* spoke to Pink Floyd's bass guitarist, Roger Waters. "It's totally anarchistic but cooperative anarchy, if you see what I mean," he said of his group's music. "It's definitely a complete realization of the aims of psychedelia. But if you take LSD what you experience depends entirely on who you are. Our music may give you the screaming horrors or throw you into screaming ecstasy. Mostly it's the latter. We find our audiences stop dancing now. We tend to get them standing there totally grooved with their mouths open."

Pink Floyd had come together during the Beatles' experimental phase and would record their debut LP, *The Piper at the Gates of Dawn,* at EMI's studio 3 while the Beatles were working on *Sgt. Pepper* in the larger studio 2. The band's main songwriter, Syd Barrett, was already steeped in LSD, Eastern mysticism, Tolkien, Miles Davis, children's literature, painting, Beat poetry, tarot cards, Bob Dylan, and the I Ching. He'd bought *Revolver* on its release and never stopped playing it. By October he'd written "The Gnome," "Matilda Mother," "Astronomy Domine," and "Let's Roll Another One" and helped to cowrite the instrumentals "Interstellar Overdrive" and "Pow R. Toc H."

As with the American West Coast happenings on which it was modeled, the *International Times* party was festive, multisensory, and disorganized. Attendees were advised to bring their "own poison," and the "all-night rave" was announced on the poster as a "Strip-Trips-Happening-Movie-Pop-Op-Costume-Masque-Drag Ball." Pink Floyd had its own liquid light show where slides of colored oils and water were shone through by powerful overhead projectors and rocked in time to the music so the group was bathed in pulsating, flowing, mingling, and dividing globules of color that appeared to be controlled by the sound. Sound poet Bob Cobbing showed art films such as *Scorpio Rising* by Kenneth Anger and *Towers Open Fire* by Antony Balch and William Burroughs onto huge screens. Yoko Ono, newly arrived in London, jumped on stage and tried to initiate a spontaneous happening by reciting her 1963 "Touch Poem for a Group of People," the text of which simply said, "Touch eachother." In the semidarkness, the people obeyed. The smell of pot and joss sticks wafted through the air, and revelers rolled in a six-foot wide plate of jelly. London had seen nothing quite like it before. Daevid Allen of Soft Machine called it "one of the most revolutionary events in the history of English alternative music and thinking. It was important because it marked the first recognition of a rapidly spreading socio-cultural revolution that had its parallel in the States. The new year would bring an inexpressible feeling of change."

BRIAN EPSTEIN HAD FLOWN OUT TO NEW YORK EARLIER IN the day hoping to be able to coax a major American act to appear on R & B / jazz singer Georgie Fame's Christmas show at the Saville Theatre (a theatre leased to Epstein) from December 26 to January 7. Fame's music was now charting, but for years he had enjoyed a cult following among London mods and US servicemen as a result of his residency at the Flamingo Club on Wardour Street.

On the flight over a stewardess surprised Epstein by asking him what he was going to be doing now that the Beatles were breaking up. "I didn't really know how this rubbishy rumor had got out," he later remarked when discussing the incident. "It was beyond the five of us." He realized that part of his task now was to reassure his various business partners in America that despite there being no plans to tour, the Beatles were not disbanding.

On the recommendation of Tony Bramwell, Epstein was also negotiating with the Four Tops to appear at the Saville in November and then tour Britain in 1967. It was all part of his attempt to fill his life now that the Beatles had no plans to perform in concert. While in New York he met with Nat Weiss, and Weiss found him much less confident since the Gillespie incident and "very difficult to work with." He noted that Epstein was now taking LSD, a drug that didn't combine well with his stimulants and sleeping pills.

Although it wasn't made public for a few weeks due to family embarrassment, this was also the day that George's friend and partner in Sibylla's, Kevin Macdonald, leapt from the roof of the West London Studios in Fulham and plunged to his death. He was twenty-nine years old and had been suffering from depression. These were among the early indications that there was a dark side to the culture of drugs and excess. LSD had been added to list of restricted drugs in Britain in September and outlawed in California in October.

Even in the absence of the Beatles the search for a suitable film script continued. On October 21, the music papers reported that an original screenplay by British TV writer Owen Holder had now replaced Richard Condon's *A Talent for Loving* as the front-runner. A 109-page first draft, titled "Beatles 3," had been submitted to Epstein and had apparently been approved. This project was subsequently referred to as "Shades of a Personality," and Michelangelo Antonioni was discussed as a potential director.

Holder was a forty-five-year-old writer from London who had been an actor in the 1950s but since 1961 had focused on writing, mostly for TV drama. His premise, as explained in an introduction to "Beatles 3," was that "each of the Beatles is an aspect of one person, Stanley Grimshaw. To make the telling of it as clear as possible," Holder wrote, "I have given these four aspects of the boys the actual names of John Paul George and Ringo (no familiarity intended, by the way) though of course each of them is Stanley and is called that by the other characters, no matter which of the Stanleys is operating at the time."

In answer to a question about their next film at the Los Angeles press conference George had said, "Well, someone has given us an idea, and he's working on the script. If the script is nice, we may do it." This must have referred to the Holder script, as the Beatles had already rejected the Condon screenplay. While in Spain John was confidently speaking about "looking forward to getting started on the film we are to make in January."

Producer Walter Shenson, who'd so far looked through over forty script submissions, said that the Beatles no longer wanted to do a historical drama. They wanted to do a "modern story set in Britain." All that was needed was a strong story line, a well-worked-out plot, and something that didn't merely cash in on their fame. They also wanted to write songs that added to the drama rather than being dropped in arbitrarily as they were in *A Hard Day's Night* and *Help!*

Despite all the positive talk "Beatles 3" didn't meet expectations, and Shenson eventually took the idea to the playwright Joe Orton, whose play *Loot* Paul had liked, and asked him to punch it up. For a fee of five thousand pounds Orton obliged and developed a screenplay he called "Up Against It" that was returned to him in April 1967. Orton wrote in his diary: "No explanation why. No criticism of the script. And apparently, Brian Epstein has no comment to make either. Fuck them."

George and Pattie returned to London from Bombay in late October after just over five weeks in India. If photographer Robert Whitaker is accurate in dating his prints, George decided to decorate the exterior walls of his bungalow in bright psychedelic designs the following week. Using Valspar masonry paints he drew crude, often childish, shapes on every available white surface—swirls, hearts, letters, orbs, flames, droplets, leaves, stars, flowers—and colored them in bright reds, yellows, greens, oranges, and blues. Each tile of the window ledges was painted a different color.

Painting the outside of a house in a multitude of colors (like painting your piano or car) was not done in Britain. Certainly there were no other bungalows in stately Esher that had been given such psychedelic treatment. George was inspired by the recent exposure to color in India, where he'd even seen cows daubed with paint. A year later the Beatles would have the façade of their Apple boutique in Baker Street painted but later because of local planning laws were forced to cover it.

George hired the Dutch artist Marijke Koger to design a psychedelic painting around the fireplace in his living room. Although using similar bright colors, this was executed more professionally than the designs on the outside walls. Within a huge circle she featured a winter scene, a rainbow, a river, stars, flying saucers, mountains, flowers, and a central figure of a Buddha-like character sitting in a meditative pose.

Koger and her partner, Simon Posthuma, who did business together as the Fool, were to become two of the most prominent psychedelic artists of the era in London, designing the cover of the Incredible String Band's album *The 5000 Spirits or the Layers of the Onion,* the inner sleeve of *Sgt. Pepper's Lonely Hearts Club Band,* and the clothes for the Apple store.

Four days after George's return Ravi Shankar flew in from Bombay to record music for a BBC TV adaptation of Lewis Carroll's *Alice's Adventures in Wonderland* directed by polymath Jonathan Miller, who, along with comedians Peter Cook and Dudley Moore and playwright

Alan Bennett, had been a leading figure in Britain's satire boom following the sketch show *Beyond the Fringe*. George, with longer hair but still sporting his mustache and wearing a Nehru jacket, drove his car to the airport to meet Shankar.

Working with two tabla players and renowned oboist Léon Goossens, Shankar improvised the soundtrack while watching the film on a screen in a dubbing theatre and listening to instructions from Miller about the required mood, pace, and intensity. *Alice's Adventures in Wonderland* was popular among potheads and acid freaks because the story of a parallel world where conventions were upturned and perceptions altered seemed to mirror their experiences. John claimed to read the book at least once a year. It would have an effect on rock songs including "White Rabbit" by Jefferson Airplane, "Hole in My Shoe" by Traffic, and the Beatles' "Lucy in the Sky with Diamonds."

Later on the same day that Shankar arrived, it was announced that British singing star Alma Cogan had died at Middlesex Hospital of ovarian cancer at the age of thirty-four. Cogan had been a chart resident in the 1950s with eighteen hit singles, but her career was damaged by the beat group revolution of the 1960s. Her music was sweet, pure, and optimistic—everything the Beatles hated. However, when they met her in January 1964 while rehearsing for *Sunday Night at the London Palladium*, they hit it off and became great friends—especially her and John.

Although few knew it at the time, according to both Cogan's sister Sandra Caron and Cynthia Lennon, the two went on to have an affair. Even though Cogan was only eight years older than John and from a different generation of musicians (she'd started out singing with big bands and at the age of fourteen had been recommended by Vera Lynn to appear on a variety show in Brighton), he saw something of his beloved mother, Julia, in her. Brian Epstein also liked her (as did many other gay men, including Noel Coward and Lionel Bart) and would take her to events as his companion.

According to Cynthia, when John heard the news of Alma Cogan's death while he was in Spain, he was "inconsolable." In an interview given in 1989 but not made public until after her death in 2015, Cynthia said, "The woman he'd earmarked to replace his Aunt Mimi in his affections was now lost. . . . Something odd happened to him. Things turned."

Penguin Books' young art director Alan Aldridge organized the cover for *The Penguin John Lennon.*

ON OCTOBER 27 JOHN'S two books, *In His Own Write* and *A Spaniard in the Works,* were published together for the first time as *The Penguin John Lennon,* with John on the cover wearing a Super-man costume. The photo, taken by photographer Brian Duffy at his studio in Swiss Cottage, North London, was the conception of Alan Aldridge, a twenty-three-year-old illustrator who in 1965 had become art director for Penguin Books.

Raised in London's East End, Aldridge had a pop art style that was playful, colorful, humorous, and surreal. He managed to capture the vibrancy of what was taking place in mid-sixties London in a way that few other artists could match, and he became the illustrator of choice for new magazines such as the *Sunday Times Magazine,* the *Observer Magazine,* and *Nova,* which wanted visuals to match the excitement of their breathless copy that was forever in pursuit of the latest thing.

Aldridge's first idea for *The Penguin John Lennon* was a painting of the Beatle as a penguin. The publishing director, who thought it was disrespectful of the great publishing house and its familiar logo, quashed this, so Aldridge contacted Duffy, one of the best-known

British photographers of the era, and asked him to do a shoot. At first Duffy demurred, saying that he'd had enough of rock 'n' roll, but then relented.

Initially John was going to pose with a birdcage built for the session, but during the shoot Aldridge had another idea. He would dress John as Superman to acknowledge his status as a world-beater in films, music, and now books. He dispatched a runner to Chelsea to pick up a costume.

When Duffy's photos were finally approved for use, there was a further glitch. DC Comics in New York, the creators and owners of the Superman franchise, refused to let the image with the giant *S* on the chest be used; it infringed on their copyright. Aldridge had to retouch the photo by replacing the *S* on his chest with a JL sticker.

The relationship between the Beatles and Alan Aldridge proved to be fruitful. The next month *Woman's Mirror* commissioned Aldridge to create a cover image of the group to go along with a feature by Maureen Cleave, drawing on her *Evening Standard* interviews. Additionally, he was asked to provide illustrations of four of the songs from *Revolver*— "Eleanor Rigby," "Yellow Submarine," "Taxman," and "Doctor Robert."

For "Taxman" he had a model of George shouldering the burden of a pile of pound notes fresh from the bank. On top, dressed in black and carrying a brief case, was Death. "Yellow Submarine" showed a submarine that looked like a large boot with a uniformed captain peering from the conning tower. For "Eleanor Rigby" he created Paul's death mask, onto which he painted images of stars, planets, church towers, flowers, and the figures of people falling through the sky.

"Doctor Robert" featured John wearing a huge black cape or overcoat that he was opening to reveal a lining crammed with spare anatomical parts. The management of *Woman's Mirror* thought potential advertisers might be put off, and so its art department replaced the parts with gleaming surgical instruments. John liked Aldridge's work so much that he visited him at his studio in Holborn and bought the original, which he had framed and hung on his wall at home. "You got it wrong though," he told Aldridge. "Doctor Robert was a New York doctor who sold speed."

The mutual appreciation between Aldridge and the Beatles would lead to other projects. John commissioned him to design a plaque for the gate of his home that read "No Hawkers, No Circuses" (a play on the traditional warning "No Hawkers, No Circulars"). In 1968, he designed the green perimeter script on the Apple label in the UK and Europe (written

Alan Aldridge interpreted Beatles songs, illustrating "Taxman," "Yellow Submarine," "Doctor Robert," and "Eleanor Rigby" for *Woman's Mirror*.

in green cursive writing and reading "Apple Records—All Rights of the Manufacturer and of the Owner of the Recorded Work Reserved" at the top and "Unauthorised Public Performance, Broadcasting and Copying of this Record Prohibited" at the bottom), and in 1969, with their permission, he authored *The Beatles Illustrated Lyrics*.

The Beatles Illustrated Lyrics was in effect an extension of what Aldridge had started with *Woman's Mirror*, although none of the original illustrations were used. Over a hundred lyrics were sent out to forty-three sculptors, illustrators, cartoonists, and photographers (including David Hockney, Peter Max, Milton Glaser, Ethan Russell, Rick Griffin, Roger Law, Stanley Mouse, and David Bailey) who each chose the songs for which they would provide a visual counterpart. Aldridge took on twenty songs that he could illustrate using photography, clay sculptures, and cartoons.

Maureen Cleave's story in *Woman's Mirror* portrayed the Beatles as being caught in a trap of celebrity, history, and their own past achievements. Ringo was quoted as saying, "We were pushed into a corner, just the four of us. A sort of a trap, really. Like Siamese quads eating out of the same bowl." John was equally grim. "We sort of half hope for the downfall," he said. "A nice downfall. Then we would just be a pleasant old memory."

For the magazine cover Aldridge focused on their feelings of entrapment. He painted the four of them, back to back, encircled by a giant roll of barbed wire. Above their heads were four tails leading to a single giant speech bubble. Inside the speech bubble, shaded from yellow to red, in large capitals was the single word "HELP!"

NOVEMBER

**From our independent experiences, we've now
got something more to offer the group.
–JOHN, 1966.**

Paul was the last Beatle to take a break from England during the hiatus between the end of the final tour and the start of the next LP. His first project outside the Beatles was to compose soundtrack music for *The Family Way*, a film directed by brothers Roy and John Boulting and based on the 1963 play *All in Good Time* written by Bill Naughton, who was the man of the moment since writing the stage play and then screenplay *Alfie*.

Despite its slightly racy title (at the time "in the family way" was a euphemism for being single and pregnant), *The Family Way* was the story of a newlywed couple that had been unable to consummate their marriage. It starred John Mills, his daughter Hayley Mills, and Hywel Bennett.

The commission had come after Paul told Brian Epstein to put the word out that he wanted to write for film. The Boulting brothers were the first to respond. Interviewed in Spain about his future, John referred to the project as something that he and Paul had been invited to work on as a team. He told Fred Robbins, "I know we've got music to write as soon as we get back. Paul's just signed us up to write music for a film. I suppose it's—off the plane, into bed, and then 'Knock! Knock! Knock! Get up and write some songs.'" Paul has since said that during the negotiations it was suggested that he partner with lyricist Johnny Mercer, who'd cowritten such classic songs as "That Old Black Magic" (with Harold Arlen) and "Moon River" (with Henry Mancini), but he let the opportunity go, because at the time he didn't know who Mercer was.

Initially, when fishing for a commission, Paul had been thinking of a theme rather than an entire soundtrack. Although a lot was made of the fact that a Beatle was "writing" for a film, his involvement in the music was minimal. He developed a short piano piece and gave it to George Martin to arrange and orchestrate. Martin then subjected the composition to enough repeats, variations, and restatements to fill out twenty-four minutes of a recording. This was later recorded at CTS Studios over three days by the George Martin Orchestra (actually a collection of session musicians including Neville Marriner and Raymond Keenlyside on violins, John Underwood on viola, and Joy Hall on cello), but Paul took the composer's credit.

"[Martin] is the interpreter," Paul explained to the *Sunday Times*. "I play themes and chords on piano or guitar, he gets it down on paper. I talk about the idea I have for instrumentation. Then he works out the arrangement. I tried to learn music once with a fellow who's a great teacher. But it got too much like homework. I have some block about seeing it in little black dots on paper. It's like Braille to me."

Another piece was required for a love scene at the heart of the film, but Paul was slow to come up with anything. This frustrated Martin, who claimed that he literally had to stand over Paul at his piano in Cavendish Avenue to coax him into tapping out a fragment of a tune that Martin could then stretch and manipulate into a full-blown score to record with his orchestra. "I need a wistful little tune," he told Paul. "You're supposed to be writing the music for this thing, and I'm supposed to be orchestrating it. But to do that I need a tune,

Paul with violinists Neville Marriner (*left*) and Raymond Keenlyside during the recording of the soundtrack for *The Family Way*.

and you've got to give me one." Paul eventually produced what Martin described as "a sweet little fragment of a waltz tune." It sufficed, and with a sprinkling of Martin's magic became "Love in the Open Air." The soundtrack album wasn't a commercial success but ironically (considering the amount of work he put into it) earned Paul an Ivor Novello Award for Best Instrumental Theme. "If it sounds like it was done in a hurry," said Martin, "it's because it was done in a hurry."

Besides supplying the key tune, Paul suggested that a brass band be used to complement the tuba and church organ that were played on it. *The Family Way* was set in England's North, an area associated at the time with gritty, working-class realism, as in the novels of John Braine (*Room at the Top*) and Stan Barstow (*A Kind of Loving*). Factories and coal mines in the region frequently had their own brass bands. Two years later Paul would produce a single by the Black Dyke Mills Band for the Apple label ("Thingumybob," written by Lennon-McCartney). Thinking about then-

Jane Asher in *Romeo and Juliet* with Gawn Grainger.

unfashionable brass bands in November 1966 may have played a part in the germination of the Lonely Hearts Club Band persona, which he would later describe as "a bit of a brass band, in a way."

With Jane Asher leaving London for Bristol to play Juliet in an Old Vic production of *Romeo and Juliet,* Paul was at liberty to take a break from England. It had been years since he'd had the freedom or opportunity to wander alone, and he relished the opportunity to be temporarily relieved of his identity as a Beatle. His fame had opened up the world to him in ways he could never have imagined, but at the same time it robbed him of the anonymity that was essential to an artist who enjoyed being an unobtrusive observer.

As a teenager in Liverpool Paul would take a bus into the city center just to watch people, overhear conversations, and make mental notes. He had a romantic idea of being a poet who observed behavior and stored experiences for later use. "I was very conscious of gathering material," he told Barry Miles. "I didn't know then what it would be for. I really fancied myself as an artist. I was preparing."

The things he saw and heard would be drawn on, but for song lyrics rather than poems. Eleanor Rigby and the lonely people, he said, were based on his memories of old people he met in Liverpool. But since the success of the Beatles it was difficult for him to spy in this way. He was now the one spied upon. The people he met were screened and behaved unnaturally in his presence because of his fame. He craved more balance in his life. He once broke down sobbing in front of Maggie McGivern, saying, "I just want to be normal."

To make things better he planned an unaccompanied drive through France and down into Spain. He would fly from Lydd in Kent to Le Touquet in northern France with Silver City Airways, whose Bristol Superfreighters each took twenty passengers and three cars. He would take his Aston Martin with him and then drive without a timetable or a fixed route. To remain incognito he would wear a theatrical mustache from Wig Creations until he could grow his own, a pair of glasses with clear lenses, and a long overcoat. He would also slick back his hair. He packed his 8 mm movie camera and some notebooks to record his journey.

He left London on November 6 with no accommodations booked. After arriving in France and clearing customs he stuck on his mustache, donned his spectacles, plastered his hair with Vaseline, and headed toward Paris and the Loire Valley beyond. He explored some chateaux on the way and stopped overnight in small hotels, where he would park some distance away and register under a false name. In each town he would amble unhindered while taking photos and shopping for antiques, and then at the end of the day retire to his room to write in his journal.

After a few days of solo travel he met up with Mal Evans at a preplanned location in Bordeaux, and together they headed for the Spanish border, where they stayed at the coastal town of San Sebas-

tian. The weather turned nasty, and so they drove on to Madrid, stopping off on the way at Ameyugo to climb up to El Monumento al
Buen Pastor, a recently erected statue of the biblical Good Shepherd.

After Madrid they headed to Cordoba and then Malaga, planning to travel east along the coast to Almeria to see John. It was then
that they learned from NEMS that John had already left Spain, and
so they changed their plans. Paul had the office arrange a safari in
Kenya through a travel agent. At Seville the Aston Martin was left for
collection by an employee who would drive it back to England while
John and Mal flew to Nairobi via Rome (where they took a bus tour
of the city and visited Saint Peter's).

In Kenya they did the normal touristy things. They stayed at a
luxury lodge in Tsavo National Park, watched hippos and crocodiles
from an underwater viewing chamber at Mzima Springs, saw Mount
Kilimanjaro while at the Maasai Amboseli Game Reserve, and spent a
night at the renowned Treetops Hotel, built on stilts around a chest-
nut tree in Aberdare National Park. Their driver, Moses, took them
everywhere in his old blue Plymouth.

Their final night, November 18, was spent at the Central YMCA
on State House Avenue in Nairobi, where Paul sang to a group of
children on the lawn outside while Mal went out shopping for gifts
in the late afternoon. Paul had been profoundly affected by the experience of leaving behind his Beatle persona and by the transformative
power of adopting a disguise. Traveling as someone else gave him a
refreshing sense of liberty. As the man with the mustache and glasses
he could do things that Paul McCartney, the man constantly under
the microscope, could never do.

He reflected on how this might apply to the whole group. How
much were they inhibited by having to be Beatles who were expected
to produce Beatles music? If they wore a corporate disguise, would
it release new dimensions of their creativity? Flying from Nairobi to
London with Mal Evans at his side, he began to draft ideas for a recording on which the Beatles would assume the identity of another

Paul with his movie camera while on holiday in Kenya.

group. "I thought—let's not be ourselves," he told Barry Miles. "Let's develop alter egos so we're not having to project an image which we know. It would be much more free. What would be really interesting would be to actually take on the personas of a different band."

While being served an airline meal, Paul noticed the small packets that came on the tray—one marked S, the other marked P. Evans asked what they were and then remembered. "Salt and pepper," he said. Paul made a quick aural joke—"Sergeant Pepper." He liked the sound. Maybe Sergeant Pepper could be the leader of the band.

Sergeant Pepper conjured up images of Edwardian or Victorian military bands in uniform. Granny Takes a Trip, the Chelsea Antique Market, and Lord Kitchener's Valet were already doing a brisk trade in old army dress jackets with brass buttons, epaulettes, high collars, and stripes. They were taking the symbols of British imperialism and turning them into contemporary art objects—reappropriating the trappings associated with discipline, submission, and hierarchy so that they became part of the culture of self-abandon, antiauthoritarianism, and equality. Pomp thus became pop.

In March, Pete Townshend had been pictured on the cover of

The Who on the cover of the *Observer Magazine.*

the *Observer Magazine* wearing a jacket made from the British Union Jack flag. In later photos of the Who John Entwistle wore military medals, and Keith Moon had a T-shirt displaying an RAF roundel. In October, Mick Jagger had appeared on *Ready, Steady, Go!* to perform "Paint It Black" dressed in a red jacket designed for a drummer of the Grenadier guards that he had picked up in Notting Hill's Portobello Road. In ads for the debut single by the new "supergroup" Cream, Eric Clapton was attired in what looked like an army bandsman's jacket.

As Paul developed his concept, he gave Sergeant Pepper an appropriately named band: Sergeant Pepper's Lonely Hearts Club

Band. This sounded legitimately Edwardian while at the same time potentially psychedelic, in line with such San Francisco groups as Quicksilver Messenger Service, Big Brother and the Holding Company, and even Dr. Humbead's New Tranquility String Band and Medicine Show.

A recent LP, sent to him by Barry Miles, would affirm the new direction Paul was considering. Called *Freak Out!* and recorded by Frank Zappa's group, the Mothers of Invention, it was a double album with a gatefold sleeve and songs all in some way dealing with aspects of American popular culture. In the centerfold Zappa printed the names of 179 people who had "contributed materially in many ways to make our music what it is." The list featured Elvis Presley, Stockhausen, Ravi Shankar, Pierre Boulez, the poet Lawrence Ferlinghetti, comic Lenny Bruce, cartoonist Jules Feiffer, novelist James Joyce, artist Salvador Dali, producer Phil Spector, actor John Wayne, and Brian Epstein. (*Sgt. Pepper* would feature a similar acknowledgment of significant influencers but would do it visually and on the front cover.)

Freak Out! by Frank Zappa's group, the Mothers of Invention.

Incidentally, November 6, 1966, when Paul left London for France, is the date that conspiracy theorists claim Paul died and was later replaced by lookalike musician William Shears Campbell (Billy Shears), who had recently won a Paul McCartney lookalike competition. They cite the lack of photographs from the trip (although there is homemade movie footage of Paul in Kenya) and the scarcity of sightings in Britain from this date until the start of the *Sgt. Pepper* sessions on November 24, by which time Paul has facial hair (because it's really Billy Shears pretending to be Paul).

Nothing about the car crash was mentioned at the time (although rumors of Beatle deaths had spread around British school playgrounds before this), but the story gained currency in America starting in October 1969. After this date believers in the swap theory had a great time finding "clues" to Paul's death from the fact that he was the only Beatle not facing the camera on the back cover of *Sgt. Pepper* and the only Beatle not wearing shoes on the cover of *Abbey Road* to hidden messages planted by John on "Strawberry Fields Forever" (some spoken words sound like "I buried Paul") and "Revolution Number 9" (played backward, the intoning voice sounds as if it's saying something like "Turn me on, dead man").

Even though almost fifty years have since passed, the theory still has the power to flare back into life. In August 2009 the Italian edition of *Wired* magazine ran a nine-page feature reporting the work of computer scientist Francesco Gavazzeni and forensic pathologist Gabriella Carlesi, who after close analysis of photos of Paul's face concluded that the Paul McCartney shown in images prior to November 1966 was not the same man as the Paul McCartney in images after that date. They reached their verdict after multiple measurements of the distances between different facial features and the discovery of "discrepancies."

In March 2015 a spoof website published a story stating that Ringo had recently given an interview in which he admitted that Paul had been replaced in 1966. He was quoted as saying, "When Paul died, we all panicked. We didn't know what to do, and Brian Epstein, our manager, suggested that we hire Billy Shears as a temporary solution. It was supposed to last only a week or two, but time went by and nobody seemed to notice, so we kept playing along. Billy turned out to be a pretty good musician, and he was able to perform almost better than Paul. The only problem was that he couldn't get along with John, at all." Unbelievably, the story was picked up by many other websites that took it as genuine news.

The day after Paul left on his travels (either to France or to eternity), John had had what would turn out to be one of the most propitious meetings of his life. Yoko Ono, who'd come to London to take part in the Destruction in Art Symposium at the Africa Centre in Covent Garden, had been invited by John Dunbar to stay on to mount a solo exhibition at the Indica Gallery. Indica Books had recently moved to bigger premises at 102 Southampton Row in Holborn, where *International Times* had its editorial offices in the basement, thus freeing up the ground floor of 6 Mason's Yard to be used for extra exhibition space.

Yoko accepted. She was with her American husband, Tony Cox, living in a flat in Camden Square loaned to them by a member of the Arts Council of Great Britain. Cox, a trained artist, built the exhibits in line with Yoko's instructions. He also designed posters advertising the show and created a guest list.

Dunbar suggested he should invite John for a preview, not because he was well known (neither Cox nor Yoko would have been impressed by the Beatles, because they were wrapped up in their own work and the avant-garde scene of New York) but because he was an art lover and a potential client. "Yoko didn't want anyone to see it before it was totally finished," says Dunbar. "But we said, he's a Beatle. He's got lots of money. He might buy something." Cox made a call to John.

John came along on November 7 as the exhibition was being set up for the next day's opening. He was still tanned from being in

Yoko Ono with her American husband, Tony Cox, around the time of her first meeting with John Lennon.

Spain and looked healthy. He took a look at the works, all of which in some way required the spectator to "complete" the art through an action or an expression of surprise, relief, or laughter. *Hammer and Nail Piece*, for example, consisted of a block of mahogany, a hammer with a gold-plated head and a small jar of gold-plated nails. The hammer was chained to the wood. *Apple Piece* was a fresh apple (renewed each day) on a Plexiglas stand with a price tag reading "£200." An all-white chess set stood on a white table next to a white chair. "John thought it was bonkers," remembers Dunbar.

The first exhibit John connected with was *Ladder Piece*. A small card was pasted to the ceiling above a white stepladder, and next to the card dangled a magnifying glass. John dutifully climbed the ladder and saw that the small card had something printed on it in a minuscule typeface. Taking the glass, he stretched up to read and discovered the single word "YES." He later said that what struck him most about the piece was that it was affirmative. It was also funny.

Noticing the *Hammer and Nail Piece*, John asked if he could have a try, but Yoko refused him because she needed the exhibition to remain untouched before the opening. Dunbar urged her to let him. She then agreed that he could if he gave her five shillings. "Well, I'll give you an imaginary five shillings," said John, "if you'll let me hammer in an imaginary nail." He later said, "That's when we really met. That's when we locked eyes and she got it and I got it and that was it." Yoko confirmed this: "It was fantastic. That was what my art was about. It was my game. The two of us were playing the same game."

Despite his art school training and his experimental bent of mind, John had not been a connoisseur of contemporary avant-garde art. Judging by the frequency of mentions in published interviews, his preference was for painters like Picasso, Dali, Renoir, and Van Gogh, and to this point he had rarely referred to anyone more modern or showed any detailed knowledge of conceptual art. He was credited with saying that "avant-garde is French for bullshit" and dismissed avant-garde artists as being "intellectual," meaning that they lived in a world of ideas rather than feelings. He was wary of being conned and as suspicious of avant-garde art as he had been suspicious of Bob Dylan's lyrics.

There was a contradiction in his attitude to art and music. He loved rock 'n' roll because it was visceral, primitive, and unpretentious, and yet he was cerebral, cultivated, and intellectual. He feared that rock 'n' roll was becoming too highbrow, self-conscious, and "artistic"—"If we want to go bullshitting off into intellectualism with rock and roll, we are going to get bullshitting rock and roll intellectualism. If we want real rock and roll, it's up to all of us to create it." And yet he'd played such a major role in making it more intellectual. He

An *International Times* advertisement for Yoko Ono's solo
exhibition at the Indica Gallery.

admitted to planting messages in songs, drew inspiration from the
compositional techniques of cubist painters and electronic experi-
mentalists, and spoke about the fact that he was only truly understood by an elite.

The confluence of conceptual art, pop art, experimental jazz,
electronic music, Beat poetry, and pop music enjoyed and promoted
by the Indica crowd was still the secret of a relative minority. In general pop musicians didn't engage with art, and artists still looked
down on pop. "The Beatles were pop stars and that was considered
beneath the realm of true artists," Tony Cox told me in 1981. "We
were at the forefront of the avant-garde. This was real art and what
everyone else was doing was relatively unimportant."

When she met John at the Indica Gallery, Yoko didn't recognize him as a Beatle. She only found out when one of the students helping to set up the show said to her, "You do know who that was, don't you?" and told her it was John Lennon. Even then it didn't impress her. Before he left the gallery she gave him a card. In the center of it was the word "breathe" all in lower case letters. At the bottom, in small print, it said "y.o. '66."

John and Cynthia had been drifting apart for years. If they hadn't married when she became pregnant in 1962, it's unlikely that they would have remained together. When they met at art school he was a teddy boy and she was a smartly attired, conventional girl from one of the middle-class areas of Birkenhead over the Mersey from Liverpool. She loved him very much and tried to meet his expectations, but their minds never met. She could be his mate, but never his soul mate.

In Yoko, John found someone he would discover to be deep, challenging, intriguing, and independent. She was older than him by almost eight years, was already on her second marriage (which was also coming apart), and had succeeded in the male-dominated arena of modern art. She had published a book of poetry (*Grapefruit*, 1964), released a film (*No. 4*, 1966), exhibited in New York and Tokyo, and was best known for performances where she would present a series of short provocative "events" in small theatres.

In one well-known event, or "piece," she would invite members of the audience to step forward and snip off small pieces of her clothing. In another she would stay concealed in a black bag. At the Jeanetta Cochrane Theatre in London she had forty cyclists moving together around a tilting stage. Sometimes she gave pieces provocative-sounding titles that would lead an audience to expect pornography, be disappointed that there wasn't any, and consequently be shamed in the act of recognizing their squalid desires.

The separate ventures of the Beatles had not gone unnoticed by the press. On November 10, John and George spoke to Don Short for a story that appeared the next day in the *Daily Mirror* under the headline "At the Crossroads" with individual headshots of each Beatle to accentuate the idea of what Short called "mounting predictions of a split-up of the world's most famous foursome." Both John and George denied that the group was ending but explained that in order to "progress" they needed to spend more time in the studio and less time on the road.

"We've been resting and thinking," explained George. "It gave us a chance to reassess things. After all, we've had four years doing what everybody else wanted us to do. Now we're doing what we want to do. But whatever we do, it has got to be real and progressive. Everything we've done so far has been rubbish, as I see it today."

John felt they now had so much time set aside for recording and making their next film that a tour was not feasible in the immediate future. But he said he didn't envisage a breakup of the group. He believed that their recent adventures as individuals could only enrich the Beatles.

Short asked if there had been a row between the group and Brian Epstein. "Row with Eppy? Not us," said George. Short contacted Epstein and asked the same question. "There have been no rows at all," he answered. "We have always seen eye to eye, but I am anxious about the growing rumors about the Beatles' future. Only last weekend, fans besieged my Belgravia home demanding another Beatles tour, but I am not at all sure that personal appearances are in their best interests. But that doesn't mean they will never appear in person again. They will. I don't think they will split up because I'm certain that they will want to do things together for a long time." (The "besieging" he referred to was when two hundred fans arrived outside his home on November 6 with a thousand-signature petition.)

On November 13 the Four Tops appeared at Epstein's Saville Theatre for two shows that marked their live British debut and acted as a promotional preview of next year's national tour. The Motown act was riding high with "Reach Out I'll Be There" and, back in Detroit, had just cut "Standing in the Shadows of Love." Singles such as "It's the Same Old Song," "Something About You," "Baby, I Need Your Loving," and "I Can't Help Myself (Sugar Pie Honey Bunch)" had made them enormously popular with mods and those who enjoyed dancing to records in the new-styled "discotheque" clubs because of their infectious beats.

Levi Stubbs of the Four Tops told Judith Simons of the *Daily Express* that although black American groups had inspired the Beatles, the inspiration was now flowing the other way. Motown music had become more melodic, poetic, and socially conscious. "Until the Beatles made their mark on us," said Stubbs, "American negro music was all rhythm and beat with very simple words. Now we have become more melodious in our approach and interested in improved harmonies."

John went to see the Four Tops, as did Mick Jagger, Donovan, Eric Burdon of the Animals, and Georgie Fame. As it was a Sunday, the traditional "dark" day for theatres, Jane Asher had been able to travel up from Bristol. There was a party afterward, at which John called over to Lawrence Payton of the Four Tops: "Tell me something man. When you cats go in the studio, what does the drummer use to get that backbeat? A bloody tree?"

Judith Simons was impressed that the Motown group played high-quality music to an audience that listened raptly to each song and applauded afterward rather than screamed. She detected the emergence of "a new kind of beat show that depends on talent rather than sex appeal." Epstein concurred with her theory. "The day of the semi-amateur beat bill is finished," he agreed. "Audiences want accomplished artists."

Earlier in the day Epstein had been rattled by a story that had appeared in the *Sunday Telegraph* suggesting that the Beatles were contemplating new management. The piece opened by revealing, "Mr. Allen Klein, the American impresario, film producer and business manager of the Rolling Stones, has been approached by two of the Beatles over their future management." The tip-off was that the two Beatles—presumably John and George—had approached Klein through a third party and that Klein was "very interested" to meet them. Diplomatically, he said that he wouldn't do anything that would come between the group and their present management.

Klein was clearly sounding them out, using the press to say that they deserved to be bigger cinema stars than they currently were but denying that he'd ever made an approach. Over the next week his lawyer, Marty Machat, was quoted as saying that he wasn't at liberty to reveal the third party liaising on behalf of the Beatles, reveal the identities of the two Beatles involved, or even confirm whether Klein would be meeting any of the Beatles while in London. Through Tony Barrow, Brian Epstein issued strong denials that there was any rupture between him and the group, claiming that the Klein story was false.

This incident hinted at a struggle that was taking place within the Beatles. John had been the original leader of the group, and it had been at his invitation that Paul had joined. But, almost imperceptibly, Paul had become his equal and was now taking over. This was not due to dictatorial tendencies but was because he had a natural interest in all levels of the business, from cover design to shares in Northern Songs and the energy to invest in them, whereas John was constitutionally lackadaisical. Paul's dominance was due to John's withdrawal.

Drugs only worsened matters. John would go on LSD binges that could last for days, during which time he couldn't be relied on to deal with business matters or make clear-minded decisions. LSD, as has already been said, affected his sense of self-worth, and he wasn't able to assert himself vigorously enough in the studio. Rather than standing up to Paul as an equal, he tended to make compromises that he later regretted.

John's next encounter with Yoko came unexpectedly, at an opening party for an exhibition of Claes Old-

TOGETHER, WORKING AGAIN—THE BEATLES LAST NIGHT

PAUL McCARTNEY

JOHN LENNON

It was front-page news when the Beatles regrouped at EMI Studios on November 24, 1966, to start recording tracks for their next LP.

enburg's work at the Robert Fraser Gallery on November 21. In works like *Soft Toilet, Floor Burger,* and *Shoestring Potatoes,* Oldenburg, a Swedish-born American based in New York, pioneered soft pop art sculptures that were both bold and humorous. John had a brief conversation with Yoko, but then Paul arrived and began talking to her, so John roughly pulled Paul away, explaining to Yoko that they both needed to go somewhere. He left her with the impression that he was harboring a lot of anger. In truth he was anxious that his more sociable and outgoing friend with avant-garde connections might make more headway with her than he had. He wanted Yoko for himself.

Still considering him a potential patron or buyer, Yoko sent him a copy of *Grapefruit* that he then kept by his bedside and dipped into at night before sleeping. Her enigmatic instructions with the brevity of haiku and the mind-twisting nature of Zen koans intrigued him. He particularly liked "Map Piece," which said simply "Draw a map to get lost." He could relate to that brevity and surrealism. "I thought I was pretty far out," he told me in 1971, "but Yoko was even further out."

When the four Beatles gathered at EMI on the evening of November 24, it was their first time in the studio in five months. John arrived wearing a parka coat with a fur-fringed hood; George had a dark raincoat with an attached shoulder cape and a raccoon hat; Ringo wore a nylon zip-up jacket; and Paul, who was carrying his guitar in a case, was dressed in a double-breasted black jacket. All were clean-shaven except for Paul, who had kept his vacation mustache.

As with other recent LPs by the Beatles, most of the songs had yet to be written, and, according to George Martin, Paul's thematic view wasn't discussed this far in advance. EMI was keen to get a single, as there hadn't been a release since "Yellow Submarine" and "Eleanor Rigby" in August. In the meantime they were planning to compensate for the lack of a Christmas single or LP from the group by releasing the first Beatles' compilation record, *A Collection of Beatles Oldies*.

In what would prove to be a productive session the Beatles recorded a rhythm track and vocals for "Strawberry Fields Forever." It took three hours, with most of that time spent "routining"—choosing instruments, deciding on an arrangement, and running through the song as John explained how he imagined it. Paul played Mellotron, George added bottleneck guitar, and Ringo introduced a muffled drum sound by covering the skins with tea towels from the EMI canteen.

This first take was faster than the version that was finally released and less convoluted. John's vocal was clear and confident, but confidence and clarity went against the spirit of a lyric that was about insecurity and confusion. The order of verses had still to be finalized, and the chorus had yet to be used at the start of the song.

That night a new club was launched on Kingly Street, close to the NEMS offices on Argyll Street. Called the Bag O' Nails and run by Rik and Johnny Gunnell, who also ran the Flamingo Club on Wardour Street, where Georgie Fame had established himself, it would soon become *the* in place for the rock aristocracy. Brian Epstein attended the opening.

The next day, at lunchtime, there was a forty-five-minute showcase featuring a new trio managed by Chas Chandler, the former bass player of the Animals. The guitarist and singer, Jimi Hendrix, had been spotted by Chandler in a Greenwich Village club and invited to London because Chandler was confident that the British press and public would be more naturally responsive to his blues-inspired music. Supported by two British musicians—bass player Noel Redding and drummer Mitch Mitchell—he performed as the Jimi Hendrix Experience.

A popular figure on the British R & B scene, Chandler had great music business connections, and the small basement club was packed with rock royalty, who'd been told to expect a musical phenomenon who would shake up the world of the electric guitar. Donovan was there, as well as Brian Jones, Keith Richards, Jeff Beck, Jimmy Page, and Eric Burdon. What they saw and heard profoundly affected many of those present. Hendrix, with his wild hair and colorful gypsy clothes, got more sound and emotion out of his guitar than anyone previously thought possible. He played "Wild Thing," "Foxy Lady," "Hey Joe," and other songs and, when he'd finished, stood his guitar by a speaker, creating feedback, so that it carried on resonating long after he'd left the stage. "Afterwards, in the dressing room, which was like a closet, John Lennon walked in," said Noel Redding in 1997. "He said, 'That's grand lads.' Then McCartney walked in and that freaked me out even more."

The Beatles went to the offices of Dick James Music on New Oxford Street at three o'clock for the recording of their 1966 Christmas disc for members of the UK Beatles fan club. Rather than the traditional greetings, they had assembled almost six minutes of songs and nonsense under the guise of a short skit. George Martin produced, Brian Epstein sat in the control room, and Neil Aspinall and Mal Evans contributed voices.

It was an ungainly recording that started with a short song called "Everywhere It's Christmas" and concluded with another music-hall-style song called "Please Don't Bring Your Banjo Back" (both of which sound as though they were written by Paul), and between these musical pieces were a series of very short sketches with titles such as "A Rare Cheese," "The Loyal Toast," and "Podgy the Bear and Jasper." There was no continuity, theme, or punch lines. The finished record would be delivered to fans in December in a psychedelic/art nouveau sleeve designed and painted by Paul.

Satirist Peter Cook, who with his performing partner Dudley Moore had a regular BBC TV sketch program, *Not Only . . . But Also,* socialized with John and Paul. He invited John to take part in a sketch being filmed in a men's room on Broadwick Street, Soho, on Sunday, November 27. It was a dig at the recent interest of the American media in Swinging London. Hiram J. Pipesucker (played by Cook) was an investigative journalist for Idaho Television, presenting a program called *The Pipesucker Report.*

In the sketch he first

Paul designed the cover for the free Beatles fan club record *Everywhere It's Christmas.*

visits a studio where a band (featuring Cook and Moore) is cutting a song called "L. S. Bumblebee." The group plays Eastern instruments and uses the sound effects of splashing water and a crowing hen. Next Pipesucker visits the Soho restroom, announcing, "This is London's most fashionable lavatory spot. Here, film stars rub shoulders with royalty in an atmosphere of cosmopolitan sophistication."

Blocking the entrance to the underground establishment is Dan (John Lennon), dressed in a doorman's coat and top hat. He explains that only members can enter but lets Pipesucker in when he flashes a five-pound note. The tough door policy was allegedly based on that of the Ad Lib Club, which had closed in January. John had four lines, and his section of the sketch lasted only fifty seconds.

The next two evenings were spent adding more layers to "Strawberry Fields Forever." The second take had no vocals but introduced a stately passage played by Paul using the flute setting on the Mellotron. The fourth take was the first to start with the chorus, and following the sixth take there was a mix down that yielded a "best" version so far, from which four acetates were cut for John, Paul, George, and Ringo to take home and listen to at their leisure.

It sounded like a finished version, but John wasn't happy with it. There was something missing, something that he would need to return to in order to fix. Unusually for a Beatles recording, it was temporarily put aside while attention was turned to another song, this time one written by Paul.

DECEMBER

We keep on doing tracks which can be any
style at all. We're not limited that way, or with
time any more. We take as much time on a
track until we get it to our satisfaction.
-PAUL, 1966

Barry Miles was one of the first people for whom Paul played his acetate of the almost complete version of "Strawberry Fields Forever." Miles had come to Cavendish Avenue to interview him for *International Times*. It was Paul's way of giving support to the new paper. A major interview with a Beatle would give the paper publicity, provide a compelling front cover, and boost circulation. It could also help secure much-needed advertising from major record companies.

It was probably the most unusual interview Paul had ever done. Miles didn't come with prepared questions, the two of them both smoked dope throughout, and the six-thousand-word conversation ranged from talk of rock 'n' roll pioneers Carl Perkins, Chuck Berry, and Bo Diddley to French theatre, classical music, materialism, peace, and Zen. Because he was with a friend his guard was down, and because he was high his mind jumped from topic to topic like a stone skimming on water. The result was an accurate reflection of the state of Paul McCartney in December 1966 with a new LP in the making and a head full of ideas.

When the piece was published, in January 1967, it increased Paul's hip quotient. Fans were familiar with reading his comments in the context of teenage fan magazines like *Fabulous, 16,* or *Datebook* or in national newspapers like the *Daily Express,* but here was an interview with a Beatle alongside a feature by Norman Mailer on war, a piece by William Burroughs on cutting up sound tapes to make aural collages, a defense of obscenity by Bengali poet Malay Roy Choudhury, a psychedelic cartoon by Jeff Nuttall, poetry reviews by Anselm Hollo, and ads for pregnancy tests, condoms, Granny Takes a Trip, Hung On You, and the Pink Floyd at UFO Club. The editorial was written while the editor, Tom McGrath, was tripping and convinced that "God is here in the simplest things, within yourself. You are God."

They began by discussing the music of the Beatles and the influences on it, Paul admitting that boredom was a propelling force. The Beatles had never wanted to atrophy. He suggested that Bob Dylan, the Who, and the Beach Boys were united in having their roots in pop and rock but currently seeking to create new music that transcended it. "We are all trying to make it into something we know *it is,* but not many people know *it is* yet. Most people think it's all just pop, which of course it isn't."

He contrasted the early days of the group, when they looked up to certain writers and performers, to their current situation, where they had largely bypassed their idols not only in record sales but also in critical acclaim. They were in the lonely position of being at the forefront of the development of contemporary pop music, with no one ahead of them that they could follow. This was uncharted territory, and they only had each other to look to for inspiration and challenge.

"The next move seems to be things like electronics because it's a complete new field and there are a lot of good new sounds to be listened to in it. But if the music itself is just going to jump about five miles ahead, then everyone's going to be left standing with this gap of five miles that they've all got to cross before they can even see what scene these people are on."

Paul began to wax philosophical, bemoaning the loss of mystery in modern life as everything was explained away by science. No more God, no more soul, no more ghosts, no more heaven, no more spirit. "I don't believe it ends with our Western logical thought," he said. "It can't do, because that's so messed up anyway. You have got to allow for the possibility of there being a lot, lot more than we know about. . . . The thing that's grown out of this materialist scene . . . is that for everything to exist on a material level you've got to be able to discount any things that happen which don't fit in with it. And they're all very neatly disposed of these days."

What Paul reiterated in different ways throughout the interview was that he'd undergone a significant change over the past two years, during which his previously secure system of categorization had been challenged. This was as true for music (this is "classical," this is "pop," this is "rock") as it was for aesthetics (this is "beautiful," that is "ugly") and morals (this is "good," that is "evil"). Everything was due to be reevaluated.

The International Times   No. 6   Jan 16-29, 1967 / 1s.
★ Paul McCARTNEY
★ Norman MAILER
★ William BURROUGHS
★ Allen GINSBERG
★ Cerebral CORTEX

Barry Miles interviewed Paul for *International Times* in December 1966 for a story published in January 1967.

"It's a beginning again," he said. "There is no end. I know I'm going to need a new set of rules and the new set of rules has got to include the rule that there aren't any rules."

As far as music was concerned, this meant being open to all genres rather than dismissing ragas as foreign, jazz as difficult, or electronic music as weird. He even questioned the unspoken rules that governed pop and rock. "Don't you think that the scene that someone like Albert Ayler or Stockhausen is getting into isn't necessarily a bad scene? It's not necessarily what you think it is. It isn't necessarily weird. What is weird? It's weird because you don't know about it, because it's a bit strange to you. It's new."

On the first two nights of the month Paul went to see the American group the Young Rascals, first at the Scotch of St James and then at Blaises in South Kensington. The Rascals specialized in "blue-eyed soul," with covers of "In the Midnight Hour" and "Mustang Sally" and a No. 1 U.S. hit with "Good Lovin'." Paul's interest was due to the Rascals being managed by Sid Bernstein, the Beatles' first American promoter, who in 1965 had used the electronic signs at Shea Stadium to announce THE RASCALS ARE COMING.

On the evening of December 6, after recording a series of Christmas greetings to be played by the pirate ships Radio London and Radio Caroline, the Beatles turned their attention to a song of Paul's, "When I'm Sixty-Four." Like "Michelle," this song had been started by Paul in his teenage years and, like "Michelle," had been a bit of a joke. Paul allegedly used to perform it as a piano instrumental at the Cavern when the speakers weren't working.

He'd now put lyrics to the tune and turned it into a vaudeville song inspired by the music that his father had performed in the 1920s when he played with a Liverpool dance band. It was an unusual choice of song if his aim, as he told Barry Miles, was to take pop music to places it had never been.

In other ways it fitted with the project still germinating in his imagination. Sergeant Pepper's band can play music from any era or culture. Also, the boom in antique clothing and old uniforms had brought about a reappraisal of early twentieth-century popular music. Contemporary groups such as the New Vaudeville Band ("Winchester Cathedral") and the Bonzo Dog Doo-Dah Band ("My Brother Makes the Noises for the Talkies") were aping the sounds of the 1920s.

Paul lightened up the song by introducing cartoonish sounding characters (Vera, Chuck, and Dave) and a comical story told in the form of a letter (as he had done previously with "P.S. I Love You" and "Paperback Writer"). Both George Martin and Paul spoke about wanting to achieve a "rooty tooty" sound, a phrase usually applied to early American jazz music and derived from the tooting noise made by the trumpet.

Recording "When I'm Sixty-Four" was as straightforward as recording "Strawberry Fields Forever" was complicated. Two takes, with Paul playing piano and bass and Ringo on drums, were done on the first day, and the next day Paul returned alone and put his vocals on the second of the takes in a three-hour session. On December 20, John, Paul, and George recorded their backing vocals and Ringo added bells. On December 28, Robert Burns, Henry MacKenzie, and Frank Reidy overdubbed their clarinets, and two days later a mix was completed during which the track was sped up slightly to raise the voice a semitone. Geoff Emerick and George Martin have both said subsequently this was to make Paul's voice appear younger—closer to what it would have sounded like when he first conceived the tune—but Paul doesn't remember it this way. "I think it was just to make it more rooty tooty," he told Barry Miles. "[It was] just to lift the key because it was starting to sound a little turgid."

After spending time with "Strawberry Fields Forever" on acetate John had been unhappy with it. He wanted to begin afresh and suggested building the sound with trumpets and cellos. "It was a very gentle song when I first heard it," George Martin told me. "The first time we recorded it, it turned out much heavier than expected. So I wasn't very surprised when he came back to me and said he'd like to do it again. That was the first time we'd ever remade anything." The remake started on the evening of December 8, right after Paul had finished singing on "When I'm Sixty-Four." For the first four hours a technical engineer, Dave Harries, had to stand in for Martin and Geoff Emerick, who were both attending the premiere of the Cliff Richard film *Finders Keepers*.

Cymbals, timpani, bongos, tambourines, and guitars were recorded backward in fifteen takes with Harries's help and two of the takes edited together to form the foundation of the new version. The next day, with George Martin back in control, Ringo's strident, clattering drum sound was added along with more backward cymbals and an Indian swarmandal played by George.

The track was now far richer than the previous "best version" that John had rejected. The additional instruments were turning it into a cauldron bubbling with musical sounds that mimicked the disarrayed thoughts that John had tried to capture when he first played it on his acoustic guitar in Spain. Trumpets and cellos were added on December 15, and John recorded two vocal tracks, both of which he liked for different reasons.

It was during the period when John was pondering which version of his vocals should be used on "Strawberry Fields Forever" that Tara Browne was killed while driving at high speed through Earl's Court, London, in the early hours of the morning. Estranged from his wife, Browne was with model Suki Potier in his Lotus Elan, returning home after a night out when a Volkswagen turned into his path from a side street. In swerving to avoid a collision he plowed into a parked van. He died on the spot from brain lacerations caused by fractures to his skull. He was twenty-one. Potier only suffered bruises and shock.

When the coroner's report was published, in January 1967, John turned aspects of the story as he learned it from a newspaper report into a fragment of song that would be incorporated into "A Day in the Life."

Tara Browne became the man who blew his mind out in a car. The story was embellished—traffic lights played no part in the incident (as in "He didn't notice that the lights had changed"), and he wasn't "from the House of Lords" (although his father was).

It was rumored that Browne had been on his way to or from a meeting with the design team of Binder, Edwards & Vaughan to

Guinness heir saved girl's life in crash

By JACK GREENSLADE

MR. TARA BROWNE, 21, heir to the £1 million Guinness fortune, was fatally injured in a London crash early yesterday after he swerved to protect the girl passenger in his car.

SUKI POTIER . . . Bruises and shock

A newspaper report about the inquest into the death of socialite Suki Potier. The tragedy would inspire part of John's contribution to "A Day in the Life."

discuss plans for the frontage of Dandie Fashions, a boutique he was a partner in that had opened two months before at 161 King's Road. Although it's true that BEV worked on the exterior of Dandie Fashions, there was no meeting between them and Browne that night

Coincidentally, Binder, Edwards & Vaughan was planning a festival of electronic music at the Roundhouse in Chalk Farm involving Paul that would be announced the day after Browne's death. Titled A Million Volt Light and Sound Rave and scheduled to take place on January 26, 1967, the festival would feature a psychedelic light show by Ray Anderson, who'd been doing lights at the Matrix and the Fillmore Auditorium in San Francisco; music by Unit Delta Plus (a freelance offshoot of the BBC's Radiophonic Workshop featuring Delia Derbyshire, Brian Hodgson, and Peter Zinovieff); and, as it said on the posters, a specially commissioned piece "composed by Paul McCartney."

The BBC Radiophonic Workshop was a unit that specialized in experimental music for radio and TV soundtracks. While working there in 1963 Delia Derbyshire had recorded the original theme music to the BBC TV series *Doctor Who* based on a composition by Ron Grainer. It would be one of the first pieces of electronic music widely known by the general public.

"Carnival of Light," recorded at EMI by the Beatles on January 5, 1967, after a "Penny Lane" session, wasn't so much "composed" by Paul as initiated by him. It was a fourteen-minute musical freakout where John, George, and Ringo were encouraged to hit, blow, shake, and strum whatever they came across in the studio in whatever fashion they chose. There was no organizing principle. The idea of avant-gardism seems to have been confused with mere cacophony and randomness. Beatles historian Mark Lewisohn, one of the few outsiders to have heard the so-far unreleased tape, has described it as "distorted, hyp-notic drum and organ sounds," "distorted lead guitar," "a church organ, various effects . . . and voices" and "various in-describable sound effects with heaps of tape echo and manic tambourine."

In December, Dud-ley Edwards had taken Paul to meet Unit Delta Plus's Peter Zinovieff at his townhouse on Deodar

A poster designed by Bob Gill advertising the Million Volt Light and Sound Rave in Camden, North London.

Engineer, composer, and inventor Peter Zinovieff at his advanced recording studio in Putney.

Road in Putney as preparation for the light and sound rave. Zinovieff, an Oxford-educated mathematician whose previous job was in nuclear physics, showed them a shed in his garden in which he had built his recording studio using ex-army electrical components including filters, noise generators, ring modulators, signal analyzers, and 384 oscillators. At the heart of it was a computer he'd bought two years previously with the proceeds from selling his wife's wedding tiara. The walls and ceiling of the shed were packed with speakers through which he played Paul and Edwards some recent recordings he had made with Delia Derbyshire. Paul was particularly interested in the unorthodox phrase lengths. Edwards says that listening to this experimental music was one of the most amazing experiences of his life. "He stood me in the centre of the room and then switched on a tape of one of his compositions. The music was played at such intense decibel frequencies that many parts of my anatomy (including internal organs) began to perform an involuntary dance. I could only describe it as 'ecstatic twitching.'"

On the night of December 20 John Edwards, a TV journalist from ITN's *Reporting 66,* caught each of the Beatles as they approached the front door of the studio. John was the first to arrive, as a passenger in a black Mini Cooper. His hair was starting to grow back, and he now had a mustache. The reporter was out to discover whether the Beatles were breaking up. Asked if he could foresee a time when the group would no longer work together, John said, "I could see us not working together for a period but we'd always get together for one reason or another. You need other people for ideas and we all get along fine."

Having been told by John that he had no ambition to do further films, Edwards asked whether he would continue writing songs, whatever course his career took. "Yeah. We'll probably go on writing music forever, whatever else we're doing, because you just can't stop. You find yourself doing it whether you want to or not," he said. As far as touring was concerned, John said, "There must be a point when tours don't work anymore, because they're not to do with what we're doing, record-wise or film-wise."

Paul, also with a mustache and carrying his guitar in a case, was asked whether he'd miss the business of touring should they retire from the stage. He said he wouldn't, because, in his words, "Performance for us has gone downhill because we can't develop when no-one can hear us. For us to perform gets more difficult each time. We want to do it but if we're not listened to, and we can't even hear ourselves, we can't get any better. So we're trying to get better with things like recording."

Ringo, who arrived with Neil Aspinall and John's old childhood pal Pete Shotton, was wearing a suit with a white shirt and necktie. He was also asked about touring. "We don't want to do what we've done already. We can't get a decent script [for the next film] and we're still trying for one. If we don't do that, we'll possibly do something different for next year. It's not like we're breaking up. We'll still come back together at the end of it."

He was asked whether he was bored with Beatlemania or even tired of the Beatles. "The thing is," said Ringo, "we can't do a tour like we've been doing all these years, because our music's progressed and we've used more instruments. It'd be soft—us going on stage, the four of us—trying to do the records we've made with orchestras and, you know, bands and things. So, if we went on stage, we'd have to have a whole line-up of men behind us."

He implied that if the Beatles' film didn't happen, he might take on a role by himself. "I'm sort of out of it because John and Paul can still write even though we're sort of not working together and George can learn his sitar. I've just been sitting around." "Getting bored?" asked the reporter. "No," said Ringo. "Getting fat."

George, bearded and again wearing his caped coat, was the only Beatle not to cooperate. He kept walking throughout his brief exchange in an attempt to dodge the microphone. Would they be going their separate ways? "No. Definitely not." By the time George was almost in the building, Edwards asked if he could have another word. George, now almost out of earshot, called back, "There aren't any more words."

The beards and mustaches were not only a fashion accoutrement that went along with the revival in pre–World War I fashion but a way of letting the world know that they were no longer boys. They had grown up. It was no longer important for them to appear youthful, fresh, or cute. Pop stars were for the most part a clean-shaven lot, but the Beatles would help to change that.

Teddy boys and rockers grew sideburns, as did Elvis and Eric Clapton, but they didn't grow mustaches or beards. These sorts of whiskers were associated with other kinds of rebels such as hippies, beats, Hell's Angels, mystics, and hermits. The sadhus George had met in India regarded shaving as a concession to pride and fashion and therefore part of the world of illusion. Revolutionaries of all different strips saw beards as antibourgeois. Fidel Castro and Che Guevara stopped shaving when fighting as guerrillas. "The beards served as a badge of identity, and as protection, until it finally became a symbol of the guerrilla fighter," said Castro. "Later, with the triumph of the revolution, we kept our beards to preserve the symbolism."

George Martin was still in discussions with John about "Strawberry Fields Forever." John had concluded that he liked the introduction of the early abandoned version but the rest of the later version. He asked whether what he considered to be the best parts of both could be joined. Martin explained that this would be technically possible, but as they were in different tempos and keys there could be no seamless transition. The result would be jarring. John's response was, "Well, you can fix that."

This exchange encapsulated the way in which the Beatles progressed. If they could imagine a sound, they assumed it could be realized. They didn't regard it as a hindrance that something had never been done before or that experienced technicians foresaw problems. Their lack of academic knowledge about music and their ignorance of many of the technical details of recording meant that their imaginations were delightfully unbounded.

In George Martin they had a sympathetic facilitator. He had everything they didn't have—classical training as a musician, sixteen years of work in the studio, and production experience with a wide variety of acts from choral and jazz to electronic and skiffle—and always responded well to a challenge.

He was able to make sense of their frequently vague descriptions of what they wanted because of the vast catalogue of musical styles he'd been involved with over the years. Additionally, he could suggest things they would never have thought of. John summed up their relationship in a 1970s interview: "George had done no rock 'n' roll when we met him and we'd never been in the studio. So we did a lot of learning together. He had a very great musical knowledge and background so he could translate for us and suggest a lot of things, which he did. . . . He taught us a lot and I'm sure we taught him a lot by our primitive musical ability."

The average age of the producers of acts like the Byrds, Stones, and Kinks was twenty-seven, and they had around three years of recording experience. Martin was already forty and had been producing since 1950. He had so much more to draw on, and as an A&R man for Parlophone his job was to get the best out of any artist he worked with rather than only involving himself with music he personally liked.

As well as being the man who could make real the Beatles' poorly expressed longings, he was someone they looked to for suggestions of unusual instruments or styles. He told me that he was their "pimp in sounds." In an interview with Marc Myers of the *Wall Street Journal* he expanded on this idea: "The Beatles were constantly coming to me and saying 'What can you give us? What instruments do you know about that we could use? What recording ideas can you give us?' Their inquisitiveness pushed us into new territory. They lapped up ideas. They were very curious people and wanted to look beyond what everyone else could do."

Confronted with John's demand to mix a new version of "Strawberry Fields Forever" from two versions in different keys and tempos, Martin faced an unusual challenge. He realized he might be able to do something, because the slower version was a semitone flatter than the faster one. He contemplated speeding one track while slowing down the other in order to get the pitches the same. He knew that if it worked, the tempos would be close enough that the difference would not be noticeable. "I did just that," he wrote in his autobiography *All You Need Is Ears*, "on a variable-control tape machine, selecting precisely the right spot to make the cut, to join them as nearly perfectly as possible." What John had imagined could be done had been done. Out of two unsatisfactory versions had come one masterpiece of modern pop.

On the day that this was achieved Paul sat with Andy Gray of *NME* to again address the issue of the Beatles' future. "One reason we don't want to tour any more is that when we're on stage nobody can hear us," he explained. "Another reason is that our stage act hasn't improved one bit since we started touring four years ago. The days when three guitarists and a drummer can stand up and sing and do nothing else must be over.

"Many of our tracks nowadays have big backings. We couldn't produce the sound on stage without an orchestra. And, if we were to do ourselves justice, we'd have to have at least three months to produce a brand new act. It would probably be very unlike what you'd expect from the Beatles." Without knowing it, he was pretty much describing the future of live rock.

This has been described as the time when the Beatles seized the studio and looked on it as another instrument to use.

> We feel that only through recording do people listen to us, so that is our most important form of communication. We have never thought of ourselves as one sound. Merseybeat wasn't our invention. We have always changed our style as we went along and we've never been frightened to develop and change. . . . We work on one song, record it, and then get tired of it. So we think up something very different.
>
> So we keep on doing tracks which can be any style at all. We're not limited that way, or with time any more. We take as much time as we want on a track, until we get it to our satisfaction. Before, we had a set time in the studio, and that was that. If it wasn't exactly as we wanted, that was too bad. Now we take time because we haven't any pressing engagements like tours to limit us. All we want is to make one track better than the last.

John's song referring to Strawberry Field may have spurred Paul to write about another local Liverpool landmark—Penny Lane. The two songs couldn't have been more different. Whereas John's was symbolic, not descriptive, Paul's was celebratory and full of detail. Yet in one significant respect they were the same. They were both written from the perspective of a mind that that had been opened or enlarged. The mundane—a Salvation Army home and a suburban intersection—were transformed into something timeless and glorious.

John and Paul had been deliberating about writing Liverpool songs since at least February 1964, when John told *Rave*, "Paul and I want to write a stage musical. That's a must. Maybe about Liverpool." The original script of "In My Life" mentioned several city sites. In an interview given in December 1965 to an American teen magazine called *flip* Paul said, "I like some of the things the Animals try to do, like the song Eric Burdon wrote about places in Newcastle on the flip of one of their hits. I still want to write a song about the places in Liverpool where I was brought up. Places like the Docker's Umbrella which is a long tunnel through which the dockers go to work on Merseyside, and Penny Lane near my old home."

The Animals song John referred to was "Club-A-Gogo," released in the UK as the B side of "Don't Let Me Be Misunderstood" in January 1966 and written by singer Eric Burdon and keyboard player Alan Price. What must have caught Paul's attention was a British group singing about its own hometown (Newcastle in this case) rather than Memphis, Chicago, or Route 66. Others were doing the same thing. Donovan had sung about Cromwell Road, Goodge Street, and Portobello Road; the Kinks about Regent Street and Leicester Square; and the Stones about Knightsbridge and St John's Wood.

In Paul's song an otherwise ordinary suburban scene was made enchanting through a cast of lovingly portrayed characters. It was as though he was surveying it through newly restored, childlike eyes rather than with the jaded perceptions of someone older. The blue skies, the clean fire engine, the pretty nurse selling poppies, and the friendly clients of the barber seemed to spring from the pages of a children's picture book. Every person and situation was taken at face value and joyfully welcomed. Nothing was rejected, judged, or overlooked.

"Penny Lane" was to become a joyous, buoyant song. As a listener you could imagine the sunlight glinting from the various brass instruments as their sounds soared up to the blue suburban skies. If nothing was real at Strawberry Field as experienced by John, everything was hyperreal on Paul's Penny Lane.

The genius of the music was that it took the lyric as its guide and enhanced its meaning. "Strawberry Fields Forever" was a journey to a netherworld to which John had to "take you down" and the sounds correspondingly descended or were distorted to give the impression of falling into a dream state. "Penny Lane," on the other hand, gave what felt like an aerial view of the life of the city, and so the instruments were used to uplift.

For the basic rhythm track Paul played pounding piano riffs on three different tracks using different treatments so that he had a range of choice. Then he added his voice, having it recorded slower than usual so it could be speeded up in the mix. The masterstroke was using the exultant piccolo trumpet of David Mason. Paul had heard his work on a TV broadcast of Bach's Second Brandenburg Concerto in which he was performing with the English Chamber Orchestra and told George Martin that this was the sound he needed to enhance "Penny Lane." Mason was invited in early in the new year to play an arrangement that Martin had written based on Paul's idea.

"Strawberry Fields Forever" and "Penny Lane" together illustrated just how far the Beatles had traveled in twelve months. Neither record was about love or could be played on stage as part of a Beatles concert. Both took days to record and between them drew inspiration from Indian ragas, Western classical, folk, orchestral, pop, rock 'n' roll, doo-wop, and electronic music. Beyond the two guitars, electric bass, and drums, sixteen additional instruments were used and eighteen session musicians were hired.

In December 1965 the Beatles had been fresh-faced touring idols widely thought of as a fad that was on the verge of dying out. Although dissatisfied with their musical progress, they had no clear idea how to con-

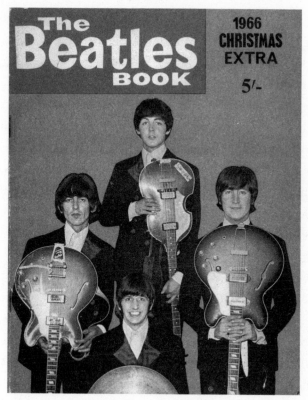

The final annual published by the *Beatles Book Monthly* in 1966.

tinue as the Beatles while simultaneously growing up as musicians and lyricists. A year later they were studio-based artists flag-waving for the avant-garde who were maturing with their audience and gaining the respect of serious music critics.

In 1965 they were interesting to sociologists as an example of postwar social mobility, the spread of informality, and the new spending power of the teenager, but as they entered 1967 they were seen as leaders in a revolutionary change of attitudes toward art, religion, authority, work, and leisure. Their experiences in Japan, America, and the Philippines had made them aware of how subversive their music could be while at the same time giving them an insight into the power of dictators, mobs, governments, radical groups, DJs, radio stations, and fundamentalist religion.

They'd gone from being a group that recorded under the supervision of a producer during time allocated between tours to a group that worked alongside a producer in open-ended sessions until everyone was happy with the result.

"When I first started in the music business, the ultimate aim for everybody was to try to re-create, on record, a live performance as accurately as possible," said George Martin. "But then we realised that we could do something other than that. In other words, the film doesn't just recreate the stage play. So, without being too pompous, we decided to go into another kind of art form, where we were devising something that couldn't be done any other way. We were putting something down on tape that could only be done on tape."

The Beatles were now in a uniquely privileged position. They had a worldwide audience that would at least listen to their next LP however good or bad it was; they had a strong revenue stream from past records; and, having retired from touring, they were able to devote all their time and attention to crafting music in the studio. They commanded respect not only as entertainers but as artists.

"We've been in the lucky position of having our childhood ambitions fulfilled," said Paul. "We've all got the big house and the big car and everything. So then, you stand on the plank, having reached the end of space, and you look across the wall and there's more space. And that's it. You get your car and house and fame and worldwide ego satisfaction, then you just look over the wall and there's a completely different scene there . . . which is really the scene."

Music critics were coming to terms with the changes, too, realizing that a new form of pop was being produced that had ambitions most recently associated with jazz, where players often used drugs, took inspiration from other cultures, went through distinct developmental periods, valued innovation, and saw their music as playing a social and political role. In December, *Melody Maker*'s Chris Welch, who'd joined the paper in 1964 and was the same age as the Beatles, tried to make sense of what was happening in a short feature entitled "Progressive Pop."

Employing categories in current use to differentiate jazz musicians ranging from Acker Bilk to Albert Ayler, he divided pop into Traditional, Mainstream, Modern, and Avant-Garde. Cliff Richard and Roy Orbison were Traditional. Tom Jones and Georgie Fame were Mainstream. The Small Faces, the Byrds, and Donovan were Modern. In the Avant-Garde category were Pink Floyd, Soft Machine, the Mothers of Invention, Love, Cream, and the Beatles. A year before it's unlikely that he would have found any groups of note to fit in this last category. Modern was about as experimental as it got.

"Jazz had been the intellectual music of the 50s," writes Michael Lydon, who was one of the first serious rock critics.

> Scholarly debates raged in *Downbeat* over Bird and Diz, Miles and Monk. 50s rock 'n' roll criticism, in contrast, was monosyllabic: "Yeah, I dig it, ya can dance to it." Now rock 'n' roll was becoming music worth taking seriously.

The Beatles and their talented peers had grabbed every riff and sound they'd heard from Muddy Waters, Bill Haley, Chuck Berry, Elvis Presley, Little Richard, Buddy Holly, Ray Charles, the Everly Brothers and the Isley Brothers, the Platters, Shirelles, Drifters, Coasters, Impressions, Miracles and Martha and the Vandellas—to name but a few—and molded them into an electric musical language that could speak intimately to millions around the world.

There was a definite feeling that pop music had now reached an important new stage, even though there may not yet have been the language available to describe it. The Beatles epitomized this stage. Reviewing 1966 and making her predictions for 1967, Judith Simons of the *Daily Express* concluded: "Honesty, experiment, art. High ideals perhaps for the 'pop' world, which is founded on mass appeal and catchy tunes. It could be an interesting year."

EPILOGUE

We just happened to become leaders of
whatever cosmic thing was going on. We came
to symbolise the start of a whole new way of
thinking.
-PAUL, 2004

So why was it that the Beatles achieved so much in one year? How did a single musical group introduce so many changes that fifty years later have become standard practice? Whenever U2, Coldplay, or Radiohead takes an extended break to work on a new album, they are doing what the Beatles did. When Adele or Taylor Swift records songs that express their feelings in their own words, they are also doing what the Beatles did. Before the Beatles, songwriters by and large didn't try singing, and singers didn't try writing. After the Beatles, it became customary for those who wrote to want to sing and for those who sang to want to write.

Whenever someone either alludes to drugs in lyrics, makes music as an accompaniment to drug-taking experiences, or simulates the disordering of the senses through musical distortion, they are following in the tradition of "Got to Get You Into My Life," "Doctor Robert," "She Said She Said," and "Tomorrow Never Knows." This stretches from the Small Faces' celebration of amphetamines ("Here Come the Nice"), the Velvet Underground's graphic description of a heroin hit ("Heroin"), and Jimi Hendrix's paean to LSD ("Purple Haze" etc.) to more recent allusions to ecstasy by Primal Scream ("Higher Than the Sun"), pot by Lil Wayne ("I Feel Like Dying"), and smack by Jay Z ("I Know").

The length of time people now spend in the studio is a direct result of what the Beatles did in 1966. Although the time spent recording (not including mixing) by the Beatles had gradually crept up from less than ten hours on their debut LP to around sixty hours on *Help!* and then just under eighty hours on *Rubber Soul,* it leapt to almost 225 hours on *Revolver.* In the early days they kept strictly to morning, afternoon, and evening shifts with appropriate breaks for refreshments, as was customary at EMI, but on *Revolver* they worked until they got the job done. "Time didn't matter to us," said George. "We had a lot to sort out and we made up a lot as we went along."

Revolver was their first album to be a piece of recorded art rather than a perfect rendition of what they anticipated being able to deliver on stage. They no longer thought that the music they wanted to make was capable of being repeated live. "It's a shame that the technology wasn't there at the time to enable them to do their new songs on stage because they were a great live band," says Tony Bramwell. "They couldn't do 'Got to Get You Into My Life' at the time because they didn't have a travelling horn section or a computerized keyboard. If they'd had that they could have blown the world away a second time with a huge sound."

Although made with all the limitations of four-track recording, *Revolver* opened the way for the later multitrack recordings of bands like Pink Floyd, Genesis, Yes, and the Electric Light Orchestra. Later on, because of advances in technology and the acceptability of using session players on stage, it became possible to play such complex songs in concert. Paul has since incorporated "Got to Get You Into My Life," "Paperback Writer," "Eleanor Rigby," "Good Day Sunshine," "For No One," "Penny Lane," "Here, There and Everywhere," "Yellow Submarine," and "Strawberry Fields Forever" into sets played around the world.

The sampling and tape manipulation developed on *Revolver* was to have a profound effect on everyone from Jimi Hendrix to Jay Z. The Beatles had heard it done by Berio, Stockhausen, William Burroughs, and Brion Gysin and brought it to mainstream pop for the first time with "Tomorrow Never Knows." Over a decade later, first in rap and later in electronic dance music and other forms of pop, sampling became widely used. Musicians sampled everything from well-known riffs created by established artists (such as the Sugarhill Gang's sampling of Chic's "Good Times" on "Rapper's Delight") and obscure vocal tracks (various tracks by Moby on his album *Play*) to recordings of exorcists, DJs, preachers, and Arabic singers (David Byrne and Brian Eno on *My Life in the Bush of Ghosts*) and movie soundtracks (Big Audio Dynamite).

In their book *Recording the Beatles* Kevin Ryan and Brian Kehew list nine changes in studio practice that they say the Beatles introduced on *Revolver,* from wearing headphones while recording and the invention of automatic double-tracking to the close miking of drums and the use of backward recording. They quote engineer Geoff Emerick as saying, "I know for a fact that, from the day it came out, *Revolver* changed the way that everyone else made records."

From this distance it's hard to appreciate what a huge step the Beatles initially took by writing songs that were not about boy-girl relationships or youthful pursuits such as dancing, driving, and listening to music. Almost all of previous pop music was essentially about love or lust. Very occasionally (as with Eddie Cochran's "Summertime Blues" or "Get a Job" by the Silhouettes) someone went beyond the boundaries, but even so these songs usually only expressed other forms of adolescent angst. On *Rubber Soul* thirteen of the fourteen songs were about love (although one of those thirteen, "The Word," was about universal love rather than romantic love), but the one that wasn't—"Nowhere Man" by John—was a pointer to the way ahead. "In My Life" was a nostalgic reflection on a disappearing Liverpool that almost avoided being a love song (except love for his cherished memories and the places connected with them), but the conventions of the day eventually prevailed.

On *Revolver* nine out of the fourteen songs weren't about love. "Got to Get You Into My Life" was disguised as a love song but was about LSD, and "Eleanor Rigby" involved longing, loneliness, and the aftermath of a wedding, but no love connections were made. The only songs directly about love were George's "I Want to Tell You" and "Love You To" (although these were also to do with confusion and death) and Paul's "For No One," "Good Day Sunshine," and "Here, There and Everywhere."

Both Dylan and the Stones were moving away from the traditional love song format. Mick Jagger was writing about boredom (presumably a result of the group's touring schedule) on *Aftermath*, and his songs about relationships were increasingly about fallouts, resentment, and disappointment rather than romantic fulfillment. Although Dylan frequently referred to a "lover" or "mama" on *Highway 61 Revisited* and *Blonde on Blonde*, his songs were too surreal to truly be "about" anything specific.

To be a pop group singing about such grown-up concerns as tax rates, death, loneliness, and letting go of your mind was novel, and it automatically increased the range of acceptable subject matter. Lyricists became more like poets in the sense that few poets confine themselves to writing only about love and teenage angst but instead record their responses to the whole of life's experiences.

It's easy to forget that in 1966, when the Beatles were in their mid-twenties, they were considered quite old to be pop stars. When they and others of their generation said that they wouldn't be prancing around on stage at thirty, they meant it. They had to think hard about playing music that was appropriate for their advanced years, and that included singing less adolescent love songs. "Too Old at 25?" a provocative headline in *Melody Maker* asked on December 3. "What is the age limit for pop success? Is it 31—or 25? The MM finds out."

It would overstate the claim to say that the Beatles were the sole cause of all the developments they were associated with or that everything they achieved was accomplished in one twelve-month period. Very often they were not the actual initiators of a trend, musical change, or attitude but popularized something that was already percolating. To use terms defined by Everett Rogers in his influential 1962 book *Diffusion of Innovations,* the Beatles were "early adopters" rather than "innovators." Brian Wilson of the Beach Boys retired from the road to devote his energies to the studio in early 1965. Jazz, folk, and classical musicians were already incorporating music from other cultures. The Kinks, Byrds, and Yardbirds had introduced Eastern tonalties to Western pop. Pete Townshend was listening to Stockhausen. The BBC Radiophonic Workshop had been working with backward tapes and tape loops.

What the Beatles were very good at was combining a number of recent and not yet widely known (or widely used) developments into one song and thereby coming up with something previously unheard in pop. Also, because of their already massive audience, when they promoted something new, it was instantly disseminated around the world. Simply mentioning Albert Ayler or John Cage in interviews meant that the keenest fans would research these other sorts of musicians little known in the world of pop, and so the influence would spread.

Singing the adapted words of a Buddhist text in "Tomorrow Never Knows" was different enough, but what made it even more extraordinary was the vocal treatment and the addition of backward chords, tape loops, and Indian instruments. Likewise, singing about the death of a lonely spinster in "Eleanor Rigby" was not what was expected from a beat group, but what made it doubly strange was giving it a string arrangement.

Any explanation of the Beatles' achievements in 1966 must start with their natural talent. Without it, none of the rest would have taken place. The bottom line is that they were great creators of memorable pop songs. They couldn't read music, had only the most basic technical knowledge of what they were doing, but nevertheless composed music that began with something that sounded familiar but always took the listener somewhere unexpected. They resisted predictability. In almost every song they wrote there was a part that was so unusual that you wanted to hear it again.

A strong work ethic accompanied this basic creative talent. They came up with fresh and original material to order without it sounding like production-line pop. Despite the demands of touring they were not only able to produce new songs for LPs and singles but between 1963 and 1965 even had leftovers that were so good they became hits for other artists. In 1963 they wrote twenty-two songs; in 1964 they wrote twenty-six; and in 1965 the total was thirty-four. Despite epitomizing the "swinging" in London they spent the majority of their time working rather than partying.

But the developments of 1966 did not lie only in more good songs but in a whole new approach to writing and recording. They challenged convention after convention and helped rewrite the rules of pop stardom. And this was no accident. Although *Revolver* wasn't part of a grand plan, they knew that they wanted it to be significantly different from anything they had done before. "We are so well established," Paul said, "that we can bring the fans along with us—stretch the limits of pop."

It was this desire to "stretch the limits" that provided the crucial motivation. By the time they recorded *Help!* in 1965 they were at the top of their game as both performers and pop songwriters and could have justifiably contented themselves with producing more of the same. They had a franchise that worked and an audience that was clamoring for more. Making extra demands on their listeners at this juncture put their career at risk. Why bother?

There was no precedent among the musicians they had always looked up to. Jerry Lee Lewis, the Everly Brothers, Gene Vincent, Chuck Berry, Carl Perkins, Little Richard, and Bo Diddley either stuck to the formula that brought their initial success or went back to the roots music that had existed before rock 'n' roll. They didn't attempt to invent the music of the future. Elvis had smoothed his rough edges and was now recording primarily for his movie soundtracks. British pop stars like Cliff Richard only changed by recording slower songs and using orchestral backings (usually a ploy to win over older listeners). The one artist who almost certainly would have experimented was Buddy Holly, who had moved from Lubbock, Texas, to live in Greenwich Village and had plans to write for film, do a gospel LP, record with Ray Charles, and set up his own studio at the time of his death in 1959.

What gave the Beatles different ambitions? It had a lot to do with their arts education—Paul studying English literature and art at school and John enrolling in art college. It enlarged their frame of reference sufficiently enough that when they came to compose music, they were able to see themselves simultaneously in the tradition of entertainers and in the tradition of painters, sculptors, filmmakers, poets, novelists, and dramatists. It was surely significant that when they made up their list of influential figures for the cover of *Sgt. Pepper,* the actors (14), writers (11), artists (8), and comedians (6) far outnumbered the musicians (4).

When they spoke about their work, they would draw comparisons not only with songwriting teams like those of Goffin and King and Leiber and Stoller but also with visual artists like Van Gogh, Matisse, and Picasso or writers like Lewis Carroll and William Burroughs. It's doubtful that Gene Vincent or Jerry Lee Lewis ever saw their work as part of such a lineage. George Martin once compared the way the Beatles built up songs in the studio to the way that Picasso created as shown in the 1956 documentary *The Mystery of Picasso* by Henri-Georges Clouzot, where he painted on glass while being filmed from the underside. As Picasso modified his initial markings, they were slowly obliterated, and the eventual painting bore no obvious connection, yet wouldn't have emerged without them.

Art colleges were largely a postwar innovation in Britain, designed to accommodate students who were intelligent and creative but perhaps not academically inclined. Typically these colleges would offer a general two-year course where students would be taught figure drawing, modeling, still life, and pictorial composition. Following an exam there would be a further two-year course in a chosen specialized subject such as lithography, lettering, illustration, or painting. From such colleges came a collection of bright young people who helped transform Britain through their skills in advertising, layout, photography, design, fashion, film, television, and PR. Graduates included people like miniskirt inventor Mary Quant (Goldsmiths College), psychedelic poster artist Michael English (Ealing School of Art), photographer Brian Duffy and spy novelist Len Deighton (Saint Martin's School of Art), pop artist Peter Blake (Royal College of Art), and illustrator Ralph Steadman (London College of Communication).

Art students were usually well ahead of their contemporaries in fashion, musical tastes, and lifestyle choices. They looked more bohemian, entertained the latest progressive ideas, and were among the first young people to pick up on jazz, blues, and folk as more authentic alternatives to mainstream pop. Their instructors knew the history of art and would be familiar with all the latest exhibitions around the world. To broaden their students' appreciation of what was going on they would introduce them to poetry, branding, European films, magazine layouts, fashion spreads, and TV commercials. Some of the most creative British pop musicians of the 1960s spent time at art colleges—Keith Richards, Pete Townshend, Ray Davies, Eric Clapton, Jimmy Page, Syd Barrett, Ronnie Wood, Eric Burdon, and John Mayall among them.

John was consequently able to make comparisons between what he was doing as a musician and how painters approached their work. His closest friend at the college (and a future Beatle) was Stuart Sutcliffe, a prize-winning painter as well a huge fan of rock 'n' roll, with whom he would have intense conversations about the intersections of art, philosophy, literature and music. They knew artists developed their characteristic styles and went through identifiable periods in which they were heavily influenced by a particular theory, color, subject, or way of seeing things. Only the worst sort of artists merely repeated themselves.

Sutcliffe was an unusual character at the time—someone who dressed like a teddy boy, admired James Dean, and loved the music of Elvis but who also read Aldous Huxley, Albert Camus, Kierkegaard, and Dostoevsky and could write perceptive essays comparing the work of Jackson Pollock with that of Cezanne. He modeled for John the possibility of reconciling the rebellious and contemplative sides of his nature as well as uniting the brash popular culture of America with the existentialist philosophical trends of Europe. "I was always torn between looking arty and looking like a rocker," John once admitted.

At the same time Paul was next door at the Liverpool Institute studying literature at an advanced level—poetry by Chaucer, Auden, Louis MacNeice, and Dylan Thomas; novels by Hardy and Steinbeck; plays by Shakespeare, Wilde, Sheridan, Beckett, Shaw, and Tennessee Williams—as well as art. His English teacher, Alan "Dusty" Durband, had been born and raised in the Dingle, a poor area of Liverpool where Ringo also lived, but had earned a scholarship to the Liverpool Institute and then to Cambridge, where one of his instructors was the influential literary critic F. R. Leavis. Durband was an inspirational educator who wrote textbooks, directed plays, and energized his pupils by making the works under discussion come alive.

Thanks to Durband, Paul was excited enough about literature to want to read far beyond the course requirements and to so identify with the life of a writer that he began to frequent the local academic bookstore, visit the theatre, and travel with a reporter's notebook at the ready. Somehow Durband had communicated to him and his fellow students what it took to be a poet, dramatist, or novelist and how works of literature were constructed. Paul has said many times how it was this training that prepared him for the transition from "Thank You Girl" to "Eleanor Rigby."

An additional push to do and see things differently came from drugs—specifically marijuana and LSD. It wasn't that the experiences simply gave the Beatles previously unexplored subject matter or introduced them to the idea of warping the sound, but that they brought about new perceptions not only about themselves but also about music and what could be done with it. John Dunbar, who knew them from 1963 onward, told me that it was their introduction to pot by Bob Dylan in 1964 that marked the beginning of the change. "From being not very educated people from Liverpool they came to London and things changed," he said. "For John, the big change was from alcohol to puff and acid and everything. It made a huge difference. It did to me. It does to everyone. It was a conscious revolution against the constraints of the fifties with its 'Yes sir, no sir' mentality."

Pot allowed their thoughts to flow more freely and opened them up to ideas previously ignored or overlooked. In his essay "Marijuana and Music," published in the *Journal of Cannabis Therapeutics* (2001), drug policy analyst Peter Webster wrote: "It is not that cannabis consciousness itself 'produces' ideas that are creative, or that valuable ideas come during the experience or because of it, but that cumulatively, over time, the kind of perception and thinking initiated by cannabis leads one to be generally more open to alternative and perhaps adventurous ways of seeing things which enrich normal consciousness. Normal consciousness, as we all admit, is limited in often involuntary, invisible ways by our times, customs, prejudices, by the necessary ignorance we must cultivate to cope with modern life."

LSD use has a similar effect. The research at Imperial College directed by Dr. Robin Carhart-Harris and published in the journal *PNAS* concluded that the drug expanded the primary visual cortex (hence the hallucinations and heightened sense of color) while at the same time decreasing connectivity between the parahippocampus and the retrosplenial cortex (hence the dissolution of ego and alterations of meaning). Participants in the experiments reported that previously unimportant things took on new significance and other previously important things felt more alien.

It's possible to see this change taking place in the interviews the Beatles gave at the time. It was dawning on them that they'd ignored a lot of experiences and cultural expressions simply because they didn't fit into their tidy way of seeing things. After they indulged in pot and LSD, these categories seemed relative rather than absolute, and they began investigating things they'd misunderstood or brushed aside, such as music from other cultures, opera, classical music, experimental cinema, and electronic music.

It also encouraged them to ask the question "Why not?" more often in the studio. Why not record a children's song or write music in the style of a 1920s band? Why not incorporate instruments that they couldn't imagine being played on stage? Why not record a whole LP in the guise of a fictional group? Suddenly everything seemed possible.

Pot and LSD affected the way they experienced music. The drugs enhanced their appreciation and made it sound more interesting. As they listened to the music of others when stoned or tripping, they noticed themselves picking up on things they'd never noticed before, and this made them more conscious of wanting to add intricacy and complexity to their own work so that there was a rich experience available to those who might hear it while in a similar state of mind. Detail became important.

The Beatles certainly weren't the first act to eulogize drugs. Cole Porter wrote about cocaine in "I Get a Kick out of You" (1934); Cab Calloway sang about opium in "Minnie the Moocher" and pot in "Reefer Man" (1931). What the Beatles did differently was allude to drugs as being sources not just of fun but of enlightenment and social transformation. These were drugs that could give you, as Paul put it, another kind of mind.

They also made music that sought to replicate the experience of using LSD rather than just making sly references to it. "Got to Get You Into My Life" was "about" drugs lyrically, but not musically. "Tomorrow Never Knows," on the other hand, was designed to bring listeners along on the trip. The sounds that attracted the Beatles, which they then pursued, were often ones that they'd first experienced while hallucinating. This is why they were appropriately intricate, distorted, or stretched.

People become more aware of sound when using pot or LSD. This led to the Beatles paying more attention to the various layers of their music and adding touches that they knew would probably only be picked up on by those already similarly turned on.

Revolver opened the doors to psychedelic rock (or acid rock), where music was made either to simulate the hallucinogenic experience or act as a friendly guide to the mind already on drugs. In *Melody Maker* Graham Nash of the Hollies explained, "Psychedelic music is trying to create an LSD session without the use of drugs. It's a question of trying to expand the consciousness to the limits." Many bands that had initially played music derived from blues adopted more freeform styles and embraced electronic gadgets that distorted guitar sounds. In San Francisco the Grateful Dead, Jefferson Airplane, Moby Grape, and Country Joe and the Fish pioneered psychedelia. In England there was Traffic, Pink Floyd, Cream, Family, and Tomorrow.

Although acid rock in this specific sense was relatively short-lived, the relationship between drugs and music persisted in such movements as rave culture, acid house, and electronic dance music, where the same combinations of lights, loud music, drugs, spacey sounds, and heavy bass rhythms were used to immerse audiences and foster feelings of unity and spirituality. Paul's contribution to the Million Volt Light and Sound Rave is often cited as a predecessor to contemporary electronic dance music events.

During this period of openness the Beatles were aided by coming into contact with similarly minded contemporaries capable of introducing them to new ideas and forms of art, literature, and music. If they'd had the appetite to develop as artists but no examples to follow or works to stimulate them, it would have been much harder for them to move forward. It was through their exposure to art from other cultures, countries, periods, and genres that they saw possibilities for their own creativity. "There are so many new sounds to take in now," said George in 1966, "and I'm listening all the time and wondering how I can adapt them into our work."

They were fortunate that at the very time they were eager to "progress," they encountered people like Ayana and Patricia Angadi, the Asher family, Maureen Cleave, Ravi Shankar, David Crosby, Barry Miles, John Dunbar, Robert Fraser, John Mayall, and Luciano Berio, who stretched their minds and gave them a far broader range of cultural experiences on which to draw. At the point at which they felt they'd exhausted all their rock 'n' roll, R & B, and soul influences, they were presented with new stimuli.

It's easy to say that the Beatles captured the spirit of the times with *Revolver,* but what the record really did was capture the spirit of the elite circle with whom they mixed. It just so happened that this circle of innovators and early adopters was at the forefront of social change, and so the Beatles were able to see the future first. They were, in John's analogy, in the crow's nest and therefore able to see land before anyone else. "We were going through changes and all we were saying was 'It's raining up here,' or 'There's land' or 'There's sun' or 'We can see a seagull,'" said John. "We were just reporting what was happening to us."

Indian music, psychedelic drugs, Tibetan Buddhism, and speed doctors were all uncommon interests in the West at the time but their influence would spread. The Beatles had access to these developments because of their position, their ability to travel, and the creative people they surrounded themselves with. The jazz musician Max Roach once said, "Two theories [of art] exist. One is that art is for the sake of art. That is true. The other theory, which is also true, is that the artist is like a secretary. . . . He keeps a record of his time." On *Revolver* the Beatles did both.

Their transformation in the studio was made possible by the expertise, experience, and patience of George Martin. No producer could have been more perfectly suited for the job. He was old enough to earn their respect, yet young enough to be a friend; sober enough to keep control, yet wild enough to embrace experiment.

When the Beatles suggested unusual sounds, he either knew who to get them from or what to do to make them. When they explained in faltering ways a mood or feeling they wanted to evoke, he was able to take their yearnings and turn them into actual music. Likewise, he could listen to them humming and write up what he heard as an orchestrated arrangement. John said of him, "He would translate. . . . He helped us develop a language to talk to musicians."

Martin had no part in the drug aspect of their lives. They didn't talk to him about LSD and hid their pot smoking from him by going elsewhere in the building when they were getting stoned and arranging for Mal Evans to guard the door so that none of the EMI operatives would discover them. Even when he eventually realized how integral drug use had become to their lives, he refused to believe that his taking drugs with them would improve the work they were making together. Their weirdness depended on his sobriety in order to get things done, provide perspective, and act as a link with the "straight" world. "The greatest of dreamers, if they're left to dream, just dream," he explained to me. "The great thing about the Beatles is they were great dreamers who were actually able to get organized. I always disapproved of drugs terribly. I don't believe in them and never have done. I don't believe drugs made them any better than they would have been anyway." Asked if we would ever have had a "Strawberry Fields Forever" if drugs hadn't been involved, he told me, "I think John had the creative ability to do an enormous amount and I think he could have done it without drugs."

Another reason why they were able to achieve so much in 1966 is that they were blessed with such great competition. If they had been on their own, they would likely have become complacent, but instead they were pursued and inspired by some of the greatest acts in the history of rock, pop, and soul, such as the Beach Boys, the Who, the Kinks, the Stones, the Byrds, the Animals, the Miracles, Donovan, and the Supremes; Booker T. and the M.G.'s, Marvin Gaye, Steve Wonder, and Bob Dylan, all of whom were creating some of the finest work of their careers.

This gave them higher standards to beat and thereby raised their game. It also suggested new approaches to pop music that they could take and develop in their own way (as with Dylan's use of language or the feedback of the Who). Many of their best songs were direct responses to new releases that they'd heard and wanted to better.

All of the acts mentioned above were inspiring each other in one of the most fertile periods in Western pop. The Motown sound inspired the Beatles, and the Beatles in turn inspired Motown. The Who were inspired by the Kinks, who in turn inspired the Beatles, who inspired the Beach Boys. All of them consequently reached heights they would not have otherwise reached.

The Beatles were able to think conceptually. They could imagine a type of song not already in existence and then work their way toward achieving it. Many acts were limited by what they already knew and couldn't think beyond it. The Beatles, on the other hand, could envisage music that had yet to be made but which, in their view, needed to be made, even though it was at times indistinct and needed the interpretative abilities of George Martin to bring shape to it. As Ringo put it, "We finished touring in '66 to go into the studio, where we could hear each other and create any fantasy that came out of anyone's brain."

This was what John must have been partly hinting at when he told Maureen Cleave that there was something he had to do but which had yet to be revealed to him and what Paul meant when he told Barry Miles in December,

I think we are being influenced at the moment by what we know we could do, and what we know we may eventually be able to do, because there is no one at the moment like Elvis was in the beginning. There are no great big idols now. That's the main pity about making it in anything—you look at things so objectively. You look at idols objectively and they are no longer idols. You just see them for what they are. This is sometimes a great thing, but you lose that sort of fan thing. You lose the bit about being influenced. So that's why I think we are now getting influenced by ourselves, more and more. I think, for instance, the Beach Boys are getting influenced by themselves.

Finally, the Beatles were fortunate to have come of age during what the ancient Chinese apparently referred to as "interesting times." The tectonic plates of different cultural outlooks were grinding against each other, releasing waves of energy that the group was able to translate into art. All the apparently secure foundations of society from family, law, and religion to the understanding of the nature of consciousness itself were being reevaluated. Had they lived in a more placid era they may never have reached the same heights of creativity.

There's a photo of John and Paul taken by Paul's brother Mike at the McCartney family home on Forthlin Road in Allerton. It's 1961, and the two boys are hunched over their acoustic guitars with the words to a new song, "I Saw Her Standing There," on the page of an open notebook on the floor in front of them. There's a pen lying on the notebook and cross-outs can be seen.

It's a poignant photo that illustrates the affection between John and Paul as well as their shared love for music. It also reveals the very ordinary postwar British surroundings out of which the Beatles and their music emerged. There's a fireplace to Paul's right that would have burned coal to heat the room in winter and wallpaper designed to look like rustic brickwork. Behind him is a television that would have had two channels available, both in black and white, with transmissions that usually ended before midnight, often with a religious epilogue by a Church of England clergyman. On the floor are a couple of carpets that don't quite meet. John is sitting on a sofa that looks as though it has an antimacassar to protect it from industrial grime and hair cream.

It's a world that no longer exists, except in period dramas, and part of what swept it away was the music and the attitude that John and Paul developed over the rest of the decade. They brought color, spontaneity, and adventure to a world largely painted in browns and grays, regulated by factory hours, and ruled over by people in suits and uniforms. It was a world of restrictions, prohibitions, and austerity into which they shouted the affirmative language of "Yeah! Yeah! Yeah!"

When I spoke to Paul in 2009, he told me about a then-recent report that claimed that two of the most significant factors in the fall of Soviet communism were the spread of contraband Levi jeans and the illicit underground distribution of Beatles records. They both opened up young people to a new way of seeing things that involved choice and freedom of expression. I reminded him of this photo of him and John writing "I Saw Her Standing There" and asked him what those two Liverpool lads working out chords in the living room of a small terraced council house would have thought if they'd been told that what they were embarking on would not just change their lives and the face of popular music but would have an impact on one of the twentieth century's most feared regimes. "It's unbelievable," he told me. "We were just four kids trying to earn a living. Someone pointed out to me the other day that the whole yoga-meditation thing—that was the Beatles too. It's astounding. As you say, to think [all this came] from Forthlin Road. It's unbelievable. The longer the story goes on, the more amazing it becomes."

APPENDIX A

CHRONOLOGY OF EVENTS

Major events connected with the Beatles and other events in culture and politics that either have some bearing on what they were doing or help set the context for the period.

DECEMBER 1965

2 Beatles drive to Berwick-upon-Tweed from London. Overnight stay at the King's Arms.

3 Drive from Berwick-upon-Tweed to Glasgow. UK release of *Rubber Soul* and "Day Tripper"/"We Can Work It Out." Opening concert at Odeon, Glasgow. Support acts are Jerry Stevens (MC), Paramounts, Moody Blues, Marionettes, Koobas, Beryl Marsden, Steve Aldo (Edward Bedford).

UK release of *My Generation* LP by the Who.

4 Concert at City Hall, Newcastle. Paul McCartney interview with Francis Wyndham is published in *London Life* magazine.

5 Concert at Empire, Liverpool (last Liverpool concert ever). Campaigners turn up trying to save the Cavern Club from closure.

7 Concert at ABC, Ardwick, Manchester.

8 Concert at Gaumont, Sheffield.

Ad Lib club closes in London.

9 Concert at Odeon, Birmingham.

10 Concert at Odeon, Hammersmith, London. Beatles are voted Best British Group and Best World Group in *NME* poll. John Lennon is voted British Vocal Personality in *NME* poll.

San Francisco group the Warlocks changes its name to the Grateful Dead.

11 Concert at Astoria, Finsbury Park, London.

12 Concert at Capitol, Cardiff, Wales (last full UK concert).

13 John, Paul, and George meet to discuss possible filming of Richard Condon's screenplay for *A Talent for Loving*. Paul takes LSD for first time at home of Tara Browne with former Pretty Things drummer Viv Prince present.

18 John's father, Freddie Lennon, poses for PR photos in advance of the release of a record.

21 Freddie Lennon turns up unannounced at John's house in Weybridge.

22 Timothy Leary is arrested for transporting marijuana over the border between Mexico and Texas.

25 George Harrison proposes to Pattie Boyd.

President Lyndon Johnson calls for a pause in the US bombing of North Vietnam.

26 Paul cuts his lip and breaks a tooth after falling off a moped near his father's home at Gayton, on the Wirral near Liverpool.

27 Jane Asher opens in John Dighton's play *The Happiest Days of Your Life* at the Theatre Royal in Bristol.

29 Stanley Kubrick commences filming *2001: A Space Odyssey* at MGM-British Studios, Borehamwood, Hertfordshire.

30 Freddie Lennon releases the single "That's My Life (My Love and My Home)" in the UK on the Pye label.

31 Photo of Paul with facial injury is published the *Daily Mirror* under the headline "No Fight, Says Injured Beatle."

JANUARY 1966

1 "The Sound of Silence" by Simon and Garfunkel makes the top spot in the *Billboard* Hot 100.

William Masters and Virginia Johnson publish *Human Sexual Response*, the book deemed by many to be the Bible of the sexual revolution.

2 Paul meets with Barry Miles and borrows his copy of the LP *The Fugs' Songbook*.

4 Brian Epstein travels to New York to plan the next US tour.

5 The soundtrack for the Shea Stadium concert TV film is partly rerecorded at CTS Studios in Bayswater. John attends a party thrown by P. J. Proby at 5 Cheltenham Terrace in Chelsea.

7 John and Ringo meet to discuss the next film. *A Talent for Loving* is rejected.

8 John, George, and Ringo go to a party of Mick Jagger's at 13a Bryanston Mews East in London's West End. Paul visits his family in Liverpool.

9 Brian Epstein leaves New York for the Bahamas.

10 Release of the single "Woman," written by Paul under the nom-de-plume Bernard Webb and recorded by Peter and Gordon. Paul drives back to London from Liverpool.

12 Ringo, Maureen, John, and Cynthia fly to Port of Spain, Trinidad, for the start of a vacation in nearby Tobago.

Batman TV series featuring Adam West launches in the US.

Isley Brothers release the single "This Old Heart of Mine."

13 George and Pattie go to Dolly's nightclub with Mick Jagger and Chrissie Shrimpton.

18 Brian Epstein flies back to London from the Virgin Islands, where he has taken a short vacation after business meetings in New York.

19 John, Cynthia, Ringo, and Maureen meet with Dr. Eric Williams, prime minister of Trinidad and Tobago, and his teenage daughter Erica.

Simon and Garfunkel release the single "Homeward Bound."

21 George marries Pattie Boyd at Esher Register Office. Paul and Brian Epstein are the best men.

Opening night of the Trips Festival in San Francisco featuring the Grateful

Dead and Big Brother and the Holding Company (with Janis Joplin) and attended by Ken Kesey and his Merry Pranksters.

23 John, Cynthia, Ringo, and Maureen return from Tobago.

25 Release of the single "Dedicated Follower of Fashion" by the Kinks.

28 The official launch of the Indica gallery and bookshop, attended by Paul.

31 Paul, Jane, George, and Pattie attend the premier of the play *How's the World Treating You* by Roger Milner at Wyndham's Theatre in London.

FEBRUARY 1966

3 Paul sees Stevie Wonder perform at the Scotch of St James and meets him afterward.

4 George and Pattie see the play *Little Malcolm and his Struggle against the Eunuchs* by David Halliwell at the Garrick Theatre.

The Rolling Stones release the single "19th Nervous Breakdown."

6 Beat poet Gregory Corso meets Marianne Faithfull in Paris and the subject of Paul writing music to his poems comes up.

7 *Crawdaddy*, the first serious magazine dedicated to pop music, is launched in the US.

The Temptations release the single "Get Ready."

8 George and Pattie fly to Barbados for their honeymoon. They stay in a villa named Benclare at Gibbs Beach.

12 John and Ringo visit the Scotch of St James.

13 Brian Epstein throws a party at 24 Chapel Street with Cilla Black, Gerry and the Pacemakers, John, Cynthia, Ringo, Maureen, Paul, and Peter Asher as guests.

15 George and Pattie are visited in Barbados by advertising man Terry Howard and his model girlfriend Venetia Cuninghame.

19 US release of the single "Daydream" by the Lovin' Spoonful.

21 Maureen Cleave interviews Paul for the *Evening Standard*.

23 Paul attends a lecture at the Italian Institute in London given by avant-garde composer Luciano Berio. George and Pattie see the launch of a weather rocket in Barbados.

Daily Express declares model Twiggy to be the "Face of 1966" after seeing pictures of her new short haircut.

24 Pattie and George leave Barbados for London.

25 The single "Shapes of Things" is released by the Yardbirds.

28 Liverpool's Cavern Club—"Birthplace of the Beatles"—closes down.

MARCH 1966

3 Brian Epstein announces that the Beatles' 1966 tour will include Germany, Japan, and America.

4 Maureen Cleave's "Jesus" interview with John appears in the *Evening Standard*.
Tara Browne's twenty-first birthday party is held at the Luggala Estate in County Wicklow, Ireland. Guests include Paul's brother Mike, Brian Jones, Anita Pallenberg, and Mick Jagger.

The Who release the single "Substitute."

6 Paul and Jane drive to Klosters in Switzerland for a skiing vacation.

8 Sam and Dave release the single "Hold On, I'm Comin'."

9 Ronnie Kray of the notorious Kray Twins gang shoots dead George Cornell at the Blind Beggar pub in London's East End. This crime eventually leads to his arrest, conviction, and imprisonment.

11 An interview with John appears in *NME*. Ringo's interview with Maureen Cleave is published in the *Evening Standard* (London).

14 The Byrds release the single "Eight Miles High."

18 Maureen Cleave's interview with George is published in the *Evening Standard*.

20 Paul and Jane Asher arrive back in London from Klosters.

21 Maureen Cleave interviews Paul. John and Paul begin writing together for *Revolver*. The first song they tackle together is "Eleanor Rigby."
The Beach Boys release the single "Sloop John B."

25 Photo shoot including pictures for the "Butcher" cover of *Yesterday and Today* with Robert Whitaker at his studio. Beatles are interviewed by Tom Lodge of Radio Caroline. Paul's interview with Maureen Cleave is published in the *Evening Standard*.
Life magazine publishes a cover story on LSD.

26 Paul goes to Aintree Racecourse to watch Drake's Drum, the horse he has bought for his father. Ringo and George go to see Roy Orbison at the Granada in Walthamstow, London. *Rave* magazine publishes Alan Freeman's interview with Paul McCartney.

28 Art Unger of *Datebook* buys the US rights to Maureen Cleave's *Evening Standard* interviews with the Beatles.

31 Brian Epstein arrives in Memphis. The *Memphis Press-Scimitar* reveals that the Beatles are planning to come to Memphis in April to record for their next album at the Stax studio.
Harold Wilson and the Labour Party win UK general election.

APRIL 1966

1 John buys *The Psychedelic Experience* by Timothy Leary from the Indica bookstore after looking for writing by Nietzsche. Maureen Cleave's interview with Brian Epstein appears in the *Evening Standard* as the last part of the series.

6 Recording "Tomorrow Never Knows."

7 Recording "Got to Get You Into My Life."

8 Recording "Got to Get You Into My Life."
Time magazine's "Is God Dead?" cover story.
British survey finds that the number of children born out of wedlock has doubled since 1956.

11 Recording "Love You To."

13 Recording "Paperback Writer."
Beach Boys complete the recording of their LP *Pet Sounds*.

14 Recording "Rain."
Mick Jagger visits the Beatles in the studio.

15 *Time* magazine's cover story "London: The Swinging City."
Rolling Stones release the LP *Aftermath*.

16 Recording "Rain."
Percy Sledge releases the single "When a Man Loves a Woman."

17 Recording "Doctor Robert."

18 John and George go to see the Lovin' Spoonful at the Marquee Club on Wardour Street. Eric Clapton is in the audience and meets George for the first time.

19 Recording "Doctor Robert."

20 Recording "And Your Bird Can Sing."
Bob Dylan releases "Rainy Day Women # 12 & 35" ("Everybody must get stoned").

21 Recording "Taxman."

26 Paul visits the Old Vic in Waterloo, London, to see *Juno and the Paycock* by Sean O'Casey.

28 Recording "Eleanor Rigby."
Musician and poet Richard Fariña (friend of Bob Dylan and brother-in-law of Joan Baez) publishes his novel *Been Down So Long It Looks Like Up to Me.*

30 Death of Richard Fariña in a motorcycle accident in Carmel, California.

MAY 1966

1 Appearance at *NME* Poll Winners Concert at Wembley Pool (last Beatles performance on a British stage).

2 BBC radio recordings (speech only) for *Saturday Club* and *Pop Profile.*

5 Adding backward guitar sounds to "I'm Only Sleeping."

6 Myra Hindley and Ian Brady are convicted of killing three children in the "moors murders" case and are sentenced to life imprisonment.

9 Recording "For No One." Bruce Johnston plays an acetate of *Pet Sounds* for John and Paul (LP not released in the UK until July 18).

14 Bob Dylan performs a concert in Liverpool. Timothy Leary, testifying before a US Senate subcommittee on drug use, declares that LSD releases "ancient" and "sacred" energies from the brain.

16 Release of *Blonde on Blonde* double LP by Bob Dylan.
US release of *Pet Sounds* LP by the Beach Boys. China's Chairman Mao announces Cultural Revolution to root out bourgeois elements from the Communist Party.

18 Horns added to "Got to Get You Into My Life."

19 Black-and-white promotional videos for "Paperback Writer" and "Rain" shot at EMI Studios.

20 Color videos for "Paperback Writer" and "Rain" are shot at Chiswick House in West London. An interview with Ringo appears in *NME.*
Aubrey Beardsley exhibition opens at the Victoria and Albert Museum.

21 John and Cynthia are seen shopping on Portobello Road with Mick Jagger and Chrissie Shrimpton. Jagger buys a military jacket from I Was Lord Kitchener's Valet.
Batman TV series gets its first UK screening on ITV.

22 Incredible String Band records their eponymous first LP.
The single "River Deep, Mountain High" by Ike and Tina Turner, produced by Phil Spector, enters the *Billboard* Hot 100.

26 Recording "Yellow Submarine."

27 Bob Dylan plays the Royal Albert Hall in London with the Beatles in the audience. This is his last live performance before an extended break.

30 "Paperback Writer" / "Rain" single is released in the US.

JUNE 1966

1 George meets Ravi Shankar after a concert at London's Royal Festival Hall. Recording sound effects for "Yellow Submarine."

2 Recording "I Want to Tell You."

3 Ad for "Paperback Writer" in *NME* uses the "butcher" photo.
The Kinks release the single "Sunny Afternoon."

4 Indica Gallery mounts its first official art exhibition.

5 Promotional videos for "Paperback Writer" are used on the Ed Sullivan Show.

6 Mixing vocal overdubs for "Eleanor Rigby."

7 Group tour rehearsals at George's house, Kinfauns.

8 Recording "Good Day Sunshine."
Ravi Shankar appears on the teen music TV program *A Whole Scene Going.*

9 "Paperback Writer" / "Rain" single is released in the UK.

10 All copies of *Yesterday and Today* with "butcher" covers are recalled by Capitol in Operation Retrieve.
Bob Dylan releases "I Want You" as a single.

11 Eric Clapton announces formation of a new band, Cream.

14 Recording "Here, There and Everywhere."

15 Rehearsal for an appearance on *Top of the Pops.*

16 Appearance on *Top of the Pops.* Interviews with *NME* and *Melody Maker.*

17 Paul buys a farm on Kintyre in Scotland.
Cliff Richard appears at a Billy Graham meeting in Earls Court.

20 *Yesterday and Today* LP is released in the US with new cover.

21 Recording "She Said She Said."

22 Final mix of LP. Beatles attend pre-opening party at Sibylla's on Swallow Street in London's West End.

23 Beatles fly to Munich and stay at Hotel Bayerischer Hof.

24 Two shows in Munich supported by Cliff Bennett and the Rebel Rousers, Peter and Gordon, and German group the Rattles. Back in England George Martin marries Judy Lockhart-Smith.

25 Beatles travel by train from Munich to Essen. Two shows in Essen. Overnight train from Essen to Hamburg.

26 Beatles arrive in Hamburg at 6:00 a.m. In Hamburg they meet with old friends Astrid Kirchherr, Bert Kaempfert, Bettina Derlien, and others.
Two shows. Overnight stay at Schloss Hotel, Tremsbüttel.
Largest civil rights march in Mississippi enters Jackson.

27 Beatles fly from Hamburg to Tokyo on polar route. Enforced stopover at Anchorage, Alaska, due to typhoon warning in the Far East.
Mothers of Invention release debut album *Freak Out!*

30 Arrival in Tokyo at 3:40 a.m. Stay at Tokyo Hilton. First show at Nippon Budokan Hall.

JULY 1966

1 Two shows at Nippon Budokan Hall.

2 Two shows at Nippon Budokan Hall. Shows filmed by NTV.

3 Beatles fly from Tokyo to Manila via a refueling stop in Hong Kong, where they conduct interviews. Party on yacht of Don Manolo Elizalde in Manila.

Anti-Vietnam protest march, four thousand strong, congregates outside American Embassy in Grosvenor Square, London.

4 Beatles fail to attend lunch party organized by Imelda Marcos at the presidential palace. Two shows at Rizal Memorial Football Stadium.

5 Press in Philippines reacts angrily to perceived snub to the Marcos family by the Beatles. Beatles are jostled at the airport and then fly from Manila to Delhi via refueling at Hong Kong.

6 Beatles, Brian Epstein, and Neil Aspinall stay at Oberoi hotel in Delhi. They purchase Indian instruments at Rikhi Ram music store.

8 Beatles fly from Delhi to London.

9 Psychedelic artists Simon Posthuma and Marijke Koger arrive in England from Holland.

11 Beach Boys release the single "God Only Knows."

12 Paul's car breaks down on Brompton Road in the early hours of the morning. He calls a mechanic to collect it, but the mechanic goes to the wrong address. Paul leaves the car and is eventually (October 27) fined one pound for "obstruction."

13 Eddie Floyd releases the single "Knock on Wood." International Society for Krishna Consciousness is incorporated in New York by Swami A. C. Bhaktivedanta Prabhupada with the aim of propagating "a knowledge of Krishna."

15 An interview with Ringo in *NME*.

Velvet Underground release the single "All Tomorrow's Parties."

18 The Byrds release the LP *Fifth Dimension*.

22 Interview with John in *NME*. Brian Epstein reported to be suffering from "glandular fever."

Bluesbreakers with Eric Clapton released.

23 Cavern Club reopens under new ownership.

24 Donovan enters *Billboard* Hot 100 with "Sunshine Superman."

27 *NME* review of *Revolver* appears.

29 *Datebook* publishes Lennon's "Jesus" interview. Alan Smith interview with Paul appears in *NME*.

30 Brian Epstein goes to Portmeirion in Wales to recuperate.

England beats West Germany 4–2 in soccer to win the World Cup.

AUGUST 1966

1 Paul interviewed by David Frost for BBC radio program *David Frost at the Phonograph*.

Charles Whitman kills twelve people at the University of Texas with a rifle.

2 George and Pattie travel to Stoodleigh, Devon, for a vacation at Pattie's mother's farmhouse.

4 Controversial comic Lenny Bruce dies in Hollywood.

5 Release of *Revolver* and "Eleanor Rigby"/"Yellow Submarine" in the UK. John and Paul record interviews for BBC radio program *The Lennon & McCartney Songbook*. Brian Epstein gives press conference in New York to explain John's comments about Jesus. LSD is added to the Drugs (Prevention of Misuse) Act in the UK Parliament, which will become law in September.

8 *Revolver* LP is released in the US.

11 Beatles fly from London to Chicago. Group press conference at their hotel to address the "Jesus" scandal.

12 Beatles play two shows in Chicago using same set list as in Germany and Japan. They are supported by US acts the Remains, Bobby Hebb, the Cyrkle, and the Ronettes. Two shows.

13 Two shows in Detroit.

14 One show in Cleveland.

15 One show in Washington, DC, and then on to Philadelphia by bus. Jefferson Airplane release debut album *Jefferson Airplane Takes Off*.

16 One show in Philadelphia; Beatles fly to Toronto. The single "Last Train to Clarksville" by the Monkees is released.

17 Two shows in Toronto.

18 One show in Boston. Four Tops release the single "Reach Out I'll Be There."

19 Two shows in Memphis then fly on to Ohio.

20 Cincinnati show is canceled due to rain.

21 Beatles play rescheduled Cincinnati show in the afternoon followed by one in Saint Louis at night and then fly to New York.

22 Staying at the Warwick Hotel in New York.

23 Beatles play one show at Shea Stadium and then fly to LA.

24 Beatles arrive in LA and stay in a private house on Curson Terrace, West Hollywood. Press conference at the Capitol Records building on North Vine Street. The Doors start recording their debut album at Sunset Sound Recorders at 6650 Sunset Boulevard.

25 Beatles fly to Seattle to play two shows and then fly back to LA.

26 A rest day at their rented property in West Hollywood. Donovan releases the LP *Sunshine Superman* in US.

27 At rest in West Hollywood. Possibly on this night Paul and George meet with Brian and Carl Wilson of the Beach Boys, who play them a copy of their next single, "Good Vibrations."

28 Beatles play Dodger Stadium, LA.

29 Beatles fly to San Francisco to play at Candlestick Park, their last concert ever. They fly back to LA after the show.

30 Beatles fly from LA to London.

SEPTEMBER 1966

1 Journalist Maureen Cleave marries Francis Nichols at St Anne's Church, Knocknarea, County Sligo.

2 Interview with George and John is published in *NME*.

5 John flies to Hanover, Germany, to start filming *How I Won the War*.

The Byrds release the single "Mr. Spaceman."

Filming of the TV series *The Prisoner* starring Patrick McGoohan begins in Portmeirion, Wales.

7 John has his hair cut short at the breakfast room of the Inn on the Heath, Celle, and is given steel-rim spectacles to wear for his role as Private Gripweed.

8 Start of filming *How I Won the War* on a NATO tank range in Celle.

LSD is outlawed in Britain.

The original series of *Star Trek* debuts on American TV.

12 *The Monkees* TV series debuts on US TV.

13 Paul and Ringo attend *Melody Maker* Pop Luncheon in a restaurant at Post Office Tower along with Dusty Springfield and Tom Jones.

14 George and Pattie fly to Bombay, where George will study sitar with Ravi Shankar.

15 Paul sees AMM performance at RCA, where Cornelius Cardew is performing. John and Neil travel by rail to Paris.

Release of Andy Warhol film *Chelsea Girls*.

16 John and Neil meet up with Paul, Brian Epstein, and Maggie McGivern in Paris.

18 John and Neil Aspinall fly to Spain from Paris.

19 John starts filming in Carboneras, Spain, while staying in Almeria.

George gives press conference at Taj Mahal hotel in Bombay.

20 George gives interview to BBC radio for *The Lively Arts*.

Launch of the underground newspaper the *San Francisco Oracle*.

23 Rolling Stones release the single "Have You Seen Your Mother, Baby, Standing in the Shadow" and begin a UK tour.

24 Jimi Hendrix arrives in London.

26 Brian Epstein is hospitalized in London clinic.

28 Yoko Ono in London for Symposium on Destruction in Art.

Ono's first UK appearance is at Africa Centre.

30 Jane Asher opens in *A Winter's Tale* at Cambridge Theatre in London.

OCTOBER 1966

1 Ringo and Maureen fly to Almeria to join John and Cynthia.

4 The New Vaudeville Band releases the single "Winchester Cathedral."

6 LSD is outlawed in California.

7 Yardbirds release the single "Happenings Ten Years Time Ago."

9 The Monkees release their debut album.

10 Beach Boys release the single "Good Vibrations."

11 George Harrison leaves houseboat in Kashmir and signs visitor book.

12 The Supremes release the single "You Keep Me Hangin' On."

14 *NME* mentions Paul writing music for a film provisionally titled "Wedlocked, or All in Good Time" and starring Hayley Mills.

15 Launch of "underground" newspaper *International Times* at the Roundhouse in Chalk Farm, London. Pink Floyd and Soft Machine play. Paul is one of the attendees.

Foundation of the Black Panther Party in Oakland, California.

21 *NME* news story says Owen Holder will write the next Beatles film, which will be titled "Shades of a Personality."

22 George and Pattie return to London from Bombay.

British double agent George Blake escapes from Wormwood Scrubs prison and flees to Moscow.

26 George picks up Ravi Shankar from London Airport.

British singer Alma Cogan dies in London.

27 Publication of *The Penguin John Lennon*.

28 *NME* runs an interview with John that took place on the set of *How I Won the War* in Spain.

29 Ravi Shankar views *Alice in Wonderland* TV production directed by Jonathan Miller in preparation for recording the soundtrack.

30 Ravi Shankar starts recording *Alice in Wonderland* soundtrack.

NOVEMBER 1966

6 Paul flies to France with a car and puts on a disguise as he embarks on a vacation. Jane Asher arrives in Bristol for a new production that will eventually tour the US.

8 John meets Yoko at Indica Gallery.

Ronald Reagan is elected governor of California.

10 Newspapers report end to Beatles tours.

11 John and Cynthia see Ben E. King at Scotch of St. James.

Ringo in *NME* says Beatles not splitting.

12 Paul and Mal Evans begin driving from Bordeaux to the southern coast of Spain, then to Nairobi.

Teenagers riot on Sunset Strip in LA to oppose the introduction of a 10:00 p.m. curfew.

13 *Sunday Telegraph* mentions that two Beatles have been sounding out Allen Klein regarding management.

Four Tops play at Savile Theatre in London on a show promoted by Brian Epstein.

16 The TV drama *Cathy Comes Home*, directed by Ken Loach, is shown in Britain and has an impact on public perception of homelessness.

19 Paul and Mal back from Kenya.

22 Claes Oldenburg exhibition opens at Robert Fraser Gallery. John and Yoko meet again. Paul is also present.

24 Recording "Strawberry Fields Forever."

Donovan releases the single "Mellow Yellow" in the US.

25 Beatles record fan club Christmas message. Pictures in newspapers of them arriving at EMI.

Jimi Hendrix plays showcase gig at Bag O' Nails in London.

27 John films appearance in *Not Only . . . But Also* sketch with Peter Cook and Dudley Moore.

28 Recording "Strawberry Fields Forever."

29 Recording "Strawberry Fields Forever."

DECEMBER 1966

1 Paul sees Young Rascals at Scotch of St James.

Science of Being and Art of Living by Maharishi Mahesh Yogi is published in New York.

2 Paul sees the Rascals at Blaises.

David Bowie releases the single "Rubber Band" backed with "The London Boys."

6 Recording "When I'm Sixty-Four."

Recording Christmas message for Radio London and Radio Caroline.

8 Recording "When I'm Sixty-Four" and "Strawberry Fields Forever."

9 Recording "Strawberry Fields Forever."

UK release of the LP *A Quick One* by the Who.

10 UK release of compilation LP "A Collection of Beatles Oldies."

13 Recording "Strawberry Fields Forever."

14 Recording "Strawberry Fields Forever."

16 Jimi Hendrix Experience releases its first single, "Hey Joe."

17 Cream single "I Feel Free" enters the UK charts.

18 Premiere of *The Family Way* with music composed by Paul at Warner Theatre in London.

Tara Browne is killed in car crash in Earl's Court, London.

19 It is announced that Paul has composed music to be played at an electronic music and light show to be held in January at the Roundhouse.

Around this date ISKCON (International Society for Krishna Consciousness) records the Hare Krishna chant in New York for Happening Records. John and George later hear this record and it stirs their interest in the Krishna movement.

20 Recording "When I'm Sixty-Four." ITV interviews all four Beatles arriving at EMI.

21 Recording "When I'm Sixty-Four."

Timothy Leary founds the League of Spiritual Discovery, a religious organization with LSD as its chief sacrament.

22 Two versions of "Strawberry Fields Forever" recorded at different speeds are patched together. Paul is interviewed by Andy Gray for *NME*.

23 Opening night of UFO Club, London's first psychedelic music venue. Final episode of UK music TV show *Ready, Steady, Go!*

29 Recording "Penny Lane."

30 Recording "Penny Lane."

31 US troop levels in Vietnam reach 389,000. More than six thousand soldiers were killed during 1966.

APPENDIX B

THE BEATLES' JUKEBOXES

These are some of the records the Beatles were listening to in 1966. John's selection is taken from the double-CD *John Lennon's Jukebox,* released in 2004. This compilation album was based on the contents of an actual 1965 jukebox belonging to John that ended up being auctioned at Christie's in 1989. The purchaser, John Midwinter, spent many years researching the forty A and B sides of the singles that John had chosen and inscribed in pen on the machine's title strips. All of them were released in 1965 or earlier.

George revealed the contents of his home jukebox (a KB Discomatic like John's) to *Record Mirror* columnist Tony Hall, and it was published in December 1965. "It's so much easier to have all my favourite records on the juke box at once," he explained to Hall. "It saves me going through piles of records to find the ones I want. Then when I get sick of them, I just throw them out and put some new ones in."

For Paul's and Ringo's selections I've had to adopt a more creative approach, because, as far as I know, they never specifically talked about the singles they loaded into their jukeboxes in 1966. To compensate I've constructed lists of singles based on what records and artists they talked about in interviews at this time or what songs they urged others to listen to. I've deliberately avoided the jazz and experimental artists that they were fans of if these musicians made LPs but not singles.

JOHN LENNON'S JUKEBOX

1. Wilson Pickett, "In the Midnight Hour"
2. Fontella Bass, "Rescue Me"
3. Smokey Robinson and the Miracles, "The Tracks of my Tears"
4. Otis Redding, "My Girl"
5. Len Barry, "1, 2, 3"
6. Tommy Tucker, "Hi Heel Sneakers"
7. Jimmy McCracklin, "The Walk"

8. Timmy Shaw, "Gonna Send You Back to Georgia"
9. The Contours, "First Look at the Purse"
10. Gary U. S. Bonds, "New Orleans"
11. Bobby Parker, "Watch Your Step"
12. Derek Martin, "Daddy Rollin' Stone"
13. Larry Williams, "Short Fat Fannie"
14. Little Richard, "Long Tall Sally"
15. Barrett Strong, "Money (That's What I Want)"
16. Bruce Channel, "Hey! Baby"
17. Bob Dylan, "Positively 4th Street"
18. The Lovin' Spoonful, "Daydream"
19. Donovan, "Turquoise"
20. Buddy Holly, "Slippin' and Slidin'"
21. Gene Vincent, "Be-Bop-A-Lula"
22. Chuck Berry, "No Particular Place to Go"
23. Paul Revere and the Raiders, "Steppin' Out"
24. The Lovin' Spoonful, "Do You Believe in Magic"
25. The Big Three, "Some Other Guy"
26. The Isley Brothers, "Twist and Shout"
27. Larry Williams, "She Said 'Yeah'"
28. Buddy Holly, "Brown Eyed Handsome Man"
29. Little Richard, "Slippin' and Slidin'"
30. Gary U. S. Bonds, "Quarter to Three"
31. Little Richard, "Ooh! My Soul"
32. Gene Vincent, "Woman Love"
33. The Miracles, "Shop Around"
34. The Animals, "Bring It on Home to Me"
35. James Ray with the Hutch Davie Orchestra, "If You Gotta Make a Fool of Somebody"
36. The Miracles, "What's So Good about Goodbye"
37. Larry Williams, "Bad Boy"
38. Edwin Starr, "Agent Double-O-Soul"
39. The Miracles, "I've Been Good to You"
40. Barrett Strong, "Oh I Apologize"
41. The Miracles, "Who's Loving You"

GEORGE HARRISON'S JUKEBOX

1. Bob and Earl, "Harlem Shuffle"
2. Chuck Jackson, "Good Things Come to Those Who Wait"
3. Booker T. and the M.G.'s, "Be My Lady"
4. Bob Dylan, "Can You Please Crawl Out Your Window"
5. Little Jerry Williams, "Baby, You're My Everything"
6. Edwin Starr, "Back Street"
7. Lee Dorsey, "Work, Work, Work"
8. The Beach Boys, "The Little Girl I Once Knew"
9. The Miracles, "My Girl Has Gone"
10. Little Richard, "I Don't Know What You've Got (But It's Got Me)"
11. Otis Redding, "I Can't Turn You Loose"
12. Otis Redding, "My Girl"
13. Jackie Wilson, "I Believe I'll Love On"
14. Booker T. and The M.G.'s, "Plum Nellie"
15. Willie Mitchell, "Everything Is Gonna Be Alright"
16. Joe Tex, "A Sweet Woman Like You"
17. The Four Tops, "Something about You"
18. James Brown, "I Got You"
19. Marvin Gaye, "Ain't That Peculiar"
20. The Byrds, "Turn, Turn, Turn"
21. Don Covay, "See Saw"
22. Sounds Incorporated, "I'm Comin' Through"
23. Wilson Pickett, "Don't Fight It"
24. Booker T. and the M.G.'s, "Bootleg"
25. The Young Rascals, "I Ain't Gonna Eat My Heart Out Any More"
26. Otis Redding, "Respect"
27. James Brown, "Try Me"
28. Otis Redding, "I've Been Loving You Too Long"
29. Patti LaBelle and the Bluebelles, "All Or Nothing"
30. Marvin Gaye, "Pretty Little Baby"
31. Fred Hughes, "Oowee Baby, I Love You"
32. The Miracles, "The Tracks of My Tears
33. Joe Tex, "Yum Yum"
34. Edwin Starr, "Agent Double-O-Soul"

35. Barrett Strong, "Money"
36. Ritchie Barrett, "Some Other Guy"
37. Chuck Berry, "It Wasn't Me"
38. Charlie Rich, "Mohair Sam"
39. The Beach Boys, "Let Him Run Wild"
40. The Lovin' Spoonful, "Do You Believe in Magic"

PAUL MCCARTNEY'S JUKEBOX

1. The Who, "Anyway, Anyhow, Anywhere"
2. The Animals, "Don't Let Me Be Misunderstood"
3. Stevie Wonder, "Uptight (Everything's Alright)"
4. The Lovin' Spoonful, "Summer in the City"
5. Little Richard, "Tutti Frutti"
6. The Coasters, "Searchin'"
7. The Jodimars, "Clarabella"
8. Elvis Presley, "All Shook Up"
9. Chuck Berry, "Sweet Little Sixteen"
10. John Mayall and the Bluesbreakers, "Parchman Farm"
11. Ben E. King, "So Much Love"
12. Gene Vincent, "Be-Bop-A-Lula"
13. Buddy Holly, "Peggy Sue"
14. The Mamas and Papas, "Monday Monday"
15. The Four Tops, "I Can't Help Myself (Sugar Pie Honey Bunch)"
16. The Beach Boys, "God Only Knows"
17. The Supremes, "You Can't Hurry Love"
18. Bo Diddley, "Crackin' Up"
19. Eddie Cochran, "Twenty Flight Rock"
20. Bob Dylan, "Mr. Tambourine Man"
21. Booker T. and the M.G.'s, "Green Onions"
22. The Fugs, "Kill for Peace"
23. The Mothers of Invention, "Trouble Comin' Every Day"
24. Donovan, "Sunshine Superman"
25. Esther Phillips, "And I Love Him"
26. B. B. King, "Eyesight to the Blind"
27. Fontella Bass, "Rescue Me"
28. Nat King Cole, "Unforgettable"

29. The Merseys, "Sorrow"

30. Bob Dylan, "Positively 4th Street"

31. Elvis Presley, "Don't Be Cruel"

32. The Beach Boys, "I Get Around"

33. Martha and the Vandellas, "Heat Wave"

34. Sam and Dave, "You Don't Know Like I Know"

35. Robert Parker, "Barefootin'"

36. Kim Fowley, "The Trip"

37. John Mayer, "Acka Raga"

38. Jimi Hendrix Experience, "Hey Joe"

39. The Young Rascals, "Good Lovin'"

40. Buddy Holly, "Rave On"

RINGO STARR'S JUKEBOX

1. Ray Charles, "Tell the Truth"

2. Elvis Presley, "Heartbreak Hotel"

3. The Johnny Otis Show, "Good Golly"

4. Eddie Cochran, "Somethin' Else"

5. The Four Aces, "Love Is a Many Splendored Thing"

6. The Shirelles, "Will You Still Love Me Tomorrow"

7. Carl Perkins, "Matchbox"

8. Gene Autry, "South of the Border"

9. Buck Owens, "Buckaroo"

10. Brook Benton, "Baby (You've Got What It Takes)"

11. Chico Hamilton, "The Dealer"

12. Yusef Lateef, "Sea Breeze

13. The Supremes, "You Keep Me Hangin' On"

14. Stevie Wonder, "Fingertips (Parts I and II)"

15. Hank Williams, "Honky Tonk Blues"

16. Cozy Cole, "Topsy II"

17. Lee Dorsey, "Holy Cow"

18. Hank Snow, "Nobody's Child"

19. Lightnin' Hopkins, "Mojo Hand"

20. Marvin Gaye, "Can I Get a Witness"

21. Little Richard, "Long Tall Sally"

22. Patsy Cline, "I Fall to Pieces"

23. Kitty Wells, "Heartbreak USA"
24. Willie Nelson, "Touch Me"
25. Della Reese, "Don't You Know"
26. The Shirelles, "Mama Said"
27. Patsy Cline, "Crazy"
28. Ernest Tubb, "Waltz Across Texas"
29. Jerry Lee Lewis, "Whole Lotta Shakin' Goin' On"
30. Johnny Burnett, "You're Sixteen"

SOURCES

I interviewed the following people specifically for this book: John Adams, Ian Albery, Alan Aldridge, Edward Bedford (aka Steve Aldo), Harry Benson, Anil Bhagwat, Kenneth Blackwell, Pattie Boyd, Tony Bramwell, Pete Brown, Garech Browne, Leslie Bryce, Gulam Butt, Tony Cartwright, Chandrika (Angadi) Casali, John Christoffel, Tony Crane, Steve Cropper, Shambhu Das, Jennifer Dunbar Dorn, George Drummond, John Dunbar, Dudley Edwards, Fred Elizalde, Lisa Elizalde, Paul Friswell (Overlanders), Bruce Higham, Eddie Holland, Venetia Howard, Adam Kinn, Marijke Koger, Michael Lydon, Tex Makin, Beryl Marsden, Sue Mautner, John Mayall, Maggie McGivern, Joe McGowan, Roy Morrison (Koobas), John Pearse, D. A. Pennebaker, Viv Prince, Michael Rainey, Eddie Thornton, John Underwood, Erica Williams, and Peter Zinovieff.

I also relied on past interviews I carried out with Al Aronowitz, David Ashton, Tony Barrow, Al Benn, William Burroughs, Maureen Cleave, Tony Cox, Donovan, Lamont Dozier, Peter Fonda, Roberta Freymann, Sarah-Jane Freymann, Frank Giardina, Allen Ginsberg, Brion Gysin, Doug Layton, Timothy Leary, Cynthia Lennon, John Lennon, Richard Lester, George Martin, Linda McCartney, Paul McCartney, Scott McKenzie, Barry Miles, Raul Nuñez, David Noebel, Yoko Ono, Simon Posthuma, Carmel Berman Reingold, Cyndy Bury Riley, Joel Schumacher, John Sebastian, Ravi Shankar, Bishan Das Sharma, Don Short, Derek Taylor, Jurgen Vollmer, Gordon Waller, J. Willoughby, and Francis Wyndham.

Several of my sources were kind enough to review relevant parts of my manuscript for accuracy. Thanks to Alan Aldridge, Anil Bhagwat, Pattie Boyd, Tony Bramwell, John Christoffel, Steve Cropper, Shambhu Das, George Drummond, John Dunbar, Dudley Edwards, Fred and Lisa Elizalde, Venetia Howard, Adam Kinn, Sue Mautner, Mike McCartney, Joe McGowan, Ralph Metzner, John Pearse, Andrew Loog Oldham, Jeff Rosen, Ralph Schoenman, Don Short, John Underwood, Klaus Voormann, and Peter Zinovieff.

There are several books I rely on when writing about the Beatles: *The Complete Beatles Recording Sessions* by Mark Lewisohn, *The Complete Beatles Chronicle* by Mark Lewisohn, *Many Years From Now* by Barry Miles, *The Beatles Off the Record* by Keith Badman, *The Beatles* by Hunter Davies, *Lennon Remembers* by Jann Wenner, *The Complete Beatles Songs* by Steve Turner, *The Playboy Interviews with John Lennon and Yoko Ono* by David Sheff, *Magical Mystery Tours* by Tony Bramwell, *The Beatles: A Diary* by Barry Miles, *NME Originals: The Beatles 1962–1970* (edited by Steve Sutherland), *Revolution in the Head* by Ian MacDonald, and *Strawberry Fields Forever: John Lennon Remembered* by Vic Garbarini, Brian Cullman, and Barbara Graustark.

Because the focus of this book is on one particular year in the group's career, there were other books that were of specific help to me:

DECEMBER 1965

Adams, Jo. *Looking Through You.* London: Omnibus, 2015.

Bicknell, Alf. *Ticket to Ride.* London: Creation, 1999.

Creasy, Martin. *Beatlemania!: The Real Story of the Beatles UK Tours, 1963–1965.* London: Omnibus, 2010.

Epstein, Brian. *A Cellarful of Noise.* London: Souvenir, 1964.

McNab, Ken. *The Beatles in Scotland.* Edinburgh: Polygon, 2008.

JANUARY 1966

Andresen, Mark. *Field of Vision: The Broadcast Life of Kenneth Allsop.* Bloomington, IN: Trafford, 2005.

Cowley, Elizabeth. *A Tender Contempt.* Lewes, UK: Book Guild, 1998.

Trynka, Paul, ed. *The Beatles: Ten Years That Shook the World.* London: Dorling Kindersley, 2004.

FEBRUARY

Boyd, Pattie. *Wonderful Today.* London: Hodder Headline, 2007.

Evans, Mike. *The Beatles Literary Anthology.* London: Plexus, 2004.

Schonfield, Hugh J. *The Passover Plot.* New York: Bernard Geis, 1965.

Thomson, Elizabeth, and David Gutman. *The Lennon Companion.* London: Macmillan, 1987.

MARCH

Gordon, Robert. *Respect Yourself: Stax Records and the Soul Explosion.* New York: Bloomsbury USA, 2013.

Green, Jonathon. *Days in the Life: Voices from the English Underground, 1961–1971.* London: Heinemann, 1988.

Krerowicz, Aaron. *The Beatles and the Avant-Garde.* Kenosha, WI: AK, 2014.

Lavezzoli, Peter. *The Dawn of Indian Music in the West.* London: Continuum, 2007.

Levy, Shawn. *Ready, Steady, Go!: Swinging London and the Invention of Cool.* London: Fourth Estate, 2002.

Miles, Barry. *In the Sixties.* London: Jonathan Cape, 2002.

Miles, Barry. *London Calling.* London: Atlantic, 2010.

Reising, Russell, ed. *Every Sound There Is: The Beatles' Revolver and the Transformation of Rock 'n' Roll.* London: Routledge, 2002.

Shotton, Pete. *John Lennon in My Life.* London: Coronet, 1983.

APRIL

Badiner, Allan, and Alex Grey, eds. *Zig Zag Zen: Buddhism and Psychedelics.* Santa Fe: Synergetic Press, 2015.

Dass, Ram, and Ralph Metzner, with Gary Bravo. *Birth of a Psychedelic Culture.* Santa Fe, NM: Synergetic Press, 2010.

Davies, Hunter, ed. *The Beatles Lyrics.* London: Weidenfeld & Nicholson, 2014.

Dr. Licks. *Standing in the Shadows of Motown: The Life and Music of Legendary Bassist James Jamerson.* Milwaukee: Hal Leonard, 1989.

Emerick, Geoff. *Here, There and Everywhere: My Life Recording the Music of the Beatles.* New York, Gotham: 2006.

Evans-Wentz, W. Y., comp. and ed. *The Tibetan Book of the Dead.* Oxford: Oxford University Press, 1927.

Harrison, George. *I Me Mine.* London: W. H. Allen, 1982.

Leary, Timothy, Ralph Metzner, and Richard Alpert. *The Psychedelic Experience.* New York: University Books, 1964.

Martin, George. *All You Need Is Ears.* New York: St. Martin's, 1979.

Pedler, Dominic. *The Songwriting Secrets of the Beatles.* London: Omnibus, 2003.

Pritchard, David, and Alan Lysaght, eds. *The Beatles: An Oral History.* New York: Hyperion, 1998.

Ryan, Kevin, and Brian Kehew. *Recording the Beatles.* Houston: Curvebender, 2006.

MAY

Aronowitz, Al. *Bob Dylan and the Beatles.* Bloomington, IN: 1st Books, 2003.

Barrow, Tony. *John, Paul, George, Ringo and Me.* New York: Thunder's Mouth, 2005.

Décharné, Max. *King's Road: The Rise and Fall of the Hippest Street in the World.* London: Weidenfeld & Nicholson, 2005.

Everett, Walter. *The Beatles as Musicians: Revolver Through the Anthology.* Oxford: Oxford University Press, 1999.

Gorman, Paul. *The Look: Adventures in Pop and Rock Fashion.* London: Sanctuary, 2001.

Granata, Charles L. *I Just Wasn't Made for These Times: Brian Wilson and the Making of Pet Sounds.* London: Unanimous, 2003.

Maymudes, Victor. *Another Side of Bob Dylan.* New York: St. Martin's, 2014.

McMillian, John. *Beatles vs. Stones.* New York: Simon & Schuster, 2013.

Oldham, Andrew. *Stoned.* London: Vintage, 2001.

Rodriguez, Robert. *Revolver: How the Beatles Reimagined Rock 'n' Roll.* Milwaukee: Backbeat, 2012.

Vyner, Harriet. *Groovy Bob: The Life and Times of Robert Fraser.* London: Faber & Faber, 2001.

JUNE

Aitken, Jonathan. *The New Meteors.* London: Secker & Warburg, 1967.

Fukuya, Toshinobu. *The Beatles' Untold Tokyo Story: Music as a Socio-Political Force.* Kawakami Ube City, Japan: Pelican Trax, 2011.

Phillips, John. *Papa John.* New York: Doubleday, 1986.

Shankar, Ravi. *Rag Mala.* Shaftesbury, UK: Element, 1999.

Spizer, Bruce. *The Beatles' Story on Capitol Records.* New York: Four Ninety-Eight Productions, 2000.

JULY

Beatles. *Anthology.* London: Cassell, 2000.

Brown, Peter. *The Love You Make: An Insider's Story of the Beatles.* London: Macmillan, 1983.

Lewis, Vic. *Music and Maiden Overs: My Showbusiness Life.* London: Chatto & Windus, 1987.

Sounes, Howard. *Fab: An Intimate Life of Paul McCartney.* London: HarperCollins, 2010.

Whitaker, Bob. *The Unseen Beatles*. London: Octopus, 1991.

AUGUST

Coleman, Ray. *Brian Epstein: The Man Who Made the Beatles*. London: Viking, 1989.

Geller, Debbie. *The Brian Epstein Story*. London: Faber & Faber, 2000.

Lefcowitz, Eric. *Tomorrow Never Knows: The Beatles' Last Concert*. San Francisco: Terra Firma, 1987.

Schwensen, Dave. *The Beatles in Cleveland*. Cleveland: North Shore, 2006.

Tashian, Barry. *Ticket to Ride: The Extraordinary Diary of the Beatles' Last Tour*. Nashville: Dowling, 1996.

Turner, Steve. *The Gospel According to the Beatles*. Louisville: Westminster John Knox, 2006.

SEPTEMBER

Higgins, Henry. *To Be a Matador*. London: William Kimber, 1972.

Giuliano, Geoffrey. *The Beatles: A Celebration*. London: Sidgwick & Jackson, 1986.

Iglesias, J. Adolfo. *Juan and John*. Almeria, Spain: Editorial Circulo Rojo, 2013.

McCabe, Peter, and Robert D. Schonfeld. *Apple to the Core*. London: Sphere, 1973.

OCTOBER

Aldridge, Alan, ed. *The Beatles Illustrated Lyrics*. London: Macdonald Unit 75, 1969.

Aldridge, Alan, ed. *The Beatles Illustrated Lyrics 2*. London: BPC, 1971.

Aldridge, Alan. *The Man with Kaleidoscope Eyes*. New York: Abrams, 2009.

Lennon, Cynthia. *A Twist of Lennon*. London: Star, 1978.

Orton, Joe. *Up Against It*. London: Eyre Methuen, 1979.

NOVEMBER

Cott, Jonathan, and Christine Doudna, eds. *The Ballad of John and Yoko*. New York: Rolling Stone, 1982.

Ono, Yoko. *Grapefruit*. London: Sphere, 1971.

Martin, George. *Summer of Love: The Making of Sgt. Pepper*. London: Pan, 1995.

Reeve, Andru J. *Turn Me On, Dead Man: The Beatles and the "Paul Is Dead" Hoax*. Bloomington, IN: AuthorHouse, 2004.

Taylor, Derek. *It Was Twenty Years Ago Today*. London: Bantam, 1987.

DECEMBER

Barratt, C. *The Beatles in the News 1966*. Colin Barratt, 2015.

Dean, Johnny, ed. *The Beatles Book Special Xmas Extra*. London: Beat, 1966.

Heylin, Clinton. *The Act You've Known for All These Years*. Edinburgh: Canongate, 2007.

I consulted many newspapers and magazines from 1966 including *NME, Melody Maker, Disc and Music Echo, Record Mirror, Music Maker, Gramophone, Musical Times, Jazz Monthly, Beatles Book Monthly, Datebook, 16, Seventeen, Fabulous, Rave, flip, Bravo, International Times, London Life, New York Times, New York Times Magazine, New York Post, San Francisco Chronicle, Los Angeles Times, Detroit Free Press, Waycross Journal-Herald, Record American, Carolina Israelite, Birmingham News, Cleveland Plain Dealer, Detroit, Guardian, Times, Daily Mail, Daily Telegraph, Sunday Telegraph, Daily Mirror, Daily Express, Billboard, Variety, Crawdaddy, Village Voice, Observer Magazine, Sunday Times, Town, Time, Newsweek, Life, Look, Daily Mirror* (Trinidad and Tobago), *Trinidad Guardian, Evening News* (Trinidad), *Woman's Mirror, Nova, Evening Standard, Private Eye, Punch, New Society, Leicester Mercury, Listener, Liverpool Echo, Liverpool Daily Post, Berwick Advertiser, Glasgow Herald, Times Literary Supplement, Birmingham Evening Mail, British Medical Journal, Yomiuri Shimbun, Manila Times, Manila Chronicle,* and *Philippines Free Press.*

I used the services of the following libraries and archives: British Library, National Archives (London), National Newspaper Library, Presidential Commission on Good Government (Manila), New York Public Library, School of Oriental and African Studies, BBC Written Archives' Centre, Western Historical Manuscript Collection at the University of Missouri, Berwick Record Office, Westminster Central Library, Chiswick Library, Rock's Back Pages, Beatle Interview Database, newspapers.com, ukpressonline.co.uk.

Much of the material on Art Unger and *Datebook,* including transcribed interviews, personal notes, and letters, was supplied courtesy of the Arthur Unger Papers, Western Historical Manuscript Collection, University of Missouri at Columbia.

Other people helped by patiently answering questions, supplying photographs and news cuttings or connecting me with interviewees: Jo Adams, Tom Adams, Shakeir Ahmed (Getty Images), Lanny Aldrich, Aurora Almendral, Keith Altham, Nancy Bacal, Linda Bankier (Berwick Record Office), Ron Brewington, Geoffrey Cannon, Chris Charlesworth, Barbara Dozier, Sasha Drummond, Alice Dunn, Vince Eager, Jane Ebdon (John Mayall), Bill Harry, Barney Hoskyns, Adolfo Iglesias, Larry Jenkins, Roger McGough, John Minford, David Mlinaric, Pete Nash, Raul Nuñez, Lietha Nuot (Destination Davos Klosters), Sean O'Mahony, Jane Ormsby-Gore, D. A. Pennebaker, Frazer Pennebaker, Morgan Perry, Lisa Power (MPL), Larry Purdom, Joanna Stephenson, Paul Wane (Tracks), Shirley Washington, Chris Welch, and Jack Williams.

CREDITS

Getty Images: 75, 83, 251, 310, 322, 342, 361

Getty Images/Robert Whitaker: 13, 123, 184, 224, 234, 238

Berwick-upon-Tweed Record Office: 19

Mark St. John: 33

Bristol Old Vic Company: 37, 362

Gerald Scarfe: 45

Chandrika Casali: 53 (both), 66

Erica Williams: 59, 60

Bristol Central Library: 63

Steve Turner: 64, 255, 259

Steve Turner Collection: 8, 9, 16, 28, 31, 57, 91, 137, 148, 153, 176, 202, 266, 271, 273, 276, 357, 366, 367, 370, 377, 380, 389, 399

Pattie Boyd: 68

Getty Images/John Hopkins: 70

Datebook: 96, 263, 286

Adam Ritchie: 111

Ace Records: 114

Tony Aspler: 139 (left)

Moya Riley: 139 (right)

Ralph Metzner and Synergetic Press: 143

Anil Bhagwat: 150

Beatles Book Photo Library: 156, 189

Klaus Voormann: 165, 210

Adam Kinn: 172

TJL Productions: 205

Edward de los Santos (Pinoy Kollektor): 243 (all), 246

Arthur Unger Papers, State Historical Society of Missouri at Columbia: 265, 301 (both)

Raul Nuñez: 279

Ravi Shankar Foundation: 327

Manzoor Ahmad Butt: 329

Douglas Kirkland: 333

Dudley Edwards/Martin Cook: 336

Dudley Edwards: 390

Adolfo Iglesias Collection: 333, 344, 347 (both)

Salvation Army: 334, 345

International Times: 372, 385

Peter Zinovieff: 391

Penguin/Random House: 355

INDEX

Page numbers in *italics* refer to illustrations. Titles are
works by Beatles unless otherwise noted.